DREAM·SINGERS

The African American Way with Dreams

ANTHONY SHAFTON

John Wiley & Sons, Inc.

*I had some dreams when I was the age of fifteen or sixteen.
I remember a dream so vividly, so clear. And I tell people about it.
I had this dream of a procession of people, walking in a funeral-
like procession, playing music. And bright colors! Very dark-
skinned. And the sun, of course. Intense, bright colors. Almost
like a Romare Bearden or Douglas Johnson painting, of the
Harlem Renaissance period, just like that. No features or
anything. And John Coltrane the saxophone player was at the
head of the procession. And he played in a kind of free style, but
very emotional! I mean, the horn was like a voice. And that's all.
That's all it was. But I could never forget how beautiful! Sunlit!
Southernish. Africanish. And the horn. Bright colors. And the
skin colors. It was like a painting that came alive.*

—Preston Jackson

*Dream-singers all,—
My people.*
—Langston Hughes, "Laughters"

CONTENTS

ACKNOWLEDGMENTS

In 1990, I interviewed a number of African American psychologists for an article, my first venture into the subject of this book. For the insights I gained from those interviews, which still shape my thinking, I thank Faheem C. Ashanti, William M. Banks, Carole "Ione" Bovoso, Edward Bruce Bynum, Loma Flowers, Gerald G. Jackson, and William D. Pierce. One psychologist, Charles Payne, later agreed to a personal interview about his own dream life for this book.

I have also profited from exchanges with medical anthropologist Loudell F. Snow, folklorists Michael Edward Bell and Carolyn M. Long, multiculturalist Michael Vannoy Adams, and dream psychologists Rosalind Cartwright, Art T. Funkhouser, Russell Gruber, and Jane White-Lewis.

The statistical analysis of the interviews is the work of Elliot Krop, who took the data I gave him and extracted statistical sense from it.

Michael Vannoy Adams, Thomas Cottle, Henry Louis Gates Jr., John Kirsch, Annamarie Poplawska, and Mado Spiegler agreed to read all or part of the manuscript at various stages and made valuable suggestions.

Two friends who are veterans in the publishing trenches, Lois Battle and Thomas Cottle, gave me important advice and kept my spirits up. Another friend and writer, Mary Lewis, shared information that led me to John Wiley & Sons. My editor there, Carole Hall, expertly set me on the right course to make revisions. I'm grateful to all these people, and in particular to Carole Hall for valuing this project.

I thank the many people who helped me as I went about arranging interviews. But above all, I thank all my interviewees. They are the heart and soul of this book. Some of the interviewees also assisted me by putting me in touch with others to interview. To single out a few, the late Marion Stamps gave me my very first interview, and later enabled me to meet with eight children as a group. Achim Rodgers was indispensable as the facilitator of my questionnaire survey of black male prisoners. And Angela Jackson and John Edgar Wideman not only guided me to other interviews, but inspired me.

PART ONE

A Reverence for Dreams

1

THROUGH THE PORTHOLE OF DREAMS

Dreams, my mama taught me, do not lie.

—Shay Youngblood

The poetry and power of dreams have attracted me since childhood. Like many people, I've always known by intuition that dreams have meanings that matter. But when I was already in my forties, a spell of particularly intense and suggestive dreams riveted my attention. I felt then that I had to learn how dreams work and what they mean.

I began going to workshops on dream interpretation. I joined groups that meet to share and discuss their dreams. I attended conferences with presentations by experts who ran the gamut from laboratory investigators to lifestyle gurus. I studied hundreds of research papers and shelves of scholarly and popular books. A preoccupation became an occupation, and eventually I turned out a book of my own, a survey of contemporary approaches to the understanding of dreams that was published in the mid-1990s.

The seed of this present book, about African Americans and dreams, was planted at the first major conference I attended. This was my first look at the collection of individuals who make dreams a career in America. And it disturbed me to see next to no black faces. I questioned the conference organizers, who told me they were also disturbed but didn't know how to recruit more black members to their organization.

The fact is, there are scarcely any African Americans among the researchers, instructors, and authors in this field. Very few blacks attend their conferences and workshops. And blacks are poorly represented among the dreamers they write about.

What, I wondered, would black psychologists say about this profile. Those I sought out recognized the situation I described to them. None blamed racism. Instead, they found the cause in black preferences. In brief, they explained that black psychologists-in-training would view dreams as a fringe field and a poor career choice. And blacks in general might perceive some of the approaches to dreams being offered as too narrowly psychological, other approaches as too New Age, too feel-good spiritual. Black culture, they emphasized, has its own lively traditions about dreams.

This drew my interest. The psychologists sketched some of these traditions as we talked, but could direct me to few books or articles. For as I soon confirmed at the library, hardly any studies have been devoted to the dreams of black Americans.

Around this time I happened to hear about the dream of a community activist named Marion Stamps in Chicago where I then lived. Her dream, which I'll describe in chapter 2, had inspired her to take a certain action to reduce gang violence. Because I had an interest in the social relevance of dreams, and because she was black, I thought I'd try to interview her. She agreed, and thus I received my first real exposure to the richness of African American beliefs and attitudes surrounding dreams. Her eloquence on the subject and her forthcomingness encouraged me to undertake this study.

Eventually I interviewed 116 African Americans. In selecting people to approach for interviews, I sought a cross section by age, occupation, and so on, while at the same time keeping an eye out for those who might be eloquent on the subject of dreams. Some of the most eloquent turned out to be ordinary folk, but I did end up with a disproportionate number of people in the arts. This appears not to have caused a bias in the sample, however. With very few exceptions, the essential characteristics of the dream experiences and beliefs of artists and nonartists were the same.

In addition to interviewing this group, I also interviewed eight youngsters at Chicago's Cabrini Green housing project, and I obtained written answers to questionnaires I submitted to twenty-five African American male prison inmates around the country.

There's a question I'm often asked by whites when I say I've done this study. "How did you get your material?" they inquire with puzzlement. What they mean is, "How did you ever manage to come in contact with enough blacks?" This question naively reflects the racial separateness of most white lives in America. But I'm happy to say I had no trouble finding people to interview, and got turned down very much less often than I expected myself.

Sometimes the "How did you get your material?" question also means, "Are black people really open with a white interviewer?" Whether the interviewees were open or not you'll judge for yourself. But one good indication is the number of them who passed me along to family or friends.

In addition to the interviews, I have taken black literature as a primary resource, weaving literary examples into discussions of the separate strands of the dream culture at almost every point. For as I quickly and happily discovered, the African American way with dreams runs like a broad vein though this literature. There for anyone to see in novels, short stories, autobiographies, plays, and poetry is plentiful evidence of the place of dreams in African American life. Fiction in particular depicts the ways families socialize their children to dreams, the reasons dreams get shared or withheld, and the sorts of interpretations they receive.

Furthermore, the existence of a literature with this vein running through it is in itself noteworthy. One function of literature is education in the broadest sense. Literature conveys values from the past into the present, often questioning them and revising them as it does so. For dreams, the treasury of African American literature performs that broad educational task amply and in many cases with full intention.

Another question I'm sometimes asked, by blacks as well as by whites, is, "Are black people's dreams really different?" This is a fair question. The short answer is, "No, but their beliefs and attitudes about dreams are different." In reality, the situation is more complicated. What we think, feel, and do while we're awake influences our dreams. So our waking-life beliefs about dreams can influence what we dream at night, which in turn reinforces what we believe. While the dreaming process is humanly universal, people can learn to be sensitive—or insensitive—to various dimensions of the dream life. Cultural groups develop their own distinct ways with dreams, seen in how they talk about dreams, in what they expect from dreams, and also to some extent in the content of their dreams.

What I want to emphasize here by way of introduction is simply this: African Americans as a group believe that dreams matter.

A Reverence for Dreams

"Dream-singers all,—/My people," Langston Hughes wrote proudly.

"I think that black people, they respect their dreams and what happens in those dreams." These are the words of interviewee Diane Dugger, a hospital lab technician. "And their life," she went on, "a lot of times revolves around dreams."

Poet Sterling Plumpp asserted that dreams are "at the core of black culture." He was speaking of hopes, but at the same time of night dreams. "I think that you are literally submerged," Plumpp continued, "and often the portholes are through dreams."

Not so many decades ago, "*everybody* talked about dreams," recalled Frances Callaway Parks, a fifty-one-year-old college professor and writer who grew up in Knoxville, Tennessee. Looking back on her childhood, she remembered:

> When people got up, they commented about the weather. They also commented about how they slept, and if they dreamed. And that was a part of the culture. People would say, "I had a dream." And then they'd go on all day. Any person coming around them, they'd share that dream with. And there were certain people, if they dreamed, everybody paid attention to what they dreamed. They had reputations for dreaming, and dreamed very accurately. . . . Those people whose dreams were observed by the community would often be true.

Fifty-seven-year-old Marva Pitchford Jolly, a ceramic sculptor, made a similar observation about the rural Mississippi of her childhood, where "folk often met each other and said, 'I've been dreaming about peas or dogs or whatever.'" But Jolly voiced contradictory views about the present status of such informal dream-sharing networks. She said that "this still happens in the black community," but later regretted that "it's all gone now. 'Cause you don't really have community. People live in buildings." Jolly lives now in Chicago.

But the reality is that it does still happen, even if less regularly than before, and even if the networks have mostly been reduced to family, lovers, and close friends—who in any case have always made up the core of dream-sharing networks. Writer Eileen Cherry, age forty-two, who also lives in Chicago, was describing her past when she reminisced about the custom of "playing the numbers" from dreams, but she also said:

> My mother and sisters, and people in my family, we talk about our
> dreams, all the time, like "Ooo, I dreamt about Aunt Pat last night,"
> "Ooo, I had this dream about'cha," and "What did you dream last
> night?" But it's connected to reaching out, it's connected to com-
> munity, it's connected to another level of communication. And the
> dreamwork in the African American community is connected to the
> religious experience. So it's embedded in my life.

Testimony such as this begins to convey the real texture of the African American way with dreams.

Some people have, perhaps, absorbed the indifference and skepticism that prevail in the mainstream toward dreams. Yet even a total skeptic like historian and developer Dempsey Travis acknowledged that dreams "were very important" in the family and community he came up in. "They would guide one's life." Travis dismissed traditional black beliefs about dreams as relics of the past. But the president of a museum of African American history, Kimberly Camp, embraced those beliefs and affirmed their present standing as "very much parts of an African American experience."

There are also whites, especially some of eastern European and Mediterranean descent, who value dreams through their own European ethnic traditions. Others have grown interested in dreams through trends in popular psychology and personal growth. But Judith Anne (Judy) Still, daughter of composer William Grant Still, was one of many interviewees to voice the opinion that as a whole "Afro-American people are more cordial to their dreams than white people." I was told that blacks give "a certain significance" to dreams which "Europeans" do not (Nelson Peery, political activist), are "more willing to talk about their dreams" (Darryl Burrows, civic organization director), and "feel more spiritual about them" than white people (Yolanda Scheunemann, psychotherapist). Psychologist Maisha Hamilton-Bennett said:

> Dreams have a reverence in the African American community, much
> more so than in the white community. . . . I think a lot of whites have
> more of a tendency to dismiss their dreams as just some meaningless
> incoherent nonsense that happened "when I was sleeping" and not
> connect it with their life. Whereas African Americans will connect it.

Is there evidence to support these observations about black/white differences with respect to dreams? As we'll see, there is. Despite the fact that this book is about African Americans and not about European Americans, I did want to be able to compare the two. So for that purpose I conducted brief interviews about dreams with a sample of 80 whites who roughly match the profile of the 116 African American interviewees. And I have drawn certain conclusions on the basis of that evidence, even though I realize some people disapprove of all interracial comparisons, believing that they inevitably serve to reinforce prejudices and stereotypes, no matter how well-intentioned. Obviously I don't agree. And I can only hope that any unintended outcome of that sort which arises from this book is more than offset by its value as a resource for all persons interested in dreams and culture.

To affirm that African Americans have a traditional way with dreams is not to say that African Americans all have the same dream experiences, or all think about dreams the same way. To the contrary, surrounding the core of beliefs and attitudes which this book mainly describes there exists, I believe, at least as much diversity in the African American community as in any other—in fact, probably more, as a result of the attention paid to dreams in this community. The diversity and nuances of viewpoint revealed in this book are as vital to the whole picture as the core beliefs and attitudes.

Something also to bear in mind is that people hold their beliefs with various degrees of certainty, consistency, and tolerance for ambiguity. There are hard skeptics. There are naive accepters. There are those in transition. There are those who embrace traditional beliefs as part of a broad enhancement of their identity. And there are those who hold belief and doubt in tension. Take as one example Reverend Marshall Hatch.

Reverend Hatch serves a Baptist church on Chicago's West Side. He is also working for his doctorate in divinity at a Presbyterian theological seminary affiliated with the University of Chicago:

> I'm personally not that affected by dreams, I don't believe. I've gone to school, so I've been affected by Western, rational thought. But the people that I minister to have *not* been affected. Whatever culture has evolved out of the southern culture, people still are very much a part of it. For them dreams are—and I guess I've been affected by it, because they've made pretty convincing arguments to me. And for them dreams are part of reality. And of course it's related to the

spiritual. People *believe* in it. They believe that that's how God communicates to them. That's very much a part of African American culture. So I've been influenced, you know, again.

The Ground to Be Covered

Reverend Hatch holds that his beliefs about dreams, along with his community's beliefs, are still strongly influenced by the African culture of their ancestors. I, too, as I pursued the research for this book, became convinced that the beliefs carried from Africa centuries ago still powerfully shape the African American way with dreams. Part Two gives an overview of this connection.

Then Part Three examines the fabric of the African American dream heritage. In the course of that discussion, I will point out specific African influences where appropriate.

- Nowhere is that influence more conspicuous than in the *prevalence of ancestor dreams,* the topic of chapter 3.
- Chapters 4 through 7 concern *predictive dreaming,* a prominent feature of African American dream beliefs, again showing the African influence. Chapter 4 deals with predictive dreaming generally, then the following three chapters explore dream signs, numbers dreams, and dreams connected with déjà vu.
- The African influence will again be touched upon in chapter 8 in connection with an *openness to dreamlike experiences in the waking state* that distinguishes black Americans from white Americans. Chapter 9 follows up with a discussion of specific altered states of consciousness: visions, voices, and presences, as well as several other altered states less emphasized in African American dream culture.
- The *spirituality of dreaming* is at the heart of the African American dream experience and permeates this entire book. But here we take up three special links between dreams and spirituality. And here, again, some traces of African influence will be discerned. Chapter 10 describes the place of dreams in organized religion. Chapter 11 is about dreams in hoodoo. And chapter 12 explains the folk belief in "witches riding you."
- Chapter 13 takes up a special subject, *dreaming about race.* Race dreams definitely are part of the African American experience of dreams, even though dreams on this theme aren't traditional

in the way that, for example, ancestor visitation dreams or numbers dreams are traditional. Race dreams open a window onto the private experience of race in America.

▪ Chapter 14 wraps up with a discussion of dream sharing, the main means by which beliefs and attitudes about dreams are transmitted from generation to generation. Examples of dream sharing occur abundantly throughout the book. The final chapter generalizes about the nature of dream sharing in black America and concludes with an assessment of the future of the African American way with dreams.

PART TWO

The African Connection

DREAM IS WHAT WE DO

INFLUENCES FROM AFRICA

A youth that's brought up and raised in a ghetto environment, surrounded by nothing but African American people, may have no sense of realization that the way that he's walking, or the way that he's talking, or the way that he's behaving, has a definitive and valuable root somewhere deep in some specific tribe in Africa.

—Ivan Watkins

Survivals of African Dream Beliefs

Everyone knows that the blues and jazz have African roots. Black musical style is an obvious example of what's called a *retention* or a *survival*, that is, a cultural feature that continues to exist from an earlier time and a different milieu. Scholars have examined many such African survivals in black America, ranging from folk tales to vernacular speech to gender roles. But dreaming is one area where the African connection hasn't really been sought before. Africa does in fact survive in the African American way with dreams, in spite of the centuries and the changes separating the Millennium from the Middle Passage. At the same time, the African American affinity for dreaming is also a distinctly American adaptation, an adaptation to oppression—a survival *for* survival.

Almost all traditional peoples of the world—including the folk of Europe—believe in dreams. But in Africa, trust in dreams runs especially deep. Traditional Africans hold that in dreams their spirits come in touch with ancestors, or with the spirits of other living persons, or with higher spiritual beings. Sometimes dreams serve as a means of witchcraft, or are sent by deceitful spirits. Other dreams may convey the wisdom and interests of the departed or of the gods. People therefore watch their dreams, and talk about them. And often they take them to experts for interpretation. Traditional dream interpreters include herbalists, sorcerers, diviners, and priests. As Afrocentrist psychologist John L. Johnson told me:

> Dreams are used all over Africa as part of the healing process. The statement is, "If they don't dream, I cannot heal them." That's from Zulu culture. And the healer will talk to the person, and then himself have a dream, and then use that dream as part of work with the person.

And it's not just traditionalists who honor dreams in Africa; so do Muslims and Christians. The authority dream interpreters enjoy everywhere on the continent is reinforced in Islamic Africa by the special knowledge interpreters have of Islamic dream books and dream theory. As for Christianity, the influence of traditional African dream beliefs is strongest in the so-called Independent "prophet-healing" churches, which are churches founded by Africans rather than by European missionaries. Here dreams and visions play a prominent role in worship, along with indigenous symbols and music.

What evidence can we find to show that African dream beliefs survived the Middle Passage? One strong piece of evidence comes from the black South, where "Guinea" or "Ebo rhymes," verses that mingled English with vestiges of African speech, were collected at the turn of the last century. In the 1920s, a folklorist discussed a very strange Guinea rhyme. No one remembered its meaning, but it was clearly the remnant of some long-forgotten African original. This was confirmed more than fifty years later when a linguist deciphered the verse. It turned out to be "a chant for divination purposes to determine the meaning of a dream." Here is the surviving version of the chant, then the linguist's reconstruction of the Bantu on which it is based, then her translation from Bantu into English:

Shool! Shool! Shool!	*Jula! Jula! Jula!*	Pull up, pull up, pull up (from deep
I rule!	*Aula!*	within), Relate the dream!
Shool! Shool! Shool!	*Jula! Jula! Jula!*	Pull up, pull up, pull up,
I rule!	*Aula!*	Relate the dream!
Shool! Shacker-rack!	*Jula tshiakalaka.*	Pull up the talking,
I shool bubbacool!	*E, jula bubakula,*	Yes, pull up the speaking-about-it.

Seller! Beller eel!	*Selula bubelela.*	Raise up again the truth!
Fust to ma tree!	*Pasunsumadi,*	When the word begins to burn inside,
Just came er bubba.	*Jukayi, umuambila.*	Stand up, tell him about it.
Buska! Buska-reel!	*Bushuwa, bushuseee!*	Truly, Truleee!

This profound dreamwork formula, a recipe for dream sharing long concealed in a nonsense rhyme, shows that African dream culture did indeed travel to North America.

Evidence as concrete as this dream chant is definitely rare. All the same, many of the broad features of dream culture in Africa have parallels in black America. I'll make that case in detail as I describe the features of African American dream life in the chapters to come. These parallel features include the importance placed on *ancestor* dreams, the *predictive* use of dreams, the fluidity of *boundaries* between dreams and other states of consciousness, such as visions, and the *spirituality* of dreams. Taken together, these features strongly suggest that the dream beliefs of their African ancestors continue to influence black Americans today.

This particular African influence has not been singled out in African American studies up till now. Some Americans, nevertheless, recognize a connection between their own attitudes about dreams and the African heritage. Maisha Hamilton-Bennett was deputy commissioner of health for Harold Washington in Chicago, and has taken over a dozen trips to Africa to study indigenous healing. She made this observation about African American "respect and reverence" for dreams:

> It probably comes out of the African cultural tradition, where dreams are very highly regarded, and magical, and show wisdom, and connection between those who are living and the ancestors who have died, and the spiritual world. I think many African Americans have retained some of that through the passing down of oral history and culture and traditions through the generations.

Ivan Watkins is a student of Yoruba and Kongo beliefs as well as Native American beliefs. This young man was raised in New Orleans. He identifies himself as a Black Indian. To his thinking, African influences are thinning, but unquestionably continue:

> The Africanisms in contemporary African American life are ingrained in the people, ingrained in the overall sense of community and family,

and the way that things are perceived and dealt with. A lot of those things are not as alive today as they were just in my parents' generation. But it still survives. In our speech patterns, in our way of interacting, our way of greeting each other. Just in the way that we talk and deal with dreams.

There are, of course, African Americans who make little or nothing of the African background. Essayist Stanley Crouch is a vocal example. He dissociates himself from Afrocentrism by mocking its most superficial form, the "pretentious name changing, costumes, and rituals that [turn] ethnicity into a hysterically nostalgic social club." Two of the novelists I interviewed disavowed Afrocentrism in a more measured way. Gloria Naylor *(Mama Day)* and Leon Forrest *(Divine Days)* concern themselves passionately with black American traditions, but choose not, in Forrest's words, to "get into the Africa thing." Other writers whose novels carry the exploration of roots to the South, but not as far as Africa, include Melvin Dixon *(Trouble the Water)* and Tina McElroy Ansa *(The Hand I Fan With)*.

Nevertheless, there are many black writers who encourage black Americans to embrace the African component of their identities. Playwright August Wilson, for example, "describes his theatrical aim as that of convincing his audience that Afro-Americans are an African people." Other writers who foster Afrocentrism to one degree or another include Margaret Walker *(Jubilee)*, Lance Jeffers *(Witherspoon)*, and of course Toni Morrison *(Song of Solomon)* and Ishmael Reed *(Mumbo Jumbo)*. Among my interviewees, two writers with this motivation are Ntozake Shange *(Sassafrass, Cypress and Indigo)* and Sandra Jackson-Opoku *(The River Where Blood Is Born)*.

Dreams are woven richly into the novels of all these writers, both the non-Afrocentrists and the Afrocentrists. For all of them appreciate the importance of dreams in African American tradition.

One writer who does seem to make a deliberate connection between dreams and Africa is Paule Marshall. Her moving *Praisesong for the Widow* is saturated with dream material. Marshall relates the symbolic death and rebirth of an African American woman: the death of what in North American life divides a black person from African roots, and the rebirth of an Afrocentric identity. This all commences on a luxury Caribbean cruise, and continues during a crossing she makes with island people on a native schooner on their annual excursion to their home island. During that passage she almost literally vomits up her North American identity. At the festival, the islanders dance the dances of their many African tribes of origin. The widow joins in, and is identified by her physique and spontaneous style as an Arada descendant. In addition to this, everything she undergoes keeps evoking memories of her childhood summers spent on the South Carolina islands with a great-aunt. She remembers the ring shout dances in church there, so like the shuffling circle dance of the island Africans. And now she understands fully the import of the story her great-aunt drummed into her of Ibo Landing—of the Ibos who after being landed by the slavers turned right around and walked back to Africa. The various boat passages of the novel echo that crossing as well as the Middle Passage. At the end of the novel, the widow returns to the United States to dedicate herself to teaching her fellow African Americans about her discoveries.

The widow's changes in the novel are instigated by a dream. She dreams that her dead great-aunt appears and takes her back once again to Ibo Landing, repeating the words of the spiritual: *"Come/ Won't you come . . . ?"* This lyric, which the widow had learned in South Carolina as a child, evokes an African spirituality that is expressed both in the *coming through* of black Christian redemption and in the widow's own coming back to her African origins. Her telling of this dream to a double-sighted old Caribbean island man, who recognizes it as a genuine ancestor dream, precipitates the crisis and resolution of the novel and of the woman's life.

Dreams and Survival

We've been speaking about the survival of African dream culture in North America. But cultural survival is more than just a useful concept: it is also a deep article of faith for many of those whose forebears were torn from their native ground, scattered, and deliberately stripped of their cultures. In his play *Going to Meet the Light,* interviewee Daniel Wideman links cultural survival, personal survival, and dreams. A character repeats what her grandmother taught her:

> She told me the only thing that kept Black folks going, through slavery and ever since, was that we got the power to remember what we never knew. That power is what kept our culture alive through the dark times. . . . But no matter how dark it gets, we still rise. We rise because together we can always remember a story we never knew, a dream we never dreamed, and we can ride that dream out and up into the light.

In a century-old short story, Paul Laurence Dunbar had already called attention to dreams as one device by which a slave kept going:

> To him slavery was deep night. What wonder, then, that he should dream, and that through the ivory gate should come to him the forbidden vision of freedom.

In the everyday meaning of "survival," dreaming is one of the "sophisticated coping devices" by which African Americans have "survived so well" through slavery and into the present. This is the view of Darryl Burrows. "It's a way to keep going and be a normal person, despite things that are designed to make you not a normal person."

"Our first responsibility is to survive," said Eileen Cherry, and that is the essential meaning of her exclamation, used as the title of this chapter: "Dream is what we do!" John Edgar Wideman, the father of the Daniel Wideman just quoted, puts it this way when writing about the evolution of the collective consciousness of African Americans:

> Just as swallows eventually figured out how to fly to Capistrano, the historical mind of African people captive in the American South learned how to "get over." From daily encounters with this land, its people, weather, its tasks, this "mind" fashioned visions, dreams, an immaterial, spiritual realm with the density, the hard and fast integrity of rungs on an iron ladder.

Wideman is evoking Jacob's ladder, that enduring African American symbol of "getting over" which Wideman envisions as runged with visions and dreams.

Until her early death, Marion Stamps was a community organizer at Chicago's Cabrini Green projects, and a gadfly at city hall:

> I know for myself, having been part of the whole black movement for self-determination, I've had to rely on spirits and dreams and things that might come as I've sat in a chair that I might not necessarily have thought about. I think it has a lot to do with just survival skills, living in the kind of environment that we are forced to live in.

Following an infamous episode of gang violence in which a young bystander was shot and killed, Stamps circulated an open letter to her community that eventually led to a gang truce. The letter and the community gatherings that cemented and celebrated the truce were inspired by her dream about "a four-day feast":

So when I had this particular dream, it was like I was trying to come up with a way to deal with the violence in the community, you know, the violence had just totally really gotten next to me. And I had gone to sleep, and what I had dreamed about was that the Lord told me he wanted me to plan a four-day feast. The Friday night feast was supposed to be a unity feast where *every*body in the community regardless of who they were were invited. Then on the Saturday night it was only supposed to be certain key people who had certain positions in the community, that they could make a change if they in fact wanted to do that. Then on the Sunday, we would announce this great big unity thing that we had came up with. And then that Monday, it would be a big gala celebration out in the community, okay?

This dream featured in public discourse about the situation, both in the community and on black talk radio. Stamps knew the dream would be taken seriously, would indeed be regarded by many as giving her a kind of authorization. It's difficult to imagine a white political activist approaching a constituency on such terms.

Although the story surrounding Marion Stamps's dream is obviously exceptional, her resort to dreaming as one of her "survival skills" is not. After filmmaker Zeinabu irene Davis told me an amusing dream about kicking the behind of a racist/sexist colleague, I complimented her for having "a very practical dream life." Davis responded in a way few whites in this country would: "Ha-ha, yeah! Yeah, you have to, I think, to survive sometimes. Mm-hm."

PART THREE

The Fabric of the Dream Heritage

3

GRANDMOTHER WILL COME

ANCESTOR VISITATION DREAMS

Yet people, no matter who you are, the spirits are around us all the time. Especially the old ones that know us and have gone on before—the ancestors.

—Bessie Jones

Ancestor Veneration in Africa

Have you ever dreamed about a deceased family member, and believed that the person's spirit actually visited you? Most of the African Americans I interviewed have had this experience. The ancestor visitation dream makes a good place to begin our exploration of the specific features of African American dream life. For ancestor veneration prevails virtually everywhere in Africa, and with it, the visitation dream. As an African writer says, "Africans do believe in dreams because they believe their ancestors still influence the society and help and guide the living in their day-to-day activities."

Such ideas have led Westerners to suppose mistakenly that Africans worship their ancestors. However, we shouldn't speak of African ancestor *worship*—a term loaded with old European stereotypes of tribal Africa—but instead of *veneration*. So says Maulana Karenga, the founder of Kwanzaa. "Africans worship only God, the Creator, in his many manifestations." Ancestors are merely "spiritual intercessors between humans and the Creator." So it is more accurate to say that Africans respect or venerate ancestors.

Further, it generally takes more than simply dying to qualify as an ancestor in Africa: the life lived must be worthy of veneration. This point was made by Songadina Ifatunji, an African American drama professor who has become a Yoruba priest: "Some, we don't call their names, and we hope we don't see them in our dreams, because they've been such rogues in this life. So we let them slip off into wherever souls like that go."

Also, Africans don't regard those newly dead spirits who try to linger here as ancestors. Measures are taken to dispel these clinging spirits. Before they can act as intermediaries, they must first leave this world behind. Yet once spirits become ancestors, they stay close by. In Temne villages (Sierra Leone), people don't sweep their houses after dark, in case they accidentally sweep out a benevolent ancestor.

Africans widely believe that the dead are eventually reincarnated, usually into the same family or lineage. A Zambian infant given the wrong name will cry and cry. If someone now dreams of an ancestor, the dream is discussed and taken to a diviner, who is likely to tell them to rename the child with the ancestor's name. The child is the ancestor reborn. As soon as the child gets its real name back, it stops crying.

In the African view, dreams above all else serve as a channel of communication from the ancestors to the living. "When a person dies," said Songadina Ifatunji, "part of even the funeral rite, part of the traditional thing that is said is, 'From now on, we will see you in our dreams.' " He was describing the ways of the Yoruba (Nigeria). Some groups warmly welcome ancestor dreams (Zulu, South Africa), some take a more guarded view of visitations (Tiv, Nigeria). But generally speaking, Africans believe that the dead return to offer advice to the living, warn them, give them insight into the future, correct their conduct, and admonish them for neglecting spiritual duties.

Newly converted African Christians and Muslims often reconcile their traditional beliefs about ancestor dreams with their adopted faith. The ancestors, as one Zimbabwean Christian puts it, "get permission from God to communicate their messages to us." Dreams often play a role in conversion to the new religion, and these dreams can follow the pattern of traditional ancestor dreams. For example, a woman from Sierra Leone dreamed she was stumbling over uneven ground and through thorny shrubs when her three dead children "found her, took her by the hand and brought her to a fine path." They begged her to stop trading on Sundays and to foreswear "traditional religious practices." The woman interpreted her dream "as God speaking to her." The scholar who recorded this story comments that "members of one's family appearing from the spirit world to advocate a change from one path to another is a very traditional theme."

"Throughout most of Africa," said Maisha Hamilton-Bennett, after many travels there, "even educated people, even people who are generations removed, even those who are very Christian or very Muslim, still hold on in their cores to these African beliefs that predate the Western religions."

Ancestor Veneration in Black America

African ancestor veneration marks many customs of the Caribbean and northeastern South America, where religions of unmistakably African origin flourish—Vodun (Voodoo), Santeria, Candomble, and so on. By contrast, in North America only a few traces of specific African customs remain. In parts of the Deep South, offerings are still placed on graves in the African manner. And Gullah rituals survive on South Carolina's Sea Islands for warding off spirits that linger after death: when the mother of an infant dies, the baby is passed over her coffin. This prevents the mother's spirit from haunting her child's dreams.

The fact is, however, that the average African American probably knows little if anything about grave adornment or passing babies over coffins. At the same time, there is a general mind-set toward ancestors that does reveal the ongoing influence of Africa. Think of the *respect traditionally shown to elders,* for example, and of the attention given to *funerals.* A widely held belief in *reincarnation,* discussed in later chapters, also probably has roots in Africa.

And so does the belief that *ancestors are concerned for the living.* In the 1930s, a folklorist was told that the spirits of our dead surround us and care for us, until they reincarnate. A contemporary folklorist still finds that "the spirits of dead relatives are believed to maintain a lively interest in their earthbound relatives." The dead "return as problem-solvers." Civic organizer Darryl Burrows put this same, very

African idea in a contemporary religious context without making any reference to Africa itself:

> We all [in my family] believe that prayer works. A dying ancestor who's dying in Christ and lifts a prayer to God in the name of Christ in your behalf is endowing you with something that will last your whole life. Now that is a very strong belief. I frankly never heard a white person have that point of view. And my mom believes that the dead pray for the living. That the dead are already taken care of, it's the living who have the problem. She'll say, "That's your grandmother. Your grand-mother's making sure that this happened to you."

Do African Americans themselves think their own beliefs and attitudes about dead relatives are African? Most of those who gave an opinion during my interviews both perceived and embraced the African influence. One was Marshall Hatch, a Doctor of Divinity as well as a Baptist minister:

> My aunt is ninety-two. And she'll say, "Your father came and sat on my bed last night, and I talked to him." And she's perfectly sane. You know, there's communication with the dead. People, when they dream about the dead, and the conversations they have, they never talk about it as a dream, they talk about it as reality. Which is very African, you know. So it's a way that the past—well, the ancestors are still involved in the present, through the dream.
>   *Do you personally believe that that is true in a real, spiritual sense?*
> I do, as a matter of fact. I wouldn't encourage people to overrely on that kinda thing, because I really believe that the scripture is the foundation of our community. But as an African myself, you know, I go past all of the training that I've received in Western schools. If my aunt says she's talked to my dad, I'm probably sixty or sixty-five percent convinced, 'cause I guess I'm an African in the sense that I revere her! For being ninety-two.

Zeinabu irene Davis might agree. She makes films with themes of the African American past and once lived for over a year in Africa. Davis keeps an "ancestor shrine," leaves a plate of her grandmother's favorite candies out for her, and dedicates spots around the house to other deceased relatives and friends. These rituals "make peace" with her ancestors and invite their guidance. I asked Davis if this orientation comes from learning about Africa as an adult, or from her own African American upbringing. She replied:

I think that it's a little bit of both, actually. I think that as a child I may have heard things, but not been able to explore them because I was a child. I do remember my grandparents speak. "Oh, you know, Auntie May said so-and-so," or "So-and-so came to me and told me."

Eileen Cherry remembered her mother's visitation dreams: "My mother would get up and say, 'Oh, Mama came to me last night!' And that would mean something *good* was going to happen!" Like Davis, Cherry has blended the remnants of ancestor veneration from her family life into an informed Afrocentric perspective. A year or so previously she had become involved in Lukumi, an Afro-Cuban religion. And as she explained:

I'm finding that a lot of their approach to life is sort of the way that I was brought up. The knowledge is still there in the culture: that there *is* no division between the world of the living and the world of the dead. That they are very present, and participating in our lives.

One woman arrived at an Afrocentric view of ancestors as the result of a "revelatory" visitation dream at age thirty-three. She had been raised in a family that was secularized and assimilated on both sides, with no interest in dreams whatever and "no continuation of the oral tradition and Africanisms." She told the following story:

I went to a party for all entering black graduate students at Yale. And there was a divinity student there, an American, but he was also a Yoruba priest. And he came up to me and he said, "Soon your grandmother will come to you in a dream, as a result of having made this change in your life." I just looked at him and said, "Well, she already did"—my father's mother, who was an amazing force in our life. And I still remember the dream so distinctly. She was standing in the door, and I knew that she was dead because her eyes were all glazed over. And she was holding the door open for me. And I interpreted that to be her affirmation of this change that I had made in my life.

But of course what was interesting was that this is a typical African dream. That your grandmother comes to you at important points in your life, and provides you with signals. That's what this divinity student told me. That's just amazing! You know, from four hundred years severed. Even though my grandmother was not the folksy type! She was also very antireligious.

In recent decades, some black authors have encouraged the "embrace of the African concept of the Ancestor-as-Guide," as Sydné

Mahone puts it. Earlier writers like Langston Hughes, Richard Wright, Ralph Ellison, and James Baldwin only touched the ancestor theme. But from the 1970s to the present, the theme has grown familiar. Thus the epigraph of *Sent for You Yesterday,* the third book of John Edgar Wideman's Homewood Trilogy, reads:

> Past lives live in us, through us. Each of us harbors the spirits of people who walked the earth before we did, and those spirits depend on us for continuing existence, just as we depend on their presence to live our lives to the fullest.

And in a novel from the 1990s, Wideman invokes the African past, "when our flesh was a fit vessel for the ancestral spirits. . . ."

The word itself—"ancestor"—may or may not be employed by black writers when they treat the theme. Take, for example, Toni Morrison's *Beloved,* about a house, and a world, "peopled by the living activity of the dead." Morrison doesn't actually say "ancestors," but this Afrocentric concept enlivens the novel as it does other works of hers, especially *Song of Solomon.*

But some contemporary writers do employ the word "ancestor" as a conscious expression of Afrocentrism. Thus Shay Youngblood, raised in Georgia, writes autobiographical stories about a girl whose female relatives "depended on ancestor spirits to advise." When asked, Youngblood conceded that "ancestor spirits" isn't a phrase her relatives would have used. Likewise, when Paule Marshall, whose novel affirming African roots was described in chapter 2, writes that she's "an unabashed ancestor worshipper," she is most likely using consciously adopted language.

This isn't to say that the word doesn't come spontaneously to others. Kai EL Zabar told me that when she prays before bed, "I acknowledge all of what we call our ancestors." This is the traditional way of her family, North Carolina Geechees now in Chicago. And Angela Powell learned during childhood summers spent in Alabama about communicating with "ancestors" in dreams.

As part of the literary theme of ancestors, ancestor dreams (and visions) figure in quite a lot of the theater, poetry, autobiography, and fiction of recent decades. This motif grows out of, and also grows into, a heritage of beliefs about ancestors and dreams with roots in Africa. We'll see how strong this heritage remains as we turn now to a sampling of ancestor visitation dreams from the interviews. The material is divided into sections that highlight the main characteristics of dreams of this type.

Ancestor Visitation Dreams

An "ancestor visitation dream" is experienced as a spiritual event, not simply as a dream about one's dead that comes from grief or guilt or love. Such dreams have their own psychological interest, but the dreamer doesn't regard them as spiritual visitations. Such merely psychological dreams lack the special feeling tone of visitations.

Feeling Tone

It's said that there's a "clear difference" between visitation dreams and other dreams, in the "uncanny or unearthly quality" visitations have. This special feeling colors the experience, even when the action taking place in the dream is unremarkable. Here are several examples.

A woman who liked watching sports with her father before he died dreamed of sitting in front of the TV with him again. When I asked if she thought the dead were actually present in such matter-of-fact dreams, she replied, "Whether they're there only as a dream person, kinda floating around? Uh-uh, no, they're alive."

Similarly, Winford Williams, a baker, had a dream visitation from a long-dead sister. Brother and sister were "just sitting on the couch, talking to each other, laughing." He, too, felt that her spirit was really there.

Journalist and writer Kai EL Zabar had a visitation dream set in her childhood bedroom. EL Zabar was her present age, forty-one, and her current boyfriend was sitting on the bed. Her mother came in and lectured her for having a man in her bedroom: "We just had a conversation. It wasn't necessarily predicting anything or anything. I guess that I want her to meet him." That sounds like a basic psychological interpretation of the dream such as anyone might have made. But for EL Zabar, it wasn't that simple:

> No. I felt her. That's the presence, or the aura of her, or whatever you want to call it, but it's her. And you don't understand that until you experience it.

You wouldn't know any one of these very ordinary-sounding dreams was a visitation just from hearing it told. Yet each had a special quality that the dreamer recognized.

There are some visitation dreams in which the special feeling tone seems to be almost the whole substance of the dream. While Lucius Bell, a teacher and a musician, sometimes has ordinary dreams in which his grandmother plays a role, "the two times that I *envisioned* her, were in my sleep. It was just a head shot and a bust shot. And, it was . . . *her!*"

And a woman whose mother had died four years earlier was sure that

> she has communicated with me through dreams. Not "Hi, how are you doing?" "Get your life back on track!" It's more of a sensation, almost a physical enveloping, very peaceful. Which is very different from other times when I dream *about* her, and I wake up and know it's a dream where I see her, and she's doing something. This is just more of a . . . of a presence.

Messages from the Dead

Not all, but most visitation dreams are said to contain guidance or a warning, or some other information. Secretary and writer Regina Reed speaks of "ancestors visiting through dreams. Usually mothers, deceased ancestors. Oftentimes bringing you a message. Or to give you a warning." Here are a few other reports of message dreams:

> My grandmother kept saying, "I keep telling J. R. to grow up and stop doing the things he know is wrong." My father says, "J. R., get it together, Son, we're depending on you. Look around, everybody's dying." Then I look up at my grandfather and he says, "Your life is wasting away, boy." *(A prisoner)*

> My mother was crying, and she said, "You've trusted your roommate too much." Because I was in a boardinghouse. And truly, one week later, I found out what my roommate had been doing. *(Nicole Smith)*

> *All* of them showed: my auntie, my mother, my grandmother, my grandpa, my uncle, *all* of 'em. And it was about me moving up to the North Side here. They all came, they say: "Move!" All of them had one word to say to me. They all said, "Move!" *(Yusuf Abdullah)*

These dream messages came in very direct words. But just as often the dreamer needs to interpret the dream to find its message. Writer Sandra Jackson-Opoku told me she dreamed that

> myself and my sister and my two kids went to look at my grandmother's house, that her and my step-grandfather built from scratch. And then we saw her standing in the doorway, saying, "Come on in! Come on in!" And we said, "Well, this is really weird, 'cause she's *dead,* isn't she?" And my sister said, "Yeah, she's dead, but let's go on in." So we went in, and the house was just like it used to look and everything. And she said, "Are you all hungry?" and we said, "Yeah." And she cooked us a meal, and we sat down and ate it. And then she encouraged us to

spend the night, and we spent the night. And then the next day, I had to take the kids to school, so we left very early, and she waved us away, and said, "Come back."

And so I called my mother and I said, "I had the strangest dream about M'Dear." And she said, "Oh, well you know, Johnny lost the house, and the house is being sold." So I called my sister and she said, "Well, you know, I saw, in the *Beverly Review*, M'Dear's house, that it was being auctioned off. Let's see if we can try to get it, 'cause M'Dear was probably telling you to save her *house*." And I said, "Well, maybe so."

Sometimes the personality of the ancestor shines through the message. One of Kimberly Camp's "ancestors" delivers his messages using "comic relief":

I have one uncle who's a real stitch. He thinks I'm amusing. He gets a kick outta watching me figure out how to get in and out of situations. You know, after I've gone to bed distraught. And I'll see him holding his belly and laughing hysterically. So, I know it's not really a big deal.
Is it your belief that this is your uncle's soul or spirit actually in contact?
It's not a belief, it is!
You're aware that some people would be skeptical.
Well, that's fine. They don't have an uncle like mine.

A certain number of visitation dreams bring *psychic* messages—that is, they contain (or the dreamer believes they contain) information the dreamer didn't or couldn't know in the ordinary way—such as what numbers to play. Janitorial worker Laura McKnight explained that her family of birth often talked about ancestors who came in dreams, "because we always say, 'They're trying to bring you some money.'" This tradition continues with her own five children. Similarly, writer Sheron Williams-Brooks's mother phoned her to say that

"Uncle Bill came to me 5 times, and he told me his shoe didn't fit. He had a size 13, it didn't fit: that's 5-12, I *know* it is!" So she's gonna play that number, and *not* gonna jump off of it.

Dreams foretelling deaths aren't uncommon, and sometimes the warning is brought by ancestors. For example, a prisoner noted that a dead aunt "visited my dreams. She warned of the death of her mother, my grandmother, who recently passed." And novelist Gloria Naylor is convinced that her father came with the news of his own death. She explained:

If you dreamt about someone and then they died, that was taken as some kind of message. Well, you know, but there's something to this stuff, I'm sorry. I dreamt about my father the night he died. And I'd never dreamt about him before, so. I dreamt that he was in this sort of white suit and white hat, and he looked something like J. R. Ewing in a way. Yeah, really weird. And he was in this room, and it was just foggy, it was just foggy. And normally I don't remember my night dreams. And I woke up and I said, "How strange! Why would I dream about Daddy?" 'Cause I think whenever you dreamt white, it meant death, that was the point.

In another fairly common message dream, dead relatives come back to say they're "okay" in the next world. Osuurete Adesanya, a teacher and a Yoruba priest, was seven years old when her brother drowned. The family delayed telling her, to spare her feelings. Meanwhile, she began seeing visions of her absent brother. And then he came to her in a dream and asked her to tell the family to stop crying:

> So I told my mother that "Genie came," and I asked, "Where's Genie? 'Cause he came in a dream, and told me that everybody should stop crying, 'cause everything was all right. So where's he at?" And that's when they just started looking at me.

Yolanda Scheunemann, a psychotherapist, provided another vivid example. Her son was killed in an electrocution accident outside their home just days after graduating from high school with honors and great expectations. The first time she was able to fall asleep, she dreamed of him:

> What I dreamed—except that it was almost real—was that David came into the bedroom. I was on top of the bed, sleeping. And I opened my eyes, and there was David. He came into the bedroom, dressed exactly as he had been dressed, in his gym shoes and shorts and shirt. And he simply said, "Hi, Mom." And he was fine. And when I woke up from that dream, it was the first indication that I had that I might survive this. So I must tell you that I felt that he had come to me. And though he didn't say, "I'm fine, I want you to know I'm all right," I have now this feeling that he is all right.

Ancestor Guardians

Just after a dear friend, a young white man, had died, student Illana Jordan dreamed about "a really dark, dark beautiful black man":

> And he'd tie my shoe for me. And I'd cry, and he'd hold me. And there was this friend of his with him, and the two of them followed me around, making sure I was okay. And I went and told my mom, and I'm

like, "Mom, there's this black man and there's this white man." And she's like, "Well, maybe the black man is my brother. And he's letting you know that you're not alone. And maybe the white guy is your friend Steve."

Illana Jordan's dream has a theme that runs through many of these visitation dreams, the theme of *guardianship*. The ancestor protects, guides, affirms, or comforts the dreamer. The following personal history, written by a prisoner, captures the essence of that theme:

> When I was 16 and in jail my great-grandmother died. After I became politicized in 1985 I used to reflect on all the times she tried to sit me down and talk to me, but I was young and impatient. I longed to talk to her about Our history, her past and struggles as a black womyn in amerikkka. At some point she began to appear in my dreams and it was like she was passing on to me the knowledge and legacy that she did not get a chance to pass on to me in life. She would tell me a little about her life and that I needed to be strong.

When the topic of visitations came up with professor and political activist Douglas Gills, he made these observations about his potential guardian ancestors:

> Now my father, he would have been on my aunt's side of that: "If I went to heaven, I don't want to come back, and if I went to hell, I can't come back." So I don't expect to see him. Now my mother would try. Now she's daring. She would say, "I'm gonna always be around you, messing with you. Giving you comfort when you need it. But I just like visiting."

And after telling me about the time he heard his deceased grandfather dragging his lame leg down the hall, Gills mentioned a dream visitation from this ancestor: "I think it was his head. And it wasn't like some interactive conversation, it was more like, 'You're doing an all right job.' As long as I can get those appraisals, I'll be all right."

Likewise, video artist Ayanna Udongo was reassured by a guardian dream she had after getting in trouble with her family when a work commitment forced her to miss her great-aunt's funeral:

> When you can't come to a loved one, a *great*–loved one's funeral, you really catch hell in the black community! And they just ignored me for a couple of months, because I didn't come. But *she* came to me, my Aunt Mary did, and let me know everything was okay. And it wasn't nothing for me to be upset about, and that she was happy where she was. And then she told me that she loved me, and she said something

to the effect that there's gonna be great things happening for me. And it was like she was out there like my guardian, letting me know. And all I can see is like her face, and like this great light behind her, and she's smiling. It was really wonderful!

Unwelcome Visitations

In European tradition, visitations are usually sinister events. For African Americans, by contrast, helpful and loving visitations outnumber the sinister kind. This positive view of the dead, a scholar observes, exists among African Americans today as a survival of the "African belief" that ancestors are guardians.

All the same, Africans do sometimes view their ancestors as dangerous spirits, and African Americans can see them in that light as well. Kai EL Zabar's mother sold her house when her deceased husband kept "appearing at the foot of the bed." He just made her "uncomfortable," she said. But the reason usually given for fearing visitations is that the dead bring death. Journalist Norma Adams Wade said visitations were "fairly common" in her natal family. It meant "they had come to get somebody, to welcome them home. Not necessarily the dreamer. Their appearance meant, watch out, somebody's gonna go." Accountant Angie Williams said:

> So the whole idea of crossing over, and what that's like, and who comes to get you: those are things that have been discussed a lot of times. My grandmother was in the hospital, and she saw her mother [in a dream]. And so my mother and her sisters prayed very hard, 'cause they said her mother was coming to take her, and they weren't ready for her to go.

Gallery owner Oscar Edmond dreamed of being chased by several ancestors. "If they would have caught you," his grandmother told him, "you would have died."

The danger doesn't necessarily arise from ill intentions on the part of the spirits, as another dream of Edmond's shows. These ancestors tried to protect him from the danger they themselves apparently couldn't help causing:

> I'm shooting basketball in the playground, and all of a sudden I see my grandma, my uncle, and my aunt. I went "Aw!" I jumped over the fence and started running after them, trying to catch up with them, 'cause I wanted to see them. And then, my uncle kind of turned around, and was trying to tell me, "Man, we're dead! You don't want to go with us!" And then I remember stopping in my tracks. And woke up. The interpretation of it that I got from my mom and them was basically that my

grandmother was deceased, and if I had caught up with them, I would have died in my sleep. And to keep me where I was at, in the land of the living, they ran from me!

Oscar's mother Adrienne Edmond felt endangered by her mother in a positively idyllic dream, "a spiritual dream." There were

> these flowers that I have never seen. And it was like the grass, instead of green it looked bluish. And the grass was high, and it went over, it didn't stand. It was beautiful grass. And it was a sunny day and we were like leaping. We were so happy. And she had my hand. And I was skeptical of that dream, 'cause my mother is deceased. . . . Am I going with her, or what?

Notice the element in this dream of being *touched* by the deceased. The belief that a spirit's touch is dangerous can be traced to Africa. Such a belief influences Adekola Adedapo, who has had recurring dreams in which her dead grandmother tries to hug her:

> You know, we were always taught, don't ever hug a dead person in a dream, because they're coming to get you. And you'll die, or you'll get sick. And after I started studying Yoruba, and got into African religion, I found out that truly in Africa, when you dream of a dead person, they say, "Don't let them touch you." You're either going to get sick, or you might die. It may be a sign that they're coming to get you, and if it ain't your time, then you need to do some kind of sacrifice to get it off of you. The newer the dead person is, the more dangerous it is to have physical contact with them in the dream, because it means they miss you, and they've come to get you.

Unknown Ancestors

Africans say they dream not only about ancestors they knew in life, but also about ancestors who lived and died before they were born. What about African Americans? "If they knew the dead person," commented Songadina Ifatunji, "you almost always hear stories of dreams after a funeral or during the first year. But I don't think people have a lot of sensitivity to dead people they *don't* know."

Compared to Africans, that may be true, but I did hear a number of dreams about ancestors not personally known by the dreamers. At age seven, Robert Blaine, an eighty-six-year-old minister, was first visited in a dream by his lifelong spiritual "intercessor," who announced that "he would use me." When the boy described the strange figure to his grandmother, he learned it was his grandfather. Gallery owner Nicole Smith wished for and finally received a dream visit from a grandmother who died before she was born. " 'I am your grandma,' " announced the visitor, who came "just to get acquainted." Filmmaker Zeinabu irene Davis dreamed about "this woman in a rocking chair, on a porch, smoking a pipe." She asked her father and learned that "your great-grandmother smoked a pipe."

Davis believes that "a lot of family history comes back in my dream life." So does writer Colleen McElroy. She has dreams in which she personally experiences episodes of long-ago family history previously unknown to her, such as coming to the North on a Mississippi barge. Her grandmother is usually able to tell her who actually lived the events and when they happened.

Some dreamers believe they're visited by ancestors whom nobody remembers anymore. Editor and journalist Kai EL Zabar said, "You can be spoken to by ancestors from time, but they're gonna come in a form or in a way that I can understand." Writer Sandra Jackson-Opoku has special dreams, "a lot different" from her "regular dreams," in which she gets whole stories from "ancestors whispering in my ear while I'm asleep, telling me about things that have happened." Writer Angela Jackson revealed reluctantly, out of reverence, that her father, a "very psychic" man, had dreams about "ancestors coming into the house in overalls. From slavery days. Farmers." Social worker Angela Powell learned as a child to expect messages from slave ancestors:

> I subscribe to it, and it was definitely something that my grandparents told me. That sometimes my great-great-grandmother or my great-great-great-grandmother or -grandfather, whatever, might try to tell me something through a dream.

"Ancestors" Who Aren't Relatives

Most visitations involve family. At the same time, some visiting spirits who aren't family may nevertheless be regarded as ancestors. The individuals who spoke to me in these terms all had a strong sense of the collective past of African Americans. The "ancestors" of artist Marva Pitchford Jolly's dreams are "not just relatives. It's all of the old people that I need to be in touch with, in order to do the things that I need to get done." Gwen Robinson gave an account of a visitation from Madame C. J. Walker, the pioneering black female entrepreneur and philanthropist, about whom Robinson was doing scholarly research:

> And frankly, I felt that the dream had a message. And that the person, Madame C. J. Walker, *was* speaking to me. In the dream she was sort

of coming back from the dead. I distinctly remember being conscious of that. There was an auditorium, there was a program that was going on. And I don't recall now whether she spoke to me directly or not. But the message I was getting was, there was a certain way she wanted me to deal with her life. And so I felt as if I had a special mission, that she was communicating to me that yes, she wanted me to tell her story.

Are Ancestor Visitation Dreams on the Wane?

How common is it for people to believe they've been visited by ancestors in dreams? Fully 70 percent of the interviewees in my sample say they've had the experience. By comparison, just 34 percent of whites in my sample said so. By any reckoning, all these numbers are impressively high, but clearly higher for blacks than for whites.

Apart from statistics, my impression is that visitations bringing guidance, advice, and warnings are not the commonplace to whites that they are to blacks. Dreaming in this vein just doesn't have the same place in white family life and lore. Novelist Ishmael Reed represents his own black family background as typical when he writes:

> My mother is the clairvoyant of the family. She has the gift of precognition and she communicates with apparitions of deceased relatives who bring her important news, prophecies, and, of course, fortune.
>
> Thousands upon thousands of blacks have these abilities. . . .
> I wouldn't be surprised if it turns out that Afros have a larger percentage of people with these *psi* abilities than other groups.

The findings of this and later chapters point in the direction Reed indicates.

And yet, many African Americans will tell you that ancestor dreams no longer have the same currency. "Years ago," observed retired manager Otis Grove at age sixty-four, "you talk to someone, they say, 'Oh, I had a dream, and grandma came to me.' You don't hear that. Not in *my* setting." Visitations are viewed by many as part of the past. "From time to time," recalled fifty-two-year-old radio journalist Richard Steele, "my grandmother and other people of that generation would say, "You know, my mother came to me in a dream. . . ."" Tamera Kilpatrick, age thirty-one, knows that "a lot of the African-American community believes that they've had visits from relatives in the past," but she herself has no belief in any sort of survival after death.

But in spite of observations such as these, any downward trend is very slight at most. Of my oldest interviewees (age fifty-six years and above), 73 percent reported ancestor visitation dreams; of the middle group (age thirty-six to fifty-five), it was 72 percent; while of the youngest group (eighteen to thirty-five), 64 percent had already experienced such dreams.

How, then, to account for the fairly widespread impression among African Americans themselves that ancestor visitation dreams are a fading phenomenon? The reason is that increasing levels of education and exposure to mainstream secular values have created a climate not so much of skepticism as of the *expectation* of skepticism. While some individuals have been swayed to disbelief, others simply don't want to appear "country." Therefore they talk less freely about visitations than they used to, even though as many people still experience them. Faheem Ashanti, staff psychologist at North Carolina State University and a Voodoo priest, commented about his students:

> The whole area of dreams as relates to anything having to do with ancestors coming back to speak with you, or . . . anything like that, that's taboo and they ain't gonna talk about it. But . . . on my wall as part of my regular office decor, I'll have things up that they can look at and it'll bring out their curiosity, and they will ask me, "You don't believe in *that* stuff, do you?" When I answer, "*Sure* I do!" then that's when they open up.

It's often supposed that education and prosperity reduce belief in things like visitations. But actually, anomalous experiences are, generally speaking, more rather than less common at higher education and income levels. In keeping with this pattern, ancestor dreams have been experienced more by those interviewees with middle-class childhoods (82 percent) than by those with lower/working/farm-class childhoods (63 percent).

In other words, we're not dealing here with the residues of poverty and ignorance. At the same time, some African Americans may *suppose* such is the case, and even more, they may suppose that *others* suppose it's the case. For this reason, a number of interviewees apologized a little for their beliefs. "I'm not a very religious person," said Sandra Jackson-Opoku, "or a superstitious person, but . . ." Illana Jordan exclaimed, "I hope I'm not nutty!"

On the other hand, Eileen Cherry spoke energetically for those who reject any skepticism. After she told me about her mother's visitation dreams, I asked if she, a doctoral candidate at a prestigious university, holds the same beliefs. She pointed around her room, at her stacks of books, her literary awards, her diplomas for subjects ranging from gospel to psychotherapy:

> I'm a very sophisticated person! [But] I'm very whole. I do, I embrace it. I don't think it's eclectic, I think it harmonizes. And I've never been, in my life, cynical about it.

4

THAT BOLT OF LIGHTNING

PREDICTIVE DREAMS

*All those tales about things that people sensed before they actually happened.
Tales that had been handed down and down and down until, if you tried to
trace them back, you'd end up God knows where—probably Africa. And
Granny had them all at the tip of her tongue.*

—Ann Petry

Who Believes in Predictive Dreams?

Virtually the whole world believes dreams can predict the future—the
whole world, that is, apart from modern Europe and North America.
At one time the West was as sure of predictive dreaming as everyone
else. But the scientific-rational worldview has steadily eroded belief.
Nowadays, however, a small rebound of interest in psychic dreaming
is being seen among dream scholars. They can point to the great
dream psychologists Freud and Jung, both of whom expressed guarded
belief based on their own experiences. Moreover, among the general
population belief in psychic events of one sort or another still runs
quite high—between 25 percent and 50 percent in most surveys.

Furthermore, belief in predictive dreaming definitely runs higher
among blacks than among whites in the United States. This is the
clear finding of my own survey. The belief was affirmed by fully 92
percent of the interviewees, but by a much lower 57 percent of the
white sample. Thus all but a small percentage of blacks believe in predictive dreams, while only something over half of whites do.

Above and beyond the yes-or-no question of belief, many more
blacks than whites think prediction is *the* important thing about

dreams. It tops the list of dream functions for blacks, whereas for whites, it holds an uncertain position along with psychological insight, problem solving, and the proposition that dreams have no function at all.

By contrast, listen to these characteristic comments from African Americans:

> I always think about dreams as something that's gonna happen in the future. *(Reggie Winfrey)*

> As a child, I believed that my mother was shown, through dreams, things that were gonna happen to people. *(Frances Callaway Parks)*

> I think everyone has dreams that are prophetic. *(Judy Still)*

Sculptor Preston Jackson, raised by parents from Tennessee in Decatur, Illinois, summed up the prevailing attitude. His father was a Baptist minister:

> If you started this conversation in my family, you wouldn't get out of here, because they would have dreams. My brothers and sisters and parents believed in dreams. . . . Live it. Do it. It's a prophecy. It's something you better follow up on, because it means something. And this is the educated part of my family. All of us went to college. And they *still* talk the same way about dreams.

Even the doubts expressed by some interviewees testify to the prevalence of the belief. Journalist and "concrete thinker" Richard Steele said:

> When discussion about dreams comes up in our culture, there are some people who view that as a kind of harbinger of something that's gonna happen, or there's a premonition somewhere in the dream. And I'm very much a skeptic about that.

Steele's very skepticism reflected his acquaintance with the prevailing theory. What's more, a shadow of that theory fell over a memorable dream of his. He dreamed of being shot in the stomach and then bleeding to death in an emergency room:

> And as a matter of fact, I said to my wife, even though I'm not a great believer in dreaming the thing that's gonna happen, I said, "You know, the thing was so strong, I have this feeling that I'm gonna be somewhere and somebody's gonna shoot a gun, I'm gonna get shot in the stomach and bleed to death."

African Influences

In chapter 2, we heard Maisha Hamilton-Bennett's opinion that African American dream beliefs retain African features. When I asked this student of Africa to be specific, she replied, "The most important thing is that many African Americans think that there's something in the dream that's going to tell you what's going to happen."

Notice how similar the following two statements about predictive dreams are, one written by an African, one by an American:

> Dreams convey warnings or messages pertaining to one's future. In this process, ancestor spirits act as intermediaries [for the] Supreme Being.

> Sometimes the ancestors deem certain information so important that they send it to the subconscious mind without being consciously asked. Then we have prophetic dreams, rich in symbolism and unforgettable!

The first is from *The Usefulness of Dreams: An African Perspective,* by West African Mary Chinkwita. The second is from *Jambalaya,* a handbook of African American spirituality by Luisah Teish. Teish's mention of the ancestors may be self-conscious, but she's genuinely drawing on her African American experience.

Let's look briefly at how dreams are processed in traditional Africa. When a Ngoni (Malawi), for instance, has a dream that feels important, he or she first tells the family about it. If no interpretation emerges, the family goes to a village elder or priest who knows how to interpret dreams. In most cases, the dream will be found to convey advice from an ancestor about what's going on, what to do, or what will happen.

The way Africans interpret dreams is usually called *divination.* The dream expert reads the pattern formed when a tray of shells or a chain or other material is thrown on the ground. This approach may appear simplistic, but it isn't. It's part of a modality of healing based on a comprehensive philosophy. The Yoruban (Nigeria) diviner, for example, discerns in the pattern on the ground one or more of 256 categories of human experience. These experiences belong in sixteen groups that correspond to the gods, or *orishas,* who influence the pattern that falls. Moreover, each of the 256 general types of experience is filled out by up to a hundred specific stories known to the diviner from family and tribal history. These, together with an understanding of the divine order, are brought to bear on the person's life and dream.

In the Independent "prophet-healing" churches, beliefs about dreams remain fundamentally close to tradition. Casting shells or chains is prohibited as anti-Christian, but ministers have the role of interpreting church members' dreams. This they do both in private and as part of the church service. As in traditional practice, dream divination is used both to diagnose the causes of present problems and to foretell the future.

Slavery Days and Folklore

Although the specifics of African dream divination such as casting shells or the categorization of 256 experiences didn't survive in North America, the intent of African divination did survive in the inclination of African Americans to believe that dreams sometimes predict the future.

The little we can know directly about dream beliefs in slavery days comes from a few stories out of the lives of heroes of black history. The renowned Frederick Douglass wrote about a dream foretelling the failure of his first attempt to escape from slavery. A confederate in the plan, "Sandy, the root man," dreamed some troubling dreams, one of which "somewhat damped" Douglass's spirits:

> "I saw you, Frederick, in the claws of a huge bird, surrounded by a large number of birds, of all colors and sizes. These were all picking at you, while you, with your arms, seemed to be trying to protect your eyes. . . . "
>
> I confess I did not like this dream. . . . Sandy was unusually emphatic and oracular, and his manner had much to do with the impression made upon me.

Harriet Tubman (who had dreams showing her the routes for the Underground Railroad) accounted for her calmness when emancipation was proclaimed in 1863 by explaining that she had already done her celebrating three years earlier. One morning in 1860, the unerring conductress had arisen singing

> "My people are free! My people are free!" She came down to breakfast singing the words in sort of ecstasy. She could not eat. The dream or vision filled her whole soul, and physical needs were forgotten.

Stories like these indicate that prophetic dreaming was widely taken for granted by African Americans before emancipation.

Folklore, a bridge between those times and the present, suggests a widespread belief in predictive dreaming well into the twentieth century. In the 1920s, folklorist Newbell Niles Puckett collected items about the causes for dreams coming true (such as sleeping under a new quilt) and about means to prevent that (such as throwing salt into the fire). Harry Middleton Hyatt, working in the 1930s, found many individuals who "lay down to sleep and see different things before they come to pass." For instance, a husband whose wife left him due to a hex dreamed that a man told him to go to the plum tree in his yard with a piece of white pine, call his wife's name nine times, and hit a leaf off the tree with the wood. He was to do this for three days and nights. After the third night he awoke convinced his wife was returning, for now he'd dreamed he saw her coming. And she did soon return, promising not to leave again.

Richard M. Dorson's collections from the 1950s also contain predictive dreams, including a "Treasure Dream." A man told how he and his wife regularly used to see the ghost of an Irishman in their yard. Then the Irishman appeared in a dream and told the man he would find money buried in the yard. It was guarded by the spirit of a "colored man" who'd been killed by his owner expressly to be a guard. When they attempted to dig up the treasure, they were scared off by huge spirits like "buffalo cows." Stories of this type are now rarely heard, though they do linger in the lore of some black families.

Then what are predictive dreams like, as contemporary African Americans experience them? That's the question for the rest of this chapter.

The Nature of Predictive Dreams

Literal Predictions and Symbolic Predictions

One of the most intriguing things about dreams is the inventive imagery they often bring. But not all dreams contain bizarre imagery. Some dreams are highly realistic. And this in itself becomes intriguing, when the future is what's pictured. A woman told me:

> I would dream at six o'clock in the morning that such-and-such a person would die, and by twelve noon, he's gone! [My grandfather] wondered, "Where in the hell is she getting all this information? It's just too factual. I mean, one or two a year is great, but not every morning! You're sitting around the breakfast table and she's marking off your friends! 'Well he's gone, and this one's on his way out, and guess what, Gramps? I see you slipping down there, too!'"

This woman said the predictions in her dreams were always literal: "Always. Straight out. There were never any hidden things where I had to make inferences."

A surprising number of literal predictions emerged from my interviews. Betty Rodgers Hale said of her dream predicting twins, "I do not dream symbolically, no. I dream the thing. I see twins, not two trees or something." Other examples include car accidents (Charles Payne), a grandmother's fall and hospitalization (Adrienne Edmond), Harold Washington's election as mayor of Chicago in 1983 (Nicole Smith), an aunt's death in a fire set by her husband and the telephone call of notification (Katie Jones), and literal numbers to gamble on (Edwina Ackie, Reggie Winfrey).

But many people see no real difference between a literal forecast and one in which the exact prediction is only known after events explain the dream. Consider the example of Marion Stamps, who had what at first seemed to be a literal dream about a "four-day feast" that would bring about a gang truce at the Cabrini Green projects:

> But that wasn't what the dream was saying. The dream was saying that in order for you to bring about the kind of peace that is necessary for this community to survive, there's some other kind of groundwork that must be laid. . . . Rather than them coming together up under one room for a feast, they came together up under one room for—for a program.

Eileen Cherry's predictive dream about the space shuttle explosion actually showed the shuttle and a fireworks display, like a "celebration," in a "little framed-off picture on a computer screen. Then when it happened, I flashed back to the dream." Another woman, who requested anonymity, dreamed during a Republican administration:

> I was on a train, and elephants were in the car ahead of me. And the elephants began to rumble, and they knocked the cars together, and it was a train wreck. And I ran—I got away, but I had to leave everything. I was naked but I did get away. And the next day I got a call from the IRS.

Again, people who believe that dreams can forecast the future see little if any difference between literal and nonliteral forecasts. No interviewee even raised the idea that meaning can be read into dream symbols after the fact. Instead, they spoke as if they just knew that a broken cup signified a car accident (Edward Moore), a beautiful flower meant he would meet his wife (a prisoner), the Salvation Army giving away free suits predicted someone being drafted (Ivan Watkins), or snow together with valuable antiques spelled coming prosperity after hardship (Tony Thomas).

Occasionally dreams alert us to physical illness. These dreams can be literal even to the point of pronouncing a diagnosis. In most cases, however, people find that messages about health come symbolically. Such dreams usually concern the dreamer's own health, and may be understood most easily as responses to subtle cues from the body. But dreams concerning the health of others are less easily explained. Two interviewees described dreams of this sort:

> It's a recurring dream, but there's always a little variation. I think of it as a death dream, but it's a dream about a cat. And a cat who has bulging eyes, and one of the eyes gets very red, as if it's hemorrhaging.
> *Do you still have that dream?*
> Every once in a while, and somebody dies. And the first time I had it, a brother-in-law of mine died of a stroke, and he was only like 43. I had the dream the night before, and it's documented, because I told every-body in the family about it. And he died the next day, unexpectedly, of a hemorrhage, which started in his eye. *(Shirlee Taylor Haizlip)*

> I remember having this dream last January. All these black spiders were after me. But I killed the spiders, I stomped them. And about the first week of February, I got a call from Nikki Giovanni. And I thought it was just a call that we were catching up, but she said, "I want to tell you that I got test results back and they found cancer, in my lung." And she's just so calm. But she said, "The good news is that it's peripheral, it's on the edge and they can operate. And we'll just have to see." And somehow or another, she was [literally] in that dream with those spi-ders, she was part of that dream in the beginning. When she said that, I *immediately* went back to that dream. And I said, "Oh, Nikki, you're gonna be all right." And she turned out to be fine, and that was the whole idea of killing the spiders. *(Ethel Smith)*

The Central Symbol

When African Americans interpret a symbolic dream, the interpreter as a rule looks for the single most important symbol. What this cen-tral symbol is doing, how it looks and so forth may be weighed, but the rest of the dream is generally set aside.

Sylvia Morris's mother, for example, told her and Sylvia's aunt a dream about a mouse. I asked whether her mother described the whole dream. "No, she just said, 'I had a dream about a mouse.' And my aunt knew exactly what that meant." In this family, a mouse portends a death.

The old popular dream books—some of them still in use—recommend this method: "Try to remember the most vital detail in your dreams and turn to it here, and read the signification and interpretation" (Black Herman, *Secrets of Magic, Mystery and Legerdermain* [*sic*]). Numbers players, some of whom traditionally relied on dream books, follow the same method. Haki Madhubuti described the betting he observed when, as a youth, he assisted his father, a policy runner in Chicago:

> And, primarily the women would play their dreams. You look at the text of the dream, and obviously a dream can mean more than one thing, but many of these women would pick out that which affected them the greatest, that concept of the dream.

Adekola Adedapo, who herself gives readings, described how a dream is generally told to and treated by a "reader-adviser":

> They'd mostly say, like, "I dreamt about a bus last night." They may not say, "I was on the bus, and la-di-da-di."
> *So you're saying the person wouldn't relate the whole dream?*
> No, they'd come in and say, "I dreamt about a bus last night, Miss Lucy." And she might say, "Well, was the bus going fast or slow? Or was it going up a hill, or was it going down?"

One interviewee, Marva Pitchford Jolly, at first dissented from this pattern. "The people that *I've* been around, and talking about dreams, wanted to know *all* of it. They never looked for the key word." But later, she added this interesting qualification:

> Someone who is very developed in prophecy the way we knew it [in rural Mississippi] would be given that bolt of lightning. There would be a symbol in this heap of whatever it is they dreamt, that they could pull that out.

Good and Bad Predictions

A topic of good news traditionally brought by dreams is the *gender of expected babies*. Darice Wright Camp's gender was dreamed by her grandmother. And Betty Rodgers Hale had a dream predicting that her grandchild would be a girl. She also predicted twins for her daughter-in-law the same way. Another dream of good news is the *preview of a future home.* In Diane Dugger's experience, this is how some people do their "house shopping. Because you've dreamt it, it automatically feels like home." Yet another and a very common good news dream is the *announcement that you're going to be seeing someone.* "It was not unusual," said Charles Payne, "for me to go back home and for my brothers and sisters to say, 'You know, Mother had a dream about you last week, and she thought you were gonna come.'" A number of interviewees brought up dreams of this type. And all three of these good news dreams—the gender announcement, the house preview, and the expect to see so-and-so dream—can also be found depicted in black literature.

It has to be said, however, that bad news far outweighs good news in the predictive dreams of African Americans. Most predictive dreams warn the dreamer of some threat to self or family. Nelson Peery's father told him a story

> about how my grandfather was involved with this guy's wife. And this woman apparently was a lady that was getting around town, too, 'cause the dream went that he was going down the railroad tracks to meet this woman, going over to her house, and he saw the head of his friend laying between the two tracks, and it was saying, "Don't go any further. What happened to me will happen to you." And so, he was terrified in this dream, he turned around and walked back home. And that morning he heard about how his friend had gone to see this woman, and her husband was waiting for him, and blew his head off with a shotgun.

Flash forward a century to Chicago's Cabrini Green housing project. A fifteen-year-old gang member dreamed about other gangs. Things they were doing in the dream made him suspect that the gang peace that had prevailed for several years "was going to break." A day or so after the dream, his aunt told him she'd seen some rival gang members, and warned him to avoid the place where they gathered. He thought his aunt's advice confirmed the dream's prediction, and warned his fellow gang members.

Everyone has heard stories about dreams foretelling public disasters. My interviews produced three such dreams. One foresaw a plane crash (Adrienne Edmond's daughter Janet), another the space shuttle explosion (Eileen Cherry). The third forewarned of an elevated train accident in Chicago. Joe Cheeks was on the train in 1977 when it derailed and fell. Cheeks's photo was in the paper, where he was cited for keeping everyone's spirits up during the ordeal. In the dream,

I saw these helicopters that are lined up, they have these sliding doors! These are the *train* doors I'm seeing, but I'm thinking all this time, it's helicopters. And they're flying, you know, snake-wise, like in between these buildings. And I'm looking at the reflection of the helicopters in the buildings, but something is wrong, because it's not helicopters that I'm seeing. The rotors aren't going this way, the rotors are going *this* way, like wheels, and I know something's wrong. And I remember something about the helicopters tilting to the side. That happened in the dream.

I think this was the very next day. When I got to the station, I'm realizing something is funny. I've done this. I've seen this. I get ready to run up to the front of the train, and something told me, don't get on that first car. And I got on the fourth car. Okay, so we start getting down around the buildings, and I started seeing the reflection of what I saw in the dream with the helicopters! Now I know without a shadow of a doubt that something's going on real shaky here. And the minute it hit, the dream, everything—I knew what was going on before anybody knew what was getting ready to happen. Because I knew, "The train is gonna fall over! This is what you saw!"

Can the Future Be Avoided?

Joe Cheeks believes that boarding the fourth car of the El instead of the first car saved his life. "If you have time to think about what you saw," he said, "then you can do something different from what you saw." Around the world, including Africa, views differ as to whether we can modify the future foretold by dreams. My interviews yielded opinions and stories on both sides. Among those who believe the future can be averted, Adrienne Edmond said, "We get forewarning so that we could pray about it, so that God can intercede." Ronald Childs's grandmother would say, "The Lord is trying to tell me to warn you." Stephanie Bell will "have these dreams and I will call my children and say, 'I think you should stay home tonight.' " Zeinabu irene Davis's father might say, "Okay, well, I should walk a different way to work" after a warning dream.

Former Bulls champion basketball guard Craig Hodges, whose public life since retiring as a player has been motivated by community service, related this "God-given" dream that contained a warning about deteriorating social conditions:

When I was about twelve years old, I had a dream about my community, Chicago Heights. We always played ball on the school ground. And [in the dream] after the game, this day, we were all dribbling our ball, passing it, or whatever, and all these trucks rolled by. And I mean, like damn, big old trucks! They stand up, and they got Uzies! And at this time, there ain't no Uzies! And that dream stuck with me for so long, and it would make my heart race when I thought about it. And when I think about it now, it makes me know that I have to prepare to make sure that what I saw doesn't happen.

On the other side of the question, I heard numerous stories about dream warnings believed to be inevitable. A man in his early twenties said:

Right now, I'm having dreams about getting cut with sharp objects. Like razor blades, knives, machetes. No one's cutting me! I'm just standing here, and something just *ssshhht*. My girlfriend said that I sense that something's gonna happen to me soon, I'm gonna get stabbed or something like that. And I say, "Well, maybe it's gonna happen today, tomorrow, or next week." She say, "You don't know. Might happen ten, twenty years from now."

Death is probably the most common prediction in African American dreams. And when death is what the dream predicts, the future is often respected as inalterable:

Especially my mom, and my grandmother. They might dream that somebody dies, and then later on, they find out that somebody did die or somebody's sick. They don't actually know who it is, but it's just something's gonna happen. *(Edwina Ackie)*

We had a cousin, Aunt Sis, who was known for her preview-type dreams. She dreamed she needed to wash everything in the house. And she did. And then her mother died two days later. She was going to be gone for a long time, so you had to take lots of things, you know, you didn't want to take something that wasn't clean, and you didn't want to leave anything dirty at the house. *(Betty Holcomb)*

In these cases, the dream sounded an alert but didn't reveal exactly who would die. That's a common pattern, particularly when the symbol of death in the dream is a traditional dream sign. But oftentimes it's clear ahead of time just who will die:

Aunt Lucille, my grandmother's sister, had a dream, and in the dream, she and her brother [Bill] were racing. And Aunt Lucille said, "I win." And so the whole family said "Oh"—and Aunt Lucille died before Uncle Bill, but they died within a month of each other. *(Angie Williams)*

My mother will love to dream of someone's demise. Whew! She will, "I dreamed that sonofabitch was dead. Thank God!"—ha-ha-ha! "Hey,

Ma, cool it! No, no, no! You're supposed to have compassion." "Compassion, my foot! He was a no-good so-and-so-and-so." *(Anonymous)*

Now I have dreamed dreams that have happened. Like my grandmother. I dreamed she died. In my dream, my aunt called me and said, "Mama died. She had a stroke. And she passed." And I woke up in the middle of the night, sweating, and stood up in the middle of the bed. That was last year. And a week and a half, two weeks later, she had a stroke. I told Christine [his girlfriend], "I had a dream Mama died last night." And she was like, "Do you want to tell somebody? Maybe you need to call your mother." I called my mother, and my mom, she's like, "Well, ain't nothing we can do about that, if you had that dream." My mom is deep like that, too. My mom had a dream about *her* [grand]mother. She had a dream that she got hit by a car or something. A week later, she was dead. *(Almontez Stewart)*

Finally, here's a case where an effort made to avert the future proved futile. As a teenager, Haitian-born Nicole Smith had a dream in which Jesus helped her to cross a narrow foot bridge over a chasm. On the other side, she encountered her brother-in-law lying with his head resting on a stone. She urged him to go back home, but he said he wouldn't because it was too noisy there. The next day she told him the dream:

He said, "Let's play the lottery!" I said, "No. And if I were you, I'd be very careful. Because this is not a lottery dream." My brother-in-law died within six months. Here is what happened. In fact again, three days before my brother-in-law died, I had a dream. I saw pieces of fire coming from the sky. And each piece that fell killed a person. And I said, "God! Help us! We are perishing!" It was like a nightmare. But it wasn't really a nightmare, it was something that was going to take place. Three days later, Haiti was invaded, and the town where I was, which was a summer resort, that's where the invaders came. My brother-in-law had a horse, and he took a ride in the mountains, and the rebels were in the mountains. So he was one of the first people to have been killed. He was shot, and when they found him, his head was just on a stone.

Dreams as Causes

To believe that a dream *predicts* the future sometimes spills over into believing that the dream actually *causes* the future to come about. This idea, that dreams are links in the chain of events, came up in some of my interviews:

My grandmother had a dream that my mother was gonna have me. This was before my mother was pregnant. And it turned out she was pregnant with me and I was a girl. And so, she always said that she was responsible for my being born. *(Darice Wright Camp)*

Before something can happen in your life, you must dream it, you know. And I have always found that to be *true* for me! Whether it's good or bad. It's like a step, and it takes you to another landing in your emotional life, so you are able, in the deepest way, to cope with what's going to happen. Because you have an inside metaphor or symbol for it. *(Angela Jackson)*

Most stories about dreams as causes involve negative outcomes. We find again the association between predictive dreaming and death:

I told [my great-aunt] I had dreamt about my other aunt, her sister, Aunt Carrie. And she looked at me real sternly, she said, "She didn't *die*, did she?" I said, "Well, as a matter of fact, she didn't, she was just *mad* as she could be." But I *had* dreamt her sister dead. And it was almost like, well, you know, you might wind up causing this to happen or something. I mean, it was a very strong reaction to that. *(Sandra Jackson-Opoku)*

Many families have someone like Ralph Arnold's mother, Bertha. "There used to be an expression in our family, 'Please don't let Bertha have a dream about me.' Because it'll come true." That is, you'll die.

The people most often thought to be in danger from dreams, however, are the dreamers themselves. Obviously, no dreamer gave me an account in which the death actually occurred, but the theory was advanced. Matthew Stephens said, "If you die in your dream you die in real life." He believes this, even though he himself had survived one such dream. He counted himself lucky. Daniel Wideman's family tells a story that led him as a small child to believe

that dreams had the power to kill. And I guess that was reinforced, because one of the strongest things I remember being told about when I was a kid was, if you dream that you're dying, wake up. Because if that dream completes itself, then you won't wake up.

Who told you that?

I don't remember. It came from some authority figure. Somebody who I trusted. Somebody who was trying to educate me about what dreams were. And they said, this is a rule, this is nonnegotiable. I remember from the age of four or five being terrified whenever I had a dream that I was falling. I would always wake up and say, "I almost died! I almost died."

That implies that the dream is causal, that it has an influence on subsequent events.
I believe that very strongly.

The dream of falling is the one most often mentioned as a cause of death to the dreamer. This belief is remarkably widespead among African Americans. Of course, strictly speaking, a dream of dying that makes you die isn't really a prediction. But the boundary between present and future isn't very firm. Tony Thomas first said, "You know, you may dream of dying, and maybe at that point will die, actually by getting a dream." But then he added that the fatal dream might not take effect until years or decades later, by which time it will have been forgotten.

Prediction, Telepathy, and Clairvoyance

One afternoon Charles Payne dreamed that a boat sank in Lake Michigan in a cove near where he lived. Later he learned that just this had occurred, some ten hours before he dreamed about it. Most of the stories we've heard involve dreams predicting the future. But here, information seems to come from the past. And in other cases, the dreamer seems to know about something happening at the very moment of the dream, either through telepathy (communication at a distance) or clairvoyance (seeing at a distance).

Quite often the boundary between past, present, and future isn't really meaningful to the dreamer. When young George Washington Carver found a knife he'd prayed for sticking in a watermelon in a field, just as he'd dreamed it, I doubt he even wondered whether he'd seen at a distance (clairvoyance) or seen into the future (precognition).

There were a number of interviewees, however, who were clear that certain dreams of theirs involved clairvoyance or telepathy rather than precognition. Gwen Robinson, for one, said she has "clairvoyant" dreams: "Sometimes I tune in on things. I mean, if somebody is really focusing on something, I may just pick it up. I may not even understand." She gave the example of a dream revealing a break-in at a relative's apartment. Another woman (name withheld for privacy) claimed that just when her estranged husband's car was burning in an arson fire he'd arranged for the insurance, she dreamed that his car exploded. Maisha Hamilton-Bennett was awakened by a dream of her imprisoned husband smoking. At that very moment he was breaking his commitment to quit, as he later confessed.

Parapsychologists suppose that the heightened state of mind caused by an emergency in some way excites telepathic communication. They call this *crisis telepathy*. I heard quite a few stories of telepathic dreams at the moment of a loved one's danger or death. For example, Colleen McElroy was in London when she dreamed about her son:

> In the middle of the night, I woke up screaming, "Kevin, stop! Don't!" And in Alaska, he had fallen asleep at the wheel. And he [later] said, "I heard somebody calling my name, and woke up. And I knew it was you."

Another striking story of this sort was told by Ann Eskridge:

> My mother was always very close to her doctor. And she had a number of operations. This particular night, she dreamed that Dr. Will came to her and was gonna take her to the hospital for an operation. And just as he was wheeling her into the ambulance, he hit his head and was bleeding. And she said, "Well, why don't *you* lie down." And he said, "No, I have to take you to the hospital." And then they were down in the basement of this hospital, and he was wheeling her into the operating room, when she looked back, and he was transparent. And he told her that he could not take care of her anymore, and that Dr. Frank would take care of her.
>
> And she said she woke up and she had been crying. And she told my father the dream, and Daddy read in the newspaper where Dr. Will had died. And when she took us to our pediatrician, Dr. Kunstadter told her that Dr. Will had shot himself in the left temple exactly where she had seen the blood come from his head. And she does that. She does those death things!

Psychic versus Spiritual

I've been employing certain words—*telepathy, clairvoyance, precognition*— that name different varieties of *psychic* experience. As normally used, these terms are neutral as to the source or cause of such experiences, except to imply the existence of some additional faculty of the mind.

Darryl Burrows, a civic organization director, brought up an interesting distinction that he said African Americans make between the *psychic* and the *spiritual:*

> African Americans, even the spiritual ones, tend to be very pejorative about psychics. I mean, the whole Dionne Warwick, Latoya Jackson thing, no one takes it serious.
>
> *What about readers and such?*
>
> Oh, but that's not psychic! Readers are spiritual women of God. Psychics, that's the title you use if you're not spiritual. If you claim to be

able to see the future, but you don't proclaim that your power comes from God. Now we will go and see Mother So-and-so, the Seven Sisters and all this stuff, we'll go do that in a minute. But to justify it if somebody challenges us, we say, "Well, I believe this woman is a woman of God, she gets her power from God." But Dionne Warwick's psychic friends? Latoya? These are people who have commercialized this and are trying to make money off it, they're not real. They don't look anything like Mrs. Jones, that I *know* is a woman of God, that *does* have visions.

My impression is that although the word itself—*psychic*—has actually entered the African American vocabulary through the mass media, the underlying distinction made by Darryl Burrows is genuine. For example, after Marva Pitchford Jolly said, "I can remember being extremely psychic as a little kid," she acknowledged that the word was never used in her Mississippi childhood. She said she still is psychic, then added, "It's become common in a funny kind of way." I asked what she meant:

> Well, when I watch psychic programs on television, it's always comical. Something's funny about it. It's almost like, well, here comes Shirley MacLaine with her extra power rings around her head. It's not a comfort level. The old people would say "funny," because "funny" and "fool" is kinda the same thing. We are using things that we don't understand, and we don't understand how precious they are. And maybe even sacred.

Most interviewees with whom I raised Darryl Burrows's distinction between *psychic* and *spiritual* agreed with him. "I don't think it's psychic," said Frances Freeman-Williams of her predictive dreams. "It's from God." "Those messages ultimately come from the Creator," Ivan Watkins insisted. And Daniel Wideman said:

> Right, and that's what I think I was referring to when I said there's faith. Certainly some of the messages do come from God, come from a higher force. But if you have that faith, then you don't try to flash the flash cards and get into what intellectual capacity of the mind would cause you to be able to predict. And I laugh at those psychics, too, because dreams are not something to be toyed with lightly, or put on the Home Shopping Network.

By "flash the flash cards," Wideman was referring to a famous experiment for testing psychic abilities in the laboratory. Thus he was rejecting scientific investigation along with commercial exploitation, since neither, in his view, is spiritually founded.

Even some interviewees who resisted Darryl Burrows's observation actually endorsed it in a backhanded way. Writer Gloria Naylor said, "I go to psychics" and "I'm a bit psychic myself." She denied that *psychic* and *spiritual* "are mutually exclusive. It just simply means that for the black community, they have expanded the concept." Psychologist and filmmaker Alice Stephens thinks that people who make the distinction "are just limited in their understanding of the whole phenomenon. I am not averse to the idea that the psychic is hooked up spiritually."

But there certainly are African Americans who accept the "Psychic Friends" and other such popular manifestations without thinking about spirituality. The two points of view came head-to-head when a friend dropped in on Diane Dugger during our interview. The friend attacked television psychics, while Dugger defended them. The friend held up the example of her grandmother and the generations connected to slavery days:

FRIEND: Those people had true psychic powers. Dionne Warwick is an entertainer. Why would she endorse something like that?

DUGGER: Because she talked to one of her "psychic friends," which is the lady that's in charge of the Psychic Friends Network, okay. And she was interpreting Dionne Warwick's dreams, and that's the reason why she's promoting her friend's psychic network, because the things that were interpreted to her, she felt was true.

FRIEND: People believe in that mess! And besides that, I say if she couldn't find her way to San Jose, she certainly can't tell me about my future.

Despite such variations in viewpoint on the part of African Americans, the picture drawn by Darryl Burrows is generally accurate. Not only is there widespread belief in predictive dreams (and other "psychic" phenomena) among African Americans, but the experience is also widely thought to have a spiritual foundation, and not simply to display an additional faculty of the mind.

Prediction and Psychological Insight

Most dream experts nowadays think the main benefit we can gain from dreams is insight into our true state of mind, and I myself am a great believer in this side of the dream life. So I want to stress that if African Americans see dreams as predictions, they also see them as tools for gaining psychological insight. The two ways of looking at dreams don't exclude each other.

When Diane Dugger told me about the gruesome accidental death of her boyfriend from a pistol shot through the head, I asked, "Did you dream about that?" I was wondering if she'd gone through the sort of nightmares that often follow major traumas. She assumed, however, that I wanted to know about predictive dreams, and so she replied, "I didn't dream that anything like that would happen." But when Dugger had an unrelated series of dreams involving pistol shots, she gave these dreams a psychological interpretation. In waking life Dugger worked under a racist boss. In her dreams, she shot this man with relish. She understood her dream behavior not as prediction but as the dramatized expression of simmering resentment.

The following story, told by an interviewee (name withheld for privacy), is a wonderful example of the wedding of predictive and psychological meaning in a single dream:

> I had a friend who ended up having an affair with my husband. And we had our little words, and I said, "I really want you to leave," and she did, she actually left this city. Then there was a time when she returned. And I had a dream that I went to this concert. I walk into the auditorium, and sitting in the audience is a friend of mine whose name is Maya. Maya has on a royal blue hat with a feather. And I go join her. And I say to her, "Oh, where did you get this hat?" You know, "It's wonderful." And she tells me she bought it at this store, and it was on sale. I said, "Cool." Then I look around and I see this person, this woman. And I just had this sensation of anger, and I tell Maya, I say, "Excuse me." Anyway, I end up . . . in the bathroom, and I say to her, I say, "You really just didn't believe me when I told you that I would kill you, did you?" I said, "I'm just gonna have to do it." And I grab her, and I stick her head in the toilet and just flush the toilet, just flush the toilet, just flush her drowned. She disappears, she's gone.
>
> Okay. Reality. I go to a concert, at a time my husband's performing. In the same auditorium. Now, I'm very apprehensive because I'm told that this person is back in town. So I look in the audience, and I don't see Maya in this damn hat, so I'm like, "Whew! Great!" 'Cause the dream was so real, so vivid. So I go and I sit down. I'll be darned! Maya comes and sits next to me, and she has on this damn blue hat! And I am like, "Where'd you get that hat from?" She said the same thing she said in the dream! Then, of course, I see this other woman. And I am trying to understand what is going on. I'm talking about, as a conscious human being. So, what doesn't happen is, I don't get that sensation that I had in the dream, I don't have any anger. And when

I actually face her, confront her later, all of that had dissipated and had basically disappeared.

And I explained to my mother, and my mother said, "Oh, you just worked it out in your dream. You took care of the anger there."

The fact that prediction doesn't exclude other types of interpretation should be borne in mind as we continue the discussion of predictive dreams in the following three chapters. So far we've looked at the general features of predictive dreams as experienced by African Americans. Now we'll consider three special types of predictive dreams. We'll explore *dream signs* and their traditional meanings, numbers gambling and *numbers dreams,* and the relationship between preview dreams and the *déjà vu* experience.

5

WE GOT THE SIGNS

SIGNS IN DREAMS

"Daughter got her blood this morning!" I heard Big Mama say. "We gonna have to take her to the river."

"I could've told you that. I seen the signs, I had the dream," Miss Mary put in.

—Shay Youngblood

If a bird flies into the house, it means someone's going to die.

That's an example of a sign, furnished by African American folklore. A sign is a symbolic event that lets us predict the future. According to tradition, signs can present themselves either when we're awake or when we're dreaming. This chapter is mostly about signs in dreams. But as background, we'll first look briefly at waking signs and their interpretations.

Waking Signs

A good place to search for waking signs is in the lore surrounding birth. Certain signs are supposed to predict the baby's gender. "If a little boy shows a liking for the expectant mother," reported Zora Neale Hurston, "a girl will be born, and vice versa." If the mother "acts evil," that means a boy. If the baby makes a "high and pointy" shape in the mother's belly, it's a boy, while "low and round" means a girl.

Other signs predict the spiritual endowments of the newborn. Extra toes mean wisdom and great mental powers. Infants with "holes in their ears, they see things, but only while they are little." Seventh sons have special spiritual gifts. So do those born with the "veil," or "caul," a part of the birth sac, the amnion, occasionally found covering an infant's face at delivery. The veil is a sign of "second sight," which can mean anything from being insightful to seeing spirits. Molefi Kete Asante, the chief framer of contemporary Afrocentrism in the United States, writes, "My family had three or four root men and women and I was said to have been born with a veil over my face, meaning that I would probably be a root doctor or a preacher." Several interviewees talked about gifted people in their lives who were seventh sons or born with veils.

But without a doubt, most waking signs bring dark predictions, and many portend death or illness: "The Little Man [death] he always send his sign first 'fore he come in." Traditional death signs include broken crockery, an empty rocking chair rocking, bread dropped as it comes out of the oven, a white worm on someone (measuring for a shroud), a lamp going out on its own, ringing ears, and flowers blooming out of season.

Many animals are bad signs. Birds are the worst. "When coots come afore the duck, tomorrow goin' to bring bad luck." Woodpeckers pecking on a house, roosters crowing at the wrong time, and owls hooting or screeching all spell bad luck or death. The most dangerous thing is for a bird to fly into the house. Three interviewees had stories about this death sign, and it shows up in novels and memoirs.

Spiders, by way of contrast, are often good signs. A spider on one's shoulder is "a sign of fortune." One dangling from the ceiling, writes poet Angela Jackson, means "a guest coming, / someone you haven't seen / in a long time."

Domestic animals play an oddly sinister role, given their everpresence. A stray cat or dog in the yard is a sign of death or sickness. A dog barking inappropriately is bad luck. The lowing of cattle after twilight is a death sign. And the most notorious bad animal is, of course, the black cat, as in the Ma Rainey blues verse:

> Black cat on my door-step, black cat on my window-sill, *(twice)*
> If one cat don't cross me, another black cat will.

Some signs have meanings that vary from person to person, family to family, or region to region. Take the "jumping" (twitching) eye, a common sign. There's a jingle that goes "Right eye, laugh eye; left eye, cry eye." A Ntozake Shange character agrees: "Her *left* eye always jumped when something was amiss." But a Sutton E. Griggs character knows trouble is brewing because her "'*right* eye hez been jumpin' fit to kill. . . . '" Memoirist Bessie Jones concludes that each person needs to watch such signs in action to "learn to tell what they mean for *you.*"

In addition to signs established by tradition, any striking or poignant event may be read as a sign in the right circumstances. A gang member quit the Vice Lords after his sideways cap got turned straight one day by his four-year-old son. "Had to be . . . a sign from God," he told Studs Terkel. What's traditional here is not the sign itself but the belief in signs and the readiness to detect them. ˙

Several interviewees told stories about such special signs. Kimberly Camp's great-uncles used to play poker on Sundays in defiance of their mother. One Sunday

> there was this clap of thunder, and the pennies stood up on their edges and started turning around and all turned green. Probably lightning came down the chimney. To them it was a sign from God that she was right, there should not be gambling on Sunday. It probably was! I mean, what are the odds of lightning coming down the chimney and not killing all of them?

African and European Influences

In European tradition, being born with the veil is a sign predicting spirituality in the newborn. The same belief is also found in West Africa. Similarly, the owl is a death sign in both places. European observers of Africa as early as the seventeenth century noticed signs found on both continents. When such a sign is known to African Americans, there's no way to be sure whether it comes from the European or the African influence, or from both.

There are, to be sure, some African American signs that have obvious European origins—signs involving clocks, for example. In other cases, such as sneezing signs, variants exist in both Europe and Africa, but because they're more common in Africa, an African origin is suspected. In general, whereas many folklorists used to give the benefit of the doubt to Europe, recent scholars such as Mechal Sobel tend to give it to Africa. Among the signs she attributes to Africa are a rooster crowing as a sign of death, and a spider hanging down as a sign that company is coming.

More will be said about African influences in the following discussion of dream signs.

Dream Signs

Waking signs and dream signs cover somewhat different ground. Itches, jumps, and sneezes, for instance, don't figure in dreams very often. But where waking and dreaming have the same sign, the meanings usually agree. Take animal signs: a cat traditionally means bad luck, and a howling dog means death in both states.

Appendix B provides a list of traditional African American dream signs which I've gathered from folklore collections, from African American literature, and from the people interviewed for this book. If more than one source mentions the same sign and interpretation, we can assume that the sign is not just someone's private dream language. However, a majority of items in the table do come from single sources. While I've excluded those signs I thought were probably idiosyncratic, you should nonetheless regard the "traditional" status of all single source entries with caution.

Some of the interviewees possess knowledge about traditional beliefs that they themselves don't hold. It should therefore not be assumed that interviewees necessarily do or do not believe the entries attributed to them.

You'll see that a majority of dream signs have negative meanings, just as do most predictive dreams generally, as well as most waking signs. The dream signs in the list run about two-to-one negative. But that probably understates the negativity, since not all dream signs get dreamed or discussed as often as others. Some of the more common ones—snake, baby, wedding—carry meanings of trouble, enemies, and death. Most African Americans think of dream signs as running to the bad.

Yet the single most frequently heard dream sign has a positive meaning—at least most people would say so. Fish in a dream means someone's pregnant:

> Thirty-nine-year old Jackie Forde laughed as she reported that her mother had called from Mississippi to see if she was pregnant again. "At my age!" In fact her mother had called *all* her grown daughters with the same question. The older woman had been dreaming of sitting on her front porch and fishing in a small puddle in the yard.

Pregnancy itself, however, is a death sign. So are marriage and birth. Things flowing with life, in other words, are signs of death. And by the same token, funerals, burials, and death itself are all signs of life—that is, of pregnancy and marriage.

All of these important dream signs are interpreted by reversing their surface meanings. Interpretation by *reversal,* or "by contraries," is an ancient principle of dream interpretation, found in traditional cultures around the world. A Zimbabwean tribe holds, for example, that to dream of being killed by a lion means good luck to the hunter.

Former longtime prisoner Moreese Bickham said, "People used to tell me, they said, 'Take your dream backwards.' Like if it's good, you say something bad, and if it's bad, you just say it's for good." The principle of reversal also shows up in the betting routines of numbers gambling: "Some folks say turn it around or play it upside down." Thus the number 122 can be played as 221 or as 112. Or it can be played as is.

Selective application of reversal is as venerable as the principle itself, going back at least to the first known dream book, a four-thousand-year-old Egyptian papyrus. It's also found in the *Oneirocritica,* by the Greek writer Artemidorus of the second century A.D., a book whose influence reaches to today's popular dream books. And in contemporary South Africa, for a Zulu to dream that a sick relative dies may foretell either death or recovery, depending on surrounding circumstances.

Reincarnation: An African Idea

For African Americans, the custom of reversing images of life (marriage, pregnancy, baby) and death (funeral, burial) may well have a basis beyond the general tendency for reversal. What's at the heart of the life/death reversal seems to be an underlying belief that new lives replace old lives in an endless cycle of renewal. Craig Hodges explained his grandmother's formula that "dreams of death mean birth" by saying, "If you dream of death, that means somebody is getting ready to go out, to let another life come in."

This idea of life replacing life implies reincarnation, a belief that is quite widespread among African Americans. A folklorist in the South once observed that African Americans "believe in reincarnation. For every death they believe there is a birth." This idea is captured by several fiction writers. If you live too long you're "stealing somebody else's time" (Toni Cade Bambara). When you die your soul goes "to the next person waitin to come in" (Julius Lester). And even though it wasn't something I usually asked about, reincarnation was brought up by well over a dozen interviewees. They said things like "spirits go on to become new spirits in other bodies, I don't think they just hang around" (Darice Wright Camp), and "I *know* I've lived other lifetimes" (Marva Pitchford Jolly).

Often reincarnation came up in the context of dreams. For instance, Kimberly Camp dreamed she was a no-good southern white woman burned to death in her house by her neighbors. Camp sees the "charmed life" she enjoys now as balancing out her life as the white woman of her dream "several incarnations ago." Other examples of dreams connected with reincarnation will be found in the chapter on déjà vu.

Belief in reincarnation certainly isn't unknown in Euro-American culture. However, its relative prominence among African Americans strongly suggests a survival of African ideas. Most Africans believe that "man's life has no end, that it constitutes a cycle," and that every newborn is "the 'come back' of some dead person." Unlike the better known Hindu/Buddhist idea of rebirth as a sort of punishment, in Africa it more often carries a sense of "the celebration of existence."

The cycle of rebirth, not surprisingly, is often thought by Africans to play out within the family, and some African Americans hold the same belief. We find this idea in fiction (Edwidge Danticat, Tina McElroy Ansa), and it arose in my interviews. "We all know," said Laura McKnight, "where some parts of the mother gonna come back in the form of grandkids. This is what we think." Kai EL Zabar said:

> The death means the birth. My mother always believed that when one person dies in the family, someone else is going to bring to life a grandchild or something. She said, "That's just the rhythm of life." She said, "That's the law. That's the way it is."

So the customary life/death reversal in the interpretation of dream signs by African Americans appears to express a faith—sometimes conscious, sometimes not—in the endless cycle of replacement and renewal of human life and spirit, a faith enduring from the African past. Life means death, death means life.

Signs Today

You may wonder how many people really know or care about signs today. I found that 82 percent of the African Americans I interviewed have some familiarity with dream signs. That's nearly twice the 45 percent familiarity I found among whites. The difference is even greater for the dream signs best known to blacks. Sixty-nine percent of blacks are familiar with the life/death dream signs, compared with 18 percent of whites. And for the fish-means-pregnancy dream sign, the numbers are blacks, 45 percent, whites, only 8 percent—and at least some of the 8 percent heard it from black friends. I didn't ask directly if people *believed in* dream signs, only if they *knew of* them. But it's probably safe to assume that the greater familiarity among blacks reflects a correspondingly higher level of belief.

Nevertheless, both knowledge and belief have diminished since earlier days. Knowledge of specific signs is certainly declining. Two women, Adrienne Edmond and Ethel Smith, were able to name nine dream signs apiece, and one woman came up with eleven. But much more typical are those who know only a couple of signs. Stephanie Bell is a case in point. She eagerly recalled her family's tradition of interpreting dreams by signs: "My great-grandmother used to talk about the fact that *her* grandmother and her mother used to interpret dreams, and this would mean such-and-such." And she asserted proudly that "it all goes back to African folklore." Nevertheless, "my great-grandmother's been dead now for about fifteen, twenty years, and I really don't remember an awful lot about that."

Some people hold on to a sign or so, while they reject all others. Even Bessie Jones, cited a couple of times already for her beliefs, was a skeptic about most signs:

> Like, they used to spit in the fire and if your spit dried up fast that was a sign you were going to die. Nothing but foolishness. Old folks had all kinds of junk like that. But now, the nose itch, that's a sign with me.

There are many outright nonbelievers, of course, and not only those universally skeptical about traditional beliefs, such as Dempsey Travis. Cheryl Boone, for example, knows the one about fish and pregnancy—"Black people always said that"— but she and her family didn't believe it: "No! No. That was stuff that my mother would laugh at, because that was an old wives' tale." And Moreese Bickham, a man powerfully convinced of his own predictive dreaming, nevertheless rejects signs: "My mama always used to say, 'We got the signs, and the rich man got the money.' I don't believe in all them signs."

This is not to say that belief has disappeared. "That stuff still exists," said Regina Reed, after reciting several of the life/death dream signs. "You hear that all the time." And, she added, "I believe it too." But if belief in signs were really thriving, I'm sure we'd see up-to-date signs—say, a computer crash—emerging to replace obsolete signs like falling off the barn.

Summing up, we can say that belief in signs and dream signs persists from the past, but less strongly than the more general belief in the predictiveness of dreams.

Wideman's Chinaman

In conclusion, I want to look briefly at John Edgar Wideman's story "The Chinaman," which is based on real incidents involving a dream sign from the novelist's family history. Wideman demonstrates how a sophisticated thinker can relate to signs in a nonskeptical way.

"The Chinaman" is a chapter in the first novel of Wideman's Homewood Trilogy. The narrator's grandmother, Mama, who dies at the end of the chapter, once had a dream about a Chinaman with "teeth like gold daggers" whose head "blew up like a watermelon," splattering her "with something . . . colder than anything she had ever touched. . . . "

Now, *Chinaman* is a fairly rare but nonetheless traditional African American death sign.

This very same death dream of the Chinaman revisits the grandmother when she's old and hospitalized. Then by chance "an Asian man" moves into a neighboring hospital room, and the two families become friendly. And it happens that this Asian man looks in at the door of the grandmother's room just as she's dying:

> That's just the way it happened. . . . He peeked in and Mama never woke up again. I can't tell you how many times I've asked myself how she knew. Because Mama did know. She knew that Chinaman was coming for her. . . .

The narrator of "The Chinaman" contemplates his own mother's understanding of the dream and her understanding of the death of "Mama," who is her mother:

> For her the story of the Chinaman is a glimpse of her God who has a plan and who moves in mysterious ways. For me the mystery of the Chinaman is silence, the silence of death and the past and lives other than mine.

When I spoke with Wideman, I asked if I was right to contrast the spiritual view of the incident taken by the narrator's mother with the narrator's humanistic view. I was guessing that the narrator's voice represents Wideman himself, and so I was really asking if his own take on dreams is more humanistic than spiritual. He set me straight:

> Well, one of the reasons I write novels is because I don't choose to make certain kinds of decisions. What I'm interested in is the multiplicity of meanings and significance of most things that happen. And very much as dreams do, [the novels] preserve ambiguity and ambivalence. So the narrator's voice is one that's important to me, but it doesn't control the vision. If my novel works at all, each voice has a kind of independence and veracity and truth.
>
> > *Something that struck me in that passage in contrast to the rest of the trilogy is that as far as I noticed, that's the only place you editorialize that way.*
>
> Mm-hm. Well, I don't think I'm trying to reduce or diminish the power of the dream. I'm saying that I'm not a conventional religious person. And that the power of that image of the Chinaman suggests to me something very basic about experience and the nature of reality, and the image goes directly to that mystery. And there's no way that I can sum the mystery up, or interpret the mystery. It is just mysterious.

Wideman exemplifies the capacity for simultaneous belief and disbelief, the comfort with tension between faith and nihilism, and the tolerance for ambiguity that are among the hallmarks of African American thought. Another writer in this class is poet Angela Jackson. Jackson opened her poem in tribute to Chicago's black mayor Harold Washington with a dangling spider, a sign of an unexpected and welcome guest. She was certainly conscious of the resonance this image carries in the community that gave Washington his unexpected and welcome victory, and was probably also thinking of Anansi, the honored spider trickster of African mythology. Thinker-artists of the caliber of Wideman and Jackson model for their readers how informed minds can entertain traditional beliefs at the millennium.

In case there's any doubt that a side of Wideman really does believe in signs, here is what he said in a different place in the interview about the beliefs of his mother and grandmother:

> Some of it has been transmitted very viscerally to me, in the sense that I have superstitions that are quite powerful for me. I hate to see a black cat cross my path. I will tell somebody not to open an umbrella in the house. If I would see a bird inside the house, I would worry about that a little.

6

BLACKONOMICS

PLAYING THE NUMBERS FROM DREAMS

Numbers was like a community institution. Everybody accepted and respected it. This was the way that the people got to the money.

—Claude Brown

The Numbers Game

"Lottery is dreaming and dreaming is lottery," said a man in the 1940s. "When *I* grew up, honey, dreams was everything," Eileen Cherry told me. "You dreamed numbers. And you played those numbers." The link between predictive dreaming and numbers gambling is the subject of this chapter. We'll begin with some background on the numbers game.

Legal lotteries for the benefit of public works, private colleges, and churches were commonplace during early American history. But in time, reaction against the abuse of lotteries by profiteers culminated with congressional legislation in 1890. However, the Anti-Lottery Bill of that year served to open the field for illegal lotteries.

The illegal forms closely identified with the heyday of lotteries in black America are *numbers* and *policy*. These words often get used interchangeably, but in fact numbers and policy are two different games. The numbers player bets on a three-digit number from 000 to 999. The policy player bets on various combinations from 1 to 78 (or 1 to 72).

Some people mistakenly think that the term *policy* comes from the similarity between small lottery bets and the small weekly insurance "policy" premiums of earlier times. But actually, the term first crops up in an antilottery tract from 1833, when most players were white and when neither lottery nor insurance yet stood out as features of African American life. Policy began in England or the West Indies, as a way of making small side bets on the legal lotteries. It spread to the Midwest and Chicago, its eventual capital, up the Mississippi from New Orleans in the 1880s. Policy burgeoned in the black North with the migrations following World War I, then really exploded with the Great Depression.

The origins of the three-digit system called numbers aren't clear, in spite of being recent. The game was supposedly invented in 1925 in Harlem by the game's first major figure, a West Indian janitor named Casper Holstein. Though in cities like Chicago numbers never made real headway, numbers quickly became the game of choice in the East, particularly New York City. Its appeal was that the winning three digits were taken from public sources, such as market closings and horse race results, and could not, therefore, easily be tampered with by the gambling management, as could the policy drawings.

You may be curious about the technical aspects of policy and numbers—the mechanics of determining winning numbers, the structure of the business, the betting and payment procedures, the types of bets, and other details. If so, please consult Appendix C for that information. For our purposes in tracing the connections between dreams and numbers, however, we can now proceed with the more general matters of attitudes and influences.

"Numbers was the thing," wrote Claude Brown in his autobiography, *Manchild in the Promised Land*. It would be hard to overstate the prominence numbers gambling once had in black affairs. Harlem's leading newspaper, the *New York Amsterdam News*, described in 1954 how "church-goers, domestics, white-collar workers, businessmen, laborers, social workers, and even many cops themselves, seek out numbers men to give them their daily play." New York City in 1960 had 1,500,000 daily players.

Numbers gambling is a fixture in the barbershops and beauty parlors, the restaurants and candy stores, the streets and homes painted in African American memoirs, novels, stories, and plays. Numerous authors have mentioned numbers in the various locales and eras they write about. While some of these works touch on numbers more or less incidentally, others make a special point of emphasizing the pervasiveness of numbers in the fabric of black life.

In Ann Petry's Harlem of the 1940s, for example, "the day's news" meant "the baseball scores, the number that came out, the latest neighborhood gossip." Numbers is a significant plot element in works such as Ralph Ellison's *Invisible Man*. Furthermore, works actually centering on numbers have been written by several important authors— Langston Hughes, Julian Mayfield, Richard Wright, Kristin Hunter, and Robert Deane Pharr.

My personal favorite of these works is Pharr's brilliant novel *The Book of Numbers*. Pharr tells the story of the founding of a black numbers bank in a mid-size southern town between 1935 and the start of World War II. The scriptural reference of Pharr's title tells us that numbers gambling was of biblical proportions in African American life in those years. Pharr depicts black economics, politics, manners, attitudes, and psychology, all through the prism of numbers.

Pharr chose to set his novel in a small unnamed southern city. Numbers is usually associated with the metropolitan centers, but in reality it thrived in lesser cities and towns as well. This is reflected in the stories my interviewees told of their childhoods in Indiana, downstate Illinois, Ohio, Missouri, Tennessee, and Alabama.

Moreover, many Caribbean immigrants have numbers in their backgrounds. "Haitians believe in dreams," said Nicole Smith. "I know people who'd go to bed early just to dream so that they can play the lottery—what they call the bolito. They have a book that tells them what this means." Immigrants like Smith and Beatriz Penso-Buford, a college counselor from Puerto Rico, replenish the numbers dream tradition when they settle here.

Racket or Resource?

Numbers was, and is, often tagged as a "racket." A racket, according to the dictionary, is "illegitimate," it works "by bribery and intimidation," and it is "fraudulent." How does numbers actually measure up to that definition?

Numbers was undoubtedly "illegitimate"—it broke the law. As for "bribery," in most places the authorities took payoffs to let the game operate, and even colluded by closing down wildcat competition. Turf wars brought "intimidation" and some violence.

Was numbers also "fraudulent"? Certainly fraud occurred. The small-time bankers and the so-called writers or runners who took and paid off bets might skip out to avoid paying off. Big bankers sometimes cut the odds if a number got hit hard. Or they would "back down"—put it out that the number had been fixed and leaked, and simply not pay.

A ploy the bankers resorted to more often was to fix the numbers. Policy houses, or "wheels," might remove a number before the draw if it had been heavily bet. Numbers bankers had to work harder to fix the public financial or racetrack results they used, but they had their own devices. As a dream book publisher told me off the record:

> There were many typographical errors that were made on purpose when the house was hit too heavily on a certain number. Somebody . . . was slipped about two or three hundred bucks to put the wrong piece of lead when they were printing the paper. And consequently, believe it or not, the *Wall Street Journal* had more subscribers and readers from the numbers world than it did businessmen. It was considered untainted.

But for all this, numbers wouldn't have prospered as it did if players believed they were regularly being cheated. In general, the biggest bankers had excellent reputations for the honesty of their operations. Dutch Schultz, for one, was widely thought to have cleaned up numbers in Harlem, and the same was said of the policy syndicate in Chicago, where kings such as the Jones brothers enjoyed the confidence of the community. Except upon occasion, numbers was not a racket in the respect crucial for the average player—it was not, broadly speaking, fraudulent.

But even if the game wasn't consistently dishonest, was it, in the words of one commentator, a means of "relentless and deliberate exploitation" just the same?

The moralists and social improvers and white press of the time condemned numbers as no better than robbery of the helpless poor. Some black writers also took a dim view of the game, even if many were fascinated by it. Richard Wright, especially, considered numbers gambling to be both foolish for the individual player and a symptom of oppression for the race as a whole. It galled Wright and others like Langston Hughes and sociologist Kenneth Clark that "even the numbers racket, a vital and indestructible part of Harlem's economy, is controlled by whites." The white mobs were attracted by the large profits and were able to overpower the black bankers, often with the cooperation of local governments. Of course the ultimate white takeover was the state lottery. "Lucky Lotto, they called it," mused Yusuf Abdullah, "but it wasn't nothing but the same policy."

In contrast to the white press, popular black journalism often spoke respectfully, indeed fondly, about numbers. That's because on balance the game represented a unique resource for a beleaguered community—this in spite of what everyone knew about the questionable aspects of gambling and illegality. "Blackonomics," it was dubbed, remembered Ramon Price, Harold Washington's half brother.

Numbers was "the most important occupation" in the ghetto. Even before the Depression, the in-house staff included "respectable" people—schoolteachers, wives of professional men, church deacons, retirees. Some workers—milkmen on their routes, janitors in large office buildings—wrote numbers to supplement their incomes. Eventually up to fifteen thousand people earned a living working for policy in Chicago in the course of a year. Novelist Pharr described numbers as "the only business in America that was open to every enterprising Negro." Moreover, not a few who aspired to the professions paid their ways through college working numbers.

As late as 1979, the *New York Amsterdam News* called numbers the "#1 Black and poor industry in the country," noting sadly that the business was "tragically declining." What's more, the black numbers kings had more cash than anyone else and they reinvested it in insurance, banking, real estate, hotels, sports teams, and other legitimate businesses that created jobs and kept the money circulating in the ghetto. Many of these men became known for their honesty, kindness, and even generosity. This was good business, no doubt, but it also reflected their perception of themselves, shared by many in the community, as civic leaders.

But what about the players, those whose small bets made the kings rich? Their hopes for the big hit were dismissed condescendingly in a 1960 mainstream magazine:

> Every player knows a story about someone (a friend, or a friend of
> a friend, or somebody up in the next block) who hit and made the
> escape to a better life. A Harlem housewife assured a visitor that "There
> was a lady right here, in this project, who made a big hit, and bought
> a house in the Bronx." How else can you live in the slums and buy a
> dream like that so cheap?

But the "dream" wasn't always idle. Secretary of State Colin Powell's family bought its first house with money Powell's father, Luther, won at numbers. Payoffs were usually too small for such life changes, but served real needs all the same. The players for the most part were not much hurt by their small daily losses, and could be helped materially and psychologically by occasional windfalls. "If it wasn't for policy I don't know what I'd do," remarked a typical Depression-era player. "I ain't working and that is the only way I can make some money." In August Wilson's play *Two Trains Running*, set in Pittsburgh in the late 1960s, the numbers runner says, "If it wasn't for the numbers all these niggers would be poor," and another man adds:

> It wasn't till I hit the numbers eight or nine years ago that I got to the point where I could change my clothes every day. See, most of these niggers around here can't do that. The only way they can do that is to hit the numbers or get lucky in a crap game.

And we hear an echo of this hope in a recent affirmation of life from Nikki Giovanni:

> I'm here; not necessarily crazy; looking forward to tomorrow. Maybe, the poet thinks, I'll buy a lottery ticket. The forty-first cigarette is lit. First thing in the morning. Fish and a lottery ticket. Hey . . . we're going to make it.

The Spirituality of Numbers

Adrienne Edmond had once "really believed that when I dreamed of a number, that I would get this money." But she was troubled:

> Sometimes people would say that's a blessing, it would come from God. But with me being saved, I'm afraid to say that because it wouldn't necessarily have to be that. We realize that we have principalities and evil forces, it can come from that. You know, to lead me into that.

Edmond decided to stop playing. She isn't alone, of course, in judging numbers gambling to be sinful. But what's interesting is that probably fewer African Americans have believed the game to be sinful than have believed numbers "come from God."

For many, the revelation of numbers has even been a vital part of organized religion, as Eileen Cherry vividly described:

> Honey, you went to church to listen! You had preachers that made their reputations, and built whole churches, based on their ability to prophesy, and to give numbers that they dreamed. And people would play those numbers, and those numbers would come out, or that horse would come out. And that's tax-free money, and that's the kind of thing that sent people to school, and they supplemented the welfare or the little two-dollar-and-fifty-cent hourly wage.

There would be these fad prophets or whatever that would come through, and people would be, "Oh, and she gives out good numbers," or—or you've heard about the more famous ones, like Daddy Grace. And here in Chicago, they would talk about Preacher Cobb, the First Church of Deliverance, and he'd be on the radio, and everybody would listen to him, and he'd say, you know, "John! First verse, fifteen!" He'd call out some scripture number, people would play it. And that's what they'd be listening for, for this number, for this scripture! It was the code!

Andres Visnapuu, a dream book publisher, remembers ministers who "made tremendous fortunes by giving private readings":

We had a run on *Aero* books back in '72 or '73, because there was a minister in Detroit who would have private readings for like twenty-five dollars. You'd go into this chapel, and there would be a coffin. And the lid would open up, and he would sit up in the coffin and he would look at the person—his visions, what he saw, what he read about them— and he'd read from the *Aero* book and give those people that number to play.

A few churches used to have special mediums whose role was to give numbers. Here is one description:

Before the service begins the church assistants move among the congregation selling little numbered cards for a quarter. When the time comes for the messages to be given the medium calls out a number and the individual possessing that number either raises his hand or stands. When this is done the medium raises her eyes heavenward and gets a message from God for this individual.

The medium's "message from God" either contained an explicit number, or else the medium stressed certain key words that the client was expected to look up in a dream book, such as "a beautiful *cloud* is over you. The spirit brings *cotton* to you."

Some of these practices were corrupt. In Langston Hughes's play *Tambourines to Glory,* the dishonest minister gives out four "Lucky Texts" during each service, urging the members to drop money in the passing tambourine for each verse number as she declares it. (But the minister herself, it should be noted, plays numbers she gets from her own dreams.) In known cases, numbers bankers paid fees to pastors for guiding business their way, or even owned the churches and hired the pastors themselves.

Apart from the churches, there were assorted spiritualists, numerologists, and root doctors who gave out numbers with varying degrees of larceny and good faith. Adekola Adedapo, herself a Yoruba diviner, tells how readers "got a piece of the action":

> If you hit the number, you came back and it was like a lawyer's contingency fee. If you hit the number and you *didn't* go back and give it up, then that's when the root part came in. That's when Miss Gertrude or whoever put roots on your butt, until you brought your money.

But the spirituality of numbers did not (and does not) depend on churches or readers for most players. The biggest part of the spirituality of numbers comes from a direct relationship to higher powers. And it works through prayer, through intuition, through luck, and through dreams. Memoirist Bessie Jones wrote of her mother:

> I don't know whether it was God or who it was, but when she said, "I need me some so-and-so; I sure need to take me a number," that woman would see that number. . . . She'd go right on and play it and it would hit. . . . She'd say, "I don't know when I'll get another; when I get in bad shape, I guess." Well that made me think God did it.

One interviewee is an artist whose abstract paintings incorporate her mother's handwritten columns of numbers—termed "workouts" or "rundowns"—as collage elements. At first the artist flatly denied any spiritual dimension in these paintings, or for that matter in her mother's attitude to the numbers. But later she said:

> My mother's always talking about, "Oh well, you know, I was born with a veil over my eyes," and so therefore she can see into things . . . and she knows the intentions of things. And I guess that maybe drove her in terms of her numbers. 'Cause she did these great long workouts that you saw reproduced in my work. . . . It was almost like a mantra repeats itself. And you repeat it repeat it repeat it and boom! you stop at some point. My mother doesn't talk about mantras, but all I know is, she didn't want anybody to talk or bother her while she was doing that.

Lottery players have always been great believers in special "signs." Sheron Williams-Brooks described her Trinidadian grandmother, who lives in Virginia:

> I'll say something, she says, "You know, that's the fifth time you've said that. Why did you say that five times?" Or if there's a double yolk, in a couple of eggs, she'll say, "I had two eggs, but there were two double yolks, in both eggs. That's 2, and 4, and 4. 244."

Lucky numbers can come from anywhere—from a girlfriend's address, from the letters in Joe Louis's name, from comic strips. These examples come from African American literature. Numbers associated with death, not surprisingly, have a particular appeal because of death's spiritual implications. When someone died, others would "jump on" the dead person's house address and play it for several months. (Once you find your number you need to stick to it, according to street lore.) Richard Steele said that where he grew up, "people checked the funeral car license plate." And Betty Rodgers Hale related this incident involving her terminally ill father:

> When my father was ill, frequently he was delirious. And he was talking about the leaves one day, I believe it was fall. He said something about leaves. And this nurse went and looked up the number for leaves, played it and hit!

The nurse was evidently not alone in monitoring terminal utterances. Langston Hughes's poem "Hope," from *Montage of a Dream Deferred*, goes in its entirety:

> He rose up on his dying bed
> and asked for fish.
> His wife looked it up in her dream book
> and played it.

This brings us to the main subject of this chapter. For dreams always were and still are the most fruitful source of numbers.

Numbers Dreams

The Spirituality of Numbers Dreams

A player in the 1940s said that dream numbers are good because "they comes from the spirit world which speaks to you in your dreams." Another said, "On many occasions God comes to me in a dream. That dream I will play in policy and catch it. . . . But you have to live free from sin to do this." And another:

> The Lord took me out of sin, you know, and put me in the land of
> the religious. And when the Lord shows me numbers I is bound to win.
> I eats my bananas, goes to sleep, and then I sees the Lord. He stands
> right smack before me like a natural man. He points one finger at me.
> I says, "One." He points two fingers. I says, "Two." Then He raises His
> whole hand. The Lord done told me to play one, two, five. I is filled
> with joy straight from the Lord.

My interviews confirmed the spiritual basis of numbers dreaming up to the present day. Devri Whitaker, from California, described with amusement the attitude of certain relatives there who play—and win—the lottery from their dreams: "God told you to play that number. But if you did it on your own, then that'd be *gambling!*" Here the view that numbers dreams come from God coexists uneasily with the view that gambling itself is sinful.

Likewise for Oscar Edmond's grandmother. She was a minister who read other people's dreams for them to find numbers. She "believed that God would take care of your needs. And somehow He would deliver it through dreams. And He would give her these numbers. And it was nothing wrong or dirty about it." At the same time, "she was a religious person, and she was quiet about that policy thing. Only close friends could come to her and get numbers."

Ayanna Udongo reminisced ironically about her astonishment when she realized what her fellow Baptists in Indianapolis around 1970 were up to:

> Well, you know what? There's a lot of people who were in the church, who played the numbers because of their dreams! Which was like, *that* was a contradiction! After they came out of church, or they'll be at the grocery store, and say, "God gave me a dream, and this number was in that," and she played it and got, you know, twenty-five dollars or whatever, and praise God. I'm like, "Oh my God, these people are gambling!" They saw it as a blessing from God.

LV Jordan was taught by her grandmother how to have intentional dreams, so as to keep alive the memory of Jordan's murdered mother. The grandmother, an avid player, never used her aptitude for intentional dreaming, or dream incubation, to obtain numbers dreams. Her restraint was founded on her principled attitude toward God's gifts:

> It has to do with what you ask God for. She said you never ask God for money, you never ask Him for happiness. You ask Him for the ability to create those things.
> *So she never asked for policy dreams?*
> No. But if she dreamt a number, you knew about it!
> *Did she think those dreams came from God?*
> Mm-hm. That's a gift.

Temperance in profiting from God's gifts is a spiritual principle in Sheron Williams-Brooks's family also. Her ninety-eight-year-old grandmother from Trinidad plays both the legal lottery and illegal policy in Virginia, and wins "all the time." I asked if she wins big:

> Well, you know what? She doesn't play big. Because I think from a West Indian, African perspective, money is not the focal point. The number was given. So you take what's given. Like a gift, it's given. If you had a beautiful voice, it was given. And then, you give in return. So, it's not about the money, but if a number is given, you take it.
>
> My mother plays the numbers, too. And she believes in dreams. My mother hits all the time! But like I say, it cannot be a moneymaking endeavor. 'Cause it's a gift. Like my mother says, "When it comes to the point where I'm making big money off of it, then the gift will be taken from me," so she doesn't.

Playing Someone Else's Dream

In Pharr's *The Book of Numbers,* a man dreams of seeing a "great big 350" on the movie screen and goes around talking about it. When 350 hits it costs the bank a lot of money because everyone jumped on the number. This fictional vignette dramatizes the interesting belief that someone else's dream can be as predictive for you as your own dream, and possibly more so. Many of my interviewees told stories along this line. For example, Carole Morisseau said:

> I have a friend, he works with me, he's an actor and director. He asks me whatever my dream was, what was the most outstanding thing of my dream. And he wants it hot off the press. And he hits with them! I guess we've been doing this for about three years now, every month or so. He has a dream book, and then he's got some kind of crazy system he uses! He comes in and he sits down and he devotes a half hour or a hour to working on these numbers.
> *And how did he hit on you as being his reliable oracle?*
> I have no idea how we got into this! I guess I was telling him about a dream or something one day, and he played it.
> *Does he put something down for you?*
> No, I've been trying to get him to! I said, "Listen, I'm not giving you any more dreams unless you play some of it for me." He said, "Well, no, I tell you what the number is, all you have to do is just go around there to the corner just like I do and play the number."

Adrienne Edmond related this story:

> I told a girl on my job [at a hospital], I said, "Oh, I dreamed of *all* these pennies." And she said, "Well, what does it mean?" So one lady had a dream book on the job. So they used to thin out from work, and

they would play the lotto. So, I didn't play the pennies, but one lady, *she* played the pennies. And she got the money, and I didn't play. But I told her about my dream. So then she told me, "From now on, when you dream, you come to me and tell me about your dream!"

The mother of one interviewee (name withheld) is a high state employee, a Ph.D. who sits on the board of directors of a well-known private university:

She plays numbers from dreams. She gave *me* a number from a dream that *I* played, and it hit. She told me that she had dreamed of some numbers, 1-1-7-0. I'm going, "Come to think of it, that's my grand-mother's address." I played and won $2,750. My mom doesn't know to this day! But I spent the money on her.

Children's Dreams
It's a common belief that children "are the best ones to give you win-ning gigs." The reason, as one observer noted in the 1930s, is that "children are more gifted with powers of divination than their elders." Author Shay Youngblood wrote me that her numbers-playing great-grandmother "asked me my dreams upon waking, we slept in the same bed until I was ten years old and this happened regularly." Many of my interviewees have comparable memories. For example:

I had a dream about a bunch of rats, and I told my mother and she played the number for rats and it came out that day. *(A prisoner)*

I used to have nightmares when I was a youth and my family members used to observe me and play their numbers from what I might say or do during my nightmares. *(A prisoner)*

Adults would constantly come to children and say, "Did you have any dreams last night?" They'd ask you, and you would tell them your dream.
   And you knew why?
If, indeed, that dream proved profitable, yeah. They might even reward you with an ice cream cone or something. *(Ramon Price)*

My mother used her dreams and played her policy. They had a book where they could go to and get the number, relate it to the dream. They asked you, "Well, what did *you* dream? Were you happy last night?" They'd take that number and they'd add it in. *(Yusuf Abdullah)*

At an early age, I provided my mother with a lot of information. From my dreams. I was right on the money. So much, my uncle called from New York and he said he wanted a number. And that he would buy school clothes for me. Well, I needed school clothes, because we were on welfare. I gave him the number. He won a couple thousand dollars, and I never heard from him. But another lady who played the numbers, she won a couple more thousand dollars. And she had wanted more information from me, but she was mixed up with the Mafia. So we shied away from that.

But it seemed like using the information for my own self never worked. I tried it, find people to play the number, and I'd play it till my five dollars run out. And then the number would fall the next week. *(Anonymous)*

Dream Books

Since 1862, when a book of the type first appeared in the United States, nearly all cheap popular dream books have assigned numbers to dream symbols. Eastern whites were originally the main buyers, but as the demographics of the illegal lottery changed, so did the target audience. At one time these books were sold at black drugstores, barbershops, shoeshine parlors, liquor stores, and newsstands.

Appendix D lists the dream books I looked at for this chapter. What I was able to learn about the authors and publishers of dream books is set out in Appendix E.

The books on the market today are mostly copied from plates dating to the 1940s and earlier. New titles sell less well than the reprints, which haven't been revised for decades (none I've seen has an entry for Computer, while under C you can still find Castor Oil and Collar Button). A typical book has a cheap paper cover featuring a mediocre illustration of the title (*Three Witches; Wise Ol' Owl*). It has about a hundred pages with a stapled binding, measures about five by seven inches, and costs under $5. The author's name is an obvious pseudonym (Rajah Rabo, Prof. Zonite). The back cover and inside pages carry ads for spiritual products and other dream books. There's a brief introduction citing the Bible, bringing in exotic traditions, quoting renowned authors, giving a nod to modern dream psychology, and praising the work in hand.

The actual dictionary section consists of an alphabetical list of dream symbols, each followed by several numbers and often a verbal interpretation as well. Supplementary lists give numbers for special topics (names, initials, the alphabet, national holidays, playing cards, animals, "hunches," human anatomy, birthstones).

The verbal interpretations of dreams in these books are derived from traditional signs and dream signs, from nineteenth-century dream books, from the publisher's other titles, from plagiarism, and from the author's imagination. The numbers also come from imagination, other titles, and plagiarism, but also from numerology and from popular dream numbers, sometimes called "fancies."

Fancies

As a *Jet* article described them in 1957, "fancies" are certain very popular numbers "based on dreams and dream books." But not all fancies originated in dream books. Some may have been borrowed from other occult sources, or have come into existence in a spontaneous way before being adopted by the dream book writers. In any event, the fancies transcended the dream books and circulated as common knowledge. Regular players all knew these numbers and the dreams they match up with. Fancies used to be called "barred numbers," too, because they were bet so heavily that some banks either reduced the odds for them or refused bets altogether in order to avoid huge payouts when they hit.

4-11-44. This very popular policy combination has a long history. A print from the 1870s shows a white man in a policy shop with a dream book in his back pocket and a betting slip in his hand on which appears 4-11-44. But a book called *How the Other Half Lives,* published in New York in 1890, mentions "the negro's lucky numbers, 4-11-44." Another source calls this "the nigger gig," and in different dream books it shows up as the gig for "Colored woman" (*Three Witches*) or "Negress" (*Wise Ol' Owl*). In some places it was known as the "washwoman's gig" (a song went, "if I hit this gig, ain't gonna bust these suds no more!"). The combination was so popular that in some locales it became the fancy for a dream about policy itself. In Chicago, 4-11-44 appeared on the signs of policy stations. And at least half a dozen dream books list 4-11-44 as the gig for "Policy" or "Lottery." The cover of *Aunt Sally's Policy Players Dream Book* shows Aunt Sally holding and pointing to a piece of paper with 4-11-44 written on it.

THE DEATH ROW. The protagonist of Chester Himes's autobiographical novel *The Third Generation* "unconsciously" calls "the death row" while quarterbacking football: 9-19-29. That's the policy gig for "Death" or "Dead" in many dream books, with 9-19-49 often given as the gig for "Cemetery." The standard form of the death row (or "dead roll") for numbers is 769, and so it appears in at least half a dozen dream books. As with all gigs, people sometimes vary the digits. The death row appears in other dream books as 679, 697, 767, 765, and 076. But players versed in the lore know the standard form.

FANCIES FROM THE BATHROOM AND THE BEDROOM. The majority of dream books politely avoid the topics of sex and elimination, but traditional fancies in these spheres were "generally known by the initiated." A blues verse by Blind Blake went, "I act like a fool and played 3-6-9," which is the widely known fancy for "fecal matter" (Jim Taylor). Dreaming of feces was considered a good dream (likewise, stepping in feces was a good sign).

The next verse of Blind Blake's blues is self-explanatory:

> I begged my baby, let me in her door *(twice)*
> Wanted to put my 25-50-75 in her 7-17-24.

Once an angry basketball player was heard to cuss out another who tripped him, saying "You 727, try that again and I'll give you a kick in that big 250 of yours."

This use of numbers as slang is one more demonstration of the former pervasiveness of numbers. Numbers slang is rare these days, but it remains in the memories of many. Stephanie Bell reminisced about her grandmother:

> She had numbers for everything. Whatever dream she had, there was a number for it, so she would play that. I don't remember ever seeing her with a book. I think she kept it all in her head. One is shit, actually shit. And it was 3-6-9. And a black man was 14-41-70. I remember those two because that had become part of her language. And she would say, "Oh, there's a 14-41-70." And she would say 3-6-9 instead of cursing. We all knew that when she said 3-6-9 she didn't want any stuff, she didn't want any shit.

The Dream Not Played

If you've been around black numbers or lotto players, chances are you've heard a story about someone who had the winning number but failed to play it. Versions of this story are recorded in books and articles about numbers, and told ruefully in literature and song. Almost always, the wasted foreknowledge comes from a dream. To quote Blind Blake's blues again:

> I dreamed last night the woman I love was dead, *(twice)*
> If I had played the "Dead Roll" I would-a come out ahead.
> I act like a fool and played 3-6-9, *(twice)*
> Lost my money, and that girl of mine.

An anthropologist heard the following story from a student. The young woman's mother had phoned to tell her a dream. She dreamed that she (the mother) was walking down a country road in the South with her niece Eunice, when

> a car went by on which the license number was plainly visible. The mother then woke up and immediately thought to herself that she should play the number of the license plate. However, she did not, and sure enough, the number "hit" the next day. This is what she called to tell her daughter, whose reaction was to tell her mother that obviously "Cousin Eunice" had come back expressly to give her aunt a winning number.

The interviews produced a considerable number of stories about dreams not played. For example:

> I dreamt that this number was gonna come out on a Monday. And I played the number every Monday for a little over a month. And then I didn't play it one Monday, because it was Christmas, and I didn't know you could play the number on Christmas, and my number came out! (Diane Dujon)

> I had a sister twelve years old when she passed. And I had this dream, and I told my mom, I said, "Mom, I dreamed of Nancy." Mom said, "What happened?" I said, "She was just standing there with Grandma, with this white outfit on." I said, "Mom, she told me to play the lottery. She told me, 'Play my birthday. Straight.'" My mother said, "Yeah, I'll play it," and I said I was gonna play it. Somehow we got busy in the course of the day, neither of us played it. And it came out straight. And I've been trying to have that dream again ever since then! (Oscar Edmond)

Beatriz Penso-Buford's story has a wrinkle: the same dream came out twice.

> I help students fill out their financial aid forms, and sometimes I help them interpret their award letters. And in my dream I saw the number 547. It was the amount of one of the student's checks. It came out two days later. And I was talking to one of our student workers, years later. And he doesn't play like 50-50, he'll play five dollars, ten dollars, and the numbers are gonna come like this [i.e., straight]. And I was talking to Billy, I said, "You know what happened to me so many years ago? I had this dream, and, you know, I didn't play the numbers." And Billy said, "What was the number?" I said, "547." He said, "I'm playing it tonight, and you'll get your share." I said, "Okay, it's a deal." Next

morning, Billy walked in. I said, "Billy?" He looked at me. He said, "No." I said, "Yeah." And he was furious. He didn't play it. But the number had come out again.

Here is a winning-number-not-played story seemingly fabricated by a dishonest winner. Adekola Adedapo, a U.S.–born Yoruba diviner who occasionally gives numbers, was talking about her clients:

> They all will say, "If this number comes in, sister, I'm gonna—." Honey, I had a woman, the number came out the exact way I called it: 1-2-4. And I called her and said, "Well, did you play it?" "Girl, you never know what happened. I gave that woman ten dollars and she said she didn't play my *number.* And so we didn't get it." And now she's probably sitting there counting her dollars!

Adedapo didn't say whether her prediction was drawn from the client's dream. Only one interviewee related a story in which the number definitely came from a source other than a dream. Daniel Wideman's grandmother, he told me, regularly played her street address. But

> one time she complained for about a year because she took a trip to Atlantic City for the weekend and I think got cleaned out pretty badly, and got back to discover that Saturday her number had hit in Pittsburgh. She wasn't there to play it.

Lottery, Numbers, and Policy at Present

Numbers gambling is not the conspicuous feature of black life it once was. Numbers is simply not the economic engine it once was—that function was undermined by the state lotteries from one side, and taken over by the drug trade from the other. Nevertheless, almost all African Americans know at least something about the numbers, and also something about getting numbers from dreams.

Young Reggie Winfrey may not have heard of dream books, but he knows about playing dreams. More typical is the woman who, when asked if she knew people who use dream books to play the lottery nowadays, answered, "Oh yeah! A lot of people use that." Many, such as the family of Achim Rodgers, made the switch from illegal to legal lottery. "They were still using their numbers, they were still using their dreams, and they were still using their dream books."

Legalization even brought in some recruits. Cecile Jackson's family got its first dream book when the lottery became legal. Alice Stephens, just a week before our interview, dreamed she saw some numbers written down at a bingo game. She called her mother, who said, "Oh, well, maybe we should play the lottery." Alice explained that her mother plays now, because it's legal. "Now it's the lottery, sanctioned by the United States government. When I was a child, it was the numbers racket. And that was gambling, and she definitely thought that gambling was immoral."

Even the old faith in numbers from church has been transferred to the legal lottery. Frances Freeman-Williams and Laura McKnight each volunteered comments about acquaintances who play hymn numbers and Bible verses. Reverend Marshall Hatch said, "I often chuckle and will use the line—really teaching against it—that 'Don't yo'all go out and play the hymn number!' Thinking it's sanctified, you know." And during Jesse Jackson Jr.'s first campaign for his congressional seat, the younger Jackson shared guest preaching honors with his father at Chicago's New Covenant Missionary Baptist Church. Jesse Sr. made a pitch about black people registering to vote. After trying with little success to get reluctant church members who weren't registered to stand up and admit it, he cajoled them with a call and response that concluded: "If I am lying . . . let me have . . . seven years hard luck . . . and never hit the lotto!"

Regardless of whether people play or not, numbers gambling is lodged in the collective memory. At young Zachary Brown's grandmother's house, "there was always Roman Catholic literature around, besides the Bible. And then the magic number things." Salim Muwakkil talks about his great-grandmother, who was "pretty otherworldly. She would meditate frequently, and would say she was doing it to come up with a number to pick. And dreams, too. She had a lot of dream books as well." Yusuf Abdullah remembers how "the policy man would come and take the numbers. And if you wanted it, he'd give you a book. And that's your dream book." When Haki Madhubuti was still the boy Don L. Lee, he made deliveries for his father's policy wheel in Chicago. Even individuals like Betty Holcomb, who come from families that viewed numbers gambling as "illegal and stupid" and "just obscene," were nevertheless exposed to relatives who had dream books and talked about dreams because they "used them to play numbers." Sandra Jackson-Opoku said she "didn't absorb any of it" and grew up thinking, "This is a bunch of myth." But she's fully familiar with the "whole culture around just dreaming, and interpreting signs, which usually had the purpose of making some money by betting on the policies." John Edgar Wideman does not ordinarily bet on the lottery:

> I mean, I'm not *all* kinds of fool. Now, if I go home to Pittsburgh, and everybody's gonna play a lottery number, I might do it, just for the heck of it. Because maybe I revert. Whatever. I might do it on that one occasion, but I just think it's a mug's game, so I don't do it.

One of Wideman's characters dismisses numbers and the lottery as "pie-in-the-sky. Rip-offs." Yet Wideman has drawn other characters whose spiritual insights through dreams and hunches enable them to play and win. When asked about this seeming inconsistency, Wideman replied, "Well, I'm describing the culture, partly. I'm not judging, saying whether it's right or wrong, but it turns people on, it happens. I've heard those dreams all my life, I've heard people swear that they win."

A fact not widely known outside the African American community is that illegal lotteries continue to operate in the shadow of the state lotteries. "Are you kidding?" exclaimed Adekola Adedapo. "Policy is never gonna die, okay? We're talking about street, we're talking about inner-inner-city politics. No, it'll always be, policy and prostitution, I'm sorry. They're gonna find a way to survive."

Many of today's illegal lotteries make use of the state lottery drawings, attracting customers by their larger (and tax-free) payoffs. Otis Grove called this the "sub-lottery system." One dream book publisher told me off the record:

> It's quite extensive. All throughout the South, in fact, the most popular number played they call the Chicago, which is the Illinois lottery results. I've been all over the place, and I'll tell you, there's some places that happen to have a machine which is totally legal, but I knew they were taking illegal bets on the side, and using the machine as a cover.

Sheron Williams-Brooks's grandmother plays both the state lottery and "policy" in Virginia, where "they use the same numbers off the same TV set." Winford Williams from South Bend, Indiana, and Regina Reed from Detroit referred to similar systems in those cities.

Dream book publisher Dale Silverberg informed me that in Philadelphia the "street number" is still derived from horse races. I asked her how extensive it is, in comparison to the state lottery. "In my clientele, I know a lot of people who play both numbers. My white friends don't play the street number. I don't think they even know about it."

To conclude, a few statistics from the interviews will serve to highlight the distinctive place of numbers gambling and numbers dreaming in African American life, even today.

- Asked if they were aware of the illegal lottery known as numbers or policy, 95 percent of blacks answered yes, but only 47 percent of whites.
- Asked whether they themselves or their families ever play or played either illegal or legal lottery, 71 percent of blacks said yes, only 10 percent of whites.
- Asked if they were aware of the use of dreams as a way to select numbers to play, 92 percent of blacks said yes, 61 percent of whites.
- Finally, asked if they were aware of the existence of dream books for deriving numbers from dreams, 84 percent of blacks said yes, only 25 percent of whites.

7

I KNEW YOU WERE GONNA SAY THAT

DÉJÀ VU AND PREDICTIVE DREAMS

It was as if he were reliving a forgotten dream, the hurt of the dream coming back in strange cadence.

—Chester Himes

Déjà Vu

Déjà vu is an oddly compelling *sensation of remembering*, accompanied by the thought, "This has happened before!" or "I've seen this before!"

Most of us are familiar with this experience. Over 90 percent of the people I surveyed had experienced déjà vu, blacks and whites alike. But blacks and whites do differ, I discovered, in the explanations they offer of déjà vu.

Déjà vu wasn't on my list of interview topics, until I noticed that the interviewees themselves were bringing it up. A dream, they said, is what you're remembering when you have the eerie remembering sensation of déjà vu. What's more, many regard the dream as a *prediction* of the unfolding event. In fact, predictive dreaming turns out to be the top explanation of déjà vu among African Americans. That's why a chapter on déjà vu is in place here at the end of this set of chapters on predictive dreams.

Scientifically speaking, the actual causes of déjà vu haven't been established, and the literature on the subject contains an amazing variety of speculations. These include nervous system glitches, memory errors, psychic events, various pathologies, and even quantum mechanics. I might add that the nonexperts I surveyed also produced an array of theories. Many persons waver between competing theories, or think that déjà vu has more than one cause.

Among whites, two theories contend as most popular. One is the nervous system glitch theory. The notion is that some temporary malfunction, such as a decoupling of the two halves of the brain, creates an illusion of memory. The second, equally popular theory among whites is reincarnation: what's happening feels familiar because you're being reminded of something that actually happened in a previous life.

While only a single black I interviewed mentioned the nervous system glitch theory, reincarnation proved to be the second most popular theory among blacks. This isn't at all surprising, considering how many blacks believe in reincarnation. For blacks, nevertheless, reincarnation came in a poor second as an explanation of déjà vu behind the prevailing theory, which is predictive dreaming.

Fully 57 percent of the blacks in my sample asserted that déjà vu is due to a dream that predicted the triggering event. Only 15 percent of my white sample asserted this belief. Many whites, to be sure, connect déjà vu with dreams, but in a different way—namely, coincidence. The triggering event, they suppose, must resemble some unremembered dream they once had, merely by chance. This theory of coincidence between life and dream dates to the nineteenth century and is a leading contender among "experts." Only a handful of investigators have speculated about the role of predictive dreams.

Déjà Vu and Predictive Dreams

We'll look now at déjà vu in relation to predictive dreaming, as experienced and explained by African Americans.

Unremembered Preview Dreams

Some people experience déjà vu and connect it with a predictive dream, even though they can't actually remember the dream in question. They simply surmise that a preview dream must have occurred. This differs from the coincidence theory, which says that a vague or partial resemblance between the event and an unremembered dream is enough to generate the illusion of memory. With the unremembered preview dream theory, the sense of memory is not really an illusion, because the dream, the unremembered dream, must have been a prediction. This shows a very strong faith in the reality of predictive dreaming.

Diane Dugger "wanted to talk about déjà vu dreams"—dreams she firmly believes took place but doesn't recall. "No, I automatically *know* it's something that I've dreamed. If I know good and well I've never been there before, it has to be my dream." And Diane Dujon told this story:

> The other day I did a speech, and there was a woman in the audience that said she was an artist. And she drew a picture of me, and then she drew a picture of my daughter. And then she wrote something to my daughter, and when my daughter showed it to me, the minute I looked at it I said, "Oh my God, I dreamt this before. I know just what this says: I dreamt this before."
> *Did you actually remember the dream, or was it a more general feeling that you had dreamed it?*
> It just feels like it came from a dream.

Several other interviewees drew the same conclusion, even though they may never have linked a déjà vu experience with a specific recalled dream.

One very interesting and complex account involves both predictive dreams and reincarnation. Craig Hodges, a member of the Chicago Bulls' first championship team, later a college coach, had the following déjà vu experience during the presidential reception for the champions:

> When I went to the White House, I wore African garments, okay? We were standing in the Rose Garden, okay? And I'm like, "This shit has happened *before!*" . . . In the amount of time that it took for me to feel like, "Man, I've been here *before*," it was *thssssh*, almost like a reel going past, like see-your-life-*pfoom!*
> *Do you know when you experienced it before?*
> No I don't, but I experienced that before—in the ancient times, my man.

Hodges went on to introduce the idea of ancestral memories. How exactly it all adds up isn't quite clear to me. But in some way, dreaming is the link between the present and the past. He said of déjà vu:

> I think it's a result of dreams, and it's a result of the link of us to our ancestors—is there any break in that link? And are many of the dreams handed down through historical experiences? And I think déjà vu is a link of the experiences of past lifetimes. Or past experiences of your

ancestors that are so much of your fiber that you can't help dream of some of the things.

So an unremembered dream, Hodges believes, formed the basis of his Rose Garden déjà vu experience while offering a glimpse of a past life or ancestral memory. Both the dream and the past itself, he apparently thinks, were previews of the present.

Dreams First Recalled While Déjà Vu Is in Progress

The very first recall of the preview dream most often emerges in the midst of the déjà vu episode. "I realize while it's happening that I dreamt this was gonna happen," said one person, "—like a premonition."

Michael Spencer told of a fight he'd had in fourth grade. "The dream was this person right in front of my face. And then in the fight, I remembered that very same picture just before I got hit in the mouth." This incident "woke me up" to the power of predictive dreaming, Spencer said.

Salim Muwakkil also related a boyhood experience:

> We were going fishing for catfish one evening, and this friend was sitting on top of his truck in front of us, and lightning struck a tree and he was burned. [The déjà vu sensation commenced, not with the lightning flash, but] after we drove up to the area, and we saw this friend laying out and a kind of smell in the air. And *after* it happened, I remembered it so perfectly from my dream! And that was pretty disconcerting.

Edward Moore, a cellist, is unusual in that his déjà vus can last "for hours." He gave this example of first recalling a "forecast" dream while a déjà vu was in progress:

> Last month I played a Stevie Wonder show. And when I walked into the rehearsal room, I knew who would be there, and I knew what was going to be played. Certain specific things, I knew what would happen *before* it happened, and what would be said afterwards. When I have that experience, I can usually remember when I dreamt it. If the situation really strikes me, then I tend to go over it and place it [the dream] in time.

Ronald Childs said that about once a month he has a déjà vu that brings up a lost dream. "These are like mini-dreams that I have, that last an instant, and that you usually don't remember." What's most remarkable, decades can pass between the "mini-dream" and the déjà vu. Childs commented on the preview dream to a recent déjà vu that occurred while he was clearing out his desk at the job he was leaving:

> It's always been very specific. I remember that particular dream. It must have been like '74, '75. I can usually pinpoint down to the year when I had it. And the dream, when it happened, would have been like an instant, something just thrown in.

Childs can't account for his vivid first-time recall of such a dream after more than twenty years: "I don't know. I don't know how I have it, but it happens all the time."

It's common during déjà vu to want to say aloud what's about to happen, but somehow you're tongue-tied and can't "break the spell." Some people, however, manage to speak out as things unfold. Ethel Smith is one:

> Sometimes, I can't remember my dreams. And then some snippet of a scene will appear in my life, and I feel like I'm doing déjà vu, and it will come back to me, that dream that I had two months ago that I couldn't remember when I got up. . . . Like a friend was gonna tell me he was moving in with a woman. And I knew exactly what he was gonna say, and how he was gonna say it. And I go, "Oh my God, I knew you were gonna say that." And then he goes, "What else was I gonna say?" And I said, "Well, you were also gonna tell me—" and we chuckled about it.

A couple of people went further and attempted to alter the events the dreams were warning them about. One prisoner was once at a party with his brother when he had déjà vu and remembered a dream in which his brother was killed in a car accident. He persuaded his brother, who was drinking, to let his girlfriend drive. The accident nevertheless took place, and the dream "was right about how the accident happened," but the brother was only injured. "From that day on he promised me to listen to me whenever I have another strange feeling overcome me, as I did on that night."

Dreams Recalled Prior to Déjà Vu

Occasionally someone undergoes a déjà vu that connects with a dream they already recalled clearly when they first dreamed it. This seems to be like having any predictive dream come true, with one difference: déjà vu involves that oddly compelling sensation of remembering and reexperiencing. One woman says that after déjà vu she can go back and locate old preview dreams recorded in her journals as much as twenty years earlier. And one prisoner recalled a certain dream, then forgot it, then re-recalled it during déjà vu:

> I dreamt that I was coming to prison, and I woke up and knew that I was coming to jail. I told my fiancée about it but forgot about it until the day I was arrested. Then it was a déjà vu—and here I am. I believe that's how we get forewarned of many things.

In other cases, the dream is in accessible memory before the déjà vu and is fully in mind from the beginning of the episode. Before being imprisoned, one man had many dreams about the guards he would later encounter. Upon his arrival in prison, he had a déjà vu related to those dreams. And Moreese "Pop" Bickham, imprisoned for many years until his release at age seventy-eight, had never actually heard the term *déjà vu,* but he knew the experience. Sometimes in the midst of things "it flash back that I dreamed this!" Other times, he remembers the dream beforehand. "I ain't been no place yet that I didn't see in my sleep before I went there," he claimed, and he gave the example of his transfer to Angola prison:

> And the high sheriff was carrying me up there. I said, "Where is that at you can see the river when you get on top of the hill?" He said, "Right up here. You ever been there?" I said, "No." He said, "Well, how did you know?" I said, "I dreamed-seen it."

Jim Taylor said, "I'll dream about a situation, and maybe three or four days later that same situation happens. And it's, 'Wow! I've been here before!'" He told about one such situation involving an argument with a man over money. "And whatever his last statement was going to be, I told it to him before he told it to me. And it shocked the crap out of him! He said, 'I was just gonna say that to you!' you know?"

Illana Jordan fell asleep on a car trip and dreamed about what she would experience after she and her friend got to California. Upon waking, she knew the dream was predictive. "I do that all the time," she said, and it distresses her, "because then I have expectations of what it's gonna be like." Two days later, in San Francisco, they were walking to the subway:

> And we see these two little kids on the porch, and they say, "Smoking will kill you," and we're laughing about the fact that this is what we thought we'd see in California. Right. But *I* was laughing at the fact

that I *knew* that was gonna be the thing. And everything is looking familiar. And when she says, "This is a long walk," and I say, "No, it's not, the subway's over this thing"—it happened in my head right before I said it to her, and happened in my dream two nights previous. And I told her what she was gonna say right before she said it. And she says, "Oh, my God!" because it was not even relevant to the discussion that we were having.

While this experience included the typical odd compelling sensation of déjà vu, Jordan said she had more or less abandoned the term *déjà vu* itself. She lives in a white milieu, where her friends dismiss déjà vu as a mere nervous system glitch. "And it's kind of frustrating to feel so strongly about something, and it be like knocked off."

Colleen McElroy had "dreams of prophecy" when she was younger. One was a *recurring* dream that eventuated in a déjà vu experience. For the reader's convenience I've keyed the elements in the dream to the parallel elements in the déjà vu situation—[1a] in the dream, for example, matches up with [1b] in the situation:

> [In the dream] I was in a car [1a], and there was a party [2a] going on in the backseat. I was driving [3a], but I was sitting in the passenger seat [4a], with a glass in my hand [5a]. And the person who was in the driver's seat seemed to be having difficulty [6a], and arguing with me [7a] about what it was I was doing. And suddenly, I had a choice between crashing [8a] into a mountain [9a] or hitting a train [10a]. And I would always wake up.
>
> And about six years later, I was driving [1b] into Oregon with my brand-new husband. And we were lost. And I was sitting there [in the passenger seat] [4b] with a cup of coffee [5b] and the map [3b] in my hand. The radio was playing, and there was a party record [2b], you know, one of those dance records, playing. And we could see Mount Hood [9b] in front of us. And at one point he decided to turn around. And when he did, the car had overheated, and it stalled [6b]. And behind us there was a logging truck, and it blew its horn, which sounds exactly like a train [10b]. I do not know to this day how I got out of that car. But I abandoned that car [8b]. And I had to crawl back in and explain, ha-ha. My husband was very upset [7b], very hurt that I had abandoned him. But I had no control over it. This was my dream.

McElroy indicated that she had experienced the déjà vu sensation before the car stalled. Then the truck horn reminded her of the recurring dreams.

Banal or Meaningful?

Yusuf Abdullah said that déjà vu saved his life when he was in the military. The déjà vu occurred while he was setting explosives, and the remembered dream alerted him to change what he was doing:

First you'll see it in the dream, and then you'll see it happening for real. And if you remember that it's happened in the dream, then you can control what else happens after you realize it's happening for real.

Abdullah's déjà vu experience is exceptional. The events involved in déjà vu rarely have such obvious life importance. In fact, what's usually noticed about déjà vu is the puzzling contrast between the *compelling déjà vu sensation* and the *banal quality of the déjà vu situation.* The strength of the feeling seems incongruous. Consider the example of déjà vu offered by Reggie Winfrey:

My definition of déjà vu is that I dream about something, and then, it happens in real life. Just exactly as I dreamed about it. And it always happens to me. I mean, I might be drinking my orange juice, and I look at a particular spot on the wall, and I'll be like, "Hey, I did that before."

And Ann Eskridge, who attributed déjà vu both to dreams and to past life experiences, quipped, "I wonder why we live it—it's boring now, it must have been really boring then!"

Perhaps the prosaic content of most déjà vu experiences explains the fact that in my reading of African American literature I found only nine mentions of déjà vu. By contrast, many other exceptional states are mentioned at a higher rate, even though in life they occur far less often. Out-of-body experiences, for example, are mentioned about twice as often.

And yet, quite a few interviewees affirmed the meaningfulness of their déjà vu experiences, regardless of whether the events seem banal. Thus Kai EL Zabar remarked that déjà vu is "not so trivial really, if you think about it. It could be something major." Sara Lawrence-Lightfoot and Kimberly Camp both said that déjà vu brings valuable "information." You have to look past the surface of things. Alice Stephens pointed to the warning function of déjà vu:

It doesn't *appear* to be [a warning] when I'm going into the situation, but when "B" happens, it turns out to be one of those important kinds of situations. It may be important to my career or something that's happening. But not in any kind of direct way. I have noticed that.

Ayanna Udongo views déjà vu as "preparing me for some kind of shock or something." Tony Thomas connects déjà vu with destiny, "something that was meant to happen—everything in your dreams is preparing you for the months and days ahead." Likewise, Charles Young "was given to believe that occasionally you hit these milestones that say, 'Yeah, you're on the right track.'" And Ronald Childs said that déjà vu is "like a spiritual reminder that everything that is happening to you is intended to happen. It's all written down in some great book somewhere."

The prevalence of the predictive dream explanation for déjà vu among African Americans derives from the strength of the belief in predictive dreaming overall. And the sense of meaning that many African Americans feel about déjà vu, even when it seems banal, reflects the spiritual weight given by them to predictive events in general, and especially to predictive dreams.

8

THE UNDERBEAT

DREAMING AND OTHER STATES
OF CONSCIOUSNESS

. . . none of these explain from where the voices within me hail . . . voices that appear when I dream, awake or sleeping.

—Leon Forrest

Boundaries

Night dreams are one thing, but waking visions quite another—or so claims Western culture. The West, however, didn't always separate the imagery of sleep and the imagery of waking so sharply. But with the Enlightenment, these states came to be viewed through the lens of secular, scientific rationality. The ordinary waking state became the West's strict standard of psychological reality and normalcy, while night dreaming was downgraded to the status of an excusable aberration. We're asleep when we dream, after all; we can't help ourselves, we all do it, it's sort of normal. "Daydreaming" is also acceptable, as long as we're secure that it's only fantasy at play. But having visions or hearing voices—"seeing things" or "hearing things" while we're awake—well, that's decidedly abnormal.

These attitudes put Euro-American mainstream culture at odds not only with its own history and folk traditions but with virtually all other cultures of the world, of all times.

African Americans remain more in line with the world consensus. They tend not to make the same rigid distinctions among states of consciousness as Euro-Americans. Every one of my interviewees with whom the subject came up energetically affirmed this difference.

Young Ramon Giles, for example, described his family's fluency and freedom with altered states:

> It might not necessarily be a dream where someone like my grand-mother (or Moses, or Abraham) may have gotten inspiration, but it may have been what they call a daydream. Or just by sitting and medi-tating, they got this vision. And so I get the sense that they don't separate the ways you can get these visions.

Then Giles went on to skewer the attitude of mainstream culture:

> And see, dreams are considered legitimate, because, okay, you go to sleep at night, you gotta do something, so you can have a dream. Now, if you're walking around in daytime and you get these strong visions, you're looney tunes.

Fluency with altered states may well be a deep survival of African psy-chology. A psychiatrist from the continent writes of traditional Africa that

> the line between reality and dreaming is never as sharp as the Western world may think. Waking thought is not purged of its imaginary con-tent, and there are no hard and impenetrable divisions between the various "psychological" productions of the psychic system.

This is emphatically *not* to say that Africans can't tell one state from another. It's just that the differences matter less to them. During her many visits to African countries, Maisha Hamilton-Bennett observed the mingling of different altered states:

> Being able to transform one's level of consciousness is really highly respected. There are people who will go into trance during a ceremony where they actually dream or have communications, they think, with the spirits of gods or the spirits of ancestors. But also as part of the ritual, they may talk about dreams that they had the night before. So dreams were often woven into the understanding of what was going on. The healer talks about a dream that he had that saw this already, or a dream that he had where he saw what the outcome or the solution was going to be.

Hamilton-Bennett's comments point up that while waking trance is recognized as a special state, it flows into night dreaming as far as meaning is concerned.

Reverend Marshall Hatch, a student of Africa, observed that black Americans have a low boundary between dreaming and waking, and that this comes from being an "African people." He noted

> how very much a part of reality the dream world is for African people, how ingrained it is. There's not a lot of distinction made between what

a person dreams and when they wake up. It's all seen as life . . . impacting one upon the other.

I said in chapter 2 that a penchant for dreaming is both a survival from Africa and an American adaptation to oppression—a survival *for* survival. The same can be said about fluency with altered states in general. Carl C. Bell, a black psychiatrist, believes that blacks throughout the world employ the ability to enter altered states as a "survival skill." In his community practice in Chicago, he sees this skill "utilized daily to help black people master stress." Stress he identifies as "survival fatigue," a sort of battle fatigue caused by racism.

Several interviewees made related observations. Daniel Wideman connected the "deliberate cultivation" of altered states to the conditions of slavery:

> For a long time, there were very few literal spaces that we could create for ourselves, so psychic space, and musical space, became very important territories. And I think that the *art of dreaming* became a political act during that time, because it was a way of creating and constructing a totally free space.

Douglas Gills called "liberalism" about the boundaries of different states "a sanity device" that developed under "conditions of oppression." Gills's own "liberalism" was illustrated when I later asked him whether he ever dreamed dreams with interracial themes. Gills responded with a story. Gills's grandfather had once saved his own life by flashing his Mason's ring at a pursuing Klansman, who then pretended not to see him up in the tree where he was hiding. When I tried to draw Gills back to dreams, he insisted he wasn't making a distinction between night dreams and waking dreams. I pressed him to say just what his waking dream was in this case. It was, precisely, the story he heard from his grandfather. "To have that memory come into your mind is comparable to having a dream?" I asked, and he answered, "Yes!" The story functioned for him as a kind of collective dream, a myth that helped him understand the complexities of racism in the South.

Colleen McElroy spoke about the nurturing of altered states as part of the survival strategy of black families:

> Someone will talk about Uncle So-and-so, who used to do whatever. And that presence is still felt in the house. Or a child may dream of Uncle So-and-so, without knowing who that person is, and mention it the next morning, and everyone recognizes who she dreamed about.

Being black in America means that you have to cultivate that kind of spirituality. And much of what is cultivated is through dreaming. That's what spirituality's all about: the dreamworld. And it may be dreaming as a sleep state, and it may be what is conventionally called daydreaming. I don't know if my dreams were provoked by talk at the dinner table. I have no idea. I know that after a while, it didn't matter, because they were moving on their own. But I think it's because people talk about "What do we need to do to survive?" And there *is* always that sense of making sure everyone knows that we're in this survival business together.

"I Have a Dream"

A notable illustration of free boundaries in service of survival is the great "I have a dream" speech of Martin Luther King Jr., a man sometimes referred to simply as "the dreamer." Gloria Naylor observed of King's unforgettable refrain:

> It was a brilliant stroke to use that metaphor for a political position, because with the African American community—being a people in the social and political position that they are in and have occupied throughout the history of this country—the idea of dreaming for things plays an important *cultural* part. There is always the underbeat of dreaming and hoping, and those things being quite valid.

"I have a dream" definitely means "I have a *hope*." But could it be that King's hope visited his night dreams? If so, then when he said "I have a dream," he also meant "I *had* a dream," or perhaps "I have a *recurring* dream." King had to know that some in his audience would take and would approve this double meaning.

What did the interviewees have to say about this? Only one, Norma Adams Wade, firmly rejected the possibility that King meant a night dream as well as a waking hope: "To me, anybody who thinks he was talking about a real go-to-sleep dream is crazy!" Wade thought the suggestion trivializes the speech. But everyone else with whom the question came up saw it the other way. I asked John Johnson whether King may have meant night dreams of racial justice. "Yeah, I think so," he replied. "I've always felt that he had those dreams." I said to Frances Parks that almost all white people would say King meant hope and only hope. "No, no. Nn-nn. Martin said he had that dream. I believe you have a hope, and then comes a night dream that affirms it. I think that you believe in the one [hope] when you believe in the other [night dreams]." Richard Hunt stated that the speech was "a kind of sermon," the kind in which a preacher validates her/his message or calling by telling a dream. Hunt continued:

> There always was a lot of talk about dreams of equality, dreams of freedom. And it's an interesting thing, because what a lot of the pre–Civil Rights life of blacks was, it was kind of imagining or dreaming of a time that was gonna be different.
> *Actually involving night dreams? So that "I have a dream" overlaps I had a dream"?*
> Right, right. Yeah, and it's certainly meaningful to carry that dream with you during the day. It would make it easier to get through the day, you know?

I told Sterling Plumpp that before doing this work, I myself had always assumed King was just talking about his waking wish for racial harmony. Plumpp responded:

> Well, I'm not so sure. I'm not sure when you are lying down black, it is as much of a wish as you think. You might even dream that, you see. . . . My aunt told me that when she was a little girl, she used to both pray and dream the field that she was chopping cotton in had turned to iron, so she wouldn't have to chop nowhere, or it would break the hoe.

Apart from comments directly on King's speech, some interviewees merged night dreams and waking hopes in the same way as King. One woman, the founder of a private agency aiding disadvantaged children, proposed a program to the Chicago public school system to teach children

> how dreams help you to understand who you are. And there are so many children that never have a chance to dream—ever. If their lives are always just *pain*, the lack of imagination—you know, they just feel "What's the sense of dreaming or hoping for anything?"

Bear in mind that she was collaborating with a dream expert in a program that primarily concerned night dreams.

Michael Warr touched on the dream/hope boundary in connection with a literary magazine he was starting up for ghetto youngsters, *Voices in the Hood:*

> One of the things I said in an editorial I wrote is that kids need to be able to dream beyond what has happened to them today.

You're using the word "dream" in the metaphorical sense?
Well, you know, I think that for some people, they actually dream about those things the way I dreamed about them when I was a kid. Dreaming is very critical, because you need to be able to think positively about the future somehow.

Several interviewees told me night dreams of theirs that expressed and reinforced their personal aspirations. Craig Hodges, reflecting on his youthful night dreams of being on the court and playing ball, said, "I look at them as part and parcel of what I accomplished, as far as basketball is concerned." Sylvia Morris spoke similarly, about dream-hopes of musicianship; Yusuf Abdullah, about dream-hopes of owning a business; and Michael Spencer, about dream-hopes of acquiring a special car:

> One of my goals as a broker is to get a Mitsubishi 3000GT. I had a dream that was so real, it was a shame to wake up! I was really into it, so far as the shifting gears, the screeching of the tires, everything. And if something like that sticks so well in your mind, it can either be a driving force, or some kind of subtle premonition that hey, yeah, it's in line for your future.

Spencer here connected the motivating power of dreams with their predictive power. Perhaps that's also what King had in mind, in the context of race relations. And by speaking publicly of his political "dream," King elevated prediction to prophecy.

"Dreams" and "Visions"

Euro-Americans, once again, typically make a strict distinction between "dreams," which happen during sleep, and "visions," which happen in the waking state. There are also some African Americans who make this strict distinction, and it probably isn't accidental that their use of the word "vision" is negatively tinged. LV Jordan's grandmother

> would say, "Michael [her dead grandson] came to me in a vision, and he sat at the foot of the bed." And like, "You were asleep! You dreamt it!" I didn't believe her. I don't believe in *visions*.

Many African Americans, however, think about "dreams" and "visions" in ways that blur or minimize the opposition of sleep and waking. We see this holistic attitude toward states of consciousness in the ways people talk about dreams and visions.

First of all, the word "dream" may itself be used to mean a vision in the Euro-American sense—that is, a waking event. Douglas Gills told how a man's spirit in the form of a cat visibly walked into the room where Gills's mother and the man's widow were sitting. The cat-spirit jumped up on the bed, and then left, making sounds just like the dead husband used to. "Dreams of cats," said Gills, "I could tell you a couple more." And Edward Moore told this story, using the word "dream" to signify a waking event:

> [Great Aunt Mandy] called my grandmother and told her that she had seen in this dream that one of my uncles was going to die, and that she should keep him away from cars. And indeed he did have this accident within a matter of weeks.
> *Was this awake or asleep?*
> She told me that she saw this while she was awake. It wasn't a night dream, it was a vision.

Sometimes both words, "dream" and "vision," are applied indiscriminately to one and the same waking event. "I had been having dreams," said Regina Reed, "I kept visioning this woman. Kind of like seeing her, right before I was ready to go to bed." Another woman said:

> I dreamed I saw [my great aunt] standing in my room. She was telling me, "Don't be afraid." And I wasn't, I just had this calm feeling all over me, and I went on back to sleep.
> *Were you awake when that happened?*
> Yes, I think I was awake. I would call that a vision.

In the other direction, the word "vision" can signify a sleeping dream. Ronald Childs's grandmother "would cook these elaborate big breakfasts, as a lot of grandmothers did. And then she would say, 'I had a vision last night.' Which was a dream, evidently." Childs said she used the words "interchangeably."

Often the term "vision" is used in preference to "dream" when the sleep experience in question is religious or spiritual in character. Haki Madhubuti said:

> Well, most certainly in a church, dreams were often referred to, in the category of visions more than anything else: that God or his angels came to a certain person that night, and this is what was said to that person. And he or she would share it with the congregation as a form of vision.

Composer William Grant Still kept a journal titled "Prayer, Praise and Dreams." He wrote, for example: "In a vision, I beheld a mighty cloud of angels approaching me. . . . As the angels sang I broke into tears, and awoke to find myself sobbing with joy." Judy Still clarified her father's views on dreams and visions:

> Some dreams are simply dreams, pictures that pass before your eyes, and some dreams are visions, where God gives you a sign or teaches you something. Or it could be a warning. Not all dreams are visions.

Shirlee Taylor Haizlip used "vision" to mean a spiritual visitation during sleep:

> I have, maybe, visions in dreams, but not visions in my conscious waking hours.
> *Explain what you mean by "visions in dreams."*
> An apparition that appears in a dream, as part of a dream. A vision is one-dimensional—this thing that floats within the dream, but is distinct from the full fleshed-out figures of the dream.

Several interviewees associated "vision" with predictive dreaming, which is usually assumed to have a spiritual basis. For example, Maisha Hamilton-Bennett said:

> My husband—one of his brothers killed his girlfriend and then committed suicide. And he [Hamilton-Bennett's husband] said he had a vision of that—I think it was a dream of it—before it happened. And he was in a situation [in prison] where in order to call his brother he would have had to call collect, and his brother had told him not to call him collect because it was running up his phone bill. And so he didn't call, and then he felt badly afterwards, because he had a vision of this happening. But I don't know if I've had predictive dreams.

Finally, some people talk about dreamlike experiences without bothering to say whether they occurred asleep or awake. There couldn't be a stronger manifestation of a low boundary between so-called dreams and visions.

Anthony Shy's great-aunt told the family that "Jesus appeared in the passenger seat of her car." Shy didn't know "if she meant that this actually happened to her or she dreamed that it happened."

Gwen Robinson said, "My mother would talk about her father visiting her after he had died, and he said to her this, that, and the other. And I didn't know if she was talking about a dream or a vision or just what."

Kai EL Zabar's mother phoned to say that EL Zabar's deceased father had been appearing at the foot of the bed, and that it made her "uncomfortable," so she was selling the house. I asked if her mother was asleep or awake during these visitations. She paused. "Hm! I don't know. That's the part of us [African Americans] that I was talking about that doesn't make those distinctions. 'Cause I didn't even ask her that."

After three years of struggle with breast cancer, and some months before she died, Sterling Plumpp's mother recounted to him a series of images she had experienced over the course of her illness:

> "So when I first got down [ill], it was like I was all alone. I looked out, and all I could see was the wilderness. And then every day I had gone out, I had cut down a tree here, I had dug up a sprout [bramble vine], and then I had pulled up a stump. And eventually I could see a big clearing. And I had this—I had a house! Then, I had begun to fence in my house. I had found a plank, and I had built this plank fence around my house, and it had a gate. And then I could see my way clear. I was here in this house, with the fence around it, and there was a clearing, and there was a road leading from it."

Plumpp, who based part of a poem on this eloquent record of his mother's preparation to meet death, introduced her experiences to me as "a kind of dream." But when I later asked if they were "night dreams or waking experiences that she had over this period of time," he said, "It was told almost as if it was a vision. You know . . . so it's hard for me to say." His mother had not felt a need to specify what state she was in, and Plumpp had not felt a need to ask.

Some African Americans say simply "I saw" instead of "I had a dream" or "I had a vision"—what matters is *what* you "see," not whether you're asleep or awake when you see it.

Osuurete Adesanya described how her father "will just say, 'I saw you. Are you okay?' " Adesanya was talking about her father's warning dreams.

Katie Jones said, "If I see death, I wouldn't tell them [her children] nothing about it." Jones was talking about seeing a spirit over her daughter's shoulder while awake.

Joe Cheeks's sister warned him, " 'Be careful in a car. I see something in a car. And I see two skeletons. They look like you'all'—me and my brother." I asked if she was awake or asleep. "Now with her, I'm not sure, because she can do both of them."

Stephanie Bell said:

> There were times when my grandmother would say that she "saw"
> Mother, Mother had come to her, during the night, and she had seen
> her in a vision. Her words would be, "I saw Mother last night, and she
> was in the room with me."
>   *She wouldn't necessarily say whether she was asleep or awake?*
> Right. I don't think she ever drew that line. She'd just say she "saw" her.

From Inside or Outside?

Where do dreams "come from"? At one time it was the prevailing
belief in Western culture that "dreams originated from a 'higher
order' outside the dreamer." Not a few Euro-Americans still maintain
some such spiritual belief. However, the secular mainstream as well as
most dream psychologists hold that dreams originate from inside the
mind of the dreamer, and that their meanings can be explained, if at
all, by reference to the mind.

The majority of African Americans, by contrast, believe that at
least some dreams originate from outside the mind. This was evident
in the chapters on ancestor dreams and predictive dreams. "How am
I able to do this?" one woman asked rhetorically about her predictive
dreams, and answered herself, "African Americans say, 'There's a reason: it's coming from somewhere else.' Whereas, on a European level,
that's as far as you take it." Haki Madhubuti said, "Many of our folk
feel that there's a certain amount of sacredness attached to it . . .
another force comes in*to* you, which would be the dream or the
vision, all right?"

If dreams originate inside the mind, merely as part of the process
of sleep, then it's easiest to think of waking visions either as hallucinations or, possibly, as rare spiritual events. That's the Euro-American
view. If, however, dreams originate outside the mind, from a spiritual
source, then there's less reason to differentiate them from visions.
Both appear to have the same cause, the same meaning, the same
legitimacy.

Reverend Marshall Hatch spelled out that for African Americans,
"seeing" involves beliefs about the source of what is seen:

> The dream in sleep is intimately related with what you call a vision. In
> the culture. So there wouldn't be that much difference. You could "see"
> it in a dream or a vision, and "see" it. It's who *showed* it to you, is what
> puts the veracity behind it. "The Lord showed it to me."

The Subconscious

Most people think that the outside-the-mind source of dreams and visions is God. But the source is sometimes conceived of in other ways. For Sheron Williams-Brooks, dreams come from "tapping into a collective intuition." Initially she said, "I believe that dreams come from out in," but when I asked specifically whether the "collective intuition" comes from inside or from outside, she responded, "I think it's a meeting of both those things." This is probably not an uncommon view. Marion Stamps said at different times that her various altered states emanated from "God," from "spirit," and from the "collective energy of everybody." But she included another on the list, "subconsciousness." This shows that for her, as for Williams-Brooks, the outside-the-mind source has an inside-the-mind counterpart.

The word "subconscious" came up spontaneously a number of times in the interviews. (The "*un*conscious" was mentioned only by a few interviewees who were influenced by mainstream psychodynamic theories.) Most interviewees who used the word appeared to think of the subconscious as a spiritual organ of the mind, as our spiritual receiver: "Something larger than us . . . comes to us in our subconsciousness" (Haki Madhubuti); "The subconscious is the spiritual self" (Yusuf Abdullah); "In my conscious subconscious mind, I am dealing with information from the outside I'm just tapped into" (Kai EL Zabar). "My subconsciousness is what is in touch with everything, these spirits and everything that's around me. . . . My subconsciousness is my link to eternity" (Ramon Giles).

Psychological-Mindedness

One last point before closing this chapter. To say that African Americans have an outside-the-mind theory of dreams is not to say that African Americans are not "psychologically minded." That's an old prejudice of white psychiatry. The reality is that African Americans are especially good at operating in more than a single mode toward dreams. I asked psychoanalyst Barbara Pulliam if she had any problem getting black clients with an outside-the-mind orientation to look at dreams the other way:

> No, I haven't had a problem with it at all. They're very willing to associate to the various elements in the dream. You just have to train them about day residue and teach them what's expected, and they go right along with it. And that's notwithstanding I do have some people who say that they will go to readers and all. And that's not pooh-poohed.

After talking about visitation dreams, obviously involving outside spirits, one woman added, "Sometimes something I dreamed about will have some reference to what I'm doing today. Sometimes it plays out my fears, or I work a lot of stuff out, in my sleep, that I maybe couldn't deal with."

Diane Dugger has alternative explanations for different predictive dreams:

> I think sometimes that they're coming from a higher being, someone that can foresee what's going on. And sometimes, it could come from something that somebody said in that day or that week, that can put you to thinking about what could occur.

A dream of publisher Hermene Hartman's, about a new office she was thinking of moving her newspaper to, was interpreted for her by friend and employee Kai EL Zabar in two ways simultaneously. EL Zabar viewed the dream both as a premonition of a real threat—fulfilled when their present office was broken into a week later—and as an inside-the-mind psychological expression: "You really don't like that [new] space."

Lastly, Angela Jackson had this reaction to seeing noted dream psychologist Gayle Delaney on Oprah Winfrey's show:

> [Oprah brought up] the old-way traditional African American interpretations of dreams. Oprah said she grew up being taught snakes meant a certain thing, you know, and all this. Then the woman went on to say that only you can interpret your own dreams within, you know, how they apply to your own consciousness, and your own life. And this made me kinda angry, because I know what she said is true, but it's—it's narrow. It's not the whole truth. Because I know people who have lived in the African American cultural traditional way of interpreting dreams, and they have proven accurate.

Later, Jackson said that dreams are "a divine source of information. It's God talking to you," then added, "But you know what? That doesn't contradict the one about it coming from inside. Our subconsciouses are attached to something greater."

9

DIDN'T BOTHER *ME* NONE

EXPERIENCES AT THE EDGE OF DREAMING

I have always seen things.
—Henry Dumas

Western culture, to repeat, emphasizes the boundaries between different states of consciousness. And strong boundaries discourage unorthodox experiences. But African Americans are on the whole less confined by these boundaries than are their fellow citizens of the West. African Americans still enjoy some of the fluency with states of consciousness brought from Africa by the slaves and preserved by their descendants in self-defense against oppression.

In this chapter we'll explore several states of consciousness that go beyond the ordinary waking state and beyond ordinary night dreaming. We'll look at three somewhat "dreamlike" experiences that people can undergo while awake. These dreamlike experiences are to see *visions,* to hear *voices,* and to feel *presences.* Most African Americans are familiar with these experiences—if not firsthand, then through family, friends, or church. Visions, voices, and presences belong in the standard repertoire of consciousness for those brought up in African American culture.

We'll also glance at three further types of experience that deviate from the ordinary in a variety of ways. *Out-of-body experiences, lucid dreams,* and *mutual dreams and visions* don't have the same consensus standing in the cultural repertoire as visions, voices, and presences, but nevertheless shed light on the African American aptitude for altered states.

Visions

It's striking how many of the leaders of slave rebellions in the pre–Civil War South were inspired by visions. Nat Turner's rebellion of 1831 is the most famous. Turner was driven forward by fervent visions:

> And about this time I had a vision—and I saw white spirits and black spirits engaged in battle, and the sun was darkened—the thunder rolled in the Heavens, and blood flowed in streams—and I heard a voice saying, "Such is your luck, such you are called to see, and let it come rough or smooth, you must surely bear it."

The great abolitionist Sojourner Truth, born in slavery, was often guided by predictive and inspiring dreams and visions. One impressive vision taught her how she should conduct herself toward white people. Her long account of this vision begins, "Just as I was going out to get into the wagon, I met God!" And it ends, "Lord, Lord, I can love even the white folks!"

Other slave narratives are also adorned by visions. Of the religious conversion narratives collected from ex-slaves, virtually all describe things seen and voices heard. Books about black folk beliefs also contain abundant accounts of visions. Most involve spirits or ghosts, which in those days, as one ex-slave put it, were "as common as pig tracks."

Visions are a recurring motif in African American folklore and literature. Harlem Renaissance author Countee Cullen, to quote one example, wrote:

> "When my mother died we knew for sure where she was going, because she cried out that there was lights shining all around her, and music, singing, and her own mother who'd been dead twenty years came and stood at the bed all dressed in white."

Interviewee Kai EL Zabar recalled:

> It was nothing for me to hear the older women talking about walking up the stairs one day, and a headless woman was walking down the stairs, and one said, "Well, Minnie, what did you do?" and she said, "Didn't bother *me* none." I mean, that was the kinda conversation we would have, and so we were not made afraid of that kind of thing.

When I commented to Reverend Marshall Hatch that you very rarely hear white people talk about visions, he replied, "Oh, black people all the time!" John Edgar Wideman thinks it isn't as common as that, but that "everybody had language for it and everybody would know what you were talking about if you referred to it."

In my survey I asked, "Have you ever seen something that you couldn't account for in the ordinary way?" This question drew accounts of visions from 47 percent of the interviewees, compared with 23 percent of the white comparison group. Visions may no longer be as common as pig tracks, but they're surprisingly common.

Not all of the visions I was told had occurred "out there," in physical space, as we might suppose. Many visions occur in some sort of mental space, with the eyes involved only slightly or not at all. This is, in fact, more usual than the out-there kind of vision. Joe Cheeks explained:

> It's not like you actually see something in three-dimensional sighting. To me, I can see things as vividly in my mind sometimes as I can with my eyesight, but I know the difference. I know that this is my vision, see, and this is something I'm seeing here. It's not the eyes.

It's important to realize that a vision is no less authentic because it occurs in mental space rather than physical space. In John Edgar Wideman's novel *Damballah,* the narrator has an *ancestor vision:* "That's when I saw her. When my grandmother, Freeda, came to me. She is wearing a thin, gray cardigan. . . . " Wideman, who based this passage on his own experience, elaborated during our interview:

> It's not a sense that there's a formed ghost in the space. But there's a kind of clear scene going on. So that it's not somebody I'm imagining, because the consciousness has an independence. To me, it's her. That's why I said that she "came to me." In the same way that I'm sitting here, if my son walked in and I said to you, "My son walked in." It has that kind of authority.

In addition to Wideman, a number of other interviewees also talked about ancestor visitations in visions. One woman heard her father's flip-flops in the kitchen a few days after he died. She found him there going about his usual morning routine:

> And I said, "Don't you know that you're not here anymore? Don't you know that you need to go on?" And he looked at me and he said, "I don't *know.* I don't *know* where I am right now." He was really puzzled and sad, 'cause he didn't want to go on. It was like I had to send him off.

Sterling Plumpp "actually" saw his grandfather and uncles, "with flashlights tied to their heads picking cotton at night, that they were going to steal from the white man." Angela Powell described a prolonged visitation filled with drumming, dancing, and feasting. It culminated with ceremonial gift giving:

> They put me in this little chair, and each woman came up to me and gave me a gift. Whether it was they sang me a song, or they wrote me a poem, or they told me a piece of advice, or whatever. And then when everyone was done, all the women were in a huge half-circle around me, and they all said something, then they all did this dance thing, and then two women took my hands and said, "It's time to go now."
>
> And later on I had a dream about my [Great-]grandma Belle, and she said, "Those were your female ancestors giving you gifts and letting you know that they're always with you, and that you're not alone."

Two interviewees, Sara Lawrence-Lightfoot and Shirlee Taylor Haizlip, have set down ghost stories in published family histories. Numbers of other interviewees also offered stories or comments about *miscellaneous spirits or ghosts*. For example:

> Down home, there was a great big tree out there. And at night, you could see people's lights, going around and around that tree, on account of they used to hang people from that tree. (*Katie Jones*)

> When I was a kid . . . I'd open the bathroom door, and there'd be this white woman with long, dark hair, in a pink house robe. The [family's] assumption was that I was mistaken: it was Jesus! And then a little more than five years ago, I walked into the bathroom [of the same house], I see this same white woman standing there. I was very excited about it. (*Edward Moore*)

> There's a house on California and Augusta, where it had burned down. And Shenika, the little girl with the veil, like, "Man! You got a lotta kids in this house!" It's as if she could see the kids that died in the fire still running around playing. (*Josh Taifa*)

> Now here's a vision, I'm telling you! . . . [During World War II], a marine who was bloodier than hell come to me and he says, "Don't send the men down that way. There's a machine gun nest down there." And so I thanked him and he left. (*Nelson Peery*)

Nelson Peery went on to say that the warning proved accurate. Nevertheless, he didn't think it was a real spirit, but only a trick of his mind to make his own intuition seem more "authentic." On the other hand, Peery, a committed Marxist with all that usually implies about spiritual attitudes, does believe that his younger brother repeatedly saw an actual ghost in their house as a child.

Three interviewees told stories about *living people seen while not physically present.* When William Grant Still was old, Judy Still's son "saw his hand coming around the door, and fiddling with the light switch. We *knew* he wasn't there, he was in the rest home. But we decided he was probably just traveling around a lot." Ntozake Shange was waiting for her lover in front of a bookstore when she saw him in a vision walking toward her. And Anthony Shy had an encounter with Sting, his favorite musician:

> I don't know if it was a dream. It felt like I had made a connection and I was actually having this complete conversation about the motivations behind the songs. But I kinda felt like I was awake, 'cause I could hear the music [playing on the stereo] completely as I was having the conversation. He was there. My eyes were open, and I was seeing him and I was talking to him. I'd like to talk to Sting and see if he had a conversation with *me.*

Visions, like dreams, sometimes bring *predictions and warnings.* We've heard Nelson Peery's account of the bloody marine. Joe Cheeks "saw" a gun accidentally dropped and his friend shot by it in the stomach. Later "the exact same thing happened over again" in actuality. Robert Blaine has seen his father innumerable times, and occasionally these visitations serve to warn him of "some disaster." Blaine said, "When he comes and don't say anything and just stands there looking at me, something is gonna happen to a member of the family or something. And it's not long." Blaine also told about a woman who was looking out the window at breakfast when she "had a vision" of her son drowning. She warned her son, but "that night at six o'clock, he was dead!" Another woman came to Blaine, a pastor, after seeing a pelican at the top of her front steps. "I told her it was a token [sign]. Something was going to happen. And she said, 'Well, I don't know what it is.' I said, 'Well, I don't either,' I said, 'but just build yourself up for it.'"

The interviews yielded an abundance of other stories about visions. There was a woman's vision of a beautiful shaft of light from ceiling to floor in a darkened hotel room. There was Michael Warr's childhood vision of a "huge gray, metallic ship, outside my window!" And many more. I'll content myself with adding just two more intriguing accounts. Both concern *recurring visions.*

Ayanna Udongo said, "You know, we have these like little windows? Of visions of things?" On several occasions,

> I would see blurry kind of brownish grayish things, and they're about the size of my fist! And there was two of them, one behind the other, like scampering. They weren't mice! Because they had no head, no tail, they were just like these two balls of something. And they would just go along the floorboard there. I don't know, it could be my guardian, it could be anything, you know?

The second recurring vision was told to me by an interviewee's mother, who doesn't want her name used:

> I can look at the moon, and I can see myself. I see a whole picture of me, standing. And I have on a white dress. And a friend of mine would be standing like on the edge of the moon. And if I keep looking, he turns and walks away. And I'll be standing right there. And then pretty soon, it turns into . . . like being in a round casket. And I lay down there. That's when I wanta come outta that moon, then. I'll tell you what the casket is like: it's like what you might call a cradle. And a baby in the cradle. The only thing, that's *me* in that cradle.
>
> *Tell me what you make of that.*
>
> Well, I don't know what to make of it. I know one thing: every time I get a chance, if I can, I'll look to see if I see the same thing, or if it changed. And it don't change.

Voices

After asking about visions, I would ask the interviewees if they'd ever heard the voice of someone not physically present, and 46 percent answered yes. The percentage would be higher if I'd included all the voices accompanying visions, as voices frequently do (such as Nelson Peery's bloody marine's warning, "Don't send the men down that way"). In any event, of my white sample 37 percent answered yes to the question about voices. These percentages for blacks and whites aren't very different. The whites, however, told me nothing like the wealth of stories I heard from the interviewees.

Like visions, voices can be experienced either in physical space or in some sort of mental space. Marva Pitchford Jolly said she "might turn around" sometimes because she hears "a voice." The voice is "actually part of this environment," not in her head. However, "I don't call it outside, because I've probably helped to generate that, based on thought waves coming from some of the things that *I* might be thinking." Did she mean, I inquired, that she merely imagines the voice? Sometimes. But other voices, she said, "I recognize, because I'm visited by certain kinds of energies on a regular basis. Just because you don't see other entities in this room, don't think that they're not here."

For Joe Cheeks, by contrast, the experience is all interior. And we find again, as with visions, that a voice has no less spiritual authenticity if it happens to occur in mental space rather than in physical space:

> I can have voices tell me, "Don't do this." "Don't turn this corner." What that is, is just like people will say, intuition, or something. It's not a actual voice.
> *So it doesn't take the form of spoken words, even in your head.*
> In my head, it kinda does. But I know it's not a real person speaking. I don't know where it's coming from.
> *Got any theories?*
> Yeah. God.

Angie Williams is one of many interviewees to tell me about auditory *ancestor visitations*. Williams comes from a well-educated and prosperous family that openly discusses spiritual experiences. She said she herself grew up "a skeptic," but added:

> Well, not a skeptic, just that it didn't happen to me. But just recently, it really happened. I was looking for another job. I was in New York. And my godmother had recently passed away. And I heard her voice. And she just said, "Go home." It was in my head. You know, everybody has said that when you get the messages, they're very simple and succinct. It's not like you get this long, drawn-out, you know, "Here's the ten steps to happiness," or whatever. She just said, "Go home." And I drove ten hours and went home. She's in my corner.

Ann Eskridge told me about her friend Carole Morisseau's unusual ancestor visitation:

> She went to sleep, and then she woke up, and she knows she was awake. But she saw this figure in the doorway. And it had a bright light around it. And then the phone rang, and it was her mother. And she said, "Don't let him in." Or—I can't remember *what* her mother said, but Carole began to say the Lord's Prayer. I said, "Well, why did you say the Lord's Prayer?" She said, "For protection. Because my mother's dead, and she would never call me unless it was a warning."

Moreese "Pop" Bickham came up in rural Mississippi. Shortly before our interview, he'd been released after thirty-seven years in prison, fifteen of them on death row, with seven stays of execution. Bickham told this history of visions, dreams, and voices:

> I had got shot in the Delta and come home, and things weren't just like I thought it ought to be, and I'm laying there studying and thinking, and I'm talking to Mama and them through the walls. All of a sudden, Grandma appears at the foot of my bed, and I raised up and said, "What you doing here?" She said, "The promise you made me [to live better], you can't keep it, go on about your business." And Mama said, "Who you talking to?" I said, "I'm talking to Grandma."
>
> Now I didn't dream about her, didn't see her, I ain't heard no more about her until the night I got in this trouble six years later. I got into it with two policemen, and they come to my house, and I walked out to hide my gun, and one of them shot me, and we just shot it out in the streets. The night I got in trouble, everything was answered. Voice was talking just like that, say, "Well, you didn't do no more than you had to." I said, "What must I do?" Said, "Leave." Say, "How I gonna go?" Said, "Take that car and go." Say, "Where I'm going?" "Just go!" And that's what I did. So all the time I was going, from about two o'clock in the morning till maybe six in the morning, I was talking, and the questions was being answered. And the last word it said, "Go ahead and do whatever I tell you to do, and everything'll be all right." I did that.
>
> Well, about three days after I'm locked up, I asked the Lord, I said, "Lord, show me that I'm gonna get outta here." And I laid down, I don't know I went to sleep or didn't go to sleep, but I had this vision or dream or whatever you want to call it. I'm standing on top of the mountain, and I could see the prettiest green trees, pretty green grass, and water running so clear you could see the fishes' tails swimming in it. And on one side of me, my mom was standing, my sister was on the other side. And Mama said, "Son, we done got you out, now you go and help others." I said, "Yeah." And Grandma said, "That's right!" She was in the background. I said, "Grandma." I said, "What are *you* doing here?" She said, "I've been with you ever since the night you got in this trouble." And then I knew that was *her* voice telling me what to do, you know. When things got bad, she was there. I knew then that the Lord had sent her spirit to watch over me and take care of me, and show me my destination. So over these thirty-seven years I've been living for that. It just took thirty-seven years for it to happen, but it happened!

Daniel Wideman's play *Going to Meet the Light* originated in a dream he dreamed while dozing as he sat alone in a Ghana slave castle dungeon. The dream seemed to continue after he awoke. He heard the voice of a *spirit,* a woman's "literal voice" addressing him:

> I mean, I didn't hear a voice echoing off the walls, but I heard a voice in my head, very clear and not my own. And people who've read the play have commented on the language: the rhythm of the language is not one of any language that I would have conscious access to.
>
>> *Were you tuning in on some real spiritual presence? Or was this an imaginative act?*
>
> Well, I haven't been able to quite determine that for sure for myself. What I do know is that there are a lot of spirits heavily present in that area. And whether this was actually one of them talking to me or not, that's kind of irrelevant. It *was* a spiritual experience.

Hearing one's name called was mentioned by a number of interviewees. The voice may be that of someone living, or dead, or unknown. Adrienne Edmond distinctly heard her husband call her name from an upstairs room, when she knew him to be downstairs at the time. Her mother told her it was "a bad omen!" Anthony Shy's mother heard her brother calling her "like he was in front of our house. And not too long after that, he died. They found him in his car in a lake in Indiana." And Douglas Gills's mother "was told by her mother, if you're walking down the street, walking along, and a voice calls out to you, never answer the voice, till you see who it is." According to folk belief, the unknown voice belongs to death, and you mustn't answer or you'll be taken.

James Cameron heard a *heavenly voice.* Cameron founded America's Black Holocaust Museum in Milwaukee. He repeated to me the story he tells in his book, *A Time of Terror,* about his near-lynching in 1930 as a teenager in Marion, Indiana. His two friends had just been taken from the jail where they were all confined. After both were beaten and hanged, one after the other, the lynchers came back for him:

> And they beat me out, and the police cleared a path through the mob so they could get me up to the tree. And I looked at the faces as they were beating me on the way, and kept crying to them and telling them I hadn't done anything to deserve this. And the beating continued. We got up to the tree and they said, "Where's the rope?" They put a rope around my neck. Then they pushed me under this limb where Tommy and Abe were hanging. The rope's around my neck, the rope has been thrown over the limb, and they're ready to hang me. Right between Tommy and Abe.

> And my mother had always told us children to pray. And I looked
> up to heaven and I prayed to God, I said, "Lord, have mercy, and for-
> give me my sins." And then, a voice came out from heaven, and said,
> "Take this boy back. He had nothing to do with any killing or raping."
> And instantly that mob, just like we was in a petrified forest, seemed
> like everything just stood still. And then a trance came over me and
> I saw this thing like a vision: I felt as if I was in a photographer's dark
> room, and I could see strips of negative films hanging down from the
> wall. They weren't these little thirty-five millimeter, they were wide, like
> wallpaper. And they had images on them, and I couldn't tell whether
> they were white or black [people]. And then all at once, things came
> back to normal, and those hands that had been rough and had already
> killed two human beings, they became soft and kind and tender, and
> they removed the rope off my neck, and I was able to stagger and
> stumble and wobble back to the jail.
>
> *What was the voice?*
>
> It was an angel. A heavenly voice. There was no human voice in the
> world could have stilled the fury and the anger of the mob that night.

In after years, Cameron made efforts to discover if any of the white
mob at the scene had heard the voice. No one else had. "You were
just lucky, that's all," they told him.

Another interviewee, Ayanna Udongo, also told a story about an
otherworldly voice, but in her case the voice was demonic:

> In my opinion, God had committed suicide and left us on our own,
> you know, and I wasn't interested in going to church or anything. And
> I was walking past the Gospel Book Store. This guy [from the store]
> called out to me, and before I got to the bookstore, a voice said, "Go
> around!" And I'm like, "*What!*" And the voice said, "Go around the
> Gospel Book Store!" And what was so bizarre is, I ran—I walked real
> quick! And then, after I'd been at my girlfriend's, I had to go this way
> again. And that voice came back again and said, "Go around!" And the
> reason why is because, I was about to be called to be a Christian. And
> this spirit was like sitting on my shoulder, and it's telling me in my ear,
> "Don't go in there." I can't tell you what it was! It was something that
> knew that I was about to participate in something against *it*. Okay,
> and God was telling this guy, "Bring her into the shop today." And it
> happened. I got saved in a bookstore!

Udongo is no longer a practicing Christian. She jokes about her conversion experience, but still credits it as authentic. She reinterprets it
now according to eclectic spiritual ideas, leaning heavily on Native
American beliefs.

It's curious that with the possible exception of Moreese Bickham (see page 110), no interviewees described *predictions* offered by voices. On the other hand, quite a number—certainly Bickham—did receive *guidance* from voices.

Creative guidance comes to some writers in the form of voices. Sheron Williams-Brooks says she is able to "tap into the collective voice that's out there." What she hears "are energies left behind after people have lived their lives. I feel as though I'm simply the microphone they come through, and not really the possessor of the writing. They're not audible, but if I heard that person's voice, I would know it." John Edgar Wideman and Ishmael Reed have both reported experiences in a similar vein.

In fact, all of the voice phenomena highlighted in this section are to be found in African American literature and folklore. Anyone interested can follow up with the references given in the notes for this chapter.

Presences

In contrast to a vision, which is seen, or a voice, which is heard, a *presence* usually means a spiritual entity felt to be near without being either seen or heard. But these classifications are somewhat fluid. Presence sometimes runs together with voice or vision. Here are some examples. Devri Whitaker's mother once told her:

> "Oh yeah, Granddaddy talked to me today. I was feeling real low, and I just felt his presence, and he told me he loved me, and I really felt strong," and da-da-da-da. He never actually said words, but she knew he was "saying" words. [There would be] an infusion of Grandpa's good will. A benevolent sort of comfort that is Granddaddy.

Tamera Kilpatrick's grandfather was killed by a hit-and-run driver: "And one day, I really felt his presence, and I sensed that I heard his voice, just saying, 'Tam.'" She concluded the presence was either an "angel" or a "demon, because I don't believe that the dead come back."

For the first year after Winford Williams's sister died, his father sensed her "presence" in the house. But after the first year, "he claimed he could see her, or hear her. He just does: 'I talked to your sister.'"

In spite of such overlaps of presences with voices and visions, for purposes of comparison I counted as "presences" only felt entities

that were neither seen nor heard. My survey found a striking difference between blacks and whites: 60 percent of blacks had experienced presences, but only 35 percent of whites.

How are unseen, unheard presences known? The awareness of a
presence is most often described simply as a *feeling:*

> Almost like, you know, somebody's in the room. *Feeling* somebody's in
> that chair is comfortable. But *hearing* them in that space makes me
> want to leave. *(Regina Reed)*

> Sometimes when I'm doing things, I feel like there's a feminine pres-
> ence with me of some sort, a female relative, nearby, but I don't know
> who. And I don't know *why* I feel it, but sometimes I do. And it hap-
> pens a lot when I cook. So maybe it's, you know, "Make it this way, not
> that way. Don't be a knucklehead, do this," or something like that,
> yeah. *(Zeinabu irene Davis)*

> There's a strength in people that did escape slavery. I can feel empow-
> ered by that. And there's a presence there, but I don't necessarily
> dream them, as much as I can feel them there. *(Angela Shannon Preston)*

Another way presences are known is by *movements of air,* especially
winds:

> When my grandmother's mother died, she used to always talk about
> her being around. She'd say that she felt her presence. *I've* felt wind
> before. *(Almontez Stewart)*

> Many times, you walk down the street, and you feel a cold breeze.
> That's a person just went into the spirit world. *(Robert Blaine)*

> When Minnie's sister died, after having given birth to her niece, there
> was an experience when the baby was just crying at the top of her
> lungs, and there was like a wind that came in the room, and the baby
> just became quiet, and Minnie could feel what she thought was the
> presence of her sister. *(Kai EL Zabar)*

> One of my aunts, she would often be visited by someone. She could
> even feel a breath on her face, because they would come close. She
> thought it was her mother. *(Regina Reed)*

Experiencing a cold *chill,* or "a clamminess" (Joe Cheeks), is another
standard way of sensing a presence:

> Sometimes I go to do something, it might not be quite right, and my
> mother will tell me, "Don't do that." She doesn't say it in words or any-
> thing like that, but I might get a chill. *(Jim Taylor)*

That's what the older people said. Like if you get a chill, that means the spirit of a soldier just passed you. And I think *I* got a chill, when we went into my aunt's apartment, when we had to pack her stuff up. *(Anthony Shy)*

Several people had stories about presences known by *touch.* Don St. Cyr Toups's mother "felt a pat on her behind. And she knew that it was her mother indicating to her that 'Yes, there is a spiritual life, and I'm all right.'" LV Jordan thinks the touches she sometimes feels are her dead brother. And a prisoner "several times felt the presence of older people that were gone long before my birth. The feeling of being touched on the shoulder."

A few people said that presences *move things.* Stephanie Bell's grandmother said her own mother "was a haint now. And if things would fall down, it was because Mother Crump didn't like a particular thing." Colleen McElroy has lived in houses with "other presences." One way she's aware of them is when "something would get moved. I would put it down on one table, and it wouldn't be there." Almontez Stewart will "feel the bed move" when his grandmother's spirit sits down on it.

Stewart said also, "I *smell* her all the time." One woman senses her father's presence from the smell of his cigar smoke.

Other Boundary States

The altered states we'll take up now lack the firm roots in folklore, family lore, and communal spirituality possessed by visions, voices, and presences. So they give us a slightly different angle on the African American aptitude for states of consciousness beyond the boundaries of ordinary experience.

Each of these other states transcends consensual reality in a different way. *Out-of-body experiences* transcend the unity of the self. *Lucid dreaming* transcends the boundary between sleeping and waking. And for *mutual dreams and visions,* the boundary crossed is the one between self and other.

Out-of-Body Experiences

In a classic out-of-body experience, a person's consciousness seems to separate from the body and leave the body behind. The conscious part then spends some time doing things away from the body. Then eventually it returns and reenters the body. Some people experience the leaving or the returning, but not both. Out-of-body experiences can occur during sleep or waking, or in various liminal states such as shock or anaesthesia. Most occur during sleep, in dreams. The experience is often pleasant and intense, even "phenomenal" (Norma Adams Wade).

The percentage of interviewees who had experienced out-of-body experiences was 36 percent (and of black male prisoners, 48 percent). The percentage of whites was 26 percent.

Not all out-of-body experiences have obvious causes, particularly not those that occur in dreams. However, many are brought on by powerful circumstantial factors. The interviewees described a range of these, including life-threatening illness (Nelson Peery), massive physical trauma (Almontez Stewart), fear for a child's safety (Stephanie Bell), a Native American sweat lodge (Ivan Watkins), and a religious crisis (Charles Payne). Colleen McElroy had the kind of operating room experience one occasionally hears, in which she saw what was happening while anaesthetized during surgery. "My surgeon said, 'You couldn't possibly have seen that.' I said, 'You had an itch behind one ear, and you finally had to lean over and let the nurse take care of it.'"

One precipitating factor worthy of special note in the context of this book is stressful consciousness of race. In her autobiography, Shirlee Taylor Haizlip tells this story:

> I was riding with the president [of the WNET Board] to New Haven in a rented limousine so that he could speak [at Yale]. . . . As we began to drive, he said, "The damnedest thing happened to me last night." . . .
>
> He proceeded to relate how the preceding evening he had found a handsome young shirtless black man talking to his wife in his kitchen. As soon as I heard the word "black," I felt as if I were having an out-of-body experience there on the Merritt Parkway. It was as if I were looking down on a black limousine carrying a white man telling a black woman about some weird experience his family had had with a man of color—without once acknowledging her own.

Haizlip added these thoughts during our interview:

> I was so uncomfortable, and feeling emotionally abused, and I didn't want to deal with the situation. Because I was very fond of this man, and he just did something that was so uncharacteristic. I just withdrew. And in withdrawing, I went out of myself and away. And I was looking down through the back window of the limousine at myself sitting there talking with him, as if he were talking to somebody else.

A number of interviewees made an association between out-of-body experiences and death. They suppose that the spirit not only leaves the body when we die, but can sometimes leave the body and return without the finality of death. Beatriz Penso-Buford, for example, said "I felt almost like the spirit just *wshhhhhh*—just becoming very, very light, almost like the soul coming out of the body. It was a *very* beautiful experience. Sometimes I feel that perhaps death is like that." Half a dozen more interviewees expressed similar thoughts about out-of-body experiences.

Lucid Dreaming

To have a lucid dream means that you know you're asleep and in the midst of a dream while the dream is happening. To put it another way, you seem to be "awake" while asleep. You might say to yourself, "I'm dreaming!"

Few interviewees were familiar with the term "lucid dreaming." What's more, in the course of telling dreams that happened to be lucid, the interviewees rarely mentioned the fact unless prompted by a question. This suggests that lucidity is a side of dream life not commonly focused on or discussed by African Americans.

I found that only 70 percent of the interviewees had ever experienced lucid dreams (and 76 percent of the prisoners), in contrast to 85 percent of whites. But this finding must be viewed cautiously, since two other surveys have found equal or higher rates of lucid dreaming in blacks as compared with whites. Moreover, I did discover one important way in which blacks clearly exceed whites as lucid dreamers. Blacks who do dream lucidly do so with great frequency: 78 percent of the black lucid dreamers said that between 21 percent and 100 percent of all their dreams are lucid. Only 25 percent of whites dream lucidly with such frequency.

Recently, lucid dreaming has been a hot topic in the world of dream psychology. Lucidity is claimed to confer many benefits, everything from deliberate problem solving while asleep to spiritual enlightenment. Most of the benefits are said to come from the lucid dreamer's enhanced ability to control the dream in progress. There's another camp, however, which regards deliberate dream control as a way of avoiding the hard truth about oneself, or which says that control interferes with the spontaneous healing properties of dreams, that we should trust the dreaming mind and not get in its way.

I found a similar division of opinion among the interviewees. On the side favoring control, Devri Whitaker and Edward Moore were both taught as children to overcome dangers in lucid dreams. Douglas Gills, who calls himself "a dream master," learned on his own to control lucid dreams, and passed along the art to his five-year-old stepson:

> I used to say, "Sometimes dreams are a payback for how you've been during the rest of the day. Things bad that you don't talk about and apologize for and get off of you, they can stay in your mind. You understand what I'm saying?" And he say, "Yeah, you mean like if I did something and I didn't say I was sorry." And I say, "The bad thing is you're having these bad dreams. The good thing is, though, you can control this." And he says, "What do you mean?" Say, "You can dream what you wanta dream. Going bad? Turn the page! Go to another chapter. Pick up another book. It's your dream, right?"

Darice Wright Camp "programs" herself "for something positive to happen." Many interviewees make creative use of lucid dream control, such as writing papers (Maisha Hamilton-Bennett), composing music (Colleen McElroy), and designing sculptures (Richard Hunt).

But other interviewees gave a range of reasons for disliking or disapproving of dream control. Controlled dreams are "less fulfilling" (Leon Forrest) or "more stressful" (Zeinabu irene Davis). More importantly, control interferes with the dream's message. Sheron Williams-Brooks affirmed that "if dreams come from out in, it doesn't make sense to control them." Daniel Wideman said that dreaming is "a mystical space that I shouldn't mess with." And John L. Johnson, who has a Jungian background, said, "You wouldn't want to fool around with anything like that." Dreaming is "a gift of the spirit. This is something that's independent. It's something coming from a spirit. One accepts it for what it is, and uses it for whatever information is valuable."

Mutual Dreams and Visions

Dreams in which two or more people discover that they've dreamed dreams with striking similarities are sometimes called *mutual* (or *shared*) *dreams*. Experiences of this nature challenge many boundaries, especially the boundary between self and other. For example, the father and the older daughter of a southern black family both had "the same dream" one night. They both dreamed that the younger daughter "was going to get married." And it turned out that this young woman's elopement was in fact set for that very morning. She was restrained, and when the suitor approached, the father told him that "he already knew about it from a dream" and made him ask proper permission.

Experiences of this type aren't common and aren't clearly labeled in the language, unless it's by the phrase "the same dream." But mutual dreams, and also mutual visions, do seem to be widely taken for granted. In fact, there are enough examples in black folklore and literature to suggest that having mutual altered states may actually have a minor place in the black cultural repertoire of consciousness.

In chapter 4 (on predictive dreams), I quoted Shirlee Taylor Haizlip's dream of a cat with a hemorrhaging eye. The dream foretold her brother-in-law's death from a stroke. Haizlip continued, "All of us had cat dreams that night, the same night that I had mine."

Judy Still told about a three-way mutual visitation dream:

> After my husband passed on, I, my mother-in-law, and my sister-in-law all had the same dream on the same night. A knock came at the door and there was Lane. And we said, "You're alive! We thought you were dead! But you're alive!" And he said, "Well, I just dropped in to say good-bye," you know. He didn't say anything about being dead. He just said he had to go, but he just wanted to stop in and say good-bye. And he walked in, and he talked, and commiserated, and then he said he had to go on, and he left. And that happened to all three of us on the same evening. And *they* don't even believe in dreams!

Josh Taifa told two mutual dreams he shared with his father. In one case, father and son both had "out-of-body dreams" in which each was looking down on the family driving across a certain bridge. The dreams came to light when they actually drove across that bridge some time later. The second mutual dream was a lucid ancestor visitation:

> I was asleep. And he was asleep. And I felt this presence, right? I'm dreaming that I woke up and I covered up my head, and I come back out of my dream, and it's still there! And then I [really] woke up. And the minute I woke up, I ran to my father's room. At the same time my father jumped up and ran into my room. And I told him what had happened, and he had the same dream. And he was like, "It felt like my mother"—you know, his mother, my grandmother. Then he told me about another dream he had had back when he was in the navy, where she came to visit him. I was like, "Wow!"

In addition to these examples, five other interviewees also told stories about mutual dreams.

A surprising number of interviewees had stories about shared visions. Anthony Shy, for one, said that his mother and her two siblings

> remember sitting on a bed with their grandmother, and she was asleep. And they all remember this guy stepping out of a mirror, all dressed in black. He came out of the mirror and ran down the stairs. And they all looked at each other and said, "Did you see that?"

Half a dozen interviewees had firsthand experiences of shared visions. When one woman was a child, she and her mother went together to the outhouse one night. Suddenly a man so tall she couldn't see his head came walking toward them:

> And I remember my mother saying, "What is the matter with you?" And I just pointed. And my mother saw this, too. And then we took off running, and we got to the porch of the house. And I remember I was in front of her, and she grabbed me and pulled me back, and she ran in the door first! I'll never forget that as long as I live. Never. And this was true. I remember telling the other family about it. I had an uncle they called Shug. My grandmother said, "Well, it was probably Shug or somebody. He wasn't going to bother you or anything like that."

When Katie Jones was visiting down home in Mississippi one year,

> we went to see one of my cousins. And I happened to look. Around the church, people looked just like leaves on the tree there. I say, "Nobody tell me nothing was happening at the church this evening." And one of my sisters, she say, "Oh, yeah, sure is!" People was just like ants along a bone there. Everybody was dressed in white. I look off, and when I looked back, I didn't see nobody. When we passed there, I didn't see a soul. Church locked up!

Mutual voices and other sounds seem to be much less common than mutual visions. Regina Reed works at the African American museum in Detroit. She said the employees there regularly hear sounds together that they believe are spirits from the cemetery over which the building was supposedly built. And another woman said that as a child, she and her friend were walking to the store on a dirt road when they heard the hooves of the horse who had recently dragged a cousin of theirs fifteen miles to his death. The horse had been shot by its owner after the accident.

I didn't collect statistics about mutual dreams, visions, and sounds, but these anecdotes offer further evidence that African Americans are receptive to experiences at the boundaries of ordinary waking and dreaming.

10

TAKE ME THROUGH

DREAMS AND DREAMLIKE
STATES IN RELIGION

*And I have been possessed. And that I'm sure is because I was raised as a
colored person. I just didn't know what the rituals were. So I spent my life
learning the rituals for something that was incarnate. In the Holy Ghost
Church I got possessed. And I got possessed one time on Shango's birthday.*

—Ntozake Shange

Ancestor dreams, predictive dreams, waking "dreamlike" states—in all
these sides of African American dream life we've observed a strong
spiritual dimension. Now we'll consider the role of dreams and
altered states in church worship. We'll see, first, that dreamlike states
can actually be part of the church service. We'll also find that membership status in the religious community was historically tied to
dreams and visions, that dreams or visions sometimes call a person to
become a minister, and that people often talk publicly about their
dreams and visions when they "testify" in church.

Shouting

The Christianized slaves had their own special way of moving rhyth-
mically as they sang spirituals together, which they called "shouting."
The "shout" was an adaptation of the African ring dance, with foot
stamping and handclapping replacing the African drums forbidden
by the masters. The term "shout" may have come from an African
word, *saut*, "to walk or run around." Or "shout" may simply have been

a euphemism for dancing, an activity prohibited by the puritanical denominations.

What matters for our purposes is that shouting also signified a style of worship regularly leading to a state of possession or trance. In Africa, such altered states are often induced by religious dancing. Zora Neale Hurston pointed out that in Africa, possession is the prerogative of priests and certain followers, whereas

> in America it has become generalized. The implication is the same, however, it is a sign of special favor from the spirit that it chooses to drive out the individual consciousness temporarily and use the body for its expression.

The generalizing of possession in the United States (and elsewhere in the Americas) was no doubt enabled by the removal of African social structures. In addition to that, possession was also a feature of worship in certain white sects during slavery days, and white practices may have spread to black converts. Be that as it may, blacks undoubtedly contributed their own heritage, traceable in the shouting churches of today in what's called "getting the Holy Ghost," "getting the spirit," or "getting happy." Even some of the gestures and movement patterns still seen in black churches reveal their West African origins.

The various shouting denominations nowadays have differing views about actual dancing. Many Baptist churches allow shouting (getting the spirit), but forbid dancing to music. In the so-called sanctified, or Pentecostal Holiness churches—originally Baptist offshoots—members may dance, as well as shake, speak in tongues, or "fall out." Midway between sanctified and Baptist are the Apostolic Holiness churches.

Ayanna Udongo joined a shouting church during her temporary commitment to Christianity, as she recalled:

> It was one of the new kind of churches that was trying to come outta the old tradition. And it was black, for sure. This one guy was an apostle, Apostle Willie Wonder, he came to town. He called out this whole family of sisters. They were the Love sisters. It was about seven of them and all the girls had children out of wedlock and all that sort of stuff. And so, he said, "I see smoke over you'all's heads!" And he said, "I see a word!" And he was describing, the smoke was blue. And he said, "I see the word *SHACKIN'!*" And the oldest sister fell on the floor! And she started shaking and carrying on. And he said, "I see a black snake

wrapped around your neck! And he got red eyes!" And then he went into, "Come out, Satan!" and her just choking and carrying on.

There was a lot of this being slain in the spirit kind of thing, and, you know, you're taken into this spiritual, visionary kind of thing where God talks to you, and he can't talk to you when you're conscious, you gotta be slain, and put to sleep, so he can do some miracle on your head.

There are, of course, African American churches where shouting is disapproved of. These are likely to include congregations of Methodists, conservative Baptists, Episcopalians, and Catholics, who tend long ago to have disowned practices such as shouting associated with the southern past.

Nevertheless, almost a third (31 percent) of African Americans, it's been found, have experienced the state of consciousness "where people 'get the Holy Ghost.'" Moreover, while membership in the shouting churches may be limited, most blacks are acquainted with shouting as a familiar feature of the black church environment. Alice Stephens, for example, who was raised in the conservative Episcopal Church, was exposed to shouting by a baby-sitter:

I remember going to her church, and she got happy, next to me. And all I could do is cry, 'cause I didn't know why she fell out. But you know, the mothers of the church would come over and assist the person who, you know, the spirit has come into them. And so they comforted me and said it was okay.

The way shouting is described—you're "slain in the spirit" (Ayanna Udongo); "you die and are reborn" (Leon Forrest)—suggests a mini-conversion experience. Mostly, however, shouting is the province of those who are already converted. And as we'll see now, *initial* conversion experiences traditionally have some special traits.

Conversion, or Coming Through

The mysticism of the early Baptist revival movement had a strong appeal for the descendants of Africans. Being born again echoed the rites of passage of African religions. And the visions that at that time qualified Baptists for church membership came easily to people culturally prone to altered states. White Baptists recognized that the visions of black converts were "particularly ecstatic." Moreover, the emphasis on conversion visions persisted in black Baptist religion and its sanctified offshoots long after it had faded and conversion had become merely routinized among white Baptists.

In his novel *Go Tell It on the Mountain,* James Baldwin described a typical conversion vision in the black church tradition. In contrast to the white tradition, it characteristically involved a soul traveling to nether regions and then up to heaven, or "coming through." Baldwin devoted over ten pages to the conversion vision of his youthful character John. It occurs at an evening prayer service:

> He knew, without knowing how it happened, that he lay on the floor. . . . He was like a rock, a dead man's body, a dying bird, fallen from an awful height. . . .
>
> He was invaded, set at naught, possessed . . . with an anguish that he could never in his life have imagined, that . . . had opened him up. . . .

In his vision, John passes through the despair of the valley of the shadow of death. After encounters with the dead, and after visioning the wretched of the earth and realizing Christ's kinship with them,

> he whispered, not knowing that he whispered: "Oh, Lord, have mercy on me. Have mercy on me." And a voice, for the first time in all his terrific journey, spoke to John, through the rage and weeping, and fire, and darkness, and flood:
>
> "Yes," said the voice, "go through. Go Through."

Then, after further visionary travails:

> John saw the Lord—for a moment only; and the darkness, for a moment only, was filled with a light he could not bear. Then, in a moment, he was set free; his tears sprang as from a fountain; his heart, like a fountain of waters, burst. Then he cried: "Oh, blessed Jesus! Oh, Lord Jesus! Take me through!"

This cry is heard and seconded by the congregation gathered around John and singing in his support as he lies on the church floor. One says, "'Rise up, rise up, Brother Johnny, and talk about the Lord's deliverance'":

> "Are you saved, boy?"
>
> "Yes," said John, "oh, yes!" And the words came upward, it seemed, of themselves, in the new voice God had given him.

An element of certain versions of the travel vision not present in Baldwin's wonderful account is the out-of-body experience of some converts as they ascend to Heaven. For example, "I remember looking down on my body as my soul flew away." And "Little Mary was standing looking down on old Mary, on this temple, my body, and it lay on the very brink of hell."

One type of conversion vision is noteworthy because it mirrors the death-and-rebirth symbolism of shamans' dreams and visions from all over the world. The visionary undergoes the dismemberment of the body, followed by its renewal and reassembly:

> He laid me upon a table in my vision. I was naked and He split me open. And there was two men there—one on each side of the table. I could hear the knives clicking in me, inside. And after they got through with me, they smother they hand over the wound and I was healed.

In addition to these traditional scenarios, there are plenty of variations, both "solemn," as Zora Neale Hurston observed, and "frivolous." Here's one of the solemn variants, recorded by another folklorist:

> When she went to church and was praying, all of a sudden she had a feeling as if someone was talking to her, telling her she was free. She felt it in her breast. She looked around to see who was talking to her, because she distinctly heard a voice. But she could see no one. She knew now that she had been changed. She began crying and shouting. . . .

As for the "frivolous" variants of the conversion vision, Ernest Gaines provides an example in his novel *The Autobiography of Miss Jane Pittman:*

> Lobo's *travel,* he saw Mannie Hall running Lizzie Aaron up a tree. If that wasn't the craziest *travel* anybody ever heard. Everybody laughing, coughing, wiping their eyes. Everybody but Lizzie. Lizzie mad as she can be. Right there in church she called Lobo a lying dog. . . . Lobo standing there, sweating. "I know what the Lord showed me," he said. "Mannie was throwing clods at you. Them children was saying, 'Look. Yonder. She on that limb over yonder.' And you went hopping from limb to limb like a cat."

Hurston's account of the traditional visionary conversion includes "an unwillingness to believe—to accept the great good fortune too quickly. So God is asked for proof," a "sign." God obliges by shifting a star's position in Heaven, making a tree cross over the road, or the like. After repeated tests, God eventually wearies and threatens damnation, whereupon the panicked convert finally declares belief.

To undertake a retreat with fasting and prayer for the purpose of achieving a conversion experience was called "seeking." Quite possibly, seeking was influenced by the Native American vision quest, as well as by African rite-of-passage initiations. Some seekers, even children, went to graveyards; others chose swamps or woods. But many actually underwent their conversion visions back in church following their quests:

> The mourner . . . wearied by days of fasting and prayer—often in the graveyard—"comes through," leaps from his seat and rushes wildly into the night shouting his gladness to the stars. Later on he will tell of his vision and be baptized. . . .

An article on "getting religion" in the *Southern Workman* of December 1894 depicts seeking and conversion in a slightly different way. Someone already "converted" at a revival, the author explains, is subsequently "called a seeker." After this person prays for a long time, he will have a "dream." Probably "dream" here means either a sleep dream or a waking experience:

> [A] Christian friend . . . interprets and applies his dreams. After a length of time the seeker believes, and at a council of the leading brethren, he recounts what he has dreamed, felt or heard, which is called an *experience of grace.*

What do we hear about conversion and coming through today? James Baldwin's lengthy account of a coming through was published in the 1950s. But already in 1939 a scholar could write that full-blown conversion experiences were "increasingly rare." Most of the people I interviewed were spiritual people and many of them religious, but if any had undergone a classic conversion, I didn't learn of it. But a few had their own variations on the theme.

One interviewee, Kai EL Zabar, had gone to the woods as a seeker. She grew up in a family of Gullah descendants, who call this practice "going to meet yourself." It includes fasting, purifying colonics, and the guidance of a knowledgeable relative. But EL Zabar's account was couched more in terms of psychology than religion:

> You confront the darkness. And the darkness is all of those fears that you've created that can inhibit you from proceeding to do what you have to do. Now they say, you face your greatest nightmare. But the [Gullah] language is, that you go to meet yourself.

When I asked if dreams were involved in the process of meeting yourself, she said they were, because dreams "oftentimes reveal to you the very things that we're talking about, that you meet there."

Charles Payne, a Catholic priest and psychologist, related an out-of-body dream with some traits of a traditional conversion experience—except for its surprising ending. This dream dates back to his novitiate days:

> I dreamed I was dead. I was in the coffin, and my mother and sister were crying over me, and I was trying to say to my mother, "Don't worry, don't cry, my body is dead but my spirit is still alive." And I was frustrated, because I couldn't speak to her, and she was crying over me. At some point, I began to float. My spirit began to float out of my body, and I wasn't worried about it, I was floating and could see the coffin closed, and my mother crying. And then it gets black. And I'm floating. And I was *excited*, because I was going to meet God! And it begins to get lighter, and lighter, and lighter. And finally, it gets very bright. And I ask the question, "Where is God?" And the answer comes back, "This *light* all around you is God." Ha. I have to tell you, I said, "I did all that work for *this*?!" And I woke up! I mean, I was disappointed!

I should mention that later in his life, Father Payne had a dream of being an astronaut in space that reconciled him to the idea of God as light.

A couple of interviewees gave accounts that show how the tradition of conversion can shape experiences that aren't religious conversions in the usual sense. Darryl Burrows reflected about his

> family's thinking about conversionary experience. We believe that there are moments in your life that are planned by God, that are key junctures where you either go one way or the other. For Saul, it was getting knocked off his horse and hearing God's voice.

Burrows then mentioned his acquaintance with conversion in the African American tradition:

> You hear old people in church talk about their visions of a white horse coming down from Heaven, and bringing them physically up to Heaven. So we believe you can have these experiences.

And he went on to interpret an experience of his own as a conversion experience within this tradition:

> I remember having one, as clear as day. And it was, being really confused about something, and it was related to my work. And praying for clarity. And I was sitting with a friend. He said something. It was a

couple sentences he said, and the clarity just came. And I knew it came, and I knew the prayer had been answered. And the next day, I quit my job. That moment was like a dreamlike state, during consciousness. But it had to do with a conversionary experience. I believe that I was getting a nudge from the Father saying, "Okay, you asked for clarity, here it is. Now deal with it!" I'm telling you, I know for a *fact* that that happened!

Frances Callaway Parks was not a good dream recaller until a marriage counselor taught her that "if I call on dreams, that they do come." During counseling, her dreams provided important psychological insight and contributed to her decision to leave the marriage, as well as change careers, move to a new city, and so on. She then had an impactful dream that seems to owe something to the tradition of conversion:

> The dream was with me standing in front of a mountain. And what is closest to me is very rocky. But the distance of this very, very tall mountain is some parts which are just so green. I mean, like spring green, you know? And I noticed that there are three paths leading to this mountain. But I don't know which one of those paths to take. And I'm so confused, I'm just standing there. And then, here is this figure that I think is a lot of artists' image of who Christ would look like. The figure is taller than the mountain. And here I am, just looking like a little toothpick. And it's almost as if I'm a child again. And this voice says to me, it says, "Follow." It said, "I'll be your guide." And so this magnanimous being just takes my hand, and we start up the mountain. And that's it. Well, I tried to figure out what that meant, in terms of my life and my career. I believe that it gave me permission, to just go ahead and do whatever I wanted to.

Parks then had a second dream in which the Christ figure showed her the path back down the mountain. Significantly, Parks summed up the message of these dreams as "liberation from bondage," an interpretation that springs from the historical roots of the conversion experience in black America. These two dreams laid the groundwork for her career as an inspirational poet.

The Call to Minister

The call to become a minister and preach is quite strongly associated with dreams and altered states in African American Christianity. On her way to our appointment at a local restaurant, the same Frances

Callaway Parks happened to run into a neighbor. As Parks walked along with this man, he mentioned for the first time that he was a minister, and he told her how he got his call:

> He said he preached his first sermon when he was twelve years old. He didn't know he was gonna be a preacher, but it just happened that he had a dream. In the dream he saw himself in that role, of like a prophet. And he told his grandmother he wanted to go to the churches, and his grandmother wouldn't let him go, because she said that they would take your mind and they would just brainwash you, whitewash your thinking. She knew the value of the dream, but she did not want it tarnished. So what he would do, he would slip out of the house. He lived in the projects, and he would take the roof, and he said he *would* go.

Here is another description of a call. A preacher named Bishop Womack was interviewed in 1970. Womack had been a gangster when he was called to preach by a series of voices and visions. To the first voice, gangster Womack answered back that he'd "rather be a dog, than a preacher." But some time later,

> I got knocked out for sure. Something hit me. And when this thing hit me and I arose, people were standing over me. And I said, "Who in the hell hit me?" I heard a voice said, "I hit you. Go home and call Jesus."

After Womack got "knocked out," his call to preach was confirmed by several visions.

It's tempting to see a lingering African influence in the association of the call with dreams and altered states in African American Christianity. In Africa, the call to join a trance cult usually comes in the form of visions or dreams of a fixed type, which are taken to mean that the person is suffering from symptoms brought on by a helpful spirit and should join the appropriate cult. The call of diviners often comes, as it does for shamans everywhere, in the form of physical and mental symptoms that include disturbing dreams.

The so-called Independent churches of Africa are often "explained and legitimated" by the call dreams of their founders. Some of these dreams take their scenarios from the Bible, but call dreams hearken "most strongly to the initiatory dreams of doctors, diviners and mediums already well established in parts of pre-Christian Africa." As is the case with these traditional roles, founder dreams are often associated with illness and recovery, a theme that appears in the dreams themselves. As for the mainstream Christian churches of Africa, "most church ministers witnessed Jesus Christ calling them in a dream," writes one African of her fellow seminarians. A Nigerian minister states that in his experience over 95 percent of African ministers "claimed that they received their 'call' in their dreams. . . . "

Of the three clergymen I interviewed, one, Robert Blaine, described a call dream. At the age of seven he was called in a dream by his "intercessor," who "told me that he would use me."

Most interviewees were familiar with the fact that ministers often cite dreams when they explain how they came to the ministry. Skepticism concerning the claims of ministers about their calls came up in several interviews. But sometimes skeptics provide excellent evidence for the prevalence of a belief or practice. Preston Jackson, a sculptor raised in a traditionally religious family, is a fairly general skeptic. I asked if his minister father ever talked about dreams:

> In his sermons. Yeah. It's sort of embarrassing sometimes to hear that. Because for many years, I'm thinking, "He's *lying!*" Because my dad, he could tell some tall tales, man. You know, he can jive! But then he tells them over and over. Like my brother's a minister now. That they have a calling to become a minister.
> *Was it in a dream?*
> Yeah. Well see, I just assume it's a dream state. They always say that God came and talked to them one day. And my brother tells me about dreams a lot. He reveals his dreams in his sermons. Like my father always did.

One woman, though no cynic about God or about dreams, doubts the claims of most ministers simply because they don't have dream lives as rich as her own:

> I've met black preachers, say, "Oh yeah, I had this dream I was called." But he can't remember anything else. I mean, that's it, the only thing he dreamed was that he was called to preach. I kind of think that's what they've heard—they're mimicking other preachers. Because some of them who are "called to preach" are no more sanctified than anybody.

Ronald Childs is another skeptic:

> I have a problem with a lot of pastors. They all say it was revealed to them in a dream that they were called to the ministry! They all say that. "The Lord called me in my sleep." You would hear them preach, and it would be like, "I don't think he called *you*." But there are a few that are believable.

Childs himself, interestingly, has dreams that he interprets as calls to his own personal mission, the mission of a writer:

> Just like in the Bible: the rapture. Are you familiar with Revelation? I had these dreams where I was this winged creature. I don't know if I was an angel or not, because I couldn't see myself, but I know that I was floating or hovering above this field. And there's a field full of people that were singing in unison, hymns or praises to God, looking up waiting for me. And I was coming down like this being, into this field. And then I would wake up. I never knew what happened once I landed—ha! I would just wake up. And I kept having these visions of that. I've had this over the years, since I would say junior high school to the present.
>
> I feel that I'm imparting some wisdom or something. I hate to tie it to the work that I'm doing as a writer, but I do see that connection, that there's a purpose for what I'm writing. You have this mission, you have this duty, to educate people, to challenge people to think differently, or whatever. And that's why I've left two jobs in the last year.

A singer who also has a degree in psychology recounted another example of an unorthodox call. One morning she "woke up and heard a voice" that sounded utterly real, saying, "Whatever you touch will be healed." She has worked without charge as a healer since being called.

Testimony in Church

In *The Autobiography of Miss Jane Pittman,* by Ernest Gaines, a woman "comes through" while picking cotton in the field. The other pickers tell her to "go home and get herself ready to *talk* that night." To "talk" means to "testify" in church, to give "testimony." In earlier days, testimony centered around conversion. As a child, Zora Neale Hurston heard converts testify about their visions at revival meetings conducted by her minister father:

> These visions are traditional. I knew them by heart as did the rest of the congregation, but still it was exciting to see how the converts would handle them. Some of them made up new details. Some of them would forget a part and improvise clumsily or fill up the gap with shouting. The audience knew, but everybody acted as if every word of it was new.

While conversion is still a topic for testimony, more often nowadays people testify about God's blessings in daily life—relief from illness, release from alcoholism, or "simply having the strength needed to complete a day's work." Visions and dreams, however, are still a common feature of testimony. I found in my interviews that 22 percent of blacks remember hearing testimony about dreams from the congregation, compared with only 6 percent of whites.

Frances Freeman-Williams said:

> This older lady that was in our church, she got up one day in the middle of the congregation, said she saw an angel. I was like, "Oo, I want to hear this!" And everybody's like, "Aw!" You know, something like doubts. And she said the angel told her that everything was gonna be all right, and the angel left.

Josh Taifa, a gangbanger at the time of our interview, used to be taken to church by his mother. He recollected hearing this testimony about a dream:

> I do remember one lady saying that she had dreamt that she took a trip to Africa, and she was standing there, and they were talking about Jesus. And a black man came and approached her, put his hand on her shoulder, and uttered some words. And she had paid little attention to the words at first, until she and the rest of the congregation had turned around to see where the man was, and the man wasn't there. And the lady went to another lady, "Did you see the man that was just standing here?" And the lady pointed up toward the sky and they seen like what was left of the footsteps of a man, you know, of a black man going up. And she came in saying that Jesus was a black man. Ha-ha!

Zeinabu irene Davis was raised Catholic, but sometimes attended Baptist services with her grandmother. She remembered dreams coming up in testimony:

> Very distinctly. I remember being scared by them, too. Because the person was so powerful who was testifying. And you could see them, you know, "God came to me today! And"—really, it was a very moving experience. It was something you wanted to happen to you, too, that was for sure, but you were kind of afraid of it, because this person would be so large, or so looming, in the church. And then when they went out, they'd just be, "Well, that's Joe down the block," or whoever. So they basically transformed by relating these experiences, which was kind of interesting.

When a preacher talks from the pulpit about being called in a dream or vision, that, too, is a form of testimony. In addition, many ministers interject their other dreams and visions into sermons. "That's a big part of the moment of transcendence," reflected Leon Forrest, "when the minister stands convicted. And he will reveal some of his dreams and some of his day-to-day agonies." Shirlee Taylor Haizlip's father often talked about his visions in his sermons, "because he knew the members would relate, and would become very interested in what he was saying."

But if a white minister preaches about dreams, it usually concerns Bible stories, such as Pharaoh's dream, rather than the minister's personal experiences.

Other Religious Dreams and Visions

Among African American Christians, dreams and related experiences that do not directly relate to church life may, nevertheless, concern religious beliefs and teachings. For example, Moreese Bickham believes that dreams are God's channel of communication:

> See, I read in the Bible where it says, when man lay down slumber in a deep sleep, God programs things in his mind, you know? And I believe that. That's right. Joseph, kings, and everybody else, he tell them in dreams. That's the best way God got contact with his people. Is when they calm and sleep.

Edwina Ackie told about a dream that concerned her christening at age eight:

> My grandmother said that one night she woke up and saw like this person standing over me, and I was just talking to this person, in my sleep! It was concerning what I was supposed to wear when I was christened. My mom made the dress as how my grandmother heard the lady describing my dress.

Noted sculptor Richard Hunt has an aunt who was cured of a "blockage" when "she saw something like an angel come down and take something away from her." Hunt himself evolved his style of sculpture, turning scrap metal into organic forms, under the influence of his "dry bones dreams," which in turn were influenced by

> sermons that black preachers would preach, the Valley of the Dry Bones. And of course, the sermon is, "Can these bones live?" So in a way, the impetus lies in these early religious experiences, sort of secularized or made into this art statement.

Judy Still's father, composer William Grant Still, had countless religious experiences:

> In one dream, he heard a whole host of angels sing to him. It was an epiphany sort of thing. And he realized at that point that the whole universe is really music. That creation is really music. And that the angels were the expression of God's sound.

Adrienne Edmond "wasn't really asleep" when she had this "dream":

> I told my sister, it was like ministering angels were ministering to me. And the topic that they were ministering to me was, "Keep the body from sinking." And I think during that time I was going through a little confusion, and some problems, some transitions. And then, it was like I could see the boat where Peter was on the water. Okay? And as long as he kept the faith, he didn't go down. When he lost it, he began to sink. And this voice was like talking to me. It was saying, "Remember the golden nuggets." And then it said, "The word of God." And then quotations started coming to me from the Bible, like, "The Lord is my strength and my salvation." The quotations started coming to me in the dream.
>
> *Is it significant to you that it was the body that was to be kept from sinking, rather than the spirit?*
>
> Okay. I think it was the body *and* the spirit, at that time for me personally. Because I had had a fall, and I fell down four stairs, and I had problems with my knees, walking.

Adrienne Edmond had another dream in which, she said, she may have seen Jesus, but she won't make that claim, because "I don't want to lie on the Supreme Being." Her brother once saw "a Christlike figure" standing at the head of her bed while she slept.

Maisha Hamilton-Bennett, like Charles Payne, experienced God as light:

> I don't know if it was a nightmare, but it was frightening. There was a lot of lightning. And I'm not sure if it was a dream or real, but it seemed like the whole world was just white, and I could see like God. Really a powerful experience. It was frightening, though, it was overwhelming. I could see the whole universe, and it was white light, and I could see God there.

Momentous dreams and visions as death approaches are not uncommon. They often include the motif of being welcomed by a loved person. When Sylvia Morris's grandfather was hospitalized and about to die,

> he told my mother, he said, "Susie came in last night, and she told me to come on." Susie was his wife. And they had a very loving, faithful marriage for over fifty years. And he died like two days later.

Katie Jones said, "Most likely, if I have a dream, it's whatever the Lord showed me in my sleep." She related an apocalyptic dream, a no-hiding-place dream:

> I dreamed that the world had come to a end. And the Lord just taken the world up just like that. And this girl says, "Katie," she says, "aren't you gonna run? You're just standing there looking!" I say, "No use a'running. Where you going? You can't hide." I dreamed that twice.
>
> *And what's the meaning of that dream?*
>
> It's just telling me the world is not gonna last too much longer, I don't believe. Because I have dreamed it the second time. And so I just feel like, you know, the time ain't long.

The Nation of Islam

Dreams have had a prominent place in the Islamic faith, from Muhammad's time to the present. So I wondered whether the Nation of Islam gives dreams any special notice. I have not, in fact, been able to discover that dreams are emphasized in the Nation of Islam's teachings. Nevertheless, its three famous leaders have all testified to important dreams and visions.

The founder was Elijah Muhammad. When he was seven, Elijah Muhammad's mother "had a vision that one day she would be the mother of a very great man." As Malcolm X recounts in his autobiography, the founder himself professed that during the early years "Allah often sent him visions of great audiences who would one day hear the teachings. . . . " Visions later sustained him when he was imprisoned.

Malcolm X's own "pre-vision" occurred well after his conversion to the Nation of Islam, while he was in a state of confusion over the expulsion of his brother Reginald by Elijah Muhammad, foreshadowing his own eventual schism with the founder. Malcolm was lying awake when "suddenly" and "with a start" he "became aware of a man" seated next to him in the chair:

> I could see him as plainly as I see anyone I look at. He wasn't black, and he wasn't white. He was light-brown-skinned, an Asiatic cast of countenance, and he had oily black hair.

I looked right into his face.

I didn't get frightened. I knew I wasn't dreaming. I couldn't move, I didn't speak, and he didn't. I couldn't place him racially—other than that I knew he was a non-European. I had no idea whatsoever who he was. He just sat there. Then, suddenly as he had come, he was gone.

Malcolm X later decided that his "pre-vision was of Master W. D. Fard, the Messiah, the one whom Elijah Muhammad said had appointed him—Elijah Muhammad—as His Last Messenger to the black people of North America."

Journalist Salim Muwakkil, while not a Muslim, once worked as editor of the *Final Call,* the Nation of Islam's newspaper. I asked him whether he had ever heard dreams brought up.

Farrakhan recently [1989] made a very big production of a dream he had. He dreamt about meeting Elijah Muhammad on a spaceship. The "Mother Ship" is what it's called. And in the Nation of Islam doctrine, the Mother Ship is this headquarters area, for when the war of Armageddon takes place on the earth. The Mother Ship will be the place where the saved go to escape the destruction. And Farrakhan came out very, very strong and very openly to his followers during one Saviors' Day, which is the big convention, talking about this dream very reverently. And I'm sure many people were a little uncomfortable about him talking so grandly about a dream. But it seems to have been accepted pretty much.

What you're describing is straight out of the Muslim playbook: the prophet gets the dream.

Exactly. And I suppose Farrakhan knew that, so that's why he didn't feel at all self-conscious about being so open and candid about it.

And of course this also legitimizes his connection to Elijah Muhammad.

Exactly right. But until then, I had never heard much talk about dreaming.

In 1989, Minister Louis Farrakhan called a press conference in Washington, D.C., to announce this dream, or "Vision," which he had experienced four years earlier. In this vision he and several friends were carried to Mexico and the top of a mountain sacred to "Quetzacoatl" which, Farrakhan said, he had actually climbed several times. There, "a Wheel" appeared, into which just Farrakhan alone was lifted by "a beam of light." This vehicle transported him "to the Mother Wheel, which is a human built planet a half mile by a half mile, that the Honorable Elijah Muhammad has taught us of for nearly sixty years." Aboard the Mother Wheel, Elijah Muhammad's voice "said, 'President Reagan has met with the Joint Chiefs of Staff to plan a war. I want you to hold a press conference in Washington, DC, and announce their plan and say to the world that you got the information from me on the Wheel.'" And Elijah Muhammad told Farrakhan that at a future date he, Farrakhan, would be brought back to the Mother Wheel and he "would be permitted to see him face to face." Now the smaller wheel transported Farrakhan past "a city in the sky . . . back to Earth and dropped me off near Washington where I then proceeded into this city to make the Announcement." Whereupon he awoke from the vision.

Several months later, said Farrakhan, he came to realize that the war alluded to in the vision was Reagan's campaign against Libya. He therefore traveled to Libya to warn Gadhafi. He asserted that Elijah Muhammad's exact words to him regarding the war had reoccurred in a *New York Times* story, and that the Wheel was present and was observed at the Libyan battle scene, where it interfered with U.S. electronics. The present news conference, he said, was a fulfillment of the commandment in the vision. Further, the reason Elijah Muhammad hadn't told him what war was being planned was because the Libyan strike "was only to serve as a sign of an even more significant and consequential war which would come several years later." That war was the one being waged "against the Black people of America, the Nation of Islam and Louis Farrakhan" by the first President Bush and General Colin Powell.

After expanding upon this "war," Farrakhan concluded: "Before you will establish your mockery of me (if that is what you wish to do) for what was revealed to me in the Wheel, you will see Wheels or what you call UFO's [*sic*] in abundance over the major cities of America and the calamities that America is presently experiencing will increase in number and in intensity that you might humble yourselves to the Warning contained in This Announcement."

An internal publication of the Nation of Islam, "The Science and Teachings of the Mother Craft," gives details about the creation and operation of the Wheel. I'm not certain what of this information stems from the teachings of Elijah Muhammad, and what from Farrakhan's dream or vision. What matters for the purposes of our discussion is the dream's time-honored function of elevating the dreamer in his community of faith.

11

ALL LIFE PASSES THROUGH WATER

DREAMS IN HOODOO

The hoodoo path aint no easy road son, bigger men have fell. The water always deeper than it look.

—A. R. Flowers

Voodoo and Hoodoo

Voodoo came from Haiti to New Orleans. It was brought by the slaves of owners fleeing Toussaint-Louverture's revolution of 1791. When Haitian Voodoo (or Vodun) arrived, it was a full-fledged religion. Voodoo in this form blended elements from over a hundred different African cultures, plus Catholicism. The sources of the word "Voodoo" in the Dahomean, Fon, and Ewe languages all have meanings that relate to "a full set of religious practices"—meanings such as "life-principle," "spirit," "the unknown."

As Voodoo spread into the various slave states, it lost the character of an organized religion involving group worship, which wasn't tolerated by the masters. Nevertheless, Voodoo reinforced the remnants of African religion that U.S. slaves retained from their homelands or picked up while "seasoning" in the West Indies. American "hoodoo" is what came out of the mix. The word "hoodoo" appears to be at once a corruption of "Voodoo" and a variant of a Hausa word, *huduba,* meaning "to arouse resentment toward someone in someone else," which in the Hausa cultural context signifies to bring bad luck upon someone—hoodoo's best-known purpose.

While no longer a religion in the full sense, hoodoo evolved as the vehicle of occult spirituality. So to get a full picture of the place of dreams in African American spirituality, we need to include the occult tradition of hoodoo. In this chapter, we'll sample the role of dreams in hoodoo and look at hoodoo's standing in today's world.

The word "hoodoo" refers to a set of beliefs. It also refers to the practitioner of those beliefs, the "hoodoo" (or "hoodoo doctor") who "hoodoos" you. But there's an array of synonyms: you get "fixed," "voodooed," "conjured," "hexed," "poisoned," "tricked," "crossed," "hurt," "goofered," or have "roots worked on" you. Some people say hoodoo only protects or heals, in contrast to conjure, which does harm. Other people equate malicious hoodoo (and/or conjure) with rootwork; whereas for others still, rootwork is herbal healing. There's little consistency in the nuances attached to these terms.

The slaves regarded hoodoo as "their own separate tradition." And many hoodoo practices can in fact be traced to Africa. The use of dirt from someone's *foot track* to fix (trick, conjure) that person is one example. The use of *body products* such as sweat, urine, and blood is known from Europe, but was never as common there as in Africa. In both African belief and hoodoo, graveyard dirt is thought to contain the spirit of the deceased (the hoodoo term for graveyard dirt or any recipe enhancing that ingredient is *goofer* or *goofer dust*). Boosting the power of a *mojo*, a *toby*, or other so-called *hands* by bringing it into contact with power-giving substances is also African. So is attributing special power to twisted roots like *High John the Conqueror* (or *Conker*). "High" means "great." "John" probably comes from the Bantu word *tshianda,* meaning "place for sorcery," and "Conqueror" from *-kankila,* to "tremble with fear." Words like "mojo," "toby," and "goofer" also have African roots.

But some elements of hoodoo did come from Europe. Fixing someone by putting a charm under her or his *doorstep*, for example, is European. So is wearing *clothing inside out* for luck, and sticking *pins* in an effigy. *Crosses* probably combine African and European influences, as do *incense* and *candles*. The slaves were exposed to European beliefs, and must have admired their masters' magic—it seemed, after all, to be working. Later, many hoodoo doctors borrowed European or Euro-American texts on magic as their sourcebooks. Not to mention that hoodoo is rife with astrology and the Bible.

Notwithstanding European contributions such as these, the black occult retained an African character. Consider the attitude to sin and the devil. African American spirituality in general downplays sin, and hoodoo does so all the more. Here God and the devil are coequal powers, not irreconcilable opposites as they are in Western Christianity. This is African. Elegbara (or Legba), the trickster god of crossroads, who is the closest African counterpart to the Christian devil, is more a reconciler of good and bad than an embodiment of pure evil. This legacy has filtered down, so that followers of hoodoo could also be committed Christians. In Countee Cullen's novel *One Way to Heaven,* a Harlem socialite attempts to overcome her childlessness with visits to Rome and prayers to saints, but also with "a bit of red flannel snipped" from her husband's "undershirt, dipped in asafetida and worn . . . around her neck."

Dreams in the Practice of Hoodoo

In hoodoo, the role of dreams and visions is secondary, but significant in a number of ways. Fixes and remedies can be divined in dreams. Fixes and remedies can also be accomplished through dreams. Dreams can be used to solicit the assistance of the dead and to gain power over the spirits of the living. And some fixes are worked on people as they lie sleeping.

Harry Middleton Hyatt's *Hoodoo, Conjuration, Witchcraft, Rootwork* is far and away the best source for information about hoodoo in the twentieth century. Hyatt's massive collection of interviews consists of nearly five thousand margin-to-margin, single-spaced typescript pages printed in five volumes. Hyatt was a white Episcopalian priest who previously had published a less superhuman collection of the folk beliefs of whites and blacks in an Illinois county. The subtitle of his hoodoo collection proclaims that it also concerns beliefs of both races—and indeed, hoodoo has its white adherents, although the hoodoo doctors themselves have mostly (though not exclusively) been black. In a few places, Hyatt asked his informants about white participation. But in fact he confined himself to black informants, and the introductory comments to volume 3 show that this was his intention from the beginning.

Ishmael Reed, author of the hoodoo novel *Mumbo Jumbo,* deemed Hyatt "legendary," and for anyone interested in hoodoo Hyatt deserves that praise. But it's oddly difficult to make out what motivated Hyatt in his immense labor. The book contains hardly any analysis, just ream after ream of interview transcripts. And Hyatt characterized hoodoo as "a strange form of thought," and even as "a dangerous mental activity." And yet his zest for the material is obvious on every page.

Unfortunately, Hyatt was one of those people who don't remember their dreams, and his curiosity about this aspect of his subject was meager. He never once initiated a line of questioning about dreams or visions—unlike his black assistant. This man, in one of only two interviews not personally conducted by Hyatt, did ask directly about visions. He was obviously better attuned to this aspect of black spirituality than was his employer. But fortunately, many of Hyatt's informants gave spontaneous accounts of dreams and visions, and it's from these that most of the following material is drawn.

One other thing. Hoodoo definitely follows patterns and employs a standard pharmacy of ingredients. But any given procedure is likely to combine and introduce elements in an inventive way. Individualization is in fact a tenet of the practice. So it can't be assumed that a process or recipe described below is widespread in its particulars.

Fixes and Remedies Divined in Dreams

In the world of hoodoo, as in Africa, the first indication you're being hexed may come in a dream. Hyatt was told by a woman with dropsy that she found out what the real problem was through a dream. Her mother appeared in the dream wearing jade green jewelry and telling her, "Darling, . . . green signifies poison." "Poison" here means a hoodoo fix.

The night before another of Hyatt's informants went blind, she dreamed she saw a woman making a mark on the ground that the dreamer would have to walk over. The next day, when she went to her job as a domestic, she saw the woman from her dream at the kitchen door, and shortly afterward she fainted and became blind. She was sure the woman had fixed her.

Another woman went to a conjure doctor to take care of a chronic chafing "down there." She was given a lotion of gunpowder and whiskey, and the doctor also gave her a bag to wear containing asafetida, bluestone (blue vitriol), and gunpowder. The doctor said, "You going to get rid of your husband." She didn't know what the doctor meant, until her husband became ill. Then she dreamed he was going to die, and "something told" her to throw the bag away in running water. She did, and her husband recovered. (She kept using the malicious doctor's lotion for the chafing "down there," however, because it worked.)

In a case from the 1980s observed by a medical ethnologist, a "root doctor" diagnosed "conjuration" for a man with "jumped-up stomach" (gastroenteritis), and advised him to encircle some fresh graveyard dirt with candles to induce his dead brother to "come to you in a dream and tell you what to do." In due course, the dead brother told him in a dream to break off with the woman whom the root doctor suspected of conjure. This is a good example of a fairly common practice: the deliberate seeking, or incubation, of dreams by hoodoo means.

Doctors sometimes dream for the benefit of the client. A man whose wife had left him went to a certain hoodoo doctor, after dreaming that he should do so. The hoodoo fasted to incubate a dream, and discovered that the wife's rival had buried two treated bottles at the client's back steps.

Fixes and Remedies Accomplished in Dreams

Dreams can play an instrumental role in the work of hoodoo. As one part of an elaborate fix, a doctor advised writing a letter to the victim spelling out your grievances. If you sleep with this letter under your head for three nights, you'll dream of the victim. The purpose of the dream is to draw the victim's spirit into the letter, for then the letter is thrown in the river, a common means of causing harm or creating a compulsion to go away.

A boy called Stableboy was paralyzed. When regular doctors failed to cure him, his mother took him to a root doctor:

> The root doctor said that someone "had gone and done him in" and that only he could help. He gave Stableboy an "eight dose" [?] and asked if he could "stand it" if he visited him in his sleep. With some trepidation Stableboy agreed. The next night the root doctor visited him in his sleep in the form of "a centipede with a thousand hands" and massaged his entire body. When he could stand this no longer he screamed, and the giant centipede vanished. When Stableboy awoke in the morning, he was well.

Soliciting the Dead in Dreams

In hoodoo, benefits can be obtained from the dead, and one means of soliciting their help is by getting them to appear in dreams.

A hoodoo doctor claimed to consult with the legendary Dr. Buzzard through incubated dreams. After fasting for two days, he would take three pennies and a hen's egg to the river, then to a "certain grave" where he would leave the pennies and the egg, returning for them three days later. At home, he would place these items under his bed, and Dr. Buzzard would "come and visit me just as plain as you are."

Suppose a dream visitation from an ancestor gets interrupted. You can get the ancestor to return with the rest of the message by sleeping with two crossed matches stuck together with a pin under your pillow.

You can get "some of your peoples" to give you a number for gambling by writing a letter of request which you leave under a glass of water as you sleep. Your dream that night may feature a cow or a dog, but that's your ancestor bringing you the number.

Another way to get luck is to give the bone of a dead person to a dog to gnaw on. Then you wrap the remains of the bone in red flannel. The dead person's spirit will come to you with a tip as you sleep.

As part of obtaining power from a dead person, a dream will tell you if you've succeeded. Dig up a left index finger, or "dog finger," from the graveyard. Next, get a cup or more of dust from the center point of a crossroads and submerge the finger in it. Every morning take some of that dust and with a certain ritual make your wishes for power over it. When you get to the bottom of the cup, throw any remaining dust away. Now wrap the bone in wire so that it can be neither touched nor seen, and sleep with that bone. By the fourth night you'll "see the skeleton in your sleep. . . . That vision got to come to you to verify your power."

Power over the Living in Dreams

Hoodoo can draw the spirits of the living into dreams, as well as the spirits of the dead. The one you love or desire will "come to you" in dreams if you think and talk about the beloved before sleep—a procedure any dream psychologist would endorse for incubating a dream. But then the person's spirit is caught when it appears by telling it that you can't remember its name, though of course you can. When the spirit says its name, you write it down, and from then on you're able to catch this spirit any time merely by calling the name. All this takes place while you're asleep.

To catch a thief, burn a white candle, recite the Twenty-third Psalm, and name out loud all your suspects, then sleep on your left side. The thief's own spirit will come and point at the stash "through a vision in your sleep."

Visions

Some hoodoo practices involve waking visions. For instance, to discover where someone is at present, copy words from a tombstone onto a piece of paper. Put the paper into a bottle containing charcoal from new wood, turpentine, and seven grains of corn. After the mixture sits for three days, ask the bottle, "'Dear bottle . . . where you at?' . . . And it'll come to me just as plain as the nose on my face. . . . It's a vision, you see."

Some variants of the grisly ritual of boiling a black cat alive (with the lid held firmly down to prevent escape) require you to withstand visions of "the devil and his imps . . . a whole gang of little people" who come with lights and music to dance with you. The Lord and angels also participate, in some accounts. The object is to obtain the one bone with power by boiling the flesh off the cat. The lucky bone is usually the one that first floats in the pot, or the one that floats upstream when you toss the stew into the river. If you pass examination, you've sold yourself to the devil. The bone will float and you can use it to become invisible to commit robberies and for other shady business.

If you want to see evil spirits, take a black cat to a crossroads at 2:00 A.M. Crossroads, a locus for many hoodoo rituals, also figure in several other vision incubations recorded by Hyatt. There's one to see your future husband (or, if you're unlucky, your coffin, predicting your early death), and one to obtain a demonic helper. Acquiring the gift of playing guitar or banjo by selling yourself to the devil is the best-known crossroads ritual. If you can stand to see and hear all the frightening devils that appear, you come away able to play.

Rituals During Sleep

There are a multitude of ways to work hoodoo by placing hands or fixes in and around the bed where you or someone else sleeps. To get a spirit in your power, for example, sleep on a murdered sinner's grave dirt placed inside an envelope together with a letter stating your wish. To drive someone crazy in six days, and kill them in nine, bury nine frogs in a jar under the person's house, directly under the victim's bed. To cure impotence, mingle your urine with your woman's urine in a bottle, add sugar and cinnamon, and sleep on that in the bed you share, but don't let her know. To "draw" a man to you, tie three knots in your own dirty stocking and sleep on it for three nights. Then sprinkle it with salt and burn it, invoking the Trinity.

We've already seen that some rituals that act during sleep are meant to produce dreams. But in most cases, charms hidden in and around a bed probably work simply by proximity—just like charms placed on someone's route, hidden behind a hearth brick, buried under the doorstep, attached to a work implement, sewn into clothing, or mixed into food. Hoodoo always works through the spirit, but for practical purposes the spirit is usually treated almost like a "physical thing" without a psychological dimension.

One group of in-sleep fixes evidently does have a psychological effect, however. These fixes cause someone, say an unfaithful husband, to *sleep-talk* and reveal the truth. You can put an open pocketknife in the palm of the sleeper's hand and close his fingers over it. Or concentrate on his photo, then touch his hair lightly and ask anything you want, such as "Will you stay with me?" Or put his hand in a container of water (but he could die if the wind changes while his hand is in the water, or if it's left there too long). Such procedures apparently engage the sleeper's mind by catching the spirit.

Sleep rituals involving water all have in common the belief that water attracts spirits. For example, a whole array of rituals employ a person's photograph together with water under the bed to draw or bind a person or run them crazy. Other procedures with water allow you to catch murderers, escape prosecution, and so on. It's hard to know what the psychological dimension of these rituals might be, if any.

But one water ritual we've already looked at does expressly involve dreams: getting an ancestral ghost to bring you a number by placing a glass of water on top of a letter stating your request. And in a recent case, a woman who had a vivid dream she didn't understand told it to a "spiritualist" friend, who instructed her to "recite the Twenty-third Psalm, take a glass of water, take three swallows, and put the glass under your bed." Although skeptical, the woman performed the ritual. That night she had a waking vision of her grandmother. Also, a contemporary conjure woman, Luisah Teish, who blends hoodoo with New Age beliefs, writes that perfumed water under the bed, when combined with certain other measures, will "keep dreams clear." Finally, water can be used to prevent the dream (or dreamlike experience) of being ridden by a witch—the subject of the next chapter. The water either catches the hag, or simply distracts it.

Another practice involving water is to leave a drink out for your own spirit, to prevent it from wandering off in search of water. For if it does, you might never wake up again. This belief comes from the "very widespread African belief that souls are often thirsty and might desert one in search of water."

The European contribution to beliefs about water, sleep, and spirits is the notion that holy water protects against spirits. Holy water should be sprinkled on the bed or hung in a bottle behind it. The European belief is that water repels, rather than attracts, spirits.

The Legacy of Hoodoo

Hyatt was told in the 1970s that the young no longer believed in hoodoo. But he was also told that hoodoo was still being handed down from parent to child, even to the college educated. In the same decade, an observer noted that "hexing" wasn't confined to "isolated rural communities of the deep south . . . but is evident in large urban areas of the northeast and west." An article from the 1980s in the leading black medical journal stated that "Although most patients will not admit to believing in root doctors . . . it is well established in northern and western cities as well [as in the South]." "Every community has it," said a prominent black psychologist in the 1990s. *Jive* and *Black Romance* magazines today carry classified ads like "Have you been hoodooed?" and "Louisiana rootman Brother Harris specializes in dressing roots." Hoodoo products are readily available from local occult stores and by mail order, and even over the Internet.

Obviously hoodoo is a far less pervasive feature of African American life than it was formerly. Still, it persists to a surprising degree. What's more, hoodoo remains in the collective memory, even for the majority who have no part in it. Just as with numbers gambling, we can assess the collective memory by looking at African American literature, where we find that hoodoo comes up quite often (see the note for this paragraph). Scattered through these works are all the large features of hoodoo and a variety of specific methods and materials, including some of those just discussed.

Some authors dismiss "that old voodoo" as "nonsense," of course. But as pointed out elsewhere, the expression of skepticism itself indicates the presence of a belief within a community. Another indirect sign of its presence is that hoodoo words show up in slang. Langston Hughes called dope "goopher dust," Chester Himes used "mojo" to mean sexual prowess, and so on. Figures of speech like these have been borrowed by writers of different decades directly from black vernacular speech up to the present day.

Three novels must be singled out in connection with hoodoo: Ishmael Reed's *Mumbo Jumbo,* A. R. Flowers's *De Mojo Blues,* and Gloria Naylor's *Mama Day.* Reed's book is a farce depicting combat between African culture in the United States and the dominant European culture—between the forces of life and death. Reed presents hoodoo as "African religion [in] the Americas where it survives to this day." Reed's thesis is that the African essence of hoodoo is one and the same as the essence of blues, jazz, and the rest of black popular culture. He says of black musicians and dancers that "they have synthesized the HooDoo of VooDoo. Its blee blop essence. . . . "

In *De Mojo Blues,* Arthur Flowers weaves blunt realism with fantasy to tell the story of a veteran spiritually radicalized by Vietnam. Flowers depicts the hoodoo practitioner as the enlightened race man and "tribal shaman" of the black diaspora. Flowers gives hoodoo a place among the world's recognized spiritual traditions, and attempts to show from the inside what the practice of hoodoo is like.

Gloria Naylor's *Mama Day* portrays three kinds of hoodoo practitioners, with their different powers and motivations. There's a false Dr. Buzzard, who recognizes the real power of hoodoo but himself is nine-tenths charlatan. There's a young woman who uses hoodoo destructively. And there's Mama Day, primarily a healer. Naylor told me:

> She's a bit of the good, a bit of the bad, a bit of the charlatan herself.
> Sometimes she uses kitchen table psychology to get things done. And
> she can be destructive, if she feels indeed that something is unjust. And
> of course ninety-nine percent of what she does is to work with nature.

As different as Reed, Flowers, and Naylor are in their styles and ambitions, all three believe that the essence of hoodoo is affinity to nature and affirmation of life.

We've seen that the role of dreams in hoodoo is significant but secondary. The same may be said of the connections found between dreams and hoodoo in literature. Toni Morrison makes dreams part of the know-how of a good "evil conjure woman." Charlotte Watson Sherman's rootman says he got his "learning from dreams." And Shay Youngblood's autobiographical character kept a lock of someone's hair "in a lil bag with some roots in it round my neck and touched it when I wanted to dream." Youngblood calls this an "Africanism."

As for visions, Walter Mosley's Soupspoon tells how his mentor Robert Johnson "sold his soul" and "[g]ive up his right eye to the blues" at "the crossroads." "With that dead eye they say he could see past all that we see, into hell—where everyone knows the blues come from anyways."

As for rituals during sleep, an August Wilson rootworker gives someone "a small cloth packet" and tells her to "sleep with it under your pillow and it'll bring good luck to you." Darryl Pinckney's narrator mocks a woman for "putting a bowl of water with a fork in it under the bed in order to trap the hostile spirits that might get her while she slept." And Ralph Ellison's character remarks that when someone is "dreamin' 'bout somebody," you can get them to "say it all" by putting their hand in "warm water."

The Interviews

Evidence for the present standing of hoodoo emerged from my interviews. Even though I seldom asked direct questions about it, hoodoo came up fairly regularly in the course of conversation. For instance, Oscar Edmond mentioned that when his grandmother went to the hospital for the last time, she told the family she had been hexed and would die if not attended by someone who could take the hex off. A daughter-in-law, she believed, had fixed her for interfering. Edmond also talked about "a real strange aunt" of his, who

> gave my mother these oils, and said, "Put this in your house, it'll get away evil spirits, and also will help with the money." My mother believes in that. Not as much today, but in those days, she was like "Okay." And the money did loosen up.

I heard many allusions like this to hoodoo in family history. "Woodoo!" recalled Stephanie Bell. "My great-grandmother and my grandmother called it woodoo." Ramon Giles found "a bottle of spirit water" when his grandmother died. Osuurete Adesanya's great-great-grandmother was a rootwoman. "She knew about, you know, spit on the bush, pick the leaf, and make some medicine out of it. But they also said that she's a very mean woman, and that she would put roots *on* a person." Sheron Williams-Brooks was proud of her great-grandmother for being "one of the leading women in Trinidad in terms of understanding the herbs." This ancestor obtained a visa to the United States by "a powerful work" put on the documents after all previous applications and appeals had been refused. Kai EL Zabar said:

> My mother told me a story about her great-aunt, who was angry at some woman and I don't know what she did to her, but the woman mysteriously died. And then when they went to the funeral, they said

the casket was closed. I mean, this is the kinda stuff I used to hear, you know, as a kid. And "Oh yeah, the snakes just came out, just crawled out the casket, you just shoulda seen 'em go." I'm like, "The snakes!" They go, "Yeah! Well, not actual snakes, but you could see the snakes," you know?

Or, they talked about the little things those people did. I mean, go get somebody's panties and do something, bury them in the ground. Or like your husband died, the woman's supposed to take hair off the vagina and put it in his hand in the casket, and close it. That's so that, you know, nobody else was visiting. When my father died, somebody came up to my mother and says, "Did you so-and-so?" She said, "You know, they still get some." She's so crazy! She said, "They're still trying to get some!" And they're dead!

Cheryl Boone said:

> I went to a psychic once, and she said there was this um . . . *voodoo*, in my family, and I got *real* huffy. And *real* indignant. *Shoot!* Beg your pardon. *Now* I don't think of it negatively, but I guess then I thought of it as being something we didn't do. In our family. It was some kinda black magic stuff, and we're too . . . educated. And then I would talk to my Great-Aunt Dot from New Orleans, and she said, "Oh, honey, Great-Aunt used to sprinkle the house *all* the time!" With the salt and stuff? That was like part of their everyday routine! And I said, "Oh, well, I guess I owe that lady an apology!"

While for many, hoodoo is a feature of the family past, a certain number of interviewees grew up with hoodoo in their homes. Conjuring "wasn't explicitly talked about" in Eileen Cherry's home, "but it was very present, and it was present in the lives around me." Lill Lowry's grandparents would sweep the steps and sidewalk every morning "to get rid of evil spirits." Her mother also had "a few little things, like, if you're sweeping and you touch her with the broom? Then she has to spit on it. My father would look at her and shake his head." Cecile Jackson's mother would intimidate Cecile's father by saying, "I'll burn a candle on you." Ralph Arnold's parents "joked about it," yet "did believe sort of halfway that the scrapings of your fingernail in a man's food could kill him." Preston Jackson had this recollection:

> Gooba [goofer] dust was a bag that was handed down through my mother's mother, and her mother, all the way from Africa. They'd sweep up something every New Year's, put it in a little white sack. It has to be white cotton, tie it up, and hang it over the door. And I was a kid, playing with my little automobiles, looking up at that bag there,

just wondering about it. And my mother wouldn't talk about it. She'd just say, "Oh, that's the gooba dust bag."

For a number of interviewees, hoodoo occasionally enters their present lives. Alice Stephens has friends afraid to visit her because of her black cat. Douglas Howard believes "you maybe could be cursed" by "a person who's into that voodoo or whatever." Edwina Ackie, whose family came from Trinidad, has a beautiful cousin who was crippled when "somebody did obeah to her." Betty Rodgers Hale, a college counselor, has a colleague "who swears he sprinkles some stuff in front of some offices and keeps some other folks out. And they stayed out, for a whole year!" Frances Freeman-Williams has a neighbor with marital problems who "was told that if she put her [menstrual] blood in what he eats, that that would seal them together." Sylvia Morris's mother takes credit for causing the divorce of a cousin from a wife who was abusing their children, by "putting her in the flowerpot"—that is, burying the husband's and wife's names on separate pieces of paper in the dirt. In prison, Achim Rodgers has observed "the guys" burning hair that's come out while braiding it, to make sure no one gets hold of it. Rodgers remembers that his aunt used to do that. One of the children I interviewed at the Cabrini Green housing project in Chicago told me about a cousin who caught someone "throwing dirt" on her while she slept: "She woke up in time to save her life." Diane Dugger's aunt took credit for causing the drowning of a man at sea, "because he did something to her oldest daughter. And I sit there and listen, and like, 'She really believes it!' And then I started thinking about other things that had happened." Another woman asserted a firm conviction in the reality of hoodoo murder. She "had an aunt who could do it," and she knew a woman who predicted "exactly what would happen" to the wife of the man this woman was involved with. The rival died.

A few interviewees talked about actually practicing hoodoo themselves. Poet Angela Jackson, whose dissertation compares the Yoruba religion of Nigeria with Brazilian Candomble, acknowledged, "I've been into the shops, and I've bought a John the Conqueror root." Kimberly Camp uses salt "to purify rooms and stuff like that." One woman had experimented with menstrual blood and burning names written on papers when in her twenties. Kai EL Zabar purifies with salt if she thinks spirits are in the house: "Now that's something definitely from my mother." Lill Lowry said she's careful now because she has, she believes, twice physically harmed people she was angry with, by wishing it, and she associates this power with the hoodoo in her family past. "Well, I don't know," she admitted with a smile. "I might have, you know, stuck out two fingers and pointed in their direction." And Joe Cheeks told this story:

> I know a girl, I don't know if you'd call her a bank *robber*. She would type up a letter, she would go to banks, and she'd come out with five thousand dollars. Okay, so one of these times she got busted. So she wanted us to go to court with her, me and my buddy. And we have to chew these roots, spit 'em around the courtroom. She takes this oil, and after you rub this all on your hands, you can't touch glass, or something. You know, it was a lot of little—So the point I'm making is, people still believe this. And she would give us this damn root, we'd have to go to court—I mean, as far as there was money, I don't give a damn, I'll spit some root around here for a grand. So you go to court, and you spit the root where she tells you, around the court, and this is supposed to protect her. She got five years. But I wasn't spitting where she told me, anyway. I was going around the floor, I feel like a idiot, you know what I mean. The money was right, I didn't care.

Dreams and Hoodoo

Over a dozen interviewees made connections of different sorts between dreams and hoodoo. That's an appreciable number, considering that hoodoo is a subject I seldom probed unless it came up spontaneously.

Marva Pitchford Jolly drew a picture of the hoodoo doctor's function as a dream interpreter in the South of her childhood:

> You might go to Miss Sadie, and you say, "Well, you know, there's a big crap game tonight." If I am Miss Sadie in Mississippi, I probably asked you something about what you dreamed. And if you dreamt about cats, she's going to say to you, "Better not go down to that game."

Osuurete Adesanya repeated some bits of dream lore. If in your dreams "people are trying to harm you, then they say, light a white candle by your bed." If you're being chased, "burn incense while you go to sleep."

The night before our interview, Tony Thomas dreamed rats were crawling on him. He "talked to somebody this morning about it, she said some people believe that's witchcraft!" Did he think so, too? "Yeah!"

Achim Rodgers and Darryl Burrows both described the belief that bad dreams can be due to a fix and require expert interpretation and intervention. Burrows said:

> The idea is that other people, through some dark, satanic link, can influence your dreams. They can make you have nightmares. They can put thoughts into your mind that will lead to behaviors. One of the things you hear from some black people in New Orleans is that, they'll say, "I had this terrible dream, and I'm just gonna have to go see So-and-so to stop having this dream."

Katie Jones said she had twice divined through dreams that someone was fixed. As a child, a dream told her that an uncle who died had been "poisoned," and revealed just who the culprits were. Then, as an adult, she dreamed about a niece "down home":

> Her husband had buried some of her baby's clothes. And I told my sister, when I was down there, I said, "I dreamed Lester had buried some of her clothes out here." And it happened.
> *Why did he bury the clothes?*
> Well, he and my niece was separated, and he was staying with another lady, and see, sometimes, when people can't get to the person, they'll take it out on the child.
> *And how did it turn out?*
> It turned out outrageous. The baby died.

Ntozake Shange gave the recipe for a "binding" ritual in one of her novels. You sleep with six roses by your head and your pillow filled with a certain leaf. Shange had used this ritual in her own life for "power" over a "cavorting" lover. "This doesn't have to go through your dream life," she insisted, but then described to me an out-of-body experience during sleep. She said it was "astral travel":

> It's like very, very deep sleep. And the body's very heavy. But there's a warm vibration in your body. This is just before you can release, and the spirit will come out and go. My spirit went over to his house, and lay with him. And then I came back. And when I woke up, I felt like this woman had never happened. I felt absolutely confident, and very relaxed. And very beautiful.

Over half a dozen interviewees mentioned that they had used or heard about placing *water under or near the bed*. Regina Reed believes it helps you remember dreams. Zeinabu irene Davis learned from her grandmother to put flowers or fragrant oil in the water for "pleasant dreams." Laura McKnight had heard that water makes "people come to you" with numbers dreams. Ann Eskridge's grandmother used to say:

> "You put a pan of water underneath your bed, and the numbers will fall out." I said, "One, two, three—like that, Grandma?" She said, "No, you dream it, and then you get a dream book. And then you look up the dream, and that's your number."

Osuurete Adesanya said the purpose of the "old custom" of putting water under the bed is to "neutralize the energy" of "bad dreams." Kimberly Camp has "always done it as a way to keep negativity out of your dreams, the negative spirits away, so that you can get to the truth." She puts salt, a protective purifier, in the water. So does Kai EL Zabar. "But," she added, "you should always balance that, too. With the sweet. The bitter with the sweet. You put the sugar and you put the salt. Or honey and salt." I asked her how this all worked to influence dreams. She replied:

> Well, all life passes through water. And so, that's all I know! One of the things you have to understand about African Americans: there are some things we just accept, and we don't seek a logical explanation for everything. And then at different times, the wisdom of that is revealed to you in different stages and phases. So like they say, "All life passes through water," then you understand, even a child comes through the placenta. And it makes sense to you and you just leave it alone. My mother used to say, "All life passes through water," and for her, calling on the spirits was life. And so, I guess, for them to come to her, they had to come through the water.

12

LITTLE STIRRUPS

WITCHES RIDING YOU AND
SLEEP PARALYSIS

*"Maybe it wuz uh witch ridin' yuh, honey. Ah'll see can't Ah find some
mustard seed whilst Ah's out."*

—Zora Neale Hurston

The Folk Tradition

"Yes!" exclaimed Stephanie Bell, grateful to have her memory jogged.
"Yes! My great-grandmother used to *talk* about that. There were times
when my grandmother could not awaken my great-grandmother. And
my great-grandmother would wake up and say that she was ridden by
a witch."

Another woman told this story:

> Last week, I was laying on the sofa, and I was having this dream like
> there was a presence in the room, and something was like pressing me
> down. And I was trying to scream, and I couldn't! And I was saying,
> "Get off!" And I couldn't move, I couldn't get up off the sofa. And to
> me, I wasn't asleep. And my eyes were like open. I didn't *see* a presence,
> but I felt! I felt the pressure on my body, from my neck on down and
> where I couldn't even talk. I don't want to say "it" or whatever, it was
> holding me down.
>
> *Have you heard the expression, to be "ridden by a witch"?*
> Yes! Yes, I've heard that. I didn't want to say that! From my grandmother,
> my aunt. They just said, "A witch got on me last night and I couldn't
> move, I couldn't talk. I'm telling you, it just wouldn't let me *go!*"

These two accounts are squarely in the vein of African American folklore about witches riding people. Parallel folk traditions are found in Alaska, the Philippines, the Caribbean—in fact, around the world. Each tradition embellishes the same general experience with its own local color. The best documented of these traditions is the "old hag" tradition among descendants of English West Country settlers in New-foundland. At present, the term "old hag" has been generalized by some Newfoundlanders to mean any very bad dream, much as "night-mare" has drifted from its original meaning. For in Old English, "mare" meant not a female horse, but a demon who attacks people in their sleep.

In African American folk beliefs of former days, coincidentally, witches and horses did go together. Witches (or "hags") had a repu-tation for stealing horses, and likewise for riding their human victims as if they were horses. Afterward, the victim was left with bit marks at the corners of the mouth, or "hair plaited into little stirrups." These notions about horses no longer survive, except remotely, perhaps, in the expression "The witch riding your back," which I heard from two interviewees (Cecile Jackson and Josh Taifa) and from a child at Cabrini Green. Most people now will tell you that whatever attacks them comes from the front. (In some of the old folk accounts, the witch gets you first from the front, then flips you over and saddles you.)

It's been speculated that the old African American folklore about witches and horses derives from Africa. In Africa, being ridden like a horse is associated with divine possession. The divinity "mounts" the medium, who is known as the " 'one climbed on' or the 'horse' of the divinity."

Perhaps the slaves did bring medium possession and the notion of a spiritual rider with them from Africa. However, Africa also has a tra-dition along the lines of the general world pattern, a tradition of being set upon and held fast by evil witches. For example, a contemporary Nigerian university graduate "felt a weight on her chest" as she was about to wake up one morning. "She found she could not move her body, could not even shout for help. . . . " She "felt she saw a bird on her chest." Birds are the West African local color for witches rid-ing people. The young woman's mother took her to a "prophetess" of an Independent Christian church, then to a "native healer." Both "faith healers" told them "that witches were after the girl and that she needed protection."

In the United States, the rider is traditionally the spirit of someone living, some witch out to get you or some hoodoo paid to torment you. Or the rider may be something other than a living spirit—the devil or, more often, a dead spirit. "It's just real common," remarked Norma Adams Wade of Texas, to hear someone say, " 'That haint just rode me last night.' "

The folklore literature records myriad ways to prevent or escape from being ridden, or to catch a witch after being ridden. Witches, for example, can be delayed by exploiting their "fatal counting instinct." Most witches are stupid and can only count so high, or else they lose count and have to start over. So you leave items out for them to count, like a sifter (for its holes), a broom (for its straws), or any seeds, grains, or meal scattered on the floor.

According to one widespread folk belief, a witch has to take off its skin, either before leaving home, in order to fly, or upon arriving at the doorstep or bedside of the victim. It greases its skin with "witch oil" to remove it, exposing a slimy body "just as red and raw as beefsteak." Lying on your bed, you sense it coming at you in this "semifluid and wholly horrible condition" to take its "seat upon your chest." So a way to catch or kill a witch—and this usually happens after it rides you—is to prevent it from putting its disrobed skin back on. One technique is to place sharp objects such as scissors or needles where they'll snag the skin. But the best recourse is to put salt and pepper onto the skin, either directly or by scattering it around the room. Pepper (usually red, sometimes black) makes the skin intolerably painful to wear.

While some of the other countermeasures (such as the broom whose straws the witch must stop to count) occur in the folklore of white America and Europe, salt and pepper is a "traditional African method" of coping with witches who ride you.

Sleep Paralysis

Local embellishments aside, the world's folk traditions of being ridden by witches all describe the same core experience. A full-blown episode usually has the following characteristics:

- A waking or near-waking state, with awareness of the real environment
- Inability to move (except the eyes)

- Feelings of choking, suffocation, or strangulation
- Oppressive pressure or weight, usually on the chest
- Feelings of crying out or speaking without being heard, or of an inability to cry out or speak
- The presence or approach of a figure
- Fear

These characteristics, as it happens, comprise a "sleep disorder" known to medicine and psychology as *sleep paralysis*. Other symptoms sometimes include pressure on the limbs, tingling or vibrations in the limbs, rushing sounds, or the sound of footsteps. Rarely, the event is pleasant or even ecstatic. Occasionally, an out-of-body experience precedes or accompanies an episode. All these variations appear in folklore as well.

The cause of sleep paralysis is a brief and transitory malfunction in the nervous system. Here's how it happens. As we sleep and dream, the parts of the brain that initiate body movements are not shut down, as you might suppose. But normally we don't move, because while the brain is busy telling the body to move, at the same time a global "off" signal is being sent to the spinal cord, effectively causing paralysis. If body movements weren't blocked in this way, the dreamer would act out the dream. And there is actually a syndrome where that very thing occurs. In *REM sleep behavior disorder*, the "off" signal to the spinal cord gets switched to "on" in the midst of dreaming, often resulting in mishaps to the dreamer or even acts of violence. In sleep paralysis, a much more common and innocuous condition, just the opposite occurs: as the sleeper awakens, the "off" signal to the spinal cord temporarily fails to switch to "on," causing the frightening sensation of paralysis.

Is sleep paralysis at the bottom of the world's various folk traditions of being ridden by witches? That certainly is the view of black psychiatrists who have studied sleep paralysis in black populations here and in Africa. It must be said, however, that science has yet to explain why people sense a figure on them or approaching them. Even people unacquainted with any of the traditions have this experience. But my own belief is that a physiological explanation for this aspect of sleep paralysis will also emerge.

Just how common is sleep paralysis? The findings both internationally and in the United States differ confusingly. It appears, however, that in this country the incidence is higher among blacks than whites.

One study of college students found a rate of 50 percent in a black group, as compared with 37 percent and 32 percent in two white groups. Carl Bell, who has published several articles on sleep paralysis in blacks, concludes that the 41 percent rate he finds is "at least twice the incidence reported in whites." In my own study, the rate of 61 percent for blacks is significantly higher than the 42 percent for whites.

Bell further concludes that the *frequency* of sleep paralysis episodes is much higher in blacks than whites. Of his subjects, over 27 percent experience episodes "once or more monthly," a frequency seldom found in the best-studied white subjects.

Bell considers several factors that may contribute to the high rate and frequency of sleep paralysis in blacks. One factor is genetic predisposition. A second is low boundaries. Blacks may be "more predisposed" to "hallucinatory phenomena." The third is what Bell calls "survival fatigue." Stress can bring on episodes of sleep paralysis, and "being black in this society is associated with stress due to racism."

Something like Bell's "survival fatigue" due to racism was suggested spontaneously by several of my interviewees. When I mentioned to Jim Taylor the likelihood that blacks are predisposed to sleep paralysis, he commented, "Well, it's probably because we're being held down all the time, in real life." Judy Still said, "Maybe it's an aspect of our place in the world, which is always tenuous." And Betty Holcomb thought it's "because of our experiences of being enchained." Another woman wondered if the genetic component "could have anything to do with inheriting it from our ancestors because they were oppressed people."

The high rates of sleep paralysis will almost surely surprise most readers. That's because people are generally reluctant to discuss the experience. Bell notes "a general tendency in blacks" to avoid discussing "any problems that might indicate a nervous condition." Many of Bell's subjects had never before disclosed their own sleep paralysis experiences "for fear they would be viewed as 'crazy.'" They were undoubtedly relieved to learn that the experience is neither uncommon nor dangerous. I also encountered that reaction in my interviews. And an African researcher concludes that sleep paralysis is underreported both in Nigeria and the United States because of "the popular opinion" that it's due to witchcraft.

Remarkably, neither Barbara Pulliam, a psychoanalyst, nor Maisha Hamilton-Bennett, a clinical psychologist, has ever heard clients mention sleep paralysis, though surely many of them had gone through it.

And Alice Stephens, a clinical psychologist in her thirties at the time when she first underwent sleep paralysis, had never heard of it herself and was deeply frightened when it happened. Other interviewees who surprised me because they had never heard it discussed in their wide experience were Sara Lawrence-Lightfoot, the educator and biographer, and novelist John Edgar Wideman. Wideman, who has written both about the African tradition of medium possession by divine riders and the southern tradition of witches riding—and who himself has experienced sleep paralysis—had never heard anyone else directly describe the experience until our conversation. While sleep paralysis is fairly common, obviously it's seldom disclosed. Yet many people have heard of witches riding you. Either these people don't make the connection, or they keep it to themselves.

The Interviews

There are a few more observations I'd like to make about the manner in which the interviewees experience sleep paralysis and relate to the folk tradition of witches. We'll consider the imagery accompanying sleep paralysis in this group of contemporaries, their state of belief or disbelief concerning witches, and an alternative folk explanation offered by some of them.

The Imagery

In the African American folk tradition, the thing that does the riding usually takes the form of a *witch*, a *haint*, or a *devil*. Only a scattering of interviewees reported imagery of this sort, even though 51 percent of those questioned had heard of witches riding you (as compared to only 15 percent of white subjects).

Three interviewees had actually seen or felt the presence of *witches*. Two of them were children at the time. The family of one of these, Oscar Edmond, called the experience "the witch's broom." The other, Almontez Stewart, was told by his "old-fashioned" mother "the witch was riding" him when he had recurring episodes. Actually, the witch would tickle his feet. Only Kai EL Zabar was beset by witches as an adult.

As for *haints*, Kimberly Camp said:

> I used to live by a cemetery once. It was very difficult. That's when
> you have the witch riding your dream. That happened to me quite
> often when I lived next to that cemetery. And it took discussing it with
> several people before I found out a way to eliminate those.

As for *devils,* one interviewee's mother once told her as a child that it was "the devil" holding her down and choking her because she'd been a bad girl. Ayanna Udongo heard "demonic voices" during sleep paralysis. And Carolyn Collins, sister of Edward Moore, was napping by the hospital bed of her dying husband when

> I woke up because I thought I heard my husband say, "Oh no! I can't be dying!" There was what looked to me like a dark figure that had a black cloak and a hood over its head. I didn't see a face. I was trying to get up and come and help him, but it was like my whole body was just paralyzed, and I couldn't get up. It felt like something was holding me down. And I felt like there was a smaller figure, in the same form as the larger figure, and I saw that one, like the side of it, holding me down.
>
> *What is your explanation of this experience?*
> The distinct feeling I had was that it was maybe the angel of death or something.

On another occasion, she had a small, gray, bulgy-eyed "*gargoylelike thing* sitting on my chest and choking me." She mentally said, "Jehovah!" and it left.

Many interviewees saw or sensed a vague *somebody* walking up the stairs, approaching, standing over the bed, sitting on the side of the bed, and/or holding them down. A *black figure* held Laura McKnight down by the arms and shoulders. Jim Taylor was once held down by *God,* who was "white, with long brown hair." Two women (Regina Reed, Ayanna Udongo) each had a *giant* on her chest. Three had seen or sensed a *rapist* (Diane Dugger, Angela Powell) or a *seducer* (Ann Eskridge). One referred to the restraining figure, who was "shrouded in light and darkness at the same time," enigmatically as "*the teacher.*" And Cheryl Boone remembered a prolonged, semimystical experience from years earlier that culminated when she felt that "something evil was sitting on my chest and was trying to choke the life out of me." But her journal from the time, which she found for me at the end of the interview, revealed the strangler to be *her own hand,* a fact she had forgotten since the event.

For several interviewees, the imagery associated with the experience was "*nothing threatening*" (Alice Stephens), such as "people walking around me" (Adrienne Edmond), doctors and nurses (Zeinabu irene Davis), or someone "just playing with me" (Larry Martin).

It was almost as usual for interviewees to describe undergoing sleep paralysis without any presence, seen or sensed, and indeed without imagery of any sort apart perhaps from the room in which they were lying, or, in one case, colors covering the whole visual field (Ethel Smith). Some didn't even experience pressure or difficulty breathing, just paralysis. Some described a heaviness, a weight, a pressure, without imagery. Some spoke in images, but only as an imaginative way to convey their experiences: "a sensation like a mountain sitting on my chest" (Sandra Jackson-Opoku); "in a pit, with things piled on top of me" (Judy Still); "like suddenly all the air is vacuumed out" (Betty Holcomb); and so on. Several said they woke up with sleep paralysis following falling dreams (Josh Taifa, Devri Whitaker, Reggie Winfrey) or other bad dreams. In cases where the bad dream was a chase dream, the imagery of the pursuer did not persist as a presence into the waking state (Betty Holcomb, Norma Adams Wade), as might be anticipated.

Belief and Disbelief

Most interviewees flatly disbelieved that their experience of sleep paralysis could be blamed on anything like the witches of tradition. Norma Adams Wade said, "I don't relate that in my life at *all*." Gwen Robinson dismissed it as "part of the whole package of things people believe in." Devri Whitaker said:

> I've had witches on me before, but nobody believed there were actually witches sitting on you. And the way that my grandmother would say it was, "And that's what the old folks call having witches on you." And that's the end of it. She *knows* all the superstitions, you see. But they're absurd. [Grandmother would say,] "That's ridiculous, that don't make no sense."

Regina Reed and her family take spiritual manifestations very seriously. As for witches riding you, she has relatives who "felt it was another presence." However:

> I never felt the same thing. My mother doesn't either. The people in my family don't think it was a presence. It's almost like something within you, not that it's somebody else holding you.

A few interviewees were in a state of uncertainty or semibelief. Josh Taifa's mother told him he was having "the witch riding your back," and she believed it. Did he? "I don't know what to believe. I'm being honest. I try not to prejudge anything." Gloria Naylor said, "Maybe it *is* a spirit. It's still a mystery to me, you know. I haven't thought it through." Ayanna Udongo was uncertain what to make of the fact that saying "Jesus" made what seemed like a demonic presence disappear. After Laura McKnight asserted, "I don't believe in that, either. No supernatural thing," I mirrored back, "So you don't think it's supernatural at all." She responded, "No," then asked, "Is it?" showing that she was not entirely unaffected by the tradition she was familiar with. Another woman dismissed it as "a cliché," as "just something that the older folks would say." But after I described the physiological explanation of sleep paralysis, she asked, "So it's *not* witches riding me?" She was clearly seeking reassurance.

Only a very small number of interviewees professed outright belief. When I described the symptoms of sleep paralysis to Ivan Watkins, he asked if I meant "that I was being ridden?" Watkins "can definitely remember fighting very severe spiritual battles in my dream state." When I mentioned sleep paralysis to Kimberly Camp after she had related her encounters with cemetery spirits, she replied, "That's some of that Western European science. So okay, I was in sleep paralysis at the time. But there was a spirit in my room."

The Blood Circulation Theory

Before closing this chapter, another folk theory about the cause of witches riding you or sleep paralysis needs to be mentioned. Adrienne Edmond put forward "poor circulation" as an alternative explanation for her episodes. So did Gloria Naylor, who said, "Sometimes I think maybe it's just the circulation of your body, you know, playing tricks. And sometimes, you know, maybe it *is* a spirit." And the woman who sought reassurance that "it's *not* witches riding me?" also asked, "Is it your blood not circulating or something?" Marva Pitchford Jolly doesn't hold the theory herself, but two separate people told her it was "just probably poor circulation" when she described her episodes to them.

Two interviewees put forward impeded circulation as their sole theory. Douglas Gills said:

> Later in life, I figured out that they were physiological in nature, because of how your blood travels in your body. When I eat too much and then I go to bed and I sleep in the wrong position, then typically I'll get this presence on me.

Similarly, Ethel Smith said she believes episodes come from "circulation of your blood. That's a medical definition that I've heard about that." She has rejected the folk spiritual belief in favor of the folk medical belief.

If you believe you've been ridden by a witch—or had sleep paralysis—you should discuss it openly with trusted friends and family. You'll probably be surprised to learn that someone else has had the same thing happen. And if they're worried that the experience is dangerous or means they're mentally unbalanced in any way, you can let them know this isn't so. Children in particular should be reassured. Adolescence is the peak period in life for sleep paralysis. Tell your children that what they've undergone may be dramatic and frightening, but it's not abnormal or harmful. They should try to relax into it and let it run its course.

PART FOUR

Dreams about Race

13

THE SAME OLD NIGHTMARE

RACE IN DREAMS

The South has always frightened me. How deeply . . . was one of the things my dreams revealed to me while I was there.

—James Baldwin

Dreaming about race isn't woven into the fabric of the dream culture in the way that, for instance, predictive dreams or ancestor dreams are. The theme of race isn't traditional, as far as dreams go. There's only one type of dream involving race that you could say is common heritage: the dream of freedom and racial justice. Hopeful dreams of this type came up in connection with African American survival mechanisms (chapter 2) and again in connection with Reverend King's "I have a dream" speech (chapter 8). But even dreams with this important theme don't stand out in the collective consciousness.

This isn't to say that people don't dream about race. Perhaps the difference is that the dream themes we've discussed so far, from ancestors to numbers to witches, all are rooted in spiritual beliefs, while dreaming about race is first and foremost a reaction to the concrete world.

In any event, a profile of dreams in African American life wouldn't feel complete without coverage of the theme of race. Accordingly, this chapter will explore the various kinds of dreams about race that emerged from my interviews and, to begin, will consider just how much or little people do actually dream about race.

How Common Is It to Dream about Race?

To shed light on this question, I asked both my black interviewees and my white comparison group the same set of questions. The blacks were first asked, "Do *white characters ever* appear in your dreams?" All of 99 percent said yes. The whites were first asked, "Do *black characters ever* appear in your dreams?" Only 77 percent said yes. So while virtually all blacks have dreams in which whites appear, nearly a quarter of whites say that black characters *never* appear in their dreams.

The next question to blacks was "How *frequently* do whites appear in your dreams—never, seldom, sometimes, or often?" The corresponding question was put to whites. For blacks taken as a whole, the answers fall between "sometimes" and "often." But whites only dream of blacks a little more than "seldom." So blacks dream of whites quite a lot more frequently than whites do of blacks.

It's perfectly possible for another race to appear in a dream without race itself actually being an issue. So I next asked, "Are you ever aware of *race as an issue* in your dreams?" Only slightly more blacks than whites answered yes, 47 percent to 35 percent.

I then asked, "How *frequently* is race an issue in your dreams— never, seldom, sometimes, or often?" Both blacks and whites said race is "seldom" an issue in their dreams, but blacks dream of the issue a little more frequently.

With this information in hand, we can see whether someone whose dreams include the other race necessarily also dreams of race as an issue. And it turns out that for blacks there is *not* a significant correlation between these two factors, while for whites there is. In other words, blacks are more likely than whites to dream of someone of the other race without the race issue coming up in some way. This can be interpreted to mean that blacks can dream of whites as persons, not merely as representatives of their race, more easily than whites can dream of blacks as persons—this in spite of the fact that race issues come up a little more often in the dreams of blacks.

So to summarize what blacks and whites say about their own dreams: first, virtually all blacks dream of whites, but only some three-quarters of whites dream of blacks. Second, blacks more frequently dream of whites than whites do of blacks. And, third, blacks dream of the race issue a little more frequently than do whites. But lastly, whites are less able than blacks to dream of someone of the other race without race itself being an issue in the dream.

I had frankly expected that what John Edgar Wideman calls the "everyday nonsense, the poison . . . , the gray drizzle" of racism would show up in mostly all black people's dreams. So I was surprised by the number of blacks who said they never or almost never dream about race issues.

Don St. Cyr Toups responded to my question about race dreams by saying, "I would never have thought of that at all. I have never had any dream having either a racial conflict or just even a contrast." Toups was by no means alone in finding the question novel. "What a fascinating question!" mused Norma Adams Wade, for example. She has plenty of whites in her dreams, but no themes of race.

Homeless Larry Martin has dreams about selling *StreetWise* in the mostly white neighborhood where I met him, but never registers race in those or any other dreams. Charles Payne is a candidate Jungian analyst and a trained dream watcher. He can say that he has no dreams with race themes. LV Jordan and Devri Whitaker are each in interracial relationships, while Kai EL Zabar and Judy Still were born to interracial couples. They all say race is never an issue in their dreams.

Even people whose work brings them up against race issues on a daily basis don't, by their own assessment, necessarily ever dream about race. Interviewees in this group include the author of a book about her racially divided family (Shirlee Taylor Haizlip), the director of a museum of African American history (Gwen Robinson), the director of an African film festival (Alice Stephens), a black nationalist poet and educator (Haki Madhubuti), an imprisoned activist (Achim Rodgers), the publisher of a black magapaper (Hermene Hartman), and two journalists who specialize in African American issues (Salim Muwakkil, Richard Steele).

Even exposure to gross racism doesn't necessarily evoke the topic of race in dreams (but of course it sometimes does, as we'll see later). Darryl Burrows "lived through" the integration of the New Orleans public school system. "In my *conscious* mind," said Burrows, "this was major traumatic. But I never, ever, that I remember, dream about that." Oscar Edmond was a boy on the West Side of Chicago during the riots in 1968 following King's assassination. "I watched white people being thrown out of their cars and beaten," he recalled, "I saw National Guards, I saw flames—but I've never had bad dreams about white people or anything like that."

The interviewees offered several interesting conjectures about why African Americans don't dream about race issues more than they apparently do.

Osuurete Adesanya suggested that racism is "something that we don't see that we can change. So, I guess, we're not connected to it. It's not *on* our minds, like." The opposite point was also made: "Blacks talk about this problem, whites deny it. We deal with it with our eyes open, and it's not something we have to deal with while we're asleep."

Sara Lawrence-Lightfoot, who herself has race dreams, wondered "if dreaming's the one place where you can escape and not have that be the primary agenda."

Several interviewees surmised that the dreaming mind functions in "a truer reality" (Ivan Watkins) where the "socially constructed category" of race "doesn't make the cut" (John Edgar Wideman), or at least "isn't such a charged issue" (Maisha Hamilton-Bennett).

Wideman also speculated that blacks don't dream about race issues more than they do because race is less essential to their identities when compared with whites. "*We* haven't made this construction of race. We don't need it to tell us something about our identity. We don't *use* it in the same way that white people do." Toni Morrison talks about "the parasitic nature" of white identity. Whites, even in broad-minded families, grow up absorbing the idea at a very deep level that there's a group of people out there inferior to them. Whites incorporate the illusion of superiority. Black families, on the other hand, make a point of shielding their small children from affronts and of avoiding the mentality of comparison. Many whites will be surprised to learn that black children often first become aware of race at a later age than do white children. Consequently, black children carry a basic assumption of equality through their early development. This realistic assumption is built into the deep layers of personality where many dreams are spawned. Yet as we've seen, blacks dream about race issues a little more than whites do. That's presumably because the assumption of equality later gets challenged and sometimes defeated by the assaults of racism.

It's possible, of course, that people actually dream about race more, or less, than they remember or are willing to say. I can imagine whites underreporting race dreams to avoid an appearance of race antagonism—or overreporting to avoid an appearance of race exclusivity. As for blacks, Darice Wright Camp couldn't remember dreaming about race but deduced that she *must*, because "when you're very affected by something, you dream about it." LV Jordan was embarrassed that she had no race dreams to report. She supposed that all other black people do. Other interviewees with feelings like these may have claimed race dreams they didn't really remember. But on the other hand, some interviewees definitely underestimated their race dreams.

Winford Williams illustrates this. He said he never dreams about race, because he "never really let race be a major issue" in his life. Yet later, when I asked about dreams with anonymous transgressors in them (discussed later in this chapter), he remarked, "When I was [living] at home, we would say something like, 'I dreamed about this white man trying to chase me down the street,' or something like that." Similarly, Gloria Naylor, who boasted of an excellent memory for past dreams, could recollect none about race. But again, when I asked about anonymous transgressors, she remembered that in one dream there were house invaders who were "*white* men, thug-type people," and added, "Now that's interesting." Obviously she hadn't focused on the race of the invaders at the time, though it certainly struck her as significant now that she thought about it.

But regardless of how little or much people dream about race, the dreams they do have on this theme are important, because the issue itself is as persistent as it is in the waking world. Awareness of the theme of race in dreams will help individual dreamers to know themselves, and help all of us as observers of dreams to take the measure of our times. Now to the dreams.

Race Dreams

We'll first take our bearings by looking at symbolism in dreams—at race itself as a symbol of other things, and at other things as symbols of race.

Race as a Symbol of Something Else

Dreams often use symbols. A car may stand for the dreamer's progress through life. Is the road smooth or rough? Who is driving? Is the car under control? A house may represent the dreamer's own mind—a place with many layers, a place of deepest familiarity, but often with neglected or unexplored rooms. Some symbols seem to be universal, others get their meanings from cultural conventions, while most are generated from the personal life experience of the dreamer. Anything can be made into a symbol by the dreaming mind. And therefore race, like anything else, may stand for something other than itself in a dream.

Here's an example of race standing for something else. Ramon Giles related a couple of dreams about violent white men. In one, a white woman is pursued by her "angry, insanely violent" white husband. A female friend of the wife crushes the husband by toppling a huge alabaster statue onto him, but he rises and tries to crush his wife and the frightened dreamer in return.

Giles shared this dream with a friend, who suggested that it "had to do with fear, maybe not of white people per se, but of the changes in my life." Giles continued:

> You know, it's not even like you're dealing with the racial question.
> It's a personal issue. White people are usually manifestations of fear
> and anxiety in my dreams. The racial question of it is real vague. It's
> definitely using objects or people from your daily reality in your dreams
> to express something. They become part of a dream language.

Giles is very perceptive. But there's another angle to this. Symbols don't arise arbitrarily. When race does stand for something other than itself, there are reasons why the dreaming mind chooses that symbol. If skin color weren't loaded with conflict in this society, race couldn't have emerged as a symbol for Giles's nonracial conflicts. So even though Giles's dream isn't directly concerned with race, it nevertheless carries a racial, a societal meaning.

Furthermore, dream symbols very often carry more than just one meaning. The dreaming mind spontaneously spins out images and stories in which multiple currents of thought, memory, and feeling converge. Thus dreams in which race is a feature can easily be about race and about something else at the same time.

Ralph Ellison aptly described the convergence of personal and racial concerns in a fever dream that Richard Wright recorded in his autobiographical novel *Black Boy*:

> While delirious from this beating [by his mother] Wright was haunted
> "by huge wobbly white bags like the full udders of a cow, suspended
> from the ceiling above me and I was gripped by the fear that they were
> going to fall and drench me with some horrible liquid . . . "

> It was as though the mother's milk had turned acid, and with it the whole pattern of life that had produced the ignorance, cruelty and fear that had fused with mother-love and exploded in the beating. It is significant that the bags were of the hostile color white. . . .

In *Invisible Man,* Ellison himself craftily employed the taboo against black-man/white-woman sex as a dream symbol for the incest taboo.

A word of caution is in order here. When interpreting race as a symbol of something else, there's the danger of taking real concerns about society and distorting them into something merely personal, merely psychological. African Americans have historical reasons for associating dream interpretations of this kind with racism. The time isn't long past when a psychiatrist (a white psychiatrist) might construe a dream about "social rebellion," for example, as showing "upsurging of sexual impulses" or something of that sort, without even considering the dreamer's desire for social change. I'm sure Ralph Ellison meant to parody this posture with that dream about the incest taboo.

John Edgar Wideman told me an old dream of his about seducing Lady Bird Johnson on stage while President Johnson is giving a civil rights speech. The dreamer "gets away" with it, and takes "great satisfaction" from compromising Johnson. A psychiatrist might say the dream was an incest fantasy (president = father, president's wife = mother). But even if that element was there, Wideman was fully justified in thinking his dream was "about the sixties and integration, and Lyndon Johnson, and black-white sexual roles."

Something Else as a Symbol of Race

Just as race can symbolize some other thing in a dream, so other things can symbolize race. Eileen Cherry said that her rage about racism doesn't come out directly in her dreams. Instead, she dreams about "raw meat. You know, like rawness?"

Reggie Winfrey has dreams about Farmer Vincent from the horror movie *Motel Hell.* Farmer Vincent cuts the insides out of a pig's head, puts it on, and comes after him. Winfrey said these dreams are about "civil rights" and "blacks being abused by whites."

Leon Forrest talked about "the nightmarish quality" for blacks of "getting shortchanged on the American Dream." He has dreams of "attempting to get over a certain abyss, hump, or something that symbolizes that travail. And only to run into a maze."

Dorothy Carter had a dream symbolically revealing to her the beauty or specialness of all the lives hidden behind the bleak walls of housing projects in segregated Chicago. Or perhaps the dream was simply blessing those lives:

> I had a dream where I was driving down Cottage Grove, past this housing project, and in every window there was a huge orchid. You know, like as big as the window? If you looked in, it was just a huge orchid, in these housing projects in every window.

Several interviewees told of dreams in which colors symbolize race themes in various ways. Until she was twenty, Kimberly Camp had "terrifying" dreams about "little orange men that live in the walls." They smelled like Aqua Velva and had crew cuts, and would "try to get" her. Why orange? "In school [we were] told that orange was the crayon for white people."

Another woman related a self-explanatory dream with symbolic colors that recurred through her adolescence. She said the dream felt both playful and stressful:

> It was just all these little white dots, and this one black dot. And they would just form all of these various configurations, and the black dot was trying to figure out how to fit into the configurations that the white dots were making.

Angela Jackson had a dream in which symbolic colors were combined with another racially meaningful symbol, flying:

> I was involved in the black student movement. I had a dream of flying then. And wearing red, black, and green, the black national colors— flying and wearing those colors. It was a very happy dream. A confident dream. A victorious dream. Some confidence in my ability to overcome as an African American person. Then, confidence in our collective ability to transcend, to fly.
>
> I understand that flying dreams are important to most people, but flying as a motif in African American cultural tradition is very important. Look at Toni Morrison's novel *Song of Solomon*, where the character in the end learns how to fly, and that was the secret of the ancestors that he had gone in search of. Where flying is a part of our overall Western articulation of the idea of victory, it has an additional meaning in African American tradition.

Jackson was referring to the folk motif, upon which Morrison improvised, of captive Africans who reversed the Middle Passage by flying home over the ocean to freedom. While blacks dream of flying no more than do whites—about three-fourths of both races have flown in dreams—the motif carries special associations for black dreamers.

There is a grim companion to this dream of Jackson's in James Baldwin's novel *Another Country*. Baldwin used the black national colors to paint, not "victorious" flight, but a defeated fall. The dream follows the death of the black character, Rufus, who has killed himself by jumping from a bridge. His white friend, Vivaldo, dreams:

> Then Rufus came hurtling from the air, impaling himself on the far, spiked fence which bounded the meadow. . . . Vivaldo watched Rufus' blood run down, bright red over the black spikes, into the green meadow.

Dreams about Black Identity

While every dream sheds light on the identity of the dreamer, some dreams have identity as their organizing theme. Such dreams epitomize who the dreamer "is" at that moment in time, and may give the dreamer a direction for future change. Race, as one component of identity, occasionally appears as the lead motif of identity dreams.

Angela Jackson's "victorious" dream of flying in the black national colors is a straightforward affirmation of black identity. So is Preston Jackson's dream celebrating blackness that is at the front of this book. But the majority of dreams are driven by doubts and conflicts, and dreams about black identity are no different.

In his memoir of a journey of discovery through the South, northerner Eddy Harris tells how he dozed in a restaurant and had a dream. He hears spirituals, then blues. A black shoeshine boy approaches. Black men in a barbershop beckon—but are they beckoning him, or the boy? The boy represented the latent southern black identity Harris was searching for. The dream asked a question: Will I find my true black self?

Sara Lawrence-Lightfoot's mother, Margaret, a psychoanalyst with a successful private practice, decided to return to Harlem Hospital, where she had worked twenty-one years earlier, following a dream whose message she couldn't resist: "I was walking along happily cuddling a brown baby in my arms. I looked down. To my horror I had dropped her." The brown baby probably represented both the needy patients of Harlem whom Margaret Lawrence had "dropped," and her own neglected black identity, as she felt it to be at the moment of the dream.

Author Audre Lorde described a dream containing the striking image of an egg-shaped watermelon with turquoise glowing brilliantly at its core. The dream showed Lorde the beauty and value of black identity, as symbolized by the watermelon—a food her family disdained because of its stereotyped associations. This radiant image is "a promise of hope" embedded in a frightening dream that Lorde titled "The Last of My Childhood Nightmares." At the end of the dream, she finds herself "free to go."

Conflicts over allegiance come up in black identity dreams. Adekola Adedapo "went through the black power thing" in the 1960s, but had many good white friends:

> So I just couldn't deal with the "Let's throw all white folks out the window." And plus, I'm *looking* like one! I used to have real, real intense dreams, and I would be caught in the middle. Like maybe the revolution was happening and there would be guns pointed at the people, and I might be sitting there at the gate. Or there would be some division, a divided room, or an aisle, or even a barbed wire fence. And it was like, make a choice. And I used to wake up tense.

Today black people are still having dreams about divided loyalties or being caught between. Angela Powell has a white girlfriend and considers herself "multiracial." She's "had nightmares about black people beating me up, because I'm a honky-lover." Zachary Brown works in mainstream institutions, mostly dates white women, and has two half sisters whose father is white. He dreamed that South African rioters reprimand him for his white associations, then kill him, along with the well-meaning white American student whose death at the hands of rioters had just been in the news. The rioters represented unfair black disapproval—or Brown's own bad conscience. Brown also had a dream in which one of his sisters berates him for preferring white women.

Another set of conflictual black identity dreams involve conflicts around money and status. After her divorce, Frances Callaway Parks's life went through many changes. She took a job teaching at Howard University. While staying with her children at her ex-mother-in-law's house in a poor neighborhood of Washington, D.C., she had the following dream. She's taking the garbage out when she finds herself in a totally strange place, and "lost." Soon she's standing in front of "two displays." One shows "a room out of the twenties or thirties," miserably furnished, where "everything is gray." The second display shows a brilliant lobby "like the Kennedy Center" where elegantly dressed people "of all races" are "just talking!" They're "having a great time." The dreamer is now distracted by a rich white yuppie couple. They look at the gray "showcase of poverty" and say, "Oh. That's how they [blacks] used to live." Eventually the dreamer enters the "happy" display. But "of course, nobody could see me."

On one side was displayed the dreary poverty that had "always been a big fear" for Parks, who grew up in a poor black neighborhood—like the part of Washington she was staying in. On the other side was displayed the secure, cultured world she aspired to, a world where she still felt like a spectator ("nobody could see me"). At that transition point in her life, Parks felt "lost" between, and at risk of relapse into black poverty.

Here is another black identity dream involving money and status conflict. Sylvia Morris is a classical musician who also runs her own agency that contracts prominent names in popular music for performances. She dreams she's driving to her violin lesson, but gets lost because she's "very tired" and "not focused," and "not that familiar with Chicago streets." Now she finds herself standing on the roadside without a car. A "huge black car" drives up:

> The car door opens and they say, "Get in." But it was a hearse! And inside the hearse was a very friendly gentleman, black, with a baseball cap. Very slight, very unthreatening in his demeanor, very smiley, and he just says to me, "Come on in." And there's a woman in the backseat. She looks like she's been drinking. They seem like they've been out partying. And she's also like . . . watching him pick me up, kinda like they're friends or brother and sister, and she's like, "Oh boy, look at this!" And she says, "Come on! Come on!"

The dreamer gets in, because she's lost and she doesn't want to walk. But then she gets out again, because these people make her uncomfortable. And then she gets back in again. "And I don't remember what happens."

Morris said the woman in the backseat reminded her of a drunken, toothless older woman she sees selling newspapers. She identified the man as the type working for her valet service: "At least once a day, black gentlemen who are slight and wear baseball caps pick me up in my car, which is a black car and has been nicknamed the Hearse."

Morris is ambitious and successful, but "not that familiar" with the strange territory her career has placed her in. If she gets "tired" and loses "focus," she could lose herself. Temptation enters, in the guise of lower-class blacks who party and offer sexual adventure. She vacillates, getting into and out of and into the car, the "hearse," and in the end doesn't know what happens. The dream depicted what for the moment was an unresolved dilemma: the hearse represented the dead end she saw as the fate of blacks who lose focus and don't get ahead, but also represented a lifeless alienation from impulse and spontaneity which felt to her like the price her ambition was exacting.

Finally, let's look at a dream that shows race just beginning to surface as an identity issue. Matthew Stephens is a bright eighteen-year-old of mixed black and white parentage, and a "hip-hopper." He asserted that race has never been very much of an issue in his life, much less a negative issue, and that he's never aware of the race of dream characters. Stephens told me that since he was small, he's had recurring dreams of being half immersed in a "humongous" living machine. "It's almost like liquid—biological—machinery." In these dreams he feel restricted, "without freedom." Stephens then told a recent dream that began in the huge tunnel of a supercollider, near the device that fires the molecule. It was "kinda cool" there, he said, but he was anxious about being hit by the molecule. The dream scene then shifted:

> Next thing I knew, I was in a building. It didn't have any windows. It was set up very much like my high school, in terms of different floors and corridors. There were rooms with doors, connecting with each other. I was walking through these rooms. I was seeing these people, just kinda being there. Both female and male, white and black, and any other difference that you can think of. It was not necessarily as tense as the other dream I was talking about, but also some sort of unsureness, but kind of adventurous, and real curiosity.

This dream strikes me as an evolution of the earlier, recurring dreams of being half trapped in a living machine. The living machine was, I imagine, both a symbol of the womb and of Stephens's identity, his self. Those dreams showed him struggling but unable to break out of a childlike attachment to reach the next stage of his development. The supercollider, another self symbol, is also huge and confining, but it contains a strong masculine symbol, the molecule shooter, which is at the same time an engine of transformation. And suddenly he finds himself in a higher space, a "high school." He still has no clear way to relate to the world—there are no windows—but there are at least differentiations—levels, corridors, and doors. And now his self has room for other people. He's still unsure of himself, but things are "connecting with each other." This self-state dream shows Stephens maturing, moving from childhood to manhood, and from unconsciousness to consciousness. But what's of interest here, he's now aware in his dream of black and white people. Race isn't a focus of the dream, but it emerges as one of the factors he must deal with in the development of his personality from its simpler child state.

Race-Change Dreams

This type of dream gives an interesting twist to the issue of black identity. During his childhood in the South, Sterling Plumpp once dreamed a happy dream in which he and his family were white. Plumpp interpreted this dream as a wish to escape all the limitations imposed by color prejudice. Carole Morisseau has dreams about great accomplishments such as becoming president. Sometimes she's white, sometimes raceless. Both conditions wish away the obstacle of race.

But dreams of being white aren't usually so simple. Young Illana Jordan dreamed in high school of "wearing a white mask and just going about my daily business." She first recalled this dream when she observed white masks like the one in the dream actually being made by an acting class. But she also told me it was an almost daily feature of her school life for other blacks to accuse her of "acting white." So this seems to be a wishful dream that pushes the dreamer to evaluate the wish.

Regina Reed dreamed she was a little white girl going to a state fair with her father and sister, also white in the dream. "Everything was beautiful, except for us." The family was "very poor." She and her sister had on "raggedy dresses." Perhaps this dream says, Be careful what you wish for, you may get it. In another dream, Reed was white and flying with three white angels, who were her family. They wanted her to go on with them, but "I was like, 'No, I need to stay.'" Her angel family "just flew away to heaven, and I stayed on earth." In this dream white is idealized, but Reed resists the idealization and stays "on earth," that is, stays grounded in reality. For her to identify too closely with white, pictured as flying high, would—to combine these two dreams—prove impoverishing.

The message of staying grounded in her own heritage and community was again conveyed to Reed by another race-change flying dream, this one from just a week before our interview. It marked the first return of a recurring dream after many years. In those dreams from Reed's childhood, she would find herself in Europe, always in some grand setting such as a cathedral. The current dream pictured the grandeur of nature. Reed was flying above European mountain peaks. And on all the peaks stood "people who were different parts of myself, but they were white! And everyone was painting and just basically artistically expressing themselves. And I thought, 'This is beautiful. I'm glad to be back.'"

Now the dream took a novel turn. Two white men flew into the scene, attempting to spy on her in her "sacred place." So she flew away. They chased her to an institution where men were in control and women served. She felt sorry for the women, but knew she didn't "belong in an institution." So she escaped. Suddenly she was home, and "everybody was black." She had a "beautiful day." She went to dinner with friends, then to a park with her family. There, as she was teaching her niece magic to make balloons fly, one "stubborn" balloon "became *me*." After refusing to respond, the balloon suddenly "turned into a bird, and into the lady that I was originally on the flight."

Reed, who wants to be a poet, had just recently returned to Detroit from the East, where for several years she had risen successfully in a mainly white corporation. The racist, sexist institution of the dream represents her new perception of the "European" (white) grandeur she idealized as a child. In going east she had, she said, "forced myself to be in structures that didn't fit," that didn't allow her to be "as free as I need to be." The dream told her that flying high in some faraway place wouldn't make her free; she had to come back to her roots. "And you know," she said, "that's why I'm here."

In a variant of the race-change dream, instead of anyone changing skin color, the races exchange roles. "I've dreamed about *them* having no power, period," one woman gloated. "My race had all of the power, and they were like the subjects. Everything was reversed, totally! Everything!" Langston Hughes's ironic poem "Cultural Exchange" begins, "Dreams and nightmares!/Nightmares, dreams, oh!/Dreaming that the Negroes/of the South have taken over—" And in one of Hughes's Simple stories, Simple hilariously describes a delightful recurring dream in which he's "the ruler of Dixie." But it's only a dream: "It were daybreak in Harlem, and I woke up to the same old nightmare."

Dreams Assessing Racism

Judy Still's father, composer William Grant Still, dreamed he was "trying to talk about brotherhood to a white southerner who was badly disposed, and awoke crying." Still had recurring dreams about being refused service in stores and diners, and about having to use back entrances at hotels or at concert halls where his own music was being performed.

Still's dreams predate the Civil Rights movement. Today, people continue to have dreams directly about racism. In Colleen McElroy's recurring dreams, there's violence in the streets, sometimes a race riot. She's in danger because she's black. She flees toward a gate, or a border. McElroy said these dreams are "reality based":

> Sometimes it's because I'm working through a situation [involving racism] that really is occurring. Sometimes it's alerting me to the possibility of what can occur—Be careful! I know it's always sort of under the surface of any number of situations. People say, "I'm so surprised that conservatism is on the rise," and I say, "You know, I don't think it ever went away."

Carole Morisseau's husband dreamed they were having a big party in a hotel room. Someone knocked. He went to the door. It was a little white girl. She was lost:

> And so he told her, "You've got to find your mother and father," and closed the door! He didn't want no trouble! And then she knocked again, and I opened the door. And I said, "Your mother and father, are they here?" And she said that she couldn't see her family. And so my husband said, "Okay, we're getting out of here!" So we packed up our stuff, and we just left. Closed the door, left all the people in there partying and the little girl and everything else, and we left.

This dream invites various psychological interpretations. But whatever the dream may reflect at the personal level about Morisseau's husband, it sheds a glaring light on race relations. Morisseau herself made this plain by empathizing with her husband's response in the dream. "That was his safety mechanism working for him," she said:

> If there's a lost white child, I'm not gonna do anything for that lost white child. I want to help, but out of your own self-preservation as a black person, you'll go and say, "Hey, So-and-so, look, there's that child over there, they need help." I'm not gonna take that child by the hand.

At this point, Morisseau suddenly remembered something. "That's funny," she mused, "I had almost that little experience just yesterday." And she told me about a situation that had arisen at the "very nice yacht club" she belongs to in which she responded essentially like her husband in his dream:

> There was a little white girl asleep on two chairs, and her mother—they went over to the poolside. And so there were about three black people

sitting there together, and there was a white friend, he was sitting with us, too. And so anyway, the child woke up and just looked around and didn't recognize anybody—and she probably saw all these black faces and freaked out, too. But I'm the first one that saw the child crying, but my guard went up, I said, "*I'm* not gonna take care of that child!" I hit my white friend, I said, "Hey, she's crying! I think that's her mother over there."

Sheron Williams-Brooks dreamed about racism when she was up for a full-time professorship and preparing herself for the final interview, a dinner meeting with the college president. Her rival was a white man. She dreamed that she and her family were seated at a large table across from the white rival, who was flanked by everyone in the administration reviewing her for the position—all white. Instead of food, spread out on the table was the professorship along with everything else she wanted in life. The rival cried, "It's mine!" and scooped it all up:

And I said, "But there's nothing left on the table for me. What's for me?" And I felt left out, and I was hungry. And the guy across the table says, "You have to go to bed hungry." And I said, "I'll be *damned* if I'll be hungry." And so, as they were leaving the table, I began to pick up the scraps, and to try to make myself something edible from what was left.

Williams-Brooks is one of the few interviewees to say she dreams about race "all the time." She told this dream as an example, but also commented upon it as a predictive warning dream. Her grandmother, with whom she shared the dream, said, "It doesn't look good for you," and advised her to change the date of her final interview. The date couldn't be changed. The position went to the white candidate.

When I met with a group of children at the Cabrini Green housing project, a boy related his dream about "a war between white people and black people":

White people were trying to come take CHA [Chicago Housing Authority] high-rises, and all the black people come outside, be protesting. We were like "Hell no, we won't go!" But it was a scary dream. There was blood, everywhere.

I asked how the dream ended. "A lot of people died. We kept the buildings. And then Bill Clinton came, and we popped him in the head." When I asked what the dream might be about, the children had no hesitation connecting it to the very real plans afoot to demolish Cabrini Green, supposedly for the good of the residents. But the children viewed the plans as a threat, and the dream as a prediction. The dreamer said, "It's gonna be true, I know that. They're already trying to get at it." Another child: "They've already torn two buildings down!" And another: "They're taking black people off public aid, all that. Trying to have us move to the suburbs. When we go out to the suburbs, they're gonna come take that. And if they put us out with no place to live, there's gonna be a war for real."

Dreams of Interracial Harmony

In the early 1950s, a depressed patient dreamed she was being poisoned by the little black and white elephants she was eating. She thought the dream symbolized her poisonous hatred for both blacks and white—blacks, because she hated seeing herself as one, and whites, because that was the way they saw her, as black. But further along in treatment, the woman dreamed she was down home and walking along "with her arms around a white and a Negro. She was able to turn a corner without looking backward and without anxiety."

Dreams like this one depicting interracial harmony are unusual. The only other straight-out example I've come across belongs to a prisoner. He described himself as coming from the poorest county of the poorest state, Mississippi. He wrote:

> I growed up in a town totally segregated from white. The only contact with them came on a job site. I never had any contact with white boy or girl my age. I didn't notice it until later on in life. In this dream I go to school with whites, I play with them. I also bring them home with me to play and I visit their house to play. In this dream there is no racism.

Ethel Smith, a novelist, was reading Dorothy West's *The Wedding*, and was touched by West's dedication of the novel to Jacqueline Kennedy Onassis, who as an editor at Doubleday had encouraged West to write the book, her first since the Harlem Renaissance. That night Smith dreamed of Jacqueline Kennedy receiving guests in the remodeled White House, with Dorothy West as the guest of honor. Possibly the dream expressed Smith's desire for recognition by the *white*-dominated publishing *houses*, or some more personal issue, but it also concerned interracial respect and friendship.

Here is a qualified example of interracial harmony in a dream. Dorothy Carter claimed she never has dreams with "racial content," and if she dreams of whites at all, it is never as main characters. Yet whites were conspicuous in one of her most fondly remembered dreams.

> I was in a cabin, like out in the woods, or on a mountain, and there were all these people and we were having this great party, and there was so much love and affection, it was the greatest. Just a great gathering of . . . of people. And the top came off of the house, and all the stars in the sky rained down on all of us, all the people. It was beautiful.

However, the dream treated white people differently from the rest. They looked "like Veronica [from *Archie* comics], like TV figures, or something." Her dreaming mind could not produce an image of universal love without conceding a place to white people, but they were only admitted to the party in a caricatured or stylized form that kept them psychologically distanced.

Dreams of Whites as Contaminants

The following dream was published in 1939. The dreamer, a long-time Baptist, had recently become a "Holy Roller" convert:

> She dreamed that she went to the home of a Sanctified woman whom she knew slightly, and that it was a fine large house. She walked back into the kitchen, and the woman told her to go to the spring and get some water. She went to the spring, but when she got there the heads and upper parts of the dead bodies of white men were floating in it. Some child whom she did not know told her to drink of the water, but she felt that she could not with the dead men in it. Among others there was the head of Master Ronald, the son of the white mistress on the plantation where she had sharecropped. The strange child kept telling her she must drink. She did not want to drink but finally forced herself to do so, and it was terrible to taste.

The house of religion is welcoming, but spirituality (the spring) is contaminated for the dreamer by her experience of whites. And the white corpses are all men. I'd guess that the dreamer was molested by Master Ronald when she was the age of the child in the dream. She had to integrate that trauma in order to purge herself of fear and hatred. The child is both her "inner child" and the Christ child, guiding her toward acceptance.

Ann Eskridge thought the following dream was warning her to watch out for some white woman, either "somebody I knew, or somebody I *would* meet." Be that as it may, the dream seems to express feelings Eskridge has about white people in general:

> There were these beautiful steps that led down to water and mountains and trees. I was the only black person there, and these three or four people were white, and they were getting sick around me. And they kept saying they had to get out. And I became very frightened. So we ran back up the steps and outside, where they continued to be sick. And I realized that I wasn't. And it just dawned on me that I was sup-posed to be in that serene place, and that *they* were the ones that weren't supposed to be there, and they had tricked me out of it. And I was looking at this woman whose face morphed! From blond, blue eyes to being very grotesque. And I realized that these people were evil! And people have told me when they've had nightmares, to say the Lord's Prayer. So I began saying the Lord's Prayer to wake myself up from this.

The spoiling of the "serene place" for Eskridge by sick whites parallels the fouling of the spring in the previous dream. The sickness afflicting the whites is, I assume, racism.

Dreams of a White Baby

A woman in psychotherapy dreamed she was hospitalized. "Somebody forcibly reached into my vagina and brought out a white baby." The dreamer apparently harbored a fear that the psychotherapist was impregnating her with an alien white identity. In a Cecil Brown novel, a woman pregnant by her white lover has "nightmares about having a white baby." Her dreams prompt her to embrace her blackness. In these dreams about the birth of white babies to black mothers, we can see an element of race change and also an element of white contamination.

During my interviews, I heard two dreams about white babies. Neither dream involves the birth of the baby, but both do involve sinister transformations—a sort of figurative birth. And again, white babies seem to represent danger to the personality from something alien. Both dreamers were children. First, Sandra Jackson-Opoku's eight-year-old son told her "this fascinating dream":

> He says that the basement of his grandmother's house represents something sinister. And that he went down there, and a white baby doll was under the stairs, and it started coming to life. It didn't get him. You know, I think he said he wound up beating it to death.

And Kimberly Camp—she who dreamed of orange men coming out of the walls—was "terrified of Frankenstein" as a child and had recurring dreams about him:

> Frankenstein always started out in my dreams as a little white baby with big brown eyes. In a crib. And the pupils in his eyes would be just a little too big. And I'd have to turn my back. For some reason, I'd have to take my eyes off that little bugger. And he'd become Frankenstein.

Dreams of Being an Outsider in a White World

Lori Kinnard lives in a white neighborhood and works among whites as an accountant's office manager. She said that the characters in her dreams are all black, because "the people who are important in my life, they're black." But she qualified this: "There are white people in my dreams. But they're usually . . . background people." As an example of this, she told me a dream where she's in a house with white women who are having a party. The women are "just talking," while she herself is "sort of a spectator." I asked what her feelings were in the dream. She felt "on the outside. Not a part of it." She wasn't even sure in the dream "if they knew I was in the room." Kinnard now reflected that she'd gone to a mostly white college, where she felt "uncomfortable, insecure." She'd first had that "uncomfortable feeling," she said, when she moved from a black grade school to a white high school.

So while the whites in her dreams may be "background figures" in the sense of not having individual identities, Kinnard really feels that *she* is a background figure as far as the white world surrounding her is concerned.

Angie Williams has similar dreams. She said "the central characters" of her dreams are always black, while the whites, if any, are "usually bystanders." But then she added, "Mostly, it's me watching them." She told a dream about sitting in the stands with a black friend watching as white athletes compete. In other words, *she* is the "bystander."

One of the board members of the private agency where Sherry McKinney is employed as a social worker gave her tickets to a philanthropic banquet. She took a white friend, and found herself the only black amid about two hundred "very wealthy people." She was "very, very uncomfortable." Later she had "the worst nightmare." She's at the banquet again, except the speaker is talking about her and pointing her out, and everyone is looking at her curiously. She's "scared," but she can't leave because her table is now in the center of the hall. McKinney was reminded of her school days, when the white students "looked at me in that way, too." This dream shows how assaultive it can be to be looked at, not as a person but as a race, even if there's no hostility.

Being looked at is also a feature in Ivan Watkins's outsider dream. Watkins is the organizer of a festival celebrating mixed African American and Native American heritage. He told me a dream he'd had during "a very difficult breakup." The girl was white. Her family liked him, but couldn't approve an interracial relationship. "And we were dealing with that in the dream, but we were like in a spirit of defiance."

In the dream, Watkins and his girl are arm-in-arm in Saks Fifth Avenue, feeling "really happy." Suddenly a white guy "catches her eye." She drifts toward the guy "in a trance." "Hey!" the dreamer protests. "What the hell you doing?" She comes to, sees the dreamer, and says sadly, sympathetically, "You know this will never last anyway." She walks away with the white guy, leaving the dreamer in a jealous fury.

> And I can remember looking around and suddenly feeling totally alienated in this environment. I realized I was probably the only black person in the store. And the people around me had seen what had happened, were looking at me like, "Huh! See what you get?" You know? And I just snapped. I was like, "Fuck you! What the hell you looking at!" And when I did that, then everybody looked at me, right? And I was like, "Fuck all of you! What're you looking at? Don't look at me!" And people started responding to me either by looking more or looking away 'cause they felt threatened or whatever.

He ends up "throwing a complete temper tantrum." He smashes everything, fights off security guards, and walks out. "And I remember waking up feeling good!"

Something this dream shares with many other outsider dreams is the symbolic significance of space—rooms, restaurants, halls, sports facilities, and so on. The dreamer, if visible at all, is a stranger, an intruder in someone else's territory.

Dreams of Humiliation

The feeling of humiliation, a feature of many outsider dreams, shows up in other dreams as well. For example, in the 1930s a man dreamed that a judge laughs superciliously down at black prisoners as he decides their fates. And in the 1960s, a friend told Claude Brown (*Manchild in the Promised Land)* about his nightmares, to persuade Brown not to work in New York's garment district:

> "Man, if you keep goin' downtown every day, you'll be a boy all your life. I used to have nightmares, man, about bein' old . . . and almost bent . . . sweeping the floors for Goldberg in that dress house of his. He's comin' in there pattin' me on my back and callin' me 'boy,' sayin' 'Come over here with your broom and sweep up this thing for me, boy.' It use to get to me. I use to jump up out of bed screamin', 'Mr. Goldberg, please, Mr. Goldberg, don't call me boy. . . . Please, Mr. Goldberg, don't pat me on my back.' "

Humiliation was expressed in the dream of a Boston child in the 1970s. The girl's family was scraping by, awaiting the unjustly delayed settlement of an insurance claim for the father's death. In the dream, a presidential candidate comes to their home and says he's there to help. But instead of the long-awaited settlement, he hands the child's mother a worthless and ridiculous toy. The mother humiliates both herself and the resentful dreamer by acting obsequiously grateful to the patronizing candidate.

Osuurete Adesanya had a dream in which humiliation is portrayed by literal belittlement. Adesanya teaches at a minority public school. The dream concerns a racist fellow teacher there who actually says things like, "These kids will never learn. They're just like all the other ones." And he criticizes Adesanya for using Afrocentric materials to complement the curriculum. In the dream

> he was pointing his finger at me and telling me to do something. And the more he pointed at me, the smaller I was getting. I was getting *small!* He was going off on me about something, I was getting smaller and smaller, and I remember I started throwing books at him. That's all I remember. I don't know if I disappeared.

Dreams of Protest

In the 1930s, a southern woman dreamed of

> being at a meeting of white people and of being introduced as "Mrs." A white man arose in the audience and objected. She was terribly angry and argued, saying that she *was* married, that she was a mother, and that her standards of personal behavior were as high in every respect as those of white women who are called "Mrs." without question.

John Dollard, the sociologist who collected this dream, deviated from the prevailing dream theories of his day—and of this day, for that matter—in recognizing that "dreams and fantasies are as much social acts as blows and manifestoes." Dollard regarded this dream as a social safety valve, a substitute for actual protest. In waking life, the woman "would not have dared to protest in this way." That's no doubt true. But in hindsight we can also see her dream, and the thousands like it we can imagine, as *practice* in sleep for the social protests of following decades.

Edward Moore is gay. At one time he had a white lover with stereotyped ideas about blacks. The lover thought that Moore's educated manner must be fake, "that at some point this veneer would crack and he would see a homeboy." Moore was offended. He finally broke it off, but without explaining why. But the whole thing continued to bother him, and he regretted his silence. Now Moore "had a number of dreams where I discussed with him specifically what bothered me." These dreams ended after

> I ran into him, and we actually had a similar conversation. He said something that offended me, and I just jumped on him immediately, where I used to ignore it.
> *Well, you'd rehearsed your lines.*
> Exactly! I knew exactly what to say!

Dreams with Historical Themes

Sandra Jackson-Opoku has written a story based entirely on a dream about a newly arrived slave, a "crazy nigger" who "refuses to be broken." Richard Hunt has also dreamed about slavery. While working on a sculpture to commemorate the Middle Passage, Hunt dreamed he escapes from a slave ship near a coast. And Diane Dujon dreams recurrently "of what it's like to be a slave," the "fear," the "work," the "other slaves," the need for "pretending you're something other than you are," and "trying to figure out what's really going on."

Osuurete Adesanya dreamed she watches from the bushes as the KKK tortures and burns someone. Several interviewees who lived through the Civil Rights era told dreams about the confrontations, lynchings, and assassinations of those years. Reggie Winfrey was born after King's "I have a dream" speech, but dreamed about being there. The scene shifts to Memphis. King is on the motel balcony, and the dreamer sees a man with a gun.

History is alive in the dreams of contemporary African Americans. I can almost imagine that the outlines of black history could be reconstructed from the evidence of dreams.

Each of the dreams just related was set in the historical past. But dreams set in the present can also contain historical themes. Historical elements show up in contemporary scenarios, adding subtle dimensions of meaning. In a dream of Angela Shannon Preston's, for example, escape from slavery was transposed to a modern city, Tampa, her hometown:

> It was before sunrise, and we were trying to sneak my brother to the airport, for some reason. And there weren't any white people around, but it was still that sense, almost—It was 1990, but it could easily have been during slavery time. You know, it was the same feeling, the same tension, that we have to sneak him away.

Preston offered no interpretation, but one is suggested by another dream of hers. She and her extended family are all captured in her grandmother's house by two white men, who beat one of her male relatives. The dreamer is aware that the fear engendered by this beating is all that prevents them from escaping. Then, in the middle of the night, a wooden carving of an old slave in the corner of the room comes alive. The old man tells her "to come through the door." The dreamer urges her sisters to join her, but they're afraid, they won't,

> so I had to leave by myself. That was one of the most upsetting things. I was running down this street, and all I could remember was, I could never go back. And I think that has a lot to do with me feeling removed now when I visit. 'Cause I only go there once a year, and I don't think I've been there within two years now. When I go, I'm not as close as I used to be.

The dream about her brother at the Tampa airport came before Preston left the South, this second dream after she'd left. Both dreams are about family, and both make reference to slavery. In addition, both are pervaded by an atmosphere of intimidation, both have male figures at risk, both move toward escape/departure, and both have symbols of transition—the airport, the door. These dreams evidently concern Preston's conflicting feelings about leaving home and establishing an independent life. The motif of slavery seems to represent the constraints of her family's character upon her drive for independence. It may well also represent the racial atmosphere of the South, and, indeed, the effect of the South and southern history upon the family character. She had to leave. A spirit from the slave past, emblematic of the thirst for freedom and spiritual transformation, helps her "come through." At the same time, she experiences something akin to survivor guilt for leaving her family behind in a condition her dreams liken to slavery.

Here is another dream set in the present but containing an historical element. Anthony Shy dreamed he's back living with his parents. A preapproved VISA card comes for him in the mail. An accompanying catalog offers all the things he likes, camping supplies, computers, and the like. But excitement turns to dismay when he finds that the back half of the catalog sells Klan apparel. The scene shifts to a cabin. A white woman from work is there. She looks like Aunt Bee from the *Andy Griffith Show*. He tells her with consternation, "They'd have to know I'm black!" Now he looks at the card. It has a picture of him in a chair flanked by men in white sheets. One is pointing a gun at his head, and he has "this really horrible grimace" on his face. He tells "Aunt Bee" that he doesn't remember taking the picture, that he doesn't want the card. But Aunt Bee tempts him: "Don't you want the cash?" He wavers, decides he'll take the cash, but will need a gun to protect himself. He runs to town half naked through snowy woods and goes from store to store trying to buy a gun. In one store, some white men playing a video game spot him: "Hey, isn't that the guy?" A pickup truck pulls up outside, "Klan guys" walk in:

> They talk to some black guys, and they're like, "Oh, wow, cool! It's the Klan! Check it out!" And I'm like, "This is bad." They were looking for me because I was gonna take their money. And one of the black guys says, "He's not the guy. That guy's with the rap group, CD-4." And at that point, my friend Steve is there, and he starts to rap, to show that I'm not the guy, that we're rappers.

This dream is a capsule of life today, from a certain angle: the flux of consumer products, virtual money, electronic images in superabundance. Like many of us, Shy is simultaneously a critic and a creature of consumer affluence. His lifestyle is highly integrated; he has suffered little from gross racism. But racism lurks in the background. Shy had this dream after inexplicably finding himself on the National Rifle Association's mailing list and receiving right-wing and paramilitary junk mail. Suddenly the old stories about the KKK acquired a new authenticity. The dream posed urgent questions, the largest being, What is real? Within that question were embedded the questions about race: Is my security an illusion? Am I really accepted by this society? Could that kind of violence happen again? Could it happen to me?

Trauma Dreams

Post-traumatic stress disorder has been much publicized in connection with combat veterans, but it can afflict anyone who undergoes a terrible experience, such as fire, invasive surgery, or violent attack. One of the chief symptoms is nightmares that replay the trauma or run variations on the theme.

Nightmares following every sort of trauma, from childhood abandonment to lynching, are described with revealing frequency in African American literature. Novelists and autobiographers testify that the lives of black Americans have been and still are beset by traumas, including traumas directly due to racism.

James Cameron's near-lynching in 1930 was described in chapter 9. His dreams show that as an old man he's still processing the terrible event. In one dream, he's running from a mob. He ducks into a shack, where people are sitting at tables. He tells them, "Something's got to be done about this mob business. It's getting out of hand." He ducks out and runs from the mob again. He finds himself at the base of a huge dam under construction. He scales its face. He can see the mob below, but they're blinded by construction lights. He climbs to the top and reaches safety.

Sherry McKinney had been one of the black children to desegregate a white school in Chicago in the 1970s. The black children were escorted to school under police protection past the white parents who picketed every day. For years afterward, McKinney dreamed that she finds herself alone, trapped inside the school by the picketers. She fears that her mother and father won't know what's become of her, and that the principal, who is angry at the blacks, will find her still there in the morning and will punish her.

Ethel Smith is "afraid of these white Bubba-guys, you know? These big—ugh!" She used to have nightmares where she's alone in her office at a Virginia college. No one else is in the building. She hears something. "Yes?" Nothing. She tries to work again. Suddenly, "There's Bubba, with a gun! And I always wake up in a cold sweat, if you can imagine." These nightmares began after a "Bubba" in one of her classes

came into my office one day and said, "I need a B out of this class, Professor Smith!" So I'm stunned, I don't know how I'm supposed to respond. Then he says to me, "I *know* where you live." So I said, "Well, we can work this out." You know, I—fuck you, I don't want you—. So for a very long time, I would dream some of those Bubbas were gonna come and kill me.

My jaw must have dropped when I learned this incident took place in the 1990s. Smith took me to school. "Where have you been? Are you kidding me? Yes! I bet if you really talk to any black professor, particularly a woman." Then she said, "That dream isn't with me anymore, I'm glad to say. But there's some of those same Bubbas."

Sheron Williams-Brooks described the traumatic impact on her dreams of witnessing racially motivated police violence:

> There was some kind of racial incident between two sets of teenagers, over the kind of music that was being played. When the police came, the black teenagers were immediately taken out. I told my husband, "I will not remain in my house, and let this go unwitnessed." And so I went outside, and they were telling all the black residents, "Get back in your damn houses!" And I'm saying, "I'm not." I said, "I will stand here on my porch and watch this." And the white officer stepped onto the black man—had him on the ground, he was handcuffed from behind—he stepped into the young black man's throat, and I heard the most awful . . . sound come from his throat. It wasn't a moan, it wasn't a scream, but it was—it was terrible. And that sound echoed in my dreams. And in my dream, not the boy, but myself, *I* was in that situation.

Dreams of Interracial Violence

White-on-black violence is a recurring theme in the dream life of black Americans. We've just seen this in trauma dreams, and we saw it in dreams with historical themes and in other dreams presented earlier. What about the reverse? Is black-on-white violence also a recurring theme for black dreamers? Not according to the evidence. My interviews yielded only a small handful of such dreams. Moreover, in all of the African American literature I surveyed, I found a mere two dreams about black-on-white violence.

Another researcher, Robert Haskell, has also found that blacks dream less of being violent toward whites than they dream of receiving violence from whites. Whites, on the other hand, his research found, dream equally of being the perpetrator and the target of interracial violence.

In the dreams of blacks, white-on-black violence is typically motivated by greed, race hatred, or some other base motive. Or else white violence toward blacks is simply treated as an arbitrary fact of life. When blacks dream of black-on-white violence, on the other hand, either the dream offers a plausible pretext for a violent response, or else white racism in the dreamer's waking life explains the motivation for violence in the dream.

Ivan Watkins dreamed of running amok in Saks, we saw, after the parents of his white girlfriend had actually rejected him. The boy who dreamed Bill Clinton gets "popped" is one of the residents defending their housing project homes against white encroachers, dream characters with real-world counterparts in white developers. Leon Forrest has dreams of being "involved in the murder of some white man." He traced this recurring dream to his abiding anger over a childhood episode when he and his father were among a group of blacks ejected from a public park by a mob of whites.

Several interviewees retaliated violently in dreams for waking-life racist affronts at the workplace. Diane Dugger said she was fired from her job as a medical technician after sixteen years because she was out front as a union organizer. She felt particularly persecuted by a six-foot-four white racist supervisor:

> I dream about doing things to him. Okay, I played it one time where he was sitting in his chair with his back turned to the door, and I came in there and pow! pow! Then I replayed the dream the next night, and I'm saying, "No, that's too damn easy. Do it differently!"

This dream recurs when something happens to revive Dugger's resentment, such as being turned down for unemployment compensation. Another woman has "totally violent" dreams about "wiping up the floor" with racist coworkers. Milder Zeinabu irene Davis only dreamed she "kicked" a sexist, racist senior colleague "in the butt."

And that is the total of all the dreams I heard from my interviewees about black-on-white violence. Moreover, even the black male prisoners follow the same pattern—that is, more white-on-black than black-on-white violence in dreams. I received only two prisoner dreams of the latter type. One prisoner and his "comrades have a shootout with FBI agents." They kill many agents and all go down fighting. The other prisoner is "attacked in prison by a group of Aryan Brotherhoods" who pull knives. His friends join in and it turns into "a race riot."

It's quite remarkable, in view of the historical provocation, that black dreams exhibit the scant amount of black-on-white violence they do. The psychological reality directly contradicts the racist stereotype according to which blacks, and particularly black males, have poor impulse control and a proclivity to violence. Lorraine Hansberry once complained bitterly about the unfairness of that stereotype:

> [W]e live in a nation where everything . . . is talked about in terms of the fact that we are going to be the mightiest, the toughest, the roughest cats going, you know. But when a Negro says something about, "I'm *tired*, I can't *stand it* no more, I want to hit somebody—" *you* say that we're sitting here, panting and ranting for violence. That's not right.

Many whites in this society project onto blacks their own darker impulses. By making this projection, whites preserve their denial that they themselves harbor forbidden tendencies such as brutality and raw desire. Ralph Ellison observed this psychological defense on the part of whites. He bemoaned the misfortune of blacks "to be shackled to almost everything" the white mind "would repress from conscience and consciousness."

Dream psychologists often say that racist projections appear in the dreams of many whites. White dreamers, they observe, falsely typecast blacks as violent and sexually aggressive transgressors, and even whites who consciously reject the racist stereotype are liable to find threatening black males in their dreams. A forty-seven-year-old educator, for example, dreamed he's in "a desolate area" when he sees "a bunch of black teenagers" coming. He feels "sort of threatened" and looks for "some way to escape." A twenty-two-year-old woman dreamed "a huge flock of black birds is flying toward my bedroom window." Now she hears voices. Black men are coming in "the front door." One has "a long, curved sword." The "front door" and the "sword" are obvious sexual symbols here. The dreamer is "frightened," even though her boyfriend is "there to protect" her.

In addition to the transgressor role, I've found that whites give blacks two other particular roles in dreams. In one of these roles, blacks appear as *figures with special virtues*. For example, a woman in her fifties, a writer, dreamed she's living in underground tunnels. A black woman is "helping" her. So is a Native American woman. They're cooking tubers for the dreamer. The dreamer is "very pleased" and is "preparing to go aboveground."

The other particular role I observed for blacks in white dreams is as *victims to be rescued*. For example, another woman in her fifties, a wealthy artist, dreamed she's with friends at a cafe. A "big strapping" black man comes in. People make fun of him because of his race, his "slurred speech." She defends him, gets into a fistfight. The black man is grateful.

What needs to be recognized about all of these roles in which whites place blacks in dreams—transgressor, figure of virtue, passive victim—is that all of them draw upon stereotypes. The black with soul and the passive, inarticulate black are no less stereotypes than the threatening black. All of these dream types, therefore, exhibit racism, to the extent that they stereotypically characterize people by skin color.

But having said that, I can also say that false typecasting of blacks in the dreams of whites is actually not all pervasive. By no means all the dreams whites have about blacks cast the blacks in stereotyped roles. In fact, a majority of white dreamers *never* put blacks in such roles, at least by their own report. Just over two-thirds of whites say that either they never dream of blacks at all, or if they do, the blacks in their dreams are simply "who they are"—friends, acquaintances, or neighbors.

Moreover, I specifically went after race stereotypes by asking my white sample about the nearly universal dream where *the dreamer is threatened, chased, or attacked by someone or something unknown.* According to the answers I received, only 21 percent of whites have *ever* dreamed about black transgressors. By contrast, 45 percent of the same white dreamers have dreamed about *white* transgressors. In other words, over twice as many whites dream of anonymous violent threats coming from their own race as dream of such threats coming from blacks.

So while racial stereotyping is undoubtedly at work in the dreams of some whites, it isn't quite as virulent as might be feared—or, conceivably, as virulent as it once was.

Now the question is, what does the transgressor look like when *blacks* have the nearly universal dream of being threatened, chased, or attacked by someone or something unknown? Just as for whites, more blacks report anonymous transgressors of their own race than of the other race. With black dreamers, however, the percentages are more nearly equal, and are considerably higher in both cases: black transgressors, 65 percent; white transgressors, 54 percent.

There are several reasons why such a high percentage of blacks would dream of anonymous transgressors of their own color. First of all, as for all dreamers, childhood experiences have a shaping influence on the imagination. Charles Young described a recurring transgressor dream. He runs from a pack of "wild coyotes," who turn into "black people." He runs harder, but he's "stuck in the mud" and "can't get away." He attributes this dream to harassment by black bullies as a youngster. A woman (name withheld) who faced hostile white crowds in a southern school district as a child dreams about white transgressors in groups. However, she has other dreams about lone transgressors, who are always black. She had undergone years of sexual abuse from a black man, her uncle.

Another factor leading blacks to dream about black transgressors is black-on-black street violence, both as media image and as urban reality. This factor presumably accounts for the fact that fully 72 percent of the male prisoners dream of black transgressors, while only 48 percent dream of white transgressors (compared to 65 percent and 54 percent for the interviewees). The transgressor dreams of the prisoners are typically set in the streets, not in prison: "I was chased into a dead end alley by two black men, who wanted to take my watch and jacket."

A further explanation for dreams of anonymous black transgressors is internalized racism. If whites make blacks the "other" onto whom they project their own fears and dark impulses, blacks living in such an environment are, as Ntozake Shange put it, "born the 'other.'" This predicament pushes black people toward disparagement of other blacks and toward a negative self-image—what Salim Muwakkil labels the "internal nigger." The anonymous transgressor of dreams is sometimes just this. For Ivan Watkins, it was "the Boo-man":

> He was the stereotype of a black man. Really full lips, a really broad nose, very, very dark complexion. He always had like overalls on, with a red plaid shirt. And he ate people. As I grew older I wanted to understand that, and often reflected upon it, and it eventually came to me that I was confronting my own Africanness. But more than Africa, it was more me confronting my Africanness through my ancestors that were right here in this land. And acknowledging that within me.

The next question is, why do 54 percent of blacks dream about *white* transgressors? *This is more than two and a half times the number of whites who put blacks in the transgressor role (21 percent).* Do whites represent the "other" for blacks, the "depreciated reciprocal," the "shadow" onto whom blacks project *their* repressed fears and urges? Certainly many dreams I heard are open to that interpretation. I've mentioned Gloria Naylor's dream about white "thug-type" house invaders. The white thugs could conceivably represent some disowned aspect of

Naylor's personality. But all of the dreams that have white transgressors, including Naylor's, immediately beg the question about racism in the real world.

There is really no way to account for the high percentage of blacks who have this type of dream without invoking the condition of society. Anthony Shy described a dream that occurred shortly after moving to Madison, Wisconsin, from Chicago for work. At one point in the dream,

> I turned into a side street and stopped at a stop sign, and there was a white kid who walked up to my car and he kept looking at me. And I said, "What are you looking at! Leave me alone!" And he just stood there, and there was this weird intense eye contact. And I had to push him away from the car in driving off. And then later in the dream, multiple kids were chasing my car. And I remember feeling that it just wasn't safe there.

Shy has many white friends "that I would trust with my life," but his new employer had just warned him not to trust the whites of Madison, they were racist. So while the dream could involve projections, it certainly reflects the dreamer's anxieties about real white racism.

Lynchings have become rare; the hoses have been put away and the dogs restrained. But as we've seen, historical violence haunts the collective memory. Moreover, racial profiling, police brutality, biased sentencing, and poverty with high infant mortality are all too commonplace today—not to speak of the psychological violence of everyday petty racism. In short, real racism, real hatred, real violence are the reasons so many blacks dream about white transgressors.

PART FIVE

Dream Sharing and the Future

14

WHAT MY MOTHER DOES

DREAM SHARING AND THE FUTURE

Every mornin when all us chillen got up, my mama Gibralter had us to take turns tellin what we had seent in our sleepwalks. This was what we talked amongst ourselves about. Mama said at night is when the secrets show.

—A. J. Verdelle

Dream Sharing

Dreams give us insight into ourselves and our relationships. They help us cope with conflicts and traumas. They produce clues to our state of health. They have a problem-solving capacity. They offer opportunities for rehearsing actions and interactions. They nourish creativity. They refresh the past, and furnish a window on the future. They monitor society. They maintain our connections with the spiritual. They keep life on course by providing a compass to the deep ocean of the psyche. And on top of all this, they entertain.

Dream sharing enhances these benefits. If nothing else, the insights of others serve to confirm or challenge our own. Sharing can improve dream recall, as well. It also increases our familiarity with the language of dreams, and even contributes to the evolution of our dream style in the direction of greater transparency. In addition, dream sharing can make it easier to talk about difficult subjects with a partner.

And building dreams into social acts by sharing them lifts their social meanings into clearer focus. In short, if we want to understand our dreams it helps to share them.

Furthermore, talk about dreams is in itself a mainstay of the traditions we've been exploring in this book. Such beliefs and attitudes can only be perpetuated in a vital way by people observing what other people say and do around dreams. Literature supports this process, by translating the values of the past for the sensibilities of the present. Fiction and poetry, drama and autobiography refurbish the fabric of dream traditions—often with irony and ambiguity—for contemporaries. However, literature can only play this supporting role if beliefs are alive and well in the everyday world. And it's chiefly through direct social interactions involving dreams that the traditions get conveyed from one person to another—including, importantly, the traditions governing the ways of talking about dreams. And so this chapter describes how African Americans share dreams with each other.

Ample evidence of dream sharing has accompanied virtually every part of this survey of dreams in African American life. For example, close to half of the interviewees (42 percent) can recall hearing dreams talked about in church during their childhoods (chapter 10). Black ministers not only make reference to biblical dreams, but share their own dreams and visions from the pulpit. What's more, dreams are shared from the floor in most churches whose members testify. This adds up to a potent institutional lesson that it's good to share dreams.

Chapter 6 described the prominence of dreams in the economic and social institution of numbers gambling. To play numbers from dreams is enshrined in the collective social memory, but also survives in lottery betting today. And talk about dreams has always been a regular part of the numbers mystique. After remarking that the middle-class branch of his family didn't talk about dreams, novelist Leon Forrest said of the Mississippi and New Orleans branches:

> They *would* talk about dreams. And, it was a cousin of mine who played policy *all* the time. And she was always talking about her dreams, and using those dreams as an index to what she would bet on. And she would use the dream book, and often win.

Regina Reed's family didn't have a dream book, but "they would know who to call, if they needed certain symbols interpreted. For the numbers or whatever in the dream." Richard Hunt remembers hearing a great deal about dreams and numbers in his father's barbershop. And Diane Dujon, who was raised in a home which never played numbers, nevertheless heard the talk of "other families around me that did a lot of stuff around dreams. Tried to interpret what they meant, and what number to hit."

Sharon Jackson Sanders is an example of someone who nowadays shares numbers dreams (her sister is poet Angela Jackson):

> I might dream of a number, or I'll dream somebody's birthday. And then I'll tell my sister. And my sister always says, "Well, look that up and see what that means." And it comes up! That's why she say, "Oh, you lucky!"

I won't go through all of the circumstances of numbers dream sharing that were touched on in chapter 6. But I will return to one belief that especially bears on dream sharing in a general way. It is the belief that *someone else's dream* can have as much or more predictive power for oneself as one's own dream. This belief obviously depends on and encourages dream sharing.

"Meant for" Dreams

"See, there's a rule in our community," said Adekola Adedapo while discussing dreams. "Very often you don't come up with your own numbers, you get your best numbers from your friends." The "rule" still holds. Alice Stephens is a Ph.D., a clinical psychologist and professor of filmmaking, and a fourth-generation college graduate in the maternal line. She recounted giving her mother in Florida a dream over the phone so that her mother could play the lottery. Then she recalled:

> I was visiting, and I was mentioning to my sister about my dreams, and my cousin happened to be at the house, and she says, "What was that number that you dreamed?" And she won money on the number that I had dreamed. So I went, "Oh. Okay." I don't play it, but if there's somebody who needs to know and they're not dreaming numbers and I *am* . . .

Children's dreams, as was explained in chapter 6, were (and still are) especially sought by some numbers players, who believe "that children are more gifted with powers of divination than their elders." Being asked in a respectful way to tell one's dreams transmits to a child a sense that dreams are valuable.

Numbers dreams are by no means the only dreams believed to carry information for someone other than the dreamer. For example, Judy Still's parents were interested in her dreams as general predictors:

> If I had a dream that something they'd done was a success, they certainly wanted to hear about it. One time, I saw something that was happening to them that was good, and I also saw myself going to meet Hopalong Cassidy. And so, when they built Hoppyland in California, my mother right away took me there, so that the rest of the dream would come true.

With adults, what usually happens is that a dream will strike the dreamer as being "meant for" another person. The dreamer then feels compelled to impart the dream or, at least, to convey the dream's meaning to that person. Half of the interviewees (50 percent) who were asked said they'd had a dream "meant for" someone else, compared with under a third (30 percent) of the white sample. While these percentages are intriguingly high for both groups, the difference is significant. So it appears that this type of dream, which carries with it such a strong impulse to dream sharing, is yet another strand in the fabric of African American dream beliefs. For example, Eileen Cherry, a writer, said:

> My sister Gloria, she's very, very sensitive like that, to people in the family. She had a dream about me. And I was in this relationship with this guy, and he was over at the house, and she called me, she said, "Are you with somebody right now?" And I said, "Yeah." She said, "Just get him outta the house." She said, "I just get this feeling. I just see you in this pool of snakes!" Pretty vivid image! She said, "Just get him out of your house." So I hung up the phone, and, you know, I got rid of him! And he ended up being—he was into armed robbery. He could have got me into a *lot* of trouble. Gloria has very, very vivid dreams. She really tunes in on everybody.

College professor Douglas Gills's mother phones him with her premonitions, which are usually based on her dreams. She doesn't actually relate the dream or give a specific warning. "She's always said, 'Check things.' And nine times out of ten, there's something to it."

Ivan Watkins has had dreams for another person "plenty times." Experience has taught this city employee and artist that he should always transmit the information. Once while his Sioux uncle was enjoying himself riding up and down the South Dakota hills on his motorcycle, Watkins fell asleep and "had this dream that he [the uncle] almost got hit by a car, and he crashed on his motorcycle." Watkins awoke, ascertained that everything was all right, and went back to sleep, only to be awakened shortly by his bleeding uncle.

> He almost got hit by a car and to dodge the car he ran into a barbed wire fence. And the first thing I said was, "I just had a dream!" And he said, "Why didn't you give me the warning?"

Three members of one family, the Edmonds, all talked about dreams for another person. Oscar Edmond spoke first about his aunt's dreams:

> She would start talking about what she would dream, and she would be telling you what's going to happen in your life. And people would take her verbatim 'cause she was so good. She was the type of person that could tell you, "Hey, look, if you got to go home, go up to State Street and come back around." And if you *didn't* take that route, you soon learned your lesson—particularly in those times when Chicago was really prejudiced and segregated. And I'll never forget, she told my uncle to go a certain route once, and he disobeyed her, and he ended up in jail.

Oscar then went on to say that his mother, Adrienne Edmond, "did the same thing." When I interviewed Adrienne, she related a recent episode when she advised her daughter Janet to warn Janet's ex-husband to be careful.

> I dreamed that Malloy and all of his friends went to a funeral. Maybe about a week or two later, one of Malloy's friends was killed. And Janet told me, she says, "Ma, that dream you had," she said, "that was Malloy's friend was killed. He was going to his car and he was shot and robbed."

Janet herself, who came in on the interview with her mother, related a dream a friend shared with her, correctly predicting Janet's own wedding within a month at a time when Janet had no thoughts about marriage. She also related a dream of her own from which she accurately warned another friend that a business partner was going to cheat her.

Other interviewees also talked about dreams "meant for" friends. Colleen McElroy told this story:

> A couple of years ago I had a dream about a friend of mine. She's now at Columbia University, doing her advanced degree. In the dream, I

walked onto campus and saw her, and she was saying, "I don't know
why I'm here. What am I doing here?" So I had to keep telling her
what she'd done: she had already completed the work. And so I called
her about the dream, and she said, "You know, they've been trying to
get me to apply for this scholarship, and I don't know if I want to or
not." I said, "I think you should."

When Norma Adams Wade was growing up,

the church folk would say these "The Lord told me" type of things
right and left! "The Lord revealed to me in my dream that you should
do so-and-so." I have a close friend, and we joke about this sometimes,
where she says, "If one more person walks up to me and says, 'The
Lord told me you oughta do so-and-so,' " she says, "I'm gonna tell
them, 'Well, it's funny to me that the Lord would come and tell *you*
what I oughta do. Why didn't he tell me?' "

It has apparently not occurred to Wade that her own conduct with
dreams may have been modeled for her by the laughable "church
folk," for later she said:

I know that I have told someone else about a dream I had, because
I wanted them to know the information within the dream. And just
one example that comes to mind: I have a close friend, and I do recall
conversations, like, "Carol, you know, I dreamed the other night that
such-and-such, and let me tell you about it, because I think this would
be good for you to know." And proceeded to tell her the dream, and
say, "So therefore, it really makes sense to me that you should do
whatever."

While dreams meant for friends are not uncommon, most "meant
for" dreams involve family members, as can be judged from the cases
that have come up in the course of this book—dreams from ancestors
with messages for the family (chapter 3), dreams predicting pregnan-
cies in the family and the genders of expected babies (chapter 4),
and others.

In fact, the largest part of all dream sharing takes place among
family members. To the question "Were dreams ever talked about in
your home as a child?" 88 percent of the interviewees said yes, as
compared with 76 percent of the white sample, a small but significant
difference. Moreover, the question didn't address the *quality* of talk
about dreams, and it's quite clear that the way dreams are handled in
black homes is much more likely to instill the idea that dreams actually matter.

To Speak or Not to Speak about Dreams

And yet, paradoxically, black homes don't necessarily communicate their dreams in a free and casual way. Indeed, there may even be reticence about dream telling. This requires explanation.

Reluctance to speak about dreams has several facets. First is *the very respect in which dreams are held.* The dream, as Alice Stephens observed of African American attitudes, "is a very private kind of thing. I suspect that it's private because it's revered. They're significant, dreams, and so you're not willing to talk."

Another restraint on open conversation about dreams is a certain *closeness about all private business,* a trait deeply seated in African American manners. "Nothing hurts a duck but his bill," the saying goes. Another adage states, "Don't say no more with your mouth than your back can stand."

Closeness was obviously ingrained as a survival skill by slavery, but the trait was also carried over from Africa, where "long ago our ancestors taught us that a man must not tell anyone more than half of what he knows about anything." Maya Angelou saw both influences, slavery and Africa, in the grandmother who raised her: "Her African-bush secretiveness and suspiciousness had been compounded by slavery and confirmed by centuries of promises made and promises broken."

Another facet of reticence about dreams is *repugnance for the southern past.* That past is so repugnant to some people that they suppress every aspect of it. When *Roots* came on television, Sandra Jackson-Opoku's aunt said, "I don't even wanta *talk* about it! I don't even wanta *watch* that kinda stuff!"—so strong was her "shame" about her "Mississippi experience." For Jackson-Opoku's father and his kin, reticence was compounded by some dark history they barely whispered about—an arson, a child fatally abused, a white man killed. As Hermene Hartman said, "There are some scars, some things that they went through that they're very determined their children not only will not go through, but you'll never even know it."

Obviously suppression of the past comes into conflict with natural desires for family continuity. Salim Muwakkil said:

> When I talk to my grandmother now, she appreciates reflecting on those things a lot more. She tells me things now that she had never told me in the past, about her past. Because a lot of it was framed by a brutal kind of segregation. So I understand why she resisted. Intellectually, she understands the need for continuity, and how that helps me figure out who I am, and get a better map of our family, who we are.

She understands that. But still, these personal inclinations that she has really still are pretty strong.

Ambivalence about remembering the repugnant southern past aloud is a motif in many African American personal histories, and it contributes to a reluctance to verbalize about traditional beliefs associated with that past, including beliefs about dreams.

Yet many of these same people carried their beliefs north with them. For these believers, still another factor contributed to reticence about dreams, the *fear of being looked down on as "countrified," as "downhomish."* The same concern caused some immigrants to shun the blues, or profess ignorance of rootwork, or drop slave names like Hannibal, or convert to Catholicism or Episcopalianism. Langston Hughes satirized this fear by having a character insist that the clerk at the market wrap a watermelon.

These qualms derive less from vanity than from a wish for oneself and, even more, for one's children to adapt and progress. Eileen Cherry's mother and aunt adhered to traditional beliefs and practices, "but we weren't supposed to be aware of that kind of stuff. You know, we were supposed to be young ladies. They split their world! They really did." Adekola Adedapo, herself a reader/adviser, gave this account of family history:

> When we were coming up, our people went through big changes to leave the country behind. And see, one of my grandmothers was from Mississippi, and her mother was a rootwoman. And that's why my mother was trying to just put it *all* away, 'cause if you were involved with voodoo, you were country! And she was trying to reach the social register in Chicago, and get her kids matriculated into the city. So this aspect of our existence was literally hidden. So there wasn't any acknowledgment of dream interpretation, or anything like that, or visions of spirits, whatever. Because this was country. This was part of the background we were trying to forget.
>
> But when people had problems, they would go at two in the morning in the back door of Miss So-and-so's house—I mean, always! I have found since then that several of my relatives went to root people or readers.

During summer stays in Mississippi, Adedapo was exposed to traditional beliefs by the grandparental generation in the persons of "Aunt Mamie, who spit tobacco in the spittoon, and all her cohorts." Adedapo added:

And I still say, How did this escape my mother, who had me as a cheerleader, who went to the Episcopal Church? Poor baby! She tried so hard to keep it away. She should have never sent me to visit the relatives, but she had five of us, and every summer farmed us out as quickly as she could! But I, you know—but I did! I got it. I did.

In sketching her own history, Adedapo's friend and associate Osuurete Adesanya brought up an old adage, that "a gift's gonna skip a generation." There's also "an old sociological law" that says, "What the second generation sought to forget, the third generation will try to remember." Hence the migrants bent on leaving the old traditions "down home" sometimes have children who absorb traditional values from the migrants' own parents and aunts. Not always, but sometimes.

A variation on this theme occurred in the family of Ntozake Shange. Shange's maternal grandmother came to St. Louis from South Carolina. She and Shange's father played the numbers "religiously," using dream books. But the grandmother was deeply ambivalent about passing along her beliefs about dreams or about hoodoo:

> She liked to distance herself from Africanisms. She's saying, "I don't believe in any of that stuff," as she's putting powder around the room. "I don't believe in anything like that, but *they* say this is good for such-and-such."

This woman's daughter, Shange's mother, *really* "didn't believe in that." But Shange herself, whose books testify to her own beliefs, feels that she absorbed a believing frame of mind from her grandmother, even if she has had to acquire much of her specific knowledge about traditional beliefs through learning as an adult.

Still one more facet of closeness with dreams involves the traditional belief that "*Dreams told before sunrise ([or] breakfast) will come true.*" A variant belief has it that telling a dream before sunrise causes it *not* to come true, or shifts the dream's "bad luck" onto someone else. But the first version is more usual.

Logic suggests that someone holding this belief might deliberately tell a dream just so that it would come true, if the dream were good. John Edgar Wideman explained why this isn't so:

> Like a lot of things, it doesn't work positively. If I dream about hitting the lottery for a million dollars, it wouldn't do me any good to talk about it before breakfast. If I dreamed about breaking my leg and talked about it before breakfast, then it would come true.

I can't estimate just how widespread this belief is, but it's certainly more than just a folklore relic. Psychoanalyst Barbara Pulliam said her mother from Virginia believes it. One of the Cabrini Green children said his aunt "always told me, if I dream something, don't ever tell it in the night, in the dark, because it's all gonna come true." Wideman himself said he "would never talk about dreams before breakfast. Because if I do, that would make them come true." And this belief has been transmitted to Wideman's son Daniel:

> There's a tradition that some dreams you keep to yourself. By speaking a dream, you bring it to light. And somehow, even though that dream has power, unless you give it word, unless you bring it to light, then you can somehow avoid or circumvent that future event from occurring. The only way that you can keep it from happening is to not reveal it. And it's not enough to just know the dream and keep it inside: you have to completely blank it out of your mind, pretend that it never happened. And suppress it so completely that it doesn't get breathed out into the world at all. Because that will bring that reality upon you.

Daniel Wideman's idea that the dream must not get "breathed out into the world" corresponds to something Alice Stephens said in connection with "the belief in our family that you don't tell the dream before sunrise":

> The Egyptians had this notion that breath was sacred, and that by giving breath to an idea, and you say it, it becomes real. And so that's part of my cosmology: one has to be vigilant and not careless about what you say. Because once you give breath to an idea, it will manifest itself. So I'm vigilant about what I say, I'm vigilant about the thoughts that I do have.

Both Stephens and Wideman imply that the power to make dreams come true by uttering them derives from the causal power of breath, of utterance in general. This helps explain why in Stephens's family, *the narrow taboo against telling bad dreams before sunrise has been broadened to discourage telling them at any time of day:*

> My sister will call me, and I'll know she's dreamed a dream where I've died in the dream. And she'll call to verify that I'm still alive. But: she won't tell me the dream. And that's a family cultural thing. Because to tell the dream will make the dream come true. She calls with this panic in her voice, and I know. She'll say, "I had a dream last night." And

sometimes I'll say, "Well, what did you dream?" And she'll say, "Oh, well, you know, I gotta go now." So the practice is not to tell it.

In chapter 4, we saw the belief that dreams don't simply predict the future, but can actually cause the future to happen. The belief that telling a dream makes it come true is obviously related. The telling is a stage of the process set in motion by the dream. Josh Taifa said:

> A girl told me two days ago—'cause I had got into a fight with about eight guys. And I called her, she was like, "Aw, well just be careful." Then she called me back, like about one-thirty the next morning, talking about she had a dream that I had went outside and something happened to me.
> *Did she tell you what the dream actually was?*
> No, she refused. She goes, "Man, be careful." Like, "Why?" She like, "Just because." And I know how she is—I was like, "Man!"

Moreese "Pop" Bickham said he once was shooting at a tree when his mother told him, "If you don't leave that gun here, somebody's going to shoot you with it just like you shot that tree." Two months later,

> I got shot twice with that same gun. I used to tell Mama, "Don't you ever tell me what you dream or see in visions." [If] she said, "You know I dreamed seeing So-and-so dead," you can bet your boots, somebody's going to bring the word, So-and-so dead! Man, I'd get scared of Mama as I would a tiger!

In the course of discussion, I asked another interviewee if the people she grew up around thought dreams caused the future to happen. She replied, "Oh yeah, they had that fear totally," then added: "I realized that people thought that I was causing things." She went on to tell a story which shows that uttering a dream is believed to be implicated in the outcome. Her mother, she said, used to help out a blind man at a neighbor's house. She dreamed one night that a disembodied voice told her that her mother would find the blind man, Mr. C., dead:

> And I told my mom on my way to school, I said, "Mom, you'd better be careful when you go to Miss G.'s house, because you're gonna find Mr. C. And you're just going to be shook up." And she says, "Oh, girl, be quiet."

Sure enough, the mother found Mr. C. dead and staring at her with open eyes:

> On the way back from school, I go up the steps to the house and I see Mom draped over the banister, totally exhausted and afraid, and then she looks up and sees me, and she's mad: "You *told* me he'd die!"

Through happenings such as this, the interviewee had acquired a reputation. "To the point where some of the neighbors would say, 'Oh, God, here she comes! *Please* don't let her say anything to me.'"

These stories show that ideas about *not* telling dreams form part of a fabric of beliefs in which dreams are respected for the information they convey and the influence they have in life. So that even when black children don't, as Frances Callaway Parks did, grow up in an environment where people share dreams freely with "any person coming around them," they nevertheless are likely to learn to respect and pay attention to dreams.

This brings us to yet another side of reticence about dreams. Many black families have a certain *style of communicating with children*. Toni Morrison writes that children "didn't initiate talk with grown-ups" and were never engaged "in serious conversation." Ethel Smith remembers that her grandmother "would look at me and say, 'That's grown folks' business, gal.'" And Luisah Teish writes:

> Often I would stand quietly nearby as some dream was being interpreted only to be dismissed with "This is a racehorse conversation and no jackasses allowed." This meant that I should leave, because their conversation was beyond my understanding. An ever-sealed lid of secrecy covered what older folks said and did.

Teish goes on to characterize this secrecy with children as a "survival mechanism" from slavery days. This strong inclination to secrecy was carried forward after slavery in family dynamics. The prevailing attitude portrayed by Toni Morrison in *The Bluest Eye* is that in the grip of hard necessity, and under chronic emergency, indulging children's curiosity is superfluous to survival, if not positively dangerous.

How can knowledge be transmitted in such an environment? Part of the explanation is hinted at in the above quote from Teish: "Often I would stand quietly nearby. . . ." *Overhearing adults* is obviously an element of any child's socialization, but in black households it is often an indispensable channel of information. As Zora Neale Hurston put it, "Nobody didn't tell 'em, but they heard." Bessie Jones writes:

Of course there were some [things] that they tried to keep from us, but my cousin and me, when we were supposed to be asleep in the other room, we would listen to them and eavesdrop while they would say things that they wouldn't tell before us, and so we learnt it.

Similar recollections were shared by interviewees spanning all age groups:

I was a kid who would always leave the door cracked so I could hear what was going on. I got a lot of education just listening. *(Dempsey Travis, age seventy-five)*

A lot of African Americans in my generation comment on it. Honey, when the grown folks was in the room talking, you was not *in* there! There was a certain way that they wanted us to perceive them. Okay? So, you couldn't sit in the room, because that would show a lack of respect. This was the adult space, so you went and stood out with the kids, or whatever, and you listened to the stories through the screen! *(Eileen Cherry, age forty-two)*

When we were all together, the kids were to go somewhere and play while they talked. They talked about dreams and stuff. So anything we ever heard was just kind of in passing, or listening to them talk on the phone. *(Sherry McKinney, age twenty-eight)*

Even when children aren't actively pushed outside the circle, they still may have to play the role of eavesdroppers. Zeinabu irene Davis (age around thirty) explained that she could sit there, but couldn't interrupt or ask questions. Moreover,

I think it did make a difference, the longer you were around people, how comfortable they felt talking to you about those kinds of things [ancestor visitation dreams, etc.]. Like I remember sitting on the porch, with my grandparents, and the information—folk wisdom—you would get. But if you were always kinda running around, and not really interested, you wouldn't get it.

Daniel Wideman (age twenty-six) made much the same point, that "if the child is interested enough and patient enough," s/he can stay and listen and learn. "And so an observant child doesn't need necessarily to approach an older person and speak about things."

Daniel Wideman then raised an important consideration about the exclusion of children. *The opportunity to overhear things isn't necessarily accidental,* but may actually reflect a method of education. "I think that's the way people got around the strict, formal notion of not telling children—was by allowing children to be in the presence of adults who were talking about all kinds of things." So what the child perceives as exclusion and eavesdropping may really involve the acquiescence or connivance of the adults. Daniel Wideman's father John Edgar Wideman also talked about the opportunity to overhear as an educational arrangement, "a kind of pedagogy":

> Because there's a belief that you can't just *tell* people things. In order for things to penetrate, the teaching that's important is a kind of internalization by the pupil, so to speak. And that cannot be effected simply by saying, "Don't put your hand on the burner." But if you open up a kid to listening and somehow learning through being a fly on the wall, things are gonna stick much better. Then you're getting at what we usually think of as "experience."

John Edgar Wideman spoke in addition about what might be called *designated transmitters*. They fulfill an instructional role:

> In a large, extended family there was always somebody who was sort of licensed, or a special case. And they were either sort of strange—and everybody knew they were strange—or they could talk in ways that other people couldn't talk. I mean, there's often an uncle who's allowed to talk about sex, even where everybody else is self-conscious about it, and puritanical about it. Well, Horton will tell bawdy stories. And Horton will pat Marsha on the ass every time he comes in the room. You know, 'cause that's Horton. And so this person functions in the family to do a lot of the work. So if you come in and look at the family in general, you might get one opinion. And if you ask everybody how ideas about sex get transmitted, they probably wouldn't mention Horton. But in fact, there's often this person who plays that role.
>
> *And the same thing, you're saying, would be true of things such as dreams and visions?*
>
> Yes, absolutely. And that person has the role of passing that stuff on more directly. And it doesn't get lost.

Men's and Women's Roles

The Widemans' extended family is apparently exceptional in one respect, for in most African American families men play a smaller part in the transmission of beliefs and attitudes about dreams than do women. Among only a few families do the males play the larger part. One such exception to the rule is the family of Shirlee Taylor Haizlip. Her father and mother both "believed in the prophecy of dreams," but her father "double-felt that dreams were important" because he was a minister. Another woman came up in a strongly patriarchal home in which family stories and other lore were jealously passed from father to eldest son. But more often, the pictures of family dream talk that I gathered during interviews minimized the role of men:

I never remember my father as a dreamer. Or ever discussing a dream. My mother, though. *(Hermene Hartman)*

Mostly my mother. I didn't hear my father talk about it much. Even though the women on his side—in fact, I never heard the men talk about it. *(Regina Reed)*

Dreams and dreaming were always important in my family. You get up in the morning, you tell people what your dream was. My grandmother, my mother, and other folks always believed in prophetic dreams, and dream symbology, as a regular part of life. It was just something everybody did, in terms of sharing the information. If my cousin has a certain kind of dream, she will call me and tell me. And she'll call my mother and tell her. And *she'll* tell *her* mother.

My grand*father*'s role: If I were to have this dream, and a cousin of mine had this dream, it likely would merge into a number, that the family would play. My father's family, I can never remember a discussion of any type of this stuff. *(Kimberly Camp)*

Most of the descriptions simply bypassed the men and centered on the women. Angela Jackson talked about her mother's interpretations of dream signs. "Is she particularly gifted at interpreting?" I asked.

Um . . . I never thought of her as being particularly gifted at interpreting. It's just what my mother does. You know, it's like, my mother cooks well.

Here are some more remarks from interviewees along these lines:

We definitely would talk about dreams and what they meant. It was with my mother's side of the family, and especially my mother's sister, my aunt. *(Beatriz Penso-Buford)*

My grandmother would always wake up in the morning, come in, and tell my ma she had this dream. And it was, one of her sisters might have been in the dream, and she would have this feeling that something's going to happen to her sister. *(Edwina Ackie)*

When [my great aunts and their friends] discussed people's personalities, they discussed them also in terms of what they dreamt about that person. And they would talk about dreams they had about men, and about what the men were doing or saying in these dreams. And that was part of their evaluation process of these men. *(Edward Moore)*

Yeah, my mother used to dream dreams. And she'd wake up and tell us about them. And she would talk to her friends. So I'd hear it over and over and over again! They would sit around and interpret their dreams. *(Diane Dugger)*

It appears from such accounts that women are the primary transmitters of beliefs and attitudes about dreams in African American families, and also that women are the primary receivers of talk on the subject. But it would be a mistake to conclude from this that beliefs and attitudes don't get adequately transmitted to men as well—they do, presumably largely through the indirect channels just described.

In fact, *there are no significant differences between African American women and men* when it comes to the fabric of beliefs and attitudes about dreams. I say this on the basis of gender comparisons for several types of dream experiences (ancestor dreams, predictive dreams, déjà vu based on predictive dreams, dreams for another person), gender comparisons for experiences at the waking/dreaming boundary (visions, voices, presences), and comparisons for knowledge of traditional beliefs (dream signs, witch riding you, numbers dreams). So while women are the primary transmitters, the knowledge they transmit is received in one way or another by boys as well as girls.

The Fabric of Tradition and the Future

Up to the present, African Americans have managed to pass along their rich fabric of beliefs and attitudes about dreams. The fabric takes its pattern from the spiritual meaning of dreams. Texture is added by an openness to dreamlike waking experiences. The traces of many African features lend a unifying color scheme. And the fabric is strengthened by an overall conviction that dreams matter.

But the social changes of the past decades have tested this mindset. There's less social isolation now to protect traditional beliefs. The community structures that preserve traditions have weakened. And many people are caught up by a mainstream that cares very little about dreams. As a result, some strands of the fabric have weakened. These include hoodoo fixes and cures, witchery, dream signs, visionary religious conversions, and that late addition, the once-ubiquitous numbers business.

On the other hand, some of the main strands of the fabric appear very strong. Seventy percent of my interviewees said they'd been visited by ancestors in dreams. Ninety-two percent affirmed that dreams are predictive. And there still is found a general openness to experiences at the waking/dreaming boundary. Moreover, even the weakened strands are more or less holding up. Not only do some individuals maintain belief, but there are many others who recognize and honor the traditions as part of their heritage without giving them full credence. Consequently, the fabric of dream traditions as a whole remains intact, if somewhat worn.

What are the prospects for the survival of the fabric of African American dream beliefs in the new century? One way to gauge is to compare the state of the fabric in younger and older individuals. This should indicate whether the fabric is weakening. So I compared interviewees twenty-nine years old and younger with those thirty and older. And the results show that there is *no significant difference between the younger and older age groups* with respect to the key factors explored in this book.

This finding does not, it should be said, eliminate the possibility of fine differences between the groups. Perhaps younger people don't have ancestor dreams as often as their elders, or know as many dream signs, or rely as much on their predictive dreams, and so on. But as a rough indicator, this statistical comparison reveals a striking degree of continuity. Only one strand of the fabric even begins to show an age difference: the interviewees twenty-nine and younger tend to be less aware than the older group of such a thing as picking numbers through dreams. But even here, the difference doesn't reach statistical significance.

Statistical conclusions naturally obscure individual differences. So I hope that a few quick portraits will convey some sense of the texture of continuity and discontinuity in younger individuals at this point in time. I've selected four young men and four young women, all in their twenties.

■ Anthony Shy, age twenty-three, is a self-trained computer consultant with one year of college. His mother frequently tells him her dreams, especially those that are either "extremely traumatic" or "very uplifting." He related to me a mutual vision his mother had experienced together with her siblings when she was a teenager. Shy wasn't sure what to make of the story, but he accepts as authentic his mother's report that she recently heard an uncle calling to her shortly before his violent death. Shy believes he himself held a conversation with the rock star Sting in a half-dream state. When the subject of presences came up, he said, "That's what the older people did, people that are no longer with us. My grandmother had visions like that, down to the most ridiculous things." But later he added, "I think *I* got a chill, when we went into her apartment, when we had to pack her stuff up." This "extremely domineering" grandmother was a Baptist minister who turned Shy's mother off organized religion, though not off faith. She has predictive dreams that she interprets by dream signs and reversal—for example, a death means something good will happen to someone. She plays the lottery from dreams using a dream book, and also plays lucky numbers such as license plates and birthdays. Shy regards his father as a skeptic about all of this. Yet it turned out that the father is "a lottery junkie" who likes to look through dream books. Shy himself has had a dream for another person and has experienced déjà vu based on predictive dreams. He has not heard of witches riding you.

■ Almontez Stewart, age twenty-eight, is an aspiring rap artist trying to launch his own record label and in the meantime earning his living doing commercials. I introduced myself to him while he was flying high-performance remote-control model airplanes in the park. Stewart's reverence for the homemade cane of his recently deceased grandmother (Mama) stands beside his awe of an associate who commutes by private jet between Chicago and Texas. Mama used to tell him "the witch was riding me," but he seems not to believe it. But she, his mother, and he himself had each experienced visitations from dead relatives, either in visions or as presences. In addition, Stewart has experienced predictive dreams, but not dreams for another person. He has relatives who play numbers from dreams, he knows about dream signs, and he believes in déjà vu based on predictive dreams. At present, he shares dreams with his girlfriend.

■ Josh Taifa, age twenty, recently served time on a weapons charge that arose in connection with cocaine dealing. When I interviewed him he was a student, but he still had one foot in the streets. Taifa never had much contact with his grandparents, who died young. He grew up between the projects, with his mother, and the suburbs, with his father. His father, a nationalist who took the family to East Africa when Taifa was five, prohibited TV and gave him mandatory reading. Through second grade he attended Haki Madhubuti's school, New Concept Betterment Center. Taifa says he didn't share dreams with his father. Nevertheless, he described two separate episodes of mutual dreaming between them, one involving a visitation from Taifa's grandmother. Taifa both admires his father and resents him for discipline verging on abuse, a frequent theme of Taifa's dreams. Through his mother, a "Baptist, Christian, something like that, I don't know," he was exposed to testimony involving dreams in church. She is into signs, and bets on the lottery from birthdays and other lucky numbers, but Taifa isn't familiar with dream signs or numbers dreams. When Taifa described his sleep paralysis to her, she told him it was "the witch riding your back." She believes it, while he is undecided. Taifa has had predictive dreams, and believes that predictive dreams are the basis of déjà vu. He has heard ghostly footsteps. He also believes that being born with the veil gives second sight, and that if you fall and hit the ground in your dream, or are called three times, you will actually die. He has not had a dream for another person. Parenthetically, Taifa described his favorite dreams as being typical for a gangbanger:

> With us, those happy dreams don't move us: we like nightmares. Because it gives you the adrenaline rush. The feel of something's happening, you know. Most of my dreams are either I'm getting shot at, or I'm running. It's something negative.

■ Daniel Wideman, age twenty-six, has experienced ancestor dreams, predictive dreams, dreams for another person, and voices. He knows about dream signs and numbers dreams, but not witches riding you. He does not connect déjà vu with predictive dreams. To what has been said already in this chapter and earlier about him, I will only add that he shares dreams regularly with his wife, and will quote his response to a question about his unusual position, growing up with a father, John Edgar Wideman, who reflects on the dream tradition as part of his own calling as a writer:

> Well, we've talked about that more in terms of my career as a writer, a storyteller, than in the specific context of dreams. But I think they're similar in a lot of ways. What we've always discussed is that it's a very unique situation, because I have now the first archival records of the family history and the family's dreams and everything else on paper, whereas he was the one who connected the notes from the field, and put those down into stories. So I have them there, and I also have them in my relationship with him as a father and what he's passed on outside of his writing, his independent persona. But the other interesting thing

that I have is the elders. The people who are his parents and brothers and sisters and aunts and uncles are still alive and actively telling these same old stories, in a new way now, to another generation. So I have my own field notes and my own experience there. Being able to sift through these various different tales and records has given me a very original perspective on things.

Now for the young women.

▪ Devri Whitaker, age twenty-five, has a graduate degree in journalism and works in public relations at a large advertising firm. She describes her grandmother as steeped in the traditional beliefs of "black southern Baptists." When Whitaker dreamed of her deceased father, she was told, "See, your father must miss you." Whitaker says that her mother manages to hold on to some of the old beliefs by translating them into mainstream terms.

> She is trying to interpret what her parents thought, but trying to say that it had some scientific basis. Because you have this immense pride in your black heritage and in your ways of doing things, and the only way for that to be right is for it to have some sort of validation by conventional standards, right? So Mom goes to school and gets a degree in psychology, and all of a sudden you've got terms and things to apply to all these weird dreams that you're having. And I guess that takes it one step further: it's not God telling you something, you're trying to tell yourself something.

Whitaker added, however, that while her mother discounts God, she still believes that dead spirits visit in dreams and as presences. As for Whitaker herself, she said, "I never had that." What does she think about her mother's experiences?

> I think my mom's kind of flaky when it comes to stuff like that! To me, that seems like a cop-out. My mother was like a step. She's a hell of a lot more practical about things than my grandmother was. And I'm even more that way. I find it much more comforting to be able to deal with what I can see and touch and feel, rather than relying on all sorts of fairy godmothers.

Whitaker added, however: "I wish I could believe that. I'm envious of people who believe that." Whitaker has had a dream for another person, but not predictive dreams. She knows about dream signs, numbers dreams, and witches riding you.

▪ Sherry McKinney, age twenty-eight, is a social worker at a private service agency for nonhospitalized psychiatric patients. Her parents, both now dead, used to have friends over all the time and "there was always something about somebody dreaming something and this was what it meant." McKinney's mother was one of six sisters who "talked on the phone every day about what dreams did they have." McKinney's own sister joined a sanctified church, and "they *always* talked about knowing something was going to happen because they had dreamed about it." On the one hand, McKinney says she finds her family's dream signs, such as fish means pregnancy, "ridiculous." But on the other, she used to avoid telling her mother her dreams for fear that her mother's predictions might come true. When McKinney dreams nowadays,

> my first thought is that it must mean something. But then I kind of try not to let myself buy into it. I have a lot of bad dreams sometimes, and so I struggle with trying to believe that they don't really mean anything, and sometimes trying to remember all those times my family said that a dream meant something that it actually happened.

She contrasts her family's serious attitude about dreams—"every time they talked about a dream, it always meant something"—with the attitude in her current circle of white friends, for whom "it's always something really goofy, or it's about dating or something." When McKinney dreams about her deceased mother,

> I think that in some way she's trying to talk to me. And not necessarily trying to tell me something or warn me about anything, but kinda letting me know that she's still around.

McKinney has not experienced visions, voices, presences, or déjà vu based on a predictive dream. She isn't familiar with numbers dreams.

■ Angela Powell, age twenty-seven, is assistant director of the African American project of an AIDS prevention organization. As a child she spent summers on the family land in Alabama with her father's parents. They were Baptists who took her to services where people "got happy" and saw visions. From these grandparents she also learned about dream signs and numbers dreams, but especially she learned that "dreams can sometimes be a way of communicating with the ancestors." Her father had moved north, become a conservative Mennonite minister, and married Powell's mother, a white fellow Mennonite. He responded to early signs of his daughter's gay sexual orientation with authoritarian threats that only hardened their already "rocky relationship." Meanwhile, she embraced her grandparents' beliefs in dreams and ancestors, which she regarded as southern and black and essentially non-Christian, in contrast with her father's style. She was therefore disconcerted when she discovered that

> he meditates and has visions of being with ancestors and communicating with them. And there have been several times where, when I asked him about something, he said he got it from a dream, or that he was told through a dream that he should do this or that.
>
> *Why don't you see that as being cut from the same cloth as the beliefs of your grandparents, who are also Christians?*
>
> Because he's a minister. And because he's had a great deal of issues with me rejecting Christianity and choosing to follow non-Christian ways of looking at spirituality. So for me, it seems like he would have issue with my grandparents' talking about ancestors—but to him, it's completely natural and it makes perfect sense.

Powell is beginning to acknowledge the similarities that bind the three generations in a common belief system, and the rift with her father is healing. He proved "amazingly open" when she officially outed herself, and at her commitment ceremony with her lover he sang "a spiritual in honor of our ancestors" at her request. Powell has experienced predictive dreams, but not in connection with déjà vu. She has had visions and felt presences. She had not heard of witches riding you.

■ Angela Shannon Preston, age twenty-nine, is a poet and a playwright, and is married to a writer, Rohan Preston. She warmly remembers dream sharing as a feature of her early life in Florida:

> As a little girl, you know, we're sitting around in the morning, and our aunts and our grandmothers are around, and somebody will be, "By the way, I had this dream last night." And it was always something that was important. If something's bothering you, and you have a dream about it, then you get up, you talk.

Dreams were usually interpreted by dream signs. Since moving to the North, Preston has had a mutual dream with a sister. They both dreamed that another sister's husband died and they were at the funeral. Shannon didn't tell anyone the dream, " 'cause you don't wanta go and say I dreamed So-and-so died." But when she talked to the first sister by phone and exchanged dreams, she immediately made the connection to a dream sign:

> And I was like, "Okay! I'm relieved! This is what this means!" You know? "Gina's pregnant!" If I had thought about it, if I had told my mother, because she's a different generation, they would stop and talk about

what this dream means. But since I'm here by myself in Chicago—
me and my husband—I don't have my family around to wake up and
say, "I had this dream."

Sure enough, Gina was pregnant. Recently, Preston mentioned her
grandmother in a poem, then dreamed that the grandmother asked
her to give greetings to the family. Her mother told her by phone
that it probably meant Grandmother was pleased with the poem. But
despite these reinforcements of interpretation through dream sharing, Preston feels that "the significance isn't as strong as it used to
be." She does share dreams with her husband, but "we don't really
interpret them, the way we did back then," when there was always an
aunt or a grandmother around "who knew all the little details. Who
could say, 'Okay, this is what this means.'" Yet her faith in dreams
remains strong:

> One of my aunts, I remember, had this dream. The world had just
> come to an end or something, and she saw the whole family on some
> ship. But it was a sign of the family being saved. So I thought that was
> nice! It's nice to be saved, because of who you're related to.
>   *It was because of her?*
> Well, she's the one who had the dream.
>   *Do you have faith in that kind of dream?*
> Oh, yes! I do.

Preston isn't familiar with numbers dreams. She has experienced
dreams for another person, presences, and déjà vu based on predictive dreams.

Let me conclude the chapter with just two more quick portraits, to
illustrate a final point. Young people who discard the beliefs and attitudes of their home environments sometimes return later and embrace
what they previously rejected. This familiar cycle is part of the process
of cultural perpetuation and renewal.

■ Charles Payne, age fifty-four, is a Catholic priest, an educator,
and a candidate Jungian analyst. Payne grew up in inner-city Detroit,
in a family where "individuals paid a lot of attention to dreams" as
predictors of good and bad. "And people *discussed* their dreams."
After he had told me some predictive dreams of his own, I asked
Payne if he thought he got that from his family.

> I connect it with my mother, particularly. My mother seemed to be a
> spiritual kind of person, and oftentimes she did things that us kids

didn't quite understand. You know. She would water pray and do different things, and she never really explained it to us. I mean, we were modern kids, teenagers. And it was only later that I appreciated it. She's dead now, and it's one of the sadnesses I have in my life, that I didn't pay much attention to what she said that's old-fashioned, and that's something from the South, you know, and I took her to be superstitious. To be honest with you, I don't know a lot about what her beliefs were, because I never *asked* her. Never thought it was important. And it was only later that things began to happen to *me* and I began to understand some of the Jungian stuff and other things, that I began to see things in a different light.

▪ Preston Jackson, age fifty, is a sculptor teaching at Chicago's Art Institute, and an avid amateur jazz musician. He was raised in Decatur, Illinois, by parents from Tennessee. His brothers and sisters, as well as his parents, "believed in dreams. They talked about them all the time." The family took the traditional view that dreams are predictive, and they lived by dream signs. But not Jackson:

Especially in the sixties and seventies, people said, "That's ignorant talk! That's backward talk!" We were ashamed of that. Just like I was ashamed of the blues. I still don't like the blues, because you want to be progressive, and the blues seems to hold you there. But we felt the same way about dreams.

As a teenager, Jackson thought his father, a Baptist minister, was "lying" about God talking to him in dreams. But when he grew older and saw his younger brother turn into an inspired preacher who spoke of dreams in the same way, Jackson became "a little bit respectful and a little fearful. I mean, I'm saying, Whoa. This is too consistent." Jackson's now intense preoccupation with dreams commenced about ten years ago:

It's interesting that people are more and more realizing the value of dreams. I guess as we get older, we realize the connections. It's nothing new, because there are religions that talk about these things. But it's a truth that automatically begins to happen to you, you know?

APPENDIX A

INDEX OF INTERVIEWEES

WITH OCCUPATIONS AND AGES WHEN INTERVIEWED

APPENDIX B

TRADITIONAL AFRICAN AMERICAN DREAM SIGNS

The last names of the interviewees who contributed dream signs during our interviews are shown below (with initials when necessary to tell them apart, and the seven anonymous interviewees designated #110, etc.). The prisoners are designated No. 1, etc. Italicized names and titles refer to the following sources, in alphabetical order: W. Demby (1972 [1950]), p. 144; J. Dollard (1988 [1937]), pp. 455–456; *Drums and Shadows* (1973 [1940]), pp. 2, 77; H. Dumas (1988), p. 27; B. Frankel (1977), pp. 38–39; S. E. Griggs (1971 [1902]), p. 15; W. D. Hand (1961), vol. 6, pp. 40, 74, 108, 405, 442, 479–481, 593–594, vol. 7, pp. 17–19, 46; J. Haskins (1974), p. 90; K. W. Heyer (1981), p. 196; H. M. Hyatt (1970–1978), pp. 1100, 1589, 4505; C. H. Johnson (1969), p. 78; T. Morrison (1981 [1973]), pp. 64, 67; P. Oliver (1990 [1960]), pp. 120–121; A. Payne-Jackson & J. Lee (1993), pp. 25–26; N. N. Puckett (1926), pp. 112–113, 463, 496–505, 570; I. Reed (1982), p. 91; L. Saxon et al. (1945), pp. 123 passim; L. F. Snow (1993), pp. 190–191; M. Sobel (1988 [1979]), pp. 72–73; *Southern Workman,* passim; L. Teish (1988 [1985]), pp. 11–12; J. E. Wideman (1992a [1981]), pp. 65 passim; S. A. Williams (1986), pp. 83–86.

Dream Sign	Meaning	Source
angel approaching	good news coming	*Puckett*
hanging back	change your ways	*Puckett*
baby/birth	death	*Puckett, Sobel,* S. Bell, Eskridge, Haizlip, A. Jackson, Jones, Reed, No. 1
	marriage	Reed
baking (bread, cake)	wonderful	#110
beautiful person	good	#110
bird	disappointment	*Hyatt*
	good	Still
whistling bird	death	*Payne-Jackson & Lee*
broom	bad luck, so change your plans	Davis
called three times	death	*Puckett, Haskins*
cat	bad luck	Jolly
	death	Haizlip

cat	enemy	A. Edmond
	vicious/jealous woman	K. Camp
	wisdom	Reed
	woman/mother coming to you	Reed
chicks, many	pregnancy	Blaine
children	good	#110
Chinaman	death	*Wideman*
cloud, floating on	good sign	No. 12
conversation, talking	people coming, meeting people	No. 5
darkness	trouble	A. Edmond
dead/death	marriage/wedding	*Hand, Williams,* A. Edmond
	pregnancy, birth	*Hand,* Haizlip, Hodges, Preston
	good	Shy, D. Wideman, #111
	transformation	EL Zabar
	rain	*So. Workman* (Feb. 1894), *Puckett, Drums*
	trouble	*Demby*
	death	W. Williams, No. 21
friend in white	friend is happy	*So. Workman* (Feb. 1894)
in black	friend is unhappy	*So. Workman* (Feb. 1894)
relative (visitation)	death of someone in family	Wade
	avoid accidental/violent death	No. 5
relative killed	that relative very ill	No. 19
your own	you will not wake up	No. 15
devil after you	you've sinned	*Puckett*
dogs	death	O. Edmond
running	backsliding	*Puckett*
howling	death	*Payne-Jackson & Lee*
dream about someone	long life for that person	Burrows
eggs	quarrel	*So. Workman* (Feb. 1894)
broken	"a big fuss"	*So. Workman* (Mar. 1894)
elephant	death	A. Edmond
falling	you need to pray more	*Puckett*
off a barn	you'll get married	*Saxon*
if you hit	you'll become albino	*Dumas*
	bad luck	E. Smith
if you don't hit	good luck	E. Smith
in ditch	you'll fall in life	*So. Workman* (Mar. 1900)
fire	death; confusion	*Heyer*
	money	anonymous informant
fish	pregnancy	*Puckett, Frankel, Teish, Snow,* numerous interviewees
	trouble	*Demby*
	you've sinned	*Puckett*
rising in the water	good fortune	EL Zabar
flowers in full bloom	very good luck	E. Smith

fruit out of season	trouble/quarrel	*So. Workman* (Mar. 1894), *Puckett*
funeral	wedding	*So. Workman* (Feb. 1894), *Hand,* K. Camp, E. Smith
	pregnancy	E. Smith
grass in winter snow	good	#110
green	money	Still
	fertility	Still
hair, long	death	Jones
horse	death	*Heyer*
	confusion	*Heyer*
black	death	*So. Workman* (Mar. 1900)
houses	moving	*So. Workman* (Mar. 1894)
light	good	Still
	death	No. 5
meat		
to eat	death or bad luck	*Dollard*
fresh	death	*Johnson*
fresh beef	white person you know will die	*Drums*
fresh pork	kin will die	*Drums*
money	trouble ahead	Bickham
large amount	bad luck	*So. Workman* (Mar. 1900)
small amount	good luck	*So. Workman* (Mar. 1900)
dollars	whipping	*Williams*
greenback money	success, good luck	*So. Workman* (Feb. 1894), *Hyatt,* E. Smith
	bad	#110
silver coins/change	trouble, bad luck	*Hyatt, Sobel, Williams,* E. Smith
	quarrel	*So. Workman* (Feb. 1894)
	good	#110
mouse	death	Morris
mud	problems, difficulties	Still
walking through	slander, but someone will help	#110
mule	death	*So. Workman* (Mar. 1900)
naked	death	Reed
	pregnancy	*Frankel*
	bad—if not "built gorgeous"	#110
name	that person sending a message	Davis
owl hooting	death	*Payne-Jackson & Lee*
party	coming into wealth	No. 5
person long not seen	that person will die; but . . .	
if you meet soon	that person will have a long life	Burrows
preacher	good luck	*Puckett*
rainbow	really good luck	E. Smith
red	death	*Hyatt*
red rose	someone in family is very ill	No. 15

reunion	coming into wealth	No. 5
road	journey/process you'll undergo	K. Camp
scuffling	death	*Heyer*
sex, engaging in	serious conversation	EL Zabar
shadow	rooting/conjure	*Payne-Jackson & Lee*
sick	sick	*Heyer*
snake	enemy	Puckett, Dollard, Drums, Saxon, Hand, K. Camp, A. Edmond, McKnight, #110
	evil person	Dugger
	evil coming to you	Freeman-Williams, Reed
	source of wisdom, information	Reed
	pregnancy	Reed
	bad luck	E. Smith
bite	death	#110
to kill	victory over enemy	*Puckett*, E. Smith
to not kill	trouble	*Griggs*
	enemy will get the best of you	*So. Workman* (Dec. 1894)
rattlesnake	you've been conjured	*So. Workman* (Feb. 1898)
little snake	the conjurer isn't very good	*So. Workman* (Feb. 1898)
snow: out of season	danger	Jones, #110
spider	mother	Reed
spouse hurt	conflict with spouse	No. 15
teeth	good fate	Martin
loss/ache	death	*Puckett, So. Workman* (Feb. 1894), Gills
loss	dishonor	A. Jackson
chew up your own	death	Gills
trees		
evergreen	good luck	*So. Workman* (May 1894)
pine tree cut down	you'll fall	*So. Workman* (Mar. 1900)
turtle, mud	wealth	*So. Workman* (May 1894)
vehicles, moving	travel	No. 5
water	good	Still
black	bad luck	*Oliver*
clear	you're doing right	*Puckett*
	good health	*So. Workman* (May 1894)
	success, good luck	*Hand*, A. Edmond, E. Smith
much	sickness	*Heyer*
muddy	death	*So. Workman* (Sep. 1895), *Puckett, Hand*
	bad luck, disappointment, etc.	*Oliver, Hand*, Lowry, E. Smith
	poor health	*So. Workman* (May 1894), *Hand*
or dirty, or cloudy	problem, obstacle	A. Edmond
body of	sensuality	EL Zabar
in, with someone	sexual intimacy with that person	EL Zabar

wedding/marriage	death/funeral	*So. Workman* (Feb. 1894), *Puckett, Hand, Morrison, Teish,* S. Bell, Bickham, K. Camp, A. Edmond, Eskridge, Haizlip, Naylor, Reed
white	death	Naylor
white woman	enemies	*Williams*
woman turned to right	that woman is pregnant	E. Jordan
yellow	jealousy	anonymous informant

APPENDIX C

TECHNICAL DETAILS ABOUT POLICY AND NUMBERS GAMBLING

The major sources (in alphabetical order) for the information in this appendix are L. A. H. Caldwell (1945), G. G. Carlson (1941), St. C. Drake & H. R. Cayton (1945), A. Q. Maisel (1949), and D. J. Travis (1987).

Additional sources include T. M. Ansa (1989), H. Asbury (1938), F. W. Egen (1959), R. Fisher (1992 [1932]), L. Hughes (1935), H. M. Hyatt (1970–1978), P. Oliver (1990 [1960]), R. D. Pharr (1969), J. S. Redding (1934), G. S. Schuyler (1989 [1931]), Andres Visnapuu (personal communication, 1995), D. Wakefield (1960), and Malcolm X (1966 [1965]).

Policy

Several devices were used to draw winning policy numbers, including numbered balls in a bag, and a roulette-type wheel. But the usual equipment was a keg or a drum containing either balls or rubberized cloths rolled up inside metal tubes. The keg or drum came to be known as a *wheel*, and by extension "wheel" also referred to the organization in charge (also called a *pool* or a *book*), as well as to the site of its drawings. Each wheel was also labeled with its own catchy name.

While originally independent, the wheels became clustered under the control of *banks* (or *companies*), the provinces of the policy *bankers* (or *barons,* or *kings*). The *controllers* (or *managers*) who ran the individual wheels seldom owned them eventually. Chicago's most famous policy kings, the Jones brothers, had the Bronx and the Rio Grande wheels, Jim Knight had the Royal Palm and the Iowa, and so on. In 1940, fifteen or sixteen kings owned some thirty wheels in Chicago. By 1955, the number of wheels had grown to forty. The kings in the metropolitan centers also controlled policy in surrounding smaller cities. Thus Detroit controlled Saginaw, Flint, Bay City, Kalamazoo, and other cities in Michigan, as well as Toledo and other cities out of state.

Prior to the time when syndicates in cities such as Chicago bought protection from the politicians and police, the wheels were mobile, setting up in different stores, garages, or vacant lots from day to day. Interested parties were kept informed. But once the fix was in, the wheels for the most part operated and advertised openly, with public spectatorship in the hundreds at each of their two or three draws (or *pulls*) per day. Only occasionally might a wheel still have the inconvenience of relocating temporarily, when the authorities put the heat on to appease public opinion.

Players placed their bets at policy *stations* (or *houses,* or *depots*). In 1940, there were about five hundred stations in Chicago, half of them situated in barber and beauty shops, restaurants, bars, shoeshine parlors, laundries, candy stores, and other businesses. Players could also bet with *walking writers*. Each wheel employed up to two hundred writers. *Runners* is another word for writers, but the term could also designate a messenger who carried bets and payoffs between the writers, the stations, and/or the bettors. (And in the East, writers were often called *collectors*.) Writers were paid from 10 to 25 percent of each bet by the wheel, which also covered their fines and bail in the event of arrest. By custom, writers additionally received from 10 to 20 percent of the winnings from the bettors.

Bets were written up on *slips* (or *tickets*), which looked something like bus transfers. The player took the original, the writer kept the duplicate, and a third copy went to the wheel. But while slips were generally employed, "there developed a whole group of people who did it without pencil and paper" (John L. Johnson). The writer in Julian Mayfield's novel *The Hit* kept all the bets in his head, to minimize his risk should he be arrested. Don King, the boxing promoter, was reputedly a numbers writer renowned for this feat in Cleveland earlier in his career. And in a famous Richard Pryor routine from the 1970s, a wino deplores the comedown of a junkie: "Nigger used to be a *genius,* I ain't lyin'. Booked the numbers, didn't need pencil or paper" (quoted by J. A. McPherson 1993, p. 186). The talented tenth of a tenth who could perform this feat are part of the lore of numbers.

The papers on which results were printed were also called *slips* (or *drawings*). One of these slips had to go to each bettor, so the wheels printed them up by the thousands immediately after every draw. Slips were of cheap paper, color coded by each wheel for its *AM, PM,* and *midnight* draws. It was the job of the *pickup man* (sometimes called a *runner*) both to gather betting slips and money from his writers before the draw, and to deliver the results slips to the writers for distribution after the draw. The pickup man got a 10 percent commission from the wheel on everything booked by the writers under him, but no cut of the winnings.

So the policy hierarchy consisted of the *bankers* on top, formed into a syndicate; the *controllers,* men who managed the separate wheels, under each banker; the *pickup men,* who acted as the controller's lieutenants; and under the pickup men, the *writers*. Other employees of the wheel were the *cashier* (or *ribbon man*), who made sure the cash handed in tallied with the betting slips; the *office clerk,* who entered bets in the books; the *operator* (or *puller*), in charge of actually drawing the numbers; and the *checkers,* who checked the betting slips for winners after the drawing.

Not only might each wheel have as many as three drawings per day, but each drawing might in fact be multiple. A drawing of one set of 12 numbers (out of 78) was called a *single leg* (or *single house*). Another drawing of two sets of 12 was called a *double leg,* and it garnered different bets. On rare occasions, there was even a *triple leg.* More often there might also be a *short leg* (or *junior leg*), consisting of 3, 4, 5, or 6 numbers. Usually the results of the single leg and the short leg were printed on one side of the slip, the results of the double leg on the other.

The basic bet in policy was called a *gig* (or *row*). The bettor won, or *hit,* if the three numbers s/he chose *came out* in any order among the twelve drawn. (A person *hits,* or *catches,* a winning number. A number *hits, falls, falls out,* or *comes out.* The expression "come out" is still current in black speech, not only for winning lottery numbers, but also for dreams which "come true.") In addition to the gig, there was an assortment of other possible bets, ranging from a simple bet on one number (a *single,* or *day number*) to complex bets on combinations, such as the *bug* (or the *spider*), a way of betting on 2, 5, or 8 gigs at a time, with certain numbers held constant. The central number of the spider was called the *carrier;* the other numbers, the *riders.*

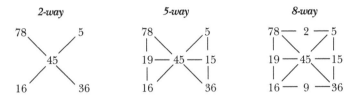

In southern Ohio and small-town Georgia and probably elsewhere, illegal lottery was called "the bug." Perhaps the name derives from the betting combination also called the bug.

Below is a table giving the names, descriptions, and payoff odds most often encountered for these and other bets.

Policy Bets

Name(s) of Bet	Description	Payoff Odds
Single/Day number	1 number falls within the 12 drawn	5-to-1
Station number	1 number in a specified position among the 12 drawn	60-to-1
Flat	2 numbers fall within the 12, in any order	30-to-1
Side	(a) 2 numbers fall consecutively within the 12	200-to-1
	(b) 2 numbers fall side by side in any of the 12 positions of a double leg	80-to-1
Cap	2 numbers fall consecutively within a given cap (each column was divided into 4 caps, or quarters)	200-to-1
Gig	3 numbers fall within the 12, in any order	100- or 200-to-1
Flat gig	3 numbers fall in specified places among the 12	1,000-to-1
Saddle	Any 2 numbers of the gig fall within the 12, in any order (played only if a gig has been played)	10-to-1
?	2 numbers of a gig fall in one leg of a double leg, 1 number in the other leg	10-to-1
Capital saddle	2 numbers fall within the first 3 drawn	800-to-1
Horse	4 numbers fall within the 12, in any order	400-to-1
Gigs-horse	3 of 4 numbers fall within the 12, in any order	50-to-1
Jack	5 numbers fall within the 12, in any order	2,000-to-1
Stovepipe	A combined bet on 8 gigs in which the first 2 numbers of all the gigs are constant	Gig odds for each gig
Bug, or Spider	A way of betting 2, 5, or 8 gigs, with certain numbers constant (see diagram above)	Gig odds for each gig

Numbers

Initially the number used was the final three digits of the Federal Reserve Clearing House report—hence, numbers was sometimes dubbed *clearing house.* The number was published every weekday afternoon in the financial pages. Newsboys cried, "Get the number" (L. Hughes 1935, p. 62). The players "anxiously perused the daily clearing house reports" (W. Thurman 1969 [1929], p. 191) to see if they had won.

Other numbers which came to be used were the closing totals for stocks or bonds (a South Carolina informant in the 1930s called numbers *stock;* in the Midwest, it was nicknamed *the big bond*). The winning three digits might be the thousands or the hundreds of various categories, or some combination. One method employed the final digits of the daily totals for stocks that advanced, declined, and remained unchanged. Mostly national markets were used for this purpose, but some places used local exchanges. Minneapolis/St. Paul used local grain trades; in the Pacific Northwest, it was the daily salmon catch; some southern areas used mining totals; in Winston-Salem, numbers was called *butter and eggs.*

When people said they were *playing the races,* some actually meant they were playing the numbers. That's because at a certain point a shift occurred from banking and market totals to racetrack pari-mutuel totals as the source of numbers. One reason was that the authorities cracked down by persuading the newspapers to round off the financial totals to render them useless for gambling purposes. The other reason was that the gambling public became dissatisfied when it realized that powerful numbers bankers could in fact rig the financial figures by bribery. Racetrack results were considered more tamper-proof.

The *1-2-3 totals* was one method of arriving at the number from racetrack results. The six dollar amounts, or odds, appearing on the tote board for win, place, and show were added together for each of the first three races separately. The winning number was the sequence of digits before the decimal for those three races. If *3-5-7 totals* were used, the winning number was comprised of the digits before the decimal in the tote board totals for the first three races summed together, for the first five races summed together, and for all seven races. Many newspapers not only showed the race results, but also did the requisite math for the benefit of numbers players, under the caption "Mutuels Paid."

The basic numbers bet was the *straight bet,* consisting of three digits in a given order. Odds varied from city to city and bank to bank, in a range from 375- to 750-to-1, but averaging about 500-to-1. As with policy, there was a variety of possible bets.

Numbers Bets

Name(s) of Bet	Description	Payoff Odds
Single/Single action	1 digit in a given position of the 3-digit winning number	8-to-1
Bolita (-ito, -eda, -eita):		
Front *or* First Bolita	First 2 digits of the 3, in order	60-to-1
Back *or* Last Bolita	Last 2 digits of the 3, in order	60-to-1
Bolita Combination	Separate bets on the front and back bolitas	60-to-1
Straight	3 digits in a given order	500-to-1
Box/Combination	Separate bets on each of the 6 possible sequences of 3 digits (e.g., 405, 450, 045, 054, 504, 540)	500-to-1
Box-in	Separate bets on a 3-digit number and its 2 neighbors (e.g., 405 with 404 and 406)	500-to-1
Run down	Separate bets on each 3-digit number in a sequence (e.g., 405, 406, 407, 408, etc.)	500-to-1

APPENDIX D

DREAM BOOKS FOR POLICY AND NUMBERS CONSULTED FOR CHAPTER 6

Andy's Dream Book. 22nd ed. Copyright 1990. Youngstown, Ohio: Eagle Supply.

Aunt Sally's Policy Players Dream Book. Copyright 1994; original copyright 1928. Chicago: Lama Temple. (Previously published by Stein Publishing House, Chicago.)

Black and White Good Luck and Dream Book. No copyright date. Chicago: Black and White.

Black Cat Lucky Number Dream Book. Copyright 1979, 1981. By "Prof. E. Z. Hitts." Mt. Vernon, N.Y.: Val Publishing.

Combination Dream Book. Copyright 1942. By "Prof. Konje" (real name: Herbert G. Parris). White Plains, N.Y.: G. Parris.

Genuine Afro Dream Book. Copyright 1939. Youngstown, Ohio: Mutuel Publishing.

Golden Dream Book. Copyright 1932. By "Prof. De Herbert" (real name: Herbert G. Parris). New York: G. Parris.

Great Professor Abdullah's Mystic Square Dream Book. No copyright date. New York: Eastern Publishing.

Gypsy's Witch Dream Book and Policy Player's Guide. Copyright 1984; original copyright 1903. Chicago: Lama Temple.

Horn of Plenty. Copyright 1995, by Calvin P. Kline. By "Madame N.A.K." Rockville, Md.: Sneaky Pete Publications.

H. P. Dream Book. Copyright 1980; original copyright 1926. By "Prof. Uriah Konje" (real name: Herbert G. Parris). West Hempstead, N.Y.: G. Parris.

Kansas City Kitty Dream Book. No copyright date. Youngstown, Ohio: Eagle Supply.

Lucky Number Dream Book. 38th ed. Copyright 1956; original copyright 193—? By Dr. Pryor. Chicago: Lama Temple.

Lucky Number Policy Players' Dream Book. Copyright 1928, by Max Stein. Chicago: Model Publishing.

Lucky Star Dream Book. Copyright 1985; previous copyright 1928. By "Prof. Konje" (real name: Herbert G. Parris). West Hempstead, N.Y.: G. Parris.

Madame Fu. Futtam's Magical-Spiritual Dream Book. Copyright 1937. By "Madame Fu. Futtam." New York: Empire Publishing.

Mother Shipton's Gypsy Fortune Teller and Dream Book. Copyright 18—? Baltimore: I. & M. Ottenheimer.

Oriental Dream Book. Copyright 1916, by Shrewsbury Publishing. Chicago: Max Stein Publishing House.

Pick'em Dream Book. Copyright 1953, by Carl Z. Talbot. By "Rajah Rabo." Mt. Vernon, N.Y.: Vernon Book Sales.

Prince Ali Lucky Five Star Fortune Telling Dream Book. Copyright 1906, by Martini; rev. ed. copyright 1980, by Dale Book. By "Martini." New York: Wholesale Book.

Queen of Gipsies Dream Book and Fortune Teller. Copyright 1922. New York: Wehman Brothers.

Rajah Rabo's New Improved 5-Star Mutuel Dream Book. Copyright 1932, by Carl Z. Talbot. (1941). New York: L. Hartmann.

Red Devil Combination Dream Book and 1995 Numerology Guide. Copyright 1995. Youngstown: Eagle Supply.

Secrets of Magic-Mystery and Legerdermain. Copyright 1967; original copyright 193—? By Black Herman. Dallas: Dorene Publishing.

Solid Gold Dream Book. Copyright 1933. By "Rex Aquarius." No publisher indicated. (Previously published by Caspar, Krueger, Dory, Milwaukee.)

Sonnyboy Dream Book. Copyright 1982. By "Sonnyboy." Detroit: Ashley Publishing.

Soul City Dream Number Book. Copyright 1977. Baltimore: Komar.

Success Dream Book. Copyright 1985; previous copyright 1931. By "Prof. De Herbert" (real name: Herbert G. Parris). West Hempstead, N.Y.: G. Parris.

Three Wise Men Dream Book. Copyright 1995. Ed. "Prof. Zonite." Youngstown, Ohio: Eagle Supply.

3 Wise Men Dream Book. Copyright 1995, by Calvin P. Kline. By "Prof. A. Z. Hitts." Rockville, Md.: Sneaky Pete Publications.

Three Witches, or Combination Dream Dictionary. Copyright 1984. Chicago: Lama Temple. (Previously published by Phoenix Publishing, Baltimore, 1941.)

True Fortune Teller. Copyright 1990. By "The Gypsy King." Youngstown, Ohio: Eagle Supply. (Previously published by Daily Press Publishing, Baltimore.)

Valmor and Sweet Georgia Brown Dream Book. No copyright date (194—?). Chicago: Valmor Products.

Wise Ol' Owl Dream Book. Copyright 1990. Detroit: Skippy Candle & Incense.

Witch Doctor's Dream Book. Copyright 1891. New York: R. H. Russell & Son.

Witches' Dream Book and Fortune Teller. Copyright 1885. New York: Wehman Bros.

Your Birthday Dream Book. Copyright 1939. Youngstown, Ohio: Mutuel Publishing.

Zolar's Occult Dream Book. No copyright date (193—?). By "Zolar" (real name: King). New York: Zolar Publishing.

APPENDIX E

DREAM BOOK AUTHORS AND PUBLISHERS

Dream book publishing may once have been a side business for certain "racketeers" (P. Oliver 1990 [1960], p. 135; K. Hunter 1964, p. 97), but for the most part the books were and are now produced by ordinary businesspeople. Today the only crooks in the business are the "unsavory bums," as Andres Visnapuu of Eagle Supply calls them, who hit-and-run with "knockoff" versions of copyrighted titles. There was one recently who "took *Three Wise Men* and made the first digit of each number one number less. And of course they sprout up like weeds. You go and chase them down, and the next thing you know they're out of business, so there's money already hidden in a jar."

The nucleus of the world of dream book publishing today is a small number of men and women who distribute each other's titles in their own regions, and who in some cases have been business partners in the past or whose fathers once worked for each other.

As far as I know, only one major dream book publishing company is black-owned at present, the G. Parris Company, founded by Herbert Gladstone Parris (born 1893) and still run by a descendant, Iona Parris. Another man in the business told me that Parris had owned a mansion in Westchester County near New York City, the first African American to own a home there. Parris wrote his own books, under the pseudonyms Prof. De Herbert and Prof. Uriah Konje. His very widely circulated books have one unique feature. At the back is a page addressed "To All Oppressed People of the World," urging readers to obtain an education and a profession: "Education can have as its function the changing of social status of [or] the preservation of the status quo. The final choice lies with each and every one of us." Parris's popular *H. P. Dream Book* has another page, addressed "To the Black People of the World," also admonishing readers to "teach your children trades and professions of all kinds," and concluding: "I want to ask you not to fight for social but political equality, and as soon as you shall have acquired political equality, there is nothing to prevent you from obtaining social equality." (*H. P.* are Herbert Parris's initials. Andres Visnapuu said that this popular book was known as "Harlem Pete.")

Another early black author and publisher, Dr. Pryor of Chicago, was described at some length by St. Clair Drake and Horace R. Cayton in *Black Metropolis* (1945, pp. 477–478). On the first floor of this entrepreneur's establishment was the Japo Oriental Company, selling hoodoo and other occult products on site and throughout the Midwest and the South. In the basement, Dr. Pryor presided at "King Solomon's Temple of Religious Science." According to the skeptical Drake and Cayton, Pryor used the temple as a further means of selling his hoodoo products to clients convinced their numbers weren't hitting because someone had crossed them.

Pryor's business was bought during the late 1940s by Lama Temple, a white concern, purveyors of "religious equipment." Pryor's *Lucky Number Dream Book,* according to Martin Mayer, present owner of Lama Temple, was the seed of that company's dream book business. In 1949, Jacob Kovinsky of Lama Temple also bought Valmor Products, which published another dream book targeted to black readers. Then, in the 1950s, Kovinsky bought out yet another Chicago publisher, Max Stein, evidently from Stein's heirs, since Stein, who also made magicians' supplies, died in 1950 (*Chicago Tribune* obituaries, May 28). This purchase brought in *Aunt Sally's* and *Three Witches.* Kovinsky's son Marvin Kane sold out to Candle Corporation of America, a maker of standard candles as well as religious supplies. Then Marty Mayer—once an employee of Lama Temple and later a partner in business with David Adler, present owner of Skippy Candle & Incense, a Detroit publisher—bought out the Lama Temple division of Candle Corporation of America. He presently owns Lama Temple as part of another firm he bought, International Imports in Los Angeles, which sells dream books in its list of fifteen hundred occult titles, as well as a line of spiritual products. (This information comes from Carolyn Long [2001] and from publishers Martin Mayer, Edward Kay, and Andres Visnapuu.)

Another black dream book author, though not a publisher, was the popular magician Herman Rucker, who styled himself Black Herman. Black Herman, who claimed he was born in Africa as a Zulu and brought to the United States by a missionary at age ten (Black Herman 1938 [?], pp. 9, 14), was cast by Ishmael Reed as a major character in *Mumbo Jumbo* (1978a [1972], pp. 39, 241 passim), Reed's satirical polemic on the confrontation between African and European civilization. Reed twice mentions the dream book (*Secrets of Magic-Mystery & Legerdermain*), and rhapsodizes that the same cultural core of life affirmation that inspires musicians like John Coltrane and Otis Redding "compelled Black Herman to write a dictionary to Dreams that Freud would have envied." Black Herman's spirituality exhibits "the ancient Vodun aesthetic" of pantheism and animism. Black Herman, an "American HooDoo man," is a spokesman in *Mumbo Jumbo* for Reed's theme that the core of hoodoo comes from the ancient religion of Egypt via West Africa, and that it lives on in popular black culture. Black Herman's signature trick was to be buried alive, making him in Reed's eyes a symbol of Osiris, to whose cult Reed traces the essence of African culture. Isis restored the buried body of her brother-lover Osiris, who had been dismembered by their brother Set, a prototype for everything wrong with Western civilization due to its suppression of erotic spirituality.

Black Herman is also made to say by Reed that "you shouldn't attempt to use any aspect of The Work for profit" (p. 58). This sentiment makes a striking contrast with the sketch of Black Herman as a "con man" dead of drink by forty drawn for me by Ed Kay, son of Joseph Kay, Black Herman's publisher.

As Ed, himself now retired, tells the story, Joe Kay was an orchestra leader on the borscht circuit. Dorene Publishing came into being after one of his musicians named Young couldn't pay some money he owed Joe, so instead gave him the copyrights to *Secrets of the Psalms* and several other occult books with dream sections which Young somehow possessed or had written. Joe printed them up and began selling them to "the gypsies" in New York storefronts. Later he acquired additional titles and also got into "oils and incenses." But he only began selling to the black trade through his association with Black Herman. According to Ed, Joe Kay became Black Herman's "promoter":

It was very unique then for a black and [a] white man to be partners. But they
used to go on the road, at these revivals. And the most amazing part of this is,
they'd dig a grave for him. And he'd get into this grave, into the box, and what
he says, he buried himself alive. And he had a pole leading down so that you
could talk to him and he could get a little air. And they'd come along, and they
would literally fill that grave up with money. And they used to take that damn
stuff up by the bushelful. This was for prayers, for the people, to save them.

At these revivals and at his establishment in Harlem, which evidently was a church,
Black Herman also sold his book with its section on dreams, published by Joe Kay.

Sherry Praytor, the current owner of the publishing company Sonny Boy, told me
that Black Herman's book was not originally Joe Kay's publication, but that Dorene
only put its imprint on a book provided by a different publisher—a common practice
in this business. When I pursued the question with Ed Kay, he reiterated that his
father was Black Herman's original publisher. Praytor's version is supported, however,
by the fact that a book titled *Black Herman's Dream Book* was advertised by a forerunner
of Eagle Supply in 1939 (H. B. Weiss 1944b, p. 642), the year Joe Kay received his first
titles from the indebted musician named Young. Praytor frankly doubts Ed Kay's
whole story about his father's partnership with Black Herman ("I'd probably not lean
on it, if I were needing a prop somewhere"). That wasn't the only time publishers I
interviewed cast doubt on each other's versions of the history of the business.

Sherry Praytor is the third owner of Sonny Boy Products, publisher of *Sonnyboy
Dream Book*. According to her, this book was written by a Black Indian woman in
Miami named Miss Dillard together with her children, one of whom, "Chief Tar," is
pictured on the cover: "And I'm sure someone interested in making a dollar collabo-
rated." Miss Dillard began as a spiritual reader. Along with the dream book, she developed Sonny Boy's line of "remedies," which sell widely in this country and even
abroad. I asked Praytor if Miss Dillard had been a sincere rootwoman. In response,
she told me that the Federal Drug Administration had visited Miss Dillard about
twenty years earlier:

> When they went down there, she came to the door in her bra and panties—
> she was an old woman, an old Indian woman—and had laundry in her hand,
> and opened the door, and walked out, and hung laundry while they talked to
> her. And I said, "What did she say about this?" And they said, "Well, it's hard to
> really know. She just kinda lives in her own world." So there you have my input
> on whether she was sincere.

Eagle Supply of Youngstown, Ohio, was started under a different name by a white
man, Ralph Anderson, in 1931. The company's main business at that time was the
wholesale distribution of magazines and newspapers. Anderson was joined in the 1940s
by his stepson, Paul Renniff, who took over when Anderson died in 1967. Renniff was
in turn joined in the 1970s by the present manager and co-owner, Andres Visnapuu.

According to Visnapuu, *Three Wise Men,* Eagle Supply's best-selling title, "was originally compiled in 1925 by a black man in Detroit, who was very spiritual, and a spiritualist." The company purchased *Kansas City Kitty* in the mid-1960s from the author, a
man in Columbus, Ohio, who may have been black; Visnapuu isn't sure. As for the
firm's other titles, Ralph Anderson himself authored *True Fortune Teller, Andy's, Billy
Bing*, and others. An employee named Trojac authored *Afro* in the 1930s (title
changed to *Aero* in the 1960s). Eagle Supply also puts out a series of statistically based
lottery prediction books, not dream related, which Visnapuu himself prepares.

As far as I know, none of the other major dream book publishers has black ante-cedents. Lady Dale dream books, for example, were written and published in Philadel-phia starting in the 1930s by Alex Silverberg, father of the present owner Dale Silver-berg. Since the mid-1950s, the family has also operated an occult shop. Joe Kay of Dorene convinced Alex to go into that business, according to Dale. Ed Kay, Marty Mayer, and Andres Visnapuu all spoke with something like adulation of Alex Silver-berg, a larger-than-life character who had died within a year of my interviews with these publishers in 1995. From these sources, I heard that Silverberg was a higher than thirty-two-order Mason; that after World War II he diverted all the military hard-ware that was supposed to be scuttled in the Mediterranean to Israel; that he had ties with the intelligence community as well as the Mafia; that he fought for the First Amendment right to publish pornography in 1952 in a case involving his importation of a Swedish magazine, and got arrested for distributing the first issue of *Playboy* in Philadelphia; and that when he had heart bypass surgery, the pope sent a special emissary to Philadelphia with a papal blessing—this for a Jewish sex and dream book purveyor.

Cynical or Sincere?

The black dream book authors and publishers all are long since gone from the busi-ness, if not dead, with the single exception of Herbert Parris's heir Iona, who wouldn't consent to be interviewed. The elder Parris was a sincere race man, who probably had a certain faith in numerology. Dr. Pryor was almost certainly a charlatan. Black Her-man and Miss Dillard are ambiguous figures. The anonymous author of *Three Wise Men* was described as "very spiritual, and a spiritualist." Beyond this, little can be said about the attitudes of the blacks in the business toward their work, whether they were cynical or sincere. But something can be said about the whites in this regard, on the basis of conversations with them.

Andres Visnapuu declared that Alex Silverberg "was a fan" of quartz crystals. "He always used to tell me, 'It's quartz, Andres! It's quartz.' " However, when I posed the implication to Dale Silverberg that her father, Alex, had been a believer in certain aspects of the work he was doing, she replied:

> No, he wasn't. Not at all. I'm much more so than he was. He had an extremely religious Jewish childhood, but his time in the army ruined religion for him forever, because, he said, both sides were praying to the same God. He did not have any time for formal religion and he did not believe in any of this. But he believed that people who believed were helped by it. . . . And we never in our store preached black magic. We always do protection and never do evil. And that was my father's belief.

Dale painted the Lady Dale occult shop as a neighborhood family business in which the Silverbergs acted as de facto social workers. I have no reason to doubt her excla-mation that "people loved my parents in that store," although the family attitude she described is paternalistic toward the black clientele whose beliefs they profit from.

Ralph Anderson of Eagle Supply wrote his books with a different outlook, accord-ing to his successor Visnapuu:

> He studied the Bible. Let's say it's an apple. So, Garden of Eden. What was the chapter and verse? He was an avid numerologist. And a brilliant statistician. He compiled a twenty-year record of every number that ever came. He had like thirty or forty people on picnic tables and benches in a hall, and he would read

the numbers, and made a human computer. And then he'd compile all this stuff, basically do a batch file, and find out the frequency patterns and which days they favored and all this stuff. But he was always biblically founded in everything.

As for Visnapuu, who authors Eagle Supply's current nondream statistically based lottery books, he is not a numerologist, he says, but professes to be working on sound statistical principles to predict future probabilities from patterns in random drawings. However, another publisher characterized Visnapuu's apparently sincere approach as sheer salesmanship on his part.

When I put it to Marty Mayer of Lama Temple that he struck me as basically a nonbeliever in the predictive power of his products, he said, "Yeah, I am. If I believed it, I would have won the lottery already. Most of my associates and the people in the business, if we all believed it, we'd go crazy."

Ed Kay of Dorene Publishing described how his father, Joe, acquired new titles:

> He would buy books, or he'd hire people to write books. I do know that we had one guy, a little later he became a writer on *Family Circle Magazine,* from their inception. And he used to get drunker than hell, and he'd go down to the library, and a couple of days later he'd come up with a book. As I understand it, he sat in his house and he wrote a bunch of stuff down, and put numbers, but he wanted to get meanings.
> *Did he look at dream interpretation books?*
> Well, a lot of that stuff he just made up. A lot of the dream stuff strictly came out of his mind.

Finally, Sherry Praytor of Sonny Boy Products made the following remarks about dream book composition:

> I think a few definitely did have roots in the black community, but for some time it has strictly been a moneymaking venture. You may rest assured, I'm thinking of writing another dream book. It's gonna be under another name. And it's gonna be just as obscure to try to trace as the ones you're working on now. Does that tell you anything?
> *How are you actually going to figure out the numbers?*
> I'm just gonna sit down and make them up, just like everybody else does. That's as honest as I know to be about it.

NOTES

1. Through the Porthole of Dreams

1 *Dreams, my mama taught me, do not lie:* S. Youngblood (1997), p. 168.

I began going to workshops: A. Shafton (1995).

4 *"Dream-singers all":* L. Hughes, "Laughters," 1922, in L. Hughes (1994), p. 27.

2. Dream Is What We Do: Influences from Africa

10 *What evidence can we find:* Folklorist N. N. Puckett (1926), pp. 16–17. Linguist W. K. Vass (1979), p. 91.

12 *There are, of course:* S. Crouch (1990), p. 222.

Nevertheless, there are many black writers: I. Reed (1990 [1988]), p. 161.

13 *We've been speaking about the survival:* D. Wideman (n.d.), p. 52.

14 *In a century-old short story:* P. L. Dunbar (1900), p. 15. It might seem that Dunbar was using "dream" simply to mean *hope.* Of course he did mean hope, but the reference to Homer's "ivory gate" of dreams tells us he meant night dreams first. According to Homer, dreams come through one of two gates: true dreams come through the gate of horn, false dreams through the gate of ivory. Dunbar apparently didn't intend the irony of giving the slave in question false (ivory) dreams, for the character eventually escapes to Canada and later fights in the Union army. See chapter 8 for further observations about the overlap of night dreams and hope dreams.

"Our first responsibility is to survive": J. E. Wideman (1995 [1994]), p. 102.

Until her early death: For a fuller account of Marion Stamps's dream, see Shafton (1996).

3. Grandmother Will Come: Ancestor Visitation Dreams

17 *Yet people, no matter who:* B. Jones (1989 [1983]), p. 83.

Have you ever dreamed: M. Chinkwita (1993), p. 54.

Such ideas have led Westerners: M. Karenga (1988), p. 20.

18 *Further, it generally takes more:* A "self-conscious renaissance" of Nigerian Yoruba religion was begun in the United States by a man from Detroit who took the

name Oseijeman Adefumni (R. F. Thompson 1984 [1983], p. 90). After being initiated in the Afro-Cuban religion Lukumi, Adefumni went on, says Songadina Ifatunji, to reconstitute a form of Yoruba religion "that took Catholicism out and returned it to its older, more traditional form." Adekola Adedapo says that "what sets our movement apart [from Lukumi] is that we have specific and very detailed rituals involved in hooking us back up with our ancestral roots." Since the 1970s, Adefumni has been headquartered near Beaufort, South Carolina, at African Village, where Yoruba architecture, dress, and social patterns as well as religion are replicated. Members such as Ifatunji and Adedapo live around the United States.

Also, Africans don't regard: M. Chinkwita (1993), p. 25. R. Shaw (1992), p. 38.

Africans widely believe: M. Chinkwita (1993), p. 59.

In the African view: H. J. Fisher (1979), p. 221. J. P. Kiernan (1985), p. 307. Akiga (1965 [1939]), p. 213.

Newly converted: N. Sithole (1977 [1970]), p. 111. P. R. McKenzie (1992), p. 130.

19 *African ancestor veneration:* M. J. Herskovits (1990 [1958/1941]), p. 150. P. Hill Jr. (1992), p. 97. R. Bastide (1971), pp. 161–162. R. F. Thompson (1984 [1983]), p. 132 passim. K. W. Heyer (1981), pp. 34–35, 42, 70. J. Haskins (1974), p. 88.

The fact is, however: R. Bastide (1971), p. 161. M. J. Herskovits (1990 [1958/1941]), p. 63. C. Joyner (1984), p. 138.

And so does the belief: H. M. Hyatt (1970–1978), pp. 20–21. L. F. Snow (1977), p. 28.

21 *One woman:* The interviewee in question is one of seven interviewees who requested anonymity. These seven individuals will be identified in the notes by their numbers, #110 through #116, on the Index of Interviewees (Appendix A). This interviewee is #115.

In recent decades: S. Mahone (1994b), p. xxxii. L. Hughes (1969 [1930]), p. 43. R. Wright (1986 [1963]), p. 71. R. Ellison (1972 [1952]), p. 33. J. Baldwin (1993 [1960]), p. 352. J. E. Wideman (1992c [1983]), p. 339 (italics omitted); see also idem (1990), p. 171.

22 *The word itself—"ancestor":* T. Morrison (1988 [1987]), pp. 29, 35–36.

But some contemporary writers: S. Youngblood (1989), p. 95; personal communication, 1995. P. Marshall (1983b), p. 95.

As part of the literary theme: For example: R. D. Pharr (1969), p. 151; J. Emanuel, in D. Randall (1971), p. 188; A. Lorde (1982), p. 104; J. Lester (1984), p. 109; C. Major (1987), pp. 75–76; R. Kenan (1990 [1989]), pp. 36, 189; J. Woodson (1990), pp. 67, 98; idem (1992), p. 98; idem (1993), p. 23; R. "C." Thurmon (1991), pp. 100–101, 121–124, 130–132; L. Forrest (1992), pp. 137, 139; A. E. Eskridge (1994), p. 25 passim; C. W. Sherman (1994 [1993]); E. Danticat (1995), pp. 167–168; T. Due (1995), pp. 230–231 passim; T. Morrison (1997), pp. 154–155; R. S. Lewis (n.d.); D. Wideman (n.d.).

23 *An "ancestor visitation dream":* M. O. Hill (1995).

It's said there's a "clear difference": E. B. Bynum (1993), p. 202.

A woman who liked watching sports: This is interviewee #114.

24 *And a woman whose mother had died:* This is interviewee #110.

Not all, but most: To preserve the anonymity of the black male prisoners who completed questionnaires, they will be identified in the notes by their numbers, No. 1 through No. 25. This is prisoner No. 4.

25 *Dreams foretelling deaths:* The prisoner is No. 14.

26 *Just after a dear friend:* Illana Jordan's mom is interviewee Elvie (LV) Jordan.

27 *Illana Jordan's dream:* The prisoner is No. 21.

28 *In European tradition:* E. D. Genovese (1974), pp. 217, 219–220.

29 *Africans say:* M. Chinkwita (1993), p. 59.

31 *How common is it:* On a 2-tailed t-test for interviewees and whites in my samples, t-value = -5.01, $p = .001$. Other surveys from the past few decades also show that blacks report contacts with the dead more than do whites. **Real contact of any kind with the dead: blacks: 57%** (R. A. Kalish & D. A. Reynolds 1973); **46%** (A. M. Greeley 1975). **Whites and mostly white samples of the general population: 36–42%** (J. A. Davis & T. W. Smith 1990); **38%** (Kalish & Reynolds, op. cit.); **27%** (Greeley, op. cit.); **17%** (G. H. Gallup & F. Newport 1991). **Contact in dreams: blacks: 37%; whites: 17%** (Kalish & Reynolds, op. cit.). These percentages for dream visitations are half of what I found, but the ratio between blacks and whites is virtually identical to my finding.

Apart from statistics: I. Reed (1978b), pp. 131–132.

32 *It's often supposed that education:* J. Dollard (1988 [1937]), p. 454. A. M. Greeley (1975), pp. 15–16. D. Hay & A. Morisy (1978), p. 258.

4. That Bolt of Lightning: Predictive Dreams

34 *All those tales:* A. Petry (1985 [1946]), pp. 15–16.

Virtually the whole world: A. Shafton (1995). S. Krippner (1995). J. King (1997), p. 5. A. M. Greeley (1975). G. H. Gallup & F. Newport (1991). J. McClenon (1993).

Furthermore, belief in predictive dreaming: The difference in rate of belief in predictive dreams between the black interviewees and the white sample is highly significant statistically: 2-tailed t-test, t-value = -5.57, $p < .001$. In the white sample, 29/80, or 36%, said they had themselves experienced at least one predictive dream. Of believers, 17/46, or 37%, had not themselves had the experience. A comparable breakdown is not available for the black interviewees.

36 *Notice how similar:* M. Chinkwita (1993), pp. 55. L. Teish (1988 [1985]), p. 80.

Let's look briefly at how dreams: M. Chinkwita (1993), pp. 23–24.

The way Africans interpret dreams: M. Chinkwita (1993), p. 65. I. Sow (1980 [1978]), pp. 77, 79 passim.

37 *In the Independent "prophet-healing" churches:* A. Omoyajowo (1965), p. 29. B. C. Ray (1993), p. 276. W. MacGaffey (1983), p. 47. L. Mullings (1984), pp. 147–148. E. T. Lawson (1984), p. 79.

The little we can know: F. Douglass (1968 [1855]), pp. 284–285. Later versions of Douglass's autobiography contain essentially the same story. Douglass and the other confederates suspected the dreamer himself, Sandy Jenkins, of being the one who betrayed their escape. A plausible interpretation of events is that his prophetic dreams prompted Jenkins to withdraw from and reveal the plan.

Harriet Tubman: Sarah Bradford, *Harriet Tubman: The Moses of Her People* (New York: Corinth Books, 1961), quoted by J. E. Noll (1991), p. 73.

Folklore, a bridge: N. N. Puckett (1926), pp. 496–497. H. M. Hyatt (1970–1978), pp. 182–185, 280. Hyatt's text reads: "Ah lay down tuh sleep an' see diff'rent things befo' dey come tuh pass." For ease of reading, I will render imitations of black vernacular such as this into standard English spelling, except in a few cases. Colloquial word forms (gonna, 'cause, etc.) will be preserved, as will be syntax and grammar, for these constitute an accurate rendering of the expressive habits and choices of the informants. But no informant would spell "I" as "Ah," or "they" as "dey."

38   *Richard M. Dorson's collections:* R. M. Dorson (1958), p. 232. Douglas Gills told how an uncle of his "had a penchant for finding money. They used to have these big black pots, huge kettle pots that you used to make soap in. If you accumulated a couple of hundred dollars, you would put the money in the pot, turn the pot upside down, so the water couldn't get into it. And so he would have dreams about pots being turned upside down, in the ground, guarded by cats. So he would then get up, that night or the next night, and he'd go follow a cat, it could have been a cat he hadn't seen before, it didn't matter, except it was usually a black cat. And the cat would lead him and sit on the ground, and he would have a shovel, and he'd dig 'em up, and lo and behold, there it was. Well, he must have done this maybe four, five, six, seven times. The other side of the coin is, while he had a penchant for finding the money, he could never keep it. There was always a crisis, that meant he had to pay at least most of what he got."

One of the most intriguing: The dreamer here is interviewee #114.

39   *A surprising number of literal predictions:* Published accounts of literal predictive dreams appear in William Grant Still's biography (J. A. Still 1990, p. 72; V. Arvey 1984, p. 77) and in Joyce Elaine Noll's collection about African American mystics and psychics (1991, p. 15 passim). While predictive dreams are actually not plentiful in African American literature—that is, apart from numbers dreams (see chapter 6)—literal or near-literal predictions are to be found from Charles Chesnutt (1969b [1899], p. 14) to Toni Morrison (1988 [1987], p. 132) and Alice Walker (1989, pp. 80–81).

Perhaps even more indicative are those works where characters tell *plausible lies* about literal predictive dreams as a way of getting over—persuading someone to place a bet (L. Hughes 1935, p. 92), or getting close to a woman (R. McKnight 1992, p. 166). Other plausible lies—about visions, visitations, and conversion experiences—are scattered through African American literature (C. Cullen 1991 [1932], pp. 366, 530; L. Hughes 1958, pp. 43, 109; C. Himes 1989a [1959], pp. 20, 24; C. Brown 1965, pp. 210–211; J. J. Phillips 1985 [1966], p. 37; T. Morrison 1972 [1970], p. 118; T. McMillan 1994 [1987], p. 241; A. Rahman 1994, pp. 312–313). The literary motif of the plausible lie about spiritual experience reflects the healthy skepticism found in the black community (and voiced by interviewees Haki Madhubuti, Ethel Smith, and #114), not so much about the possibility of such experiences as about the authenticity of all those claimed. But the very fact that such events sometimes get faked is testimony to the importance given the genuine thing. So the motif of the plausible spiritual lie is one more way in which literature substantiates the importance of the genuine thing.

Again, people who believe: The prisoner is No. 15.

40   *Occasionally, dreams alert us:* A. Shafton (1995), pp. 262–289.

41   *A topic of good news:* Additional interviewees with "expect to see So-and-so" dreams were Edwina Ackie, Darryl Burrows, Eileen Cherry, Betty Rodgers Hale, Katie Jones, Angela Shannon Preston, and Reggie Winfrey. As for good news dreams in

literature: **gender announcement:** A. J. Verdelle (1995), p. 248 (see also B. Frankel 1977, p. 41); **house preview:** E. Southerland (1979), p. 157; **expect to see So-and-so:** M. Golden (1989), pp. 185–186.

42 *Everyone has heard stories:* The following account of a vision involving the same accident was related by an African American woman not among the interviewees: "I was [driving] southbound on Michigan Avenue, about a block from Lake Street, and I saw the vision of the El falling off the track! And as soon as I got to the intersection of Lake and Michigan, I could see the El falling off the track."

43 *Joe Cheeks believes:* For the Douala people (Cameroon), for example, the dream "goes beyond a simple warning. It is the communication of a fait accompli" (E. De Rosny 1985, p. 266). But a Nigerian writes that a dreamer seeks an interpretation precisely to "avert the 'danger' if something frightful is foretold, or bring the dream to fulfillment if it promises something good" (A. Omoyajowo 1965, p. 15).

Former Bulls champion: Hodges continued: "And not only that, when I was growing up, each yard had like little chains that we used to just kinda hop over 'em, or whatever, it wasn't no biggie. Well, this day, as the trucks came by, we went to go over the little chains that we *thought* were there—Fences! Okay, so, we moved from Chicago Heights, where we lived in the projects. Then like my sophomore or junior year [of college], I would come back in the summer, went to the projects, right? Got fences up. Blew me away, man!" Although Hodges carried the dream with him during the intervening years, it was not until he saw the fences that he became conscious of the dream as a predictor of the social future. Hodges estimates he's told this story to about twenty people.

44 *Death is probably the most common prediction:* For an elaborate fictional depiction of predictive dreams which prove inevitable, see E. J. Gaines (1981 [1971]), pp. 89–97, 114–117, 121.

In these cases: The anonymous interviewee is #110.

45 *Finally, here's a case:* In Haiti, said Nicole Smith, the presence of Jesus or a priest or other such figure in a dream is taken as a sign that there is a true message in the dream. "The seeing of my brother-in-law while I still was with Jesus meant that this was going to take place in my life, too."

47 *The dream of falling:* I gathered data from the prisoners, but not the interviewees, concerning the belief that dreams of falling can cause death. For the prisoners, 80% had heard the belief, while 36% affirmed it. For the white sample, 68% had heard the belief, while only 3% affirmed it.

One afternoon: For examples in African American literature of dreams revealing the past, see J. E. Wideman (1992c [1983]), pp. 459–462 and E. Danticat (1995), p. 189.

Quite often the boundary: J. E. Noll (1991), p. 28, citing Gary E. Kremer, *George Washington Carver: In His Own Words* (Columbia: University of Missouri Press, 1987).

There were a number of interviewees: For examples of telepathy and clairvoyance in African American folklore and literature, see *Drums and Shadows* (1973 [1940]), pp. 57–58, 70; D. West (1982 [1948]), p. 38 passim; A. D. Pate (1994), p. i passim.

48 *Parapsychologists suppose:* Additional crisis telepathy dreams were told by Edwina Ackie, Kai EL Zabar, Maisha Hamilton-Bennett, and interviewees #110 and #111.

5. We Got the Signs: Signs in Dreams

53 *"Daughter got her blood"*: S. Youngblood (1989), p. 101.

That's an example of a sign: Certain signs are more than omens, they actually *cause* things to happen: if you bite off a butterfly's head, you'll get a new dress (N. N. Puckett 1926, p. 312). This chapter mostly concerns signs that are simply omens, since signs in dreams are usually of that type. But as we've seen already, the line between prediction and causation isn't always definite.

A good place to search: Z. N. Hurston (1981), p. 22. B. Frankel (1977), p. 40.

Other signs predict: H. M. Hyatt (1970–1978), p. 1094. B. Frankel (1977), p. 48. M. K. Asante (1993), p. 131. For the veil in literature, see T. M. Ansa (1989), pp. 2 passim (see also J. E. Wideman 1992c [1983], p. 456; T. C. Bambara 1993, p. 310). The interviewees who talked about seventh sons or people born with veils are Osuurete Adesanya, Nelson Peery, Josh Taifa, and Craig Hodges. Hodges's mother was born with the veil, and as a result is "a heavy person." Hodges gave a variant version of just what "a veil" is: "Her hair actually covered her face. And people say—this is what my grandmom was saying—that she was never supposed to see any evil. You know, and that they weren't supposed to cut it, but they did."

54 *But without a doubt:* M. H. B. Roberson (1983), p. 165. R. Bass (1935), p. 389. C. McKay (1928). R. Bass (1930), p. 387; idem (1935), p. 391.

Many animals are bad signs: W. Attaway (1993 [1941]), pp. 5, 43. R. Bass (1930), p. 386. B. Jones (1989 [1983]), pp. 77, 84. C. Major (1987), p. 106. C. L. Taulbert (1989), p. 106. A. Bontemps (1959 [1931]), p. 175. P. Oliver (1990 [1960]), p. 120. M. Walker (1967 [1966]), p. 3. J. M. Brewer (1968), p. 287. A. Bontemps (1968 [1936]), p. 96; idem (1959 [1931]), pp. 186–187. T. M. Ansa (1989), pp. 242 ff. V. Arvey (1984), p. 12. The three interviewees with stories about the death sign of a bird flying into the house are Carole Morisseau, Barbara Pulliam, and Judy Still.

Spiders, by way of contrast: P. Oliver (1990 [1960]), p. 120. A. Jackson (1993), p. 51.

Domestic animals: H. M. Hyatt (1970–1978), p. 4096. C. Major (1987), p. 106. P. Oliver (1990 [1960]), p. 120 (lyric by Ma Rainey).

Some signs have meanings: H. M. Hyatt (1970–1978), p. 2027. N. Shange (1985), p. 120. S. E. Griggs (1971 [1902]), p. 15. B. Jones (1989 [1983]), p. 77 (italics added).

55 *In addition to signs established:* S. Terkel (1993 [1992]), p. 247. Examples of special signs in African American literature include H. Dumas (1976), p. 110; M. Dixon (1989), pp. 17, 40; S. Youngblood (1989), p. 57; J. E. Wideman (1992e), p. 16; A. Rahman (1994), p. 288; D. West (1995), p. 6.

In European tradition: J. Haskins (1974), pp. 119–120. M. J. Herskovits (1990 [1958/1941]), p. 189. N. N. Puckett (1926), p. 482. M. Sobel (1988 [1979]), p. 72. J. Thornton (1992), p. 240.

There are, to be sure: N. N. Puckett (1926), pp. 311, 453–454. M. Sobel (1988 [1979]), pp. 72, 184.

56 *Yet the single most frequently heard dream sign:* L. F. Snow (1993), p. 191.

57 *All of these important dream signs:* A. Shafton (1995), pp. 54–55. C. Chesnutt (1969b [1899]), p. 135. F. H. Melland, *In Witchbound Africa* (London: Seeley Service, 1923), p. 247, quoted by W. Morgan (1932), p. 396. Frances Freeman-

Williams said, "If you dream about someone's having a boy, they're having the opposite, a girl." Gender reversal in the interpretation of dreams signifying births, deaths, or matters in general was mentioned by Diane Dugger, Oscar Edmond, Laura McKnight, and interviewee #113.

Former longtime prisoner: B. Jones (1989 [1983]), p. 169.

Selective application of reversal: S. G. Lee (1958), p. 266.

This idea of life replacing life: W. D. Hand (1961), p. 40. T. C. Bambara (1972), p. 146 (see also idem 1980, pp. 110, 140). J. Lester 1984, pp. 104–105 (see also N. N. Puckett 1926, pp. 112–113; E. Danticat 1995, p. 48; S. Jackson-Opoku 1997, pp. 87, 350). Reincarnation was brought up by interviewees Adekola Adedapo, Osuurete Adesanya, Darice Wright Camp, Kimberly Camp, Eileen Cherry, Kai EL Zabar, Ann E. Eskridge, Maisha Hamilton-Bennett, Craig Hodges, Cecile Jackson, Marva Pitchford Jolly, Sherry McKinney, Laura McKnight, Regina Reed, Nicole Smith, Don St. Cyr Toups, and #114.

58 *Belief in reincarnation:* W. MacGaffey (1983), p. 127. M. Sobel (1988 [1979]), p. 14. E. D. Genovese (1974), p. 212. J. T. Munday, "Spirit Names among the Central Bantu," *African Studies* 7 (1948), p. 40, quoted by W. K. Vass (1979), p. 35. A. Omoyajowo (1965), p. 8.

The cycle of rebirth: E. Danticat (1995), p. 41. T. M. Ansa (1989), p. 103.

59 *Nevertheless, both knowledge and belief:* The woman who knows eleven dream signs is interviewee #110.

Some people hold on to a sign: B. Jones (1989 [1983]), p. 83 (see also R. Fisher 1992 [1932], p. 29).

There are many outright nonbelievers: The version of Bickham's saying recorded by Zora Neale Hurston (1990 [1935], p. 95) goes, "'Niggers got all de signs and white folks got all de money.' . . ."

60 *"The Chinaman" is a chapter:* J. E. Wideman (1992a [1981]), pp. 75–77.

Now, Chinaman *is a fairly rare: Chinaman,* as Wideman has tipped the reader off in the chapter's epigraph (op. cit., p. 70), is a sign of death in traditional African American "toasts." Toasts are long, ribald narrative poems depicting contests of wits and powers. The most famous toasts are "The Signifying Monkey," "Shine," and "Stagolee." From a toast called "The Fall" comes this verse, containing the Chinaman sign: "But the deadliest blow came when this whore / Took sick and could not sin. / The Chinaman spoke, no motherfucking joke, / I knew this was the end" (W. Labov et al. 1968, p. 338).

61 *Wideman exemplifies:* A. Jackson (1993), p. 51.

6. Blackonomics: Playing the Numbers from Dreams

62 *Numbers was like a community institution:* Claude Brown (1965), p. 191.

"Lottery is dreaming": L. Saxon et al. (1945), p. 136.

Legal lotteries: F. W. Egen (1959), pp. 12–13. G. G. Carlson (1941), pp. 30–35.

Some people mistakenly think: L. A. H. Caldwell (1945), p. III. Job R. Tyson, *Brief Survey of the Great Extent and Evil Tendencies of the Lottery System as Existing in the United States* (Philadelphia, n.d., 1833), quoted by H. B. Weiss (1944a), p. 531. H. Asbury (1938). G. G. Carlson (1941). St. C. Drake & H. R. Cayton (1945).

63 *The origins of the three-digit system:* J. S. Redding (1934), p. 533. G. G. Carlson (1941), p. 47. The introduction of numbers has also been attributed to "early Italian immigrants to New York City" (G. J. McCall 1963, p. 426); to one Carlos Duran, who supposedly brought numbers to New York from Dominique around 1913 (J. R. Lawson 1979, p. 25); to Cubans who brought their game bolito (P. Oliver 1990 [1960], pp. 132–133); to staff members at the *New York Sun* (H. Asbury 1938, p. 88); and to black lottery promoters in Harlem, in 1921(I. Light 1974, p. 76, citing John Scarne, *Scarne's Complete Guide to Gambling*).

"Numbers was the thing": Claude Brown (1965), p. 191. L. Seaton (1954), pp. 1, 2. D. Wakefield (1960), p. 25.

Numbers gambling is a fixture: Black literature mentioning numbers, policy, or lottery in specific locales, not cited in the next note, includes the following (other mentions of policy, etc. are scattered through the notes of this chapter): M. Angelou (1971 [1969]), p. 51; idem (1982 [1981]), p. 47; idem (1993 [1974]), p. 126; T. M. Ansa (1989), p. 192; idem (1996), p. 24 passim; T. C. Bambara (1980), pp. 13, 109, 146; Imamu A. Baraka (1971), p. 20; P. Beatty (1996), p. 51; D. Bradley (1986), p. 40 passim; Cecil Brown (1983), p. 72; Claude Brown (1965), p. 36 passim; E. Bullins (1973), p. 58; G. Cain (1972 [1970]), p. 179; M. Charles (1971), passim; L. Clifton (1969), p. 250; P. H. Dean (1971), p. 314; W. Demby (1965), p. 31; idem (1972 [1950]), pp. 26–27 passim; W. E. B. DuBois (1974 [1928]), pp. 113, 140; T. Due (1995), p. 152; L. Elder III (1965), p. 24 passim; R. L. Fair (1966), p. 177; idem (1970), p. 73 passim; R. Fisher (1992 [1932]), p. 138; L. Forrest (1988 [1973]), pp. 16, 172; idem (1992), p. 98; D. Goines (1975), p. 41 passim; M. Golden (1989), p. 13 passim; C. (O.) Gordon (1969), p. 413; D. Greaves (1971), pp. 273, 289, 298; S. Greenlee (1969), p. 210; N. C. Heard (1978), pp. 26, 32; C. Himes (1972), p. 32; idem (1980), p. 59; idem (1988 [1966]), p. 85; idem (1989a [1959]), p. 79; idem (1989b [1954]), p. 162; idem (1990), pp. 26, 100; L. Hughes (1958), p. 20 passim; idem (1961), p. 53 passim; idem (1969 [1930]), p. 301; K. Hunter (1975), pp. 122, 124; S. Jackson-Opoku (1997), p. 114; P. James (1975), p. 152; B. Jones (1989 [1983]), p. 169; J. Lester (1970 [1969]), p. 45; D. Long (1970), pp. 310–311; A. Lorde (1982), p. 50; C. Major (1987), p. 32; P. Marshall (1981 [1959]), p. 28; C. J. McElroy (1988 [1987]), p. 30; T. McMillan (1994 [1987]), pp. 24, 153; J. A. McPherson (1973), p. 360; idem (1977), p. 64; T. Morrison (1981 [1973]), p. 32; idem (1993b [1992]), pp. 9, 10, 23; W. Mosley (1991 [1990]), p. 133; idem (1992 [1991]), p. 55; idem (1993 [1992]), p. 9; idem (1994), pp. 25–26; idem (1995), pp. 64, 198; L. Neal (1971), p. 268; R. D. Pharr (1997 [1978]), pp. 98, 158; D. Pinckney (1993 [1992]), p. 62; I. Reed (1978a [1972]), pp. 20, 113; idem (1986), p. 16; idem (1990 [1967]), p. 14; G. S. Schuyler (1989 [1931]), pp. 26–27 passim; N. Shange (1982), p. 42; idem (1985), p. 126; A. Shepp (1971), pp. 41, 70; C. L. Taulbert (1992), pp. 52–53; H. Van Dyke (1971), pp. 63, 78; idem (1985), p. 457; E. K. Walker (1970), p. 11; D. West (1940), p. 124; J. E. Wideman (1986 [1973]), pp. 45, 244–245; idem (1987), p. 20; idem (1990), p. 176; idem (1992b [1981]), pp. 181–182; idem (1992c [1983]), pp. 372–373; idem (1992h), p. 136; J. A. Williams (1968 [1967]), pp. 62, 97, 144, 209, 211; idem (1969), p. 44; A. Wilson (1986), pp. 21–22; idem (1993), pp. 1–2; Malcolm X (1966 [1965]), pp. 60, 84 ff; A. Young (1981 [1970]), p. 8 passim; S. Youngblood (1989), pp. 12–13.

64 *In Ann Petry's Harlem:* A. Petry (1985 [1946]), p. 143 (see also W. Thurman 1969 [1929], p. 133; J. Baldwin 1993 [1960], p. 6; T. C. Bambara 1966, p. 37; E. K. Walker 1970, p. 11; C. McElroy 1990, p. 122). R. Ellison (1972 [1952]), pp. 316 passim, 480. L. Hughes (1935). J. Mayfield (1989 [1957]); idem (1989 [1958]).

R. Wright (1986 [1963]). K. Hunter (1964). R. D. Pharr (1969). There is also Lewis A. H. Caldwell, whose novel *The Policy King* (1945), while perfectly readable, is actually just a thinly veiled history and sociological study of policy in Chicago up to 1945.

My personal favorite: Pharr's idiosyncratic masterpiece (1969) is part adventure, part novel of education, part love story. It continually surprises the reader by its unexpected turns of plot and its effortless ventures into new layers of meaning. Pharr delivers all this with much of the tang of Langston Hughes, the edge of Chester Himes, and the passion of James Baldwin.

Pharr chose to set his novel: The interviewees with childhood stories about numbers in lesser cities and towns are Winford Williams from Indiana, Preston Jackson from downstate Illinois, Achim Rodgers from Ohio, Ntozake Shange from Missouri, John L. Johnson and Frances Callaway Parks from Tennessee, and Otis G. Grove from Alabama.

Was numbers also "fraudulent"?: For fraud depicted in literature, see L. Hughes (1931), p. 88; idem (1961), p. 133; L. A. H. Caldwell (1945), p. 59; Claude Brown (1965), p. 214; T. C. Bambara (1972), p. 145; J. Mayfield (1989 [1957]); J. S. Redding (1934), p. 534. For cutting the odds—the so-called "cut-number"—see V. Caldwell (1933); G. J. McCall (1963), p. 424; A. Wilson (1993), pp. 83–84.

65 *A ploy the bankers resorted to:* L. A. H. Caldwell (1945), p. 87. G. J. McCall (1963), p. 423. Many fixes were aimed at rival bankers, not at the bettors. Dutch Schultz supposedly forced the black numbers kings of Harlem to come in under him in 1931 by rigging a number and breaking their banks. Later, a "Fix Syndicate" headquartered in New York and Pittsburgh specialized in altering numbers in newspapers around the country for local bankers, who would see to it that rivals were heavily hit (*Our World* 1950, p. 27; A. Q. Maisel 1949, p. 23; K. Hunter 1964, p. 285).

Dutch Schultz was passively involved in an even more notorious case of rigging. The day he was shot and killed in 1935, no one knew what was coming next, so the writers and pickup men failed to turn in the money. Those whose job it was to fix the numbers got a message from the mob: "We are broke—no money to pay anyone." That day 000 came out, a ill-omened number that was seldom played. This story was covered in *Time* (1935, pp. 16–17), and several versions of it circulated in the black urban folklore of the day (F. W. Egen 1959, pp. 65–66; G. G. Carlson 1941, pp. 135–136; R. D. Pharr 1969, pp. 154, 222).

But for all this: I. Light (1974), p. 57. St. C. Drake & H. R. Cayton (1945), p. 486.

But even if the game: P. Oliver (1990 [1960]), p. 132.

The moralists: L. A. H. Caldwell (1945), pp. 34, 63 passim. St. C. Drake & H. R. Cayton (1945), pp. 490–491. L. Hughes (1935); idem (1958), p. 20; idem (1971), p. 59. J. Mayfield (1989 [1957]), pp. 32–33. Claude Brown (1965), p. 189. J. A. Williams (1968 [1967]), p. 211. L. Forrest (1988 [1973]), p. 172. R. Wright (1986 [1963]), pp. 36–37, 41–47. K. B. Clark (1964), p. 28. M. Robinson (1975).

The theme of white takeover and control of numbers occurs often in black literature, expressing a widespread and lingering resentment (J. Mayfield 1960, p. 424; D. Wakefield 1960, p. 25; R. Ellison 1972 [1952], p. 365; K. Hunter 1964, p. 47 passim; L. Elder III 1965, p. 76; R. D. Pharr 1969, p. 24; J. A. Williams 1969, p. 44; R. L. Fair 1970, pp. 81–83; Imamu A. Baraka 1971, p. 20; C. Himes 1972, pp. 32, 37; D. Bradley 1986, p. 65; I. Reed 1986, p. 16; M. Golden 1989, p. 40).

66 *In contrast to the white press:* Our World (1950). Ebony (1953). M. Robinson (1975), p. A-2. J. S. Redding (1934), p. 539. J. Mayfield (1960), p. 425.

Numbers was "the most important": L. A. H. Caldwell (1945), p. 218. J. S. Redding (1934), p. 536. G. G. Carlson (1941), p. 50. D. J. Travis (1987), p. 174; idem (1981), p. 36. R. D. Pharr (1969), pp. 178, 233–234. C. (O.) Gordon (1969), p. 413. D. Greaves (1971). A. Shepp (1971), p. 41. V. Caldwell (1933). P. James (1975), p. 193.

As late as 1979: J. R. Lawson (1979), p. 25. St. C. Drake & H. R. Cayton (1945), passim. D. J. Travis (1987), p. 175.

But what about the players: D. Wakefield (1960), p. 25. G. Ifill (1995), citing Colin Powell, *My American Journey.* G. G. Carlson (1941), p. 140. A. Wilson (1993), p. 3. N. Giovanni (1993), p. 112. The theme of buying a house with numbers winnings is treated positively by novelists R. D. Pharr (1969), p. 43; M. Golden (1989), p. 37; and J. E. Wideman (1992c [1983]), pp. 372–373. As an historical note, Denmark Vesey, who later led the famous slave insurrection of 1822, bought his freedom in 1800 with $1,500 won in a legal lottery to finance road work (A. Fabian 1990, p. 126).

68 *A few churches:* G. G. Carlson (1941), pp. 108–109.

Some of these practices were corrupt: L. Hughes (1958), pp. 92–94, 131 passim (see also 1935, p. 80; D. Bradley 1986, p. 40).

Apart from the churches: G. J. McCall (1963), pp. 421–422. L. Hughes (1935), pp. 72, 86. A. Petry (1985 [1946]), pp. 123–124. O. Harrington (1971), p. 73. For hoodoo and numbers in the South, see L. Saxon et al. (1945), pp. 123, 125, 136; H. M. Hyatt (1970–1978), pp. 245, 546, 573, 580, 804, 1081, 1083, 1318, 4564, 4638.

69 *But the spirituality of numbers:* B. Jones (1989 [1983]), pp. 169–170.

One interviewee: The artist is interviewee #115.

Lucky numbers can come from anywhere: L. Hughes (1935), pp. 46, 58. R. D. Pharr (1969), p. 217. Claude Brown (1965), p. 286. H. M. Hyatt (1970–1978), p. 546. L. Hughes (1994), p. 425.

70 *A player in the 1940s:* G. G. Carlson (1941), p. 116. St. C. Drake & H. R. Cayton (1945), p. 476. L. Saxon et al. (1945), p. 125.

72 *In Pharr's* The Book of Numbers: R. D. Pharr (1969), p. 309 (see also W. Demby 1972 [1950], p. 217; *Pittsburgh Courier,* Dec. 8, 1934, quoted by G. G. Carlson 1941, pp. 116–117, 134–135; L. Hughes 1994, pp. 269–270).

73 *It's a common belief:* J. S. Redding (1934), p. 542. St. C. Drake & H. R. Cayton (1945), p. 475 (see also T. M. Ansa 1989, p. 233). The prisoners are No. 18 and No. 22, respectively. The anonymous dreamer is #114.

74 *Since 1862:* H. B. Weiss (1944a). R. Lucas (1949), p. 53. L. Seaton (1954), p. 2. D. J. Travis (1981), p. 36.

75 *As a Jet article describes:* F. H. Mitchell (1957), p. 50. D. J. Travis (1987), p. 176. J. Mayfield (1989 [1957]), p. 103. *Hot numbers,* by contrast, are numbers believed to be enjoying a temporary run of luck for weeks, months, or even years, but which lack any special meanings (G. G. Carlson 1941, p. 14; J. S. Redding 1934, p. 537).

4-11-44: H. Asbury (1938), facing p. 106. Jacob Riis, *How the Other Half Lives* (New York: Charles Scribner's and Sons, 1907 [1890]), p. 155, quoted by G. G. Carlson (1941), p. 40. I. Light (1974), p. 43. L. Saxon et al. (1945), pp. 121–123, 133. G. G. Carlson (1941), glossary. St. C. Drake & H. R. Cayton (1945), p. 470.

The Death Row: C. Himes (1989b [1954]), p. 162. St. C. Drake & H. R. Cayton (1945, p. 474) and D. J. Travis (1981, p. 36) both give 9-9-29 as the "Death Row" for policy. But because of the way policy numbers were drawn, there could be no repeated numbers such as 9-9. Apparently there was a misprint for 9-19-29 in Drake & Cayton, inadvertently copied by Travis.

76 *Fancies from the Bathroom:* St. C. Drake & H. R. Cayton (1945), p. 475. P. Oliver (1990 [1960]), p. 135. G. J. McCall (1963), p. 422.

Once an angry basketball player: G. G. Carlson (1941), p. 133.

If you've been around: G. J. McCall (1963), p. 423. St. C. Drake & H. R. Cayton (1945), p. 474. B. Jones (1989 [1983]), p. 101. D. Long (1970), pp. 310–311. J. Mayfield (1989 [1957]), pp. 18, 137. P. Oliver (1990 [1960]), p. 135.

77 *An anthropologist heard:* Loudell F. Snow kindly relayed this story to me in 1994.

The interviews produced: In addition to those related in the text, stories about dreams not played were told by Edwina Ackie, Adrienne Edmond, Almontez Stewart, and Devri Whitaker.

78 *Young Reggie Winfrey:* The woman with the typical comment is interviewee #112.

79 *Even the old faith:* Showcase Chicago cable TV, October 21, 1995.

Regardless whether people play or not: J. E. Wideman (1987), p. 20.

81 *To conclude:* On 2-tailed t-tests, (1) t-value = -7.78, $p = .001$; (2) t-value = -10.46, $p = .001$; (3) t-value = -4.93, $p = .001$; (4) t-value = 9.43, $p = .001$. Interestingly, the black prisoners showed less familiarity with numbers dreams (64%: t-value = 2.71, $p = .011$) and dream books (56%: t-value = 2.55, $p = .016$) than did the interviewees.

7. I Knew You Were Gonna Say That: Déjà Vu and Predictive Dreams

82 *It was as if he were reliving a forgotten dream:* C. Himes (1989b [1954]), p. 182.

Most of us are familiar: Reported percentages of people who have experienced déjà vu in various populations range from **56%** to **96%** (M. Leeds 1944; A. M. Greeley 1975; V. M. Neppe 1983; J. A. Davis & T. W. Smith 1990; H. N. Sno & D. H. Linszen 1990; G. H. Gallup & F. Newport 1991; J. S. Levin 1993; J. McClenon 1994).

As for comparative rates of déjà vu among blacks and whites, my surveys showed **blacks: 94%; black male prisoners: 96%;** and **whites: 92%.** The General Social Surveys of the National Opinion Research Center show blacks and whites even at about **65%** (T. F. Richardson & G. Winokur 1968; J. W. Fox 1992, citing J. A. Davis & T. W. Smith 1990), and a survey of two college campuses shows **black students: 80%,** and **white students: 86%**—not a significant difference (J. McClenon 1994).

Scientifically speaking: A. T. Funkhouser (1983a). H. N. Sno & D. H. Linszen (1990). R. A. White (n.d.).

83 *Among whites:* G. H. Gallup & F. Newport (1991), p. 140.

While only a single black: The nervous system glitch theory was mentioned by interviewee #111.

Fully 57 percent: By 2-tailed t-test, t-value = -6.11, $p = .000$. The percentage of black male prisoners who subscribe to the predictive dream theory of déjà vu is even higher—83%. The 15% for whites in my sample falls close to the only other statistic I've seen on this question: 18% of U.S. whites (mostly Jewish males) gave "dreams and prophecy" as their explanation for déjà vu (M. Leeds 1944, p. 42).

Unfortunately, after fifty years Leeds couldn't recall exactly what he meant by "dreams and prophecy" at the time (personal communication, 1995). Recent discussions of déjà vu in connection with predictive dreaming include Louise E. Rhine, *Hidden Channels of the Mind* (New York: William Sloane Associates, 1961), pp. 106–108, quoted by C. T. K. Chari (1964), pp. 199–200; V. M. Neppe (1983); A. T. Funkhouser (1983a, 1983b); H. N. Sno & D. H. Linszen (1990).

84 *Several other interviewees:* Unremembered preview dreams were also mentioned by Stephanie Bell, Darice Wright Camp, and Marshall Hatch.

85 *The very first recall:* The person in question is interviewee #116.

86 *It's common during déjà vu:* A. Funkhouser (1995).

A couple of people: The prisoner who dreamed about his brother is No. 23.

Occasionally someone undergoes: Interviewee #114 can locate old preview dreams in her journals. The prisoner is No. 5.

87 *In other cases:* Prisoner No. 4 dreamed about his guards.

Illana Jordan: Illana Jordan also mentioned that there had been an infinite regress of déjà vus within the dream itself. Two other interviewees also experienced illusions of infinite regress in association with déjà vu. Anthony Shy said, "I remember doing this, I dreamed that this happened. And in that dream, I remember thinking the exact same thing, that I had dreamed that it happened. But then it happened. [For example] I was sitting watching television, and I remembered that I had a dream that I was watching television, but in the dream, I remember that I had a dream." He doesn't ever remember the regress dream until the déjà vu experience is in progress. Michael Spencer spoke of "déjà déjà vu": "In the déjà vu I remember the déjà vu and I remember remembering the déjà vu. And I always try to search for the ending point as to when the loop ends. And it's usually when I branch off to another thought, and then I try to remember if I remember that, and usually I don't."

89 *Perhaps the prosaic content:* Of the nine writers who mention déjà vu, only three make a connection to dreams. Of these, two (Chester Himes 1989b [1954], p. 182; Roi Ottley 1965, p. 43) may have predictive dreaming in mind, but don't directly say so; while the third (Ralph Ellison 1972 [1952], p. 293) mentions memory error, possibly based on dreams, as the underlying cause. Two of the nine writers attribute déjà vu to other causes (Jessie Fauset 1989 [1924], p. 157; John Edgar Wideman 1995 [1994], p. 186). Four writers simply describe the déjà vu phenomenon without explanation (Al Young 1980, pp. 10–11; Sherley Anne Williams 1986, p. 82; Xam Cartiér 1992 [1991], p. 181; Tananarive Due 1995, p. 188).

Out-of-body experiences were reported by 36% of the black interviewees, 48% of the black male prisoners, and 26% of the white survey subjects (see chapter 9).

8. The Underbeat: Dreaming and Other States of Consciousness

91 *None of these explain:* L. Forrest (1992), p. 11.

92 *Fluency with altered states:* I. Sow (1980 [1978]), pp. 45–46 (see also W. MacGaffey 1983, p. 70; J. P. Kiernan 1985, p. 305).

93 *I said in chapter 2:* C. C. Bell (1982), p. 1017.

94 *A notable illustration:* V. Harding (1992 [1981]), p. xvii.

"I have a dream" definitely means: In African American literature, "dream" is a commonplace metaphor for hope, but the connection with night dreams, if any, is seldom made explicit. The hope almost always pertains to racism and social justice (Z. N. Hurston 1978 [1937], p. 31; H. Dumas 1976, p. 73; S. A. Williams 1986, p. 171), but usually the dream = hope metaphor is used ironically, to depict hopelessness or the intransigence of racist America (R. Wright 1966 [1945], pp. 186–187; idem 1987 [1958]; L. Hughes 1994, pp. 93–94, 189, 426; J. Baldwin 1993 [1960], pp. 404, 413; idem 1968, pp. 32, 157; J. Edwards 1963, p. 45; E. Bullins 1973, p. 85; R. D. Pharr 1997 [1978], pp. 23–24; W. Mosley 1994, p. 20).

The two instances I know of where waking hope is explicitly connected with hopeful night dreaming are also ironic. In Charles Chesnutt's story "Cicely's Dream" (1969b [1899]), when Cicely chances to find a young man lying unconscious in the woods, she recalls a "beautiful dream" that predicted the event as well as happiness flowing from it. Cicely and the young man fall in love and become engaged. But at the end of the story, the dream is suddenly fulfilled for her white schoolteacher from the North instead of for Cicely. It turns out that the dark-hued amnesiac she rescued and loves is not a light-skinned black after all, but a dark-skinned white, the lost beloved of the schoolteacher, wounded in the Civil War recently ended. Their improbable reunion, a coincidence that would spoil an ordinary love story, instead sharpens the irony of this parable about the disappointment of the former slaves in the hope, the dream of Reconstruction. The story concludes laconically, "For, after all, her beautiful dream had been one of the kind that go by contraries." The other instance where waking hope is explicitly and ironically linked with hopeful night dreaming comes from a recent novel by poet Paul Beatty (1996), who caps off *The White Boy Shuffle* with this verse, indicating cynically how King's prophecy stands: "Like the good Reverend King / I too 'have a dream,' / but when I wake up / I forget it and / remember I'm running late for work."

The words "dream" and "dreaming'" are used liberally in African American literature to characterize diverse aspects of waking life in addition to hope. These include, to mention a few, aspects of *time* (uncanny recurrence, sudden transformation, time distortion, time fleeing); *memory* (sharp recall, faulty recall, repressed reality, the lost past); *thought* (illusion, self-deception, uncertainty, thoughts known to others); and *mood* (total absorption, chilling out, intoxication, absence of appropriate emotion). Also frequently illuminated by the metaphor of dream are the *great verities of life:* death, love, freedom, innocence—and, of course, hope.

95 *Apart from comments:* The woman with the program for disadvantaged children is interviewee #110.

97 *Sometimes both words:* The woman who dreamed she saw her great aunt is interviewee #113.

In the other direction: "Vision" is used with almost as much latitude as "dream." Besides to mean "seeing things," interviewees used "vision" to signify a variety of other waking experiences: predictions (Maisha Hamilton-Bennett), "hunches" (Osuurete Adesanya), out-of-body experiences (Thomas Pitts), and unseen presences (Anthony Shy), as well as imagination (Frances Freeman-Williams) and just thinking (Diane Dugger).

Often the term "vision": J. A. Still (1990), p. 70.

99 *After three years of struggle:* S. D. Plumpp (1986), p. 15.

100 *Where do dreams "come from"?:* W. B. Webb (1994), p. 55. In the Freudian tradition, dreams express the energies of unconscious wishes, as transformed to disguise them from the conscious mind. Jung thought that the unconscious seeks to communicate with the ego, not to disguise itself, and he added that some aspects of dreams express a collective unconscious. But although he wavered about it, he usually regarded the collective unconscious as an organ of the individual psyche, not as an outside agency. Other dream theorists dispute the existence of the unconscious, but believe that dreams are produced by, and reflect the preoccupations of, the dreamer's own psyche, which simply operates somewhat differently in sleep than in waking. For a comprehensive survey of twentieth-century Euro-American dream theories, see A. Shafton (1995).

The majority of African Americans: The woman who said African Americans believe "it's coming from somewhere else" is interviewee #112. Her assessment is shared by black psychologists I consulted, including Edward Bruce Bynum, Gerald G. Jackson, Faheem C. Ashanti, and Charles Payne (see A. Shafton 1996, p. 77).

101 *One last point:* This prejudice of white psychiatry is discussed by M. Sabshin et al. (1970); C. C. Bell et al. (1988); and J. D. Geller (1988).

102 *After talking about visitation dreams:* The woman with dreams about her current life is interviewee #112.

9. Didn't Bother *Me* None: Experiences at the Edge of Dreaming

103 *I have always seen things:* H. Dumas (1976), p. 81.

104 *It's striking how many:* T. R. Gray (1966), pp. 233–234.

The great abolitionist: William L. Katz, ed., *Narrative of Sojourner Truth, a Bondswoman of Olden Time* (New York: Arno Press and New York Times), 1968, quoted by J. E. Noll (1991), p. 86.

Other slave narratives: L. Brent (1861), pp. 431–432. J. M. Brewer (1968), pp. 255–256. C. H. Johnson (1969), p. 97. L. W. Levine (1977), pp. 78–79, quoting WPA Slave Narratives (North Carolina).

Visions are a recurring motif: **Folklore:** H. M. Hyatt (1970–1978), pp. 26, 111; Z. N. Hurston (1981); *Drums and Shadows* (1973 [1940]); R. M. Dorson (1956); B. Frankel (1977); K. W. Heyer (1981); J. Mellon (1988). **Literature:** T. M. Ansa (1989), p. 56; idem (1996), passim; A. Bontemps (1959 [1931]); idem (1968 [1936]), passim; Cecil Brown (1993), p. 33; X. Cartiér (1992 [1991]), p. 20 passim; D. T. Clardy (1987 [1985]), pp. 227, 232; C. Cullen (1991 [1932]), p. 528; E. Danticat (1995), p. 85; W. E. B. Du Bois (1989 [1911]), pp. 19–20 passim; T. Due (1995), pp. 62, 146–147; H. Dumas (1988), p. 116; R. Ellison (1972 [1952]), p. 58; A. R. Flowers (1985), pp. 64, 151–154; M. Golden (1989), p. 60 passim; R. Hayden (1966); C. Himes (1989b [1954]), p. 32; Z. N. Hurston (1978 [1937]), p. 13; S. Jackson-Opoku (1997), p. 86; L. Jeffers (1983), p. 13; J. Kincaid (1986), p. 4; C. E. Lincoln (1989 [1988]), p. 136; C. Major (1987), p. 10; P. Marshall (1983a), pp. 87–88 passim; T. Morrison (1978 [1977]), pp. 9–10 passim; idem (1982 [1981]), pp. 257–259; idem (1988 [1987]), p. 25 passim; idem (1997), pp. 311–312; W. Mosley (1995), p. 167; A. Murray (1989 [1974]), p. 2; A. Petry (1958), p. 195; R. D. Pharr (1969), p. 302; J. J. Phillips (1985 [1966]), pp. 35, 38;

D. Pinckney (1993 [1992]), p. 45; I. Reed (1990 [1967]), p. 17; idem (1982), p. 89; N. Shange (1982), p. 5 passim; C. W. Sherman (1994 [1993]), p. 16 passim; R. "C." Thurmon (1991), pp. 93, 97; A. Walker (1989), pp. 183, 185; D. West (1982 [1948]), p. 38; J. E. Wideman (1986 [1973]), p. 173; idem (1992a [1981]), pp. 19, 72; idem (1992d), p. 247; A. Wilson (1988), pp. 78–81; idem (1990), pp. 35, 68, 69; J. Woodson (1990), pp. 67, 98; idem (1992), p. 98; idem (1993), p. 23; R. Wright (1966 [1945]), p. 104; idem (1987 [1958]), p. 340; idem (1986 [1963]), pp. 139, 143; S. Youngblood (1989), p. 106.

105 *In my survey:* By a 2-tailed t-test, t-value = -3.36, $p = .001$. Most visions are not hallucinatory—they aren't mistaken for true sensory perceptions. Nonetheless, susceptibility to hallucinations is another indicator of the same fluid boundary. Western culture, with its "rigid distinction between reality and fantasy," takes a dim view of hallucinations, suppressing their occurrence as well as recognition of them when they do occur. In cultures where "the distinction between reality and fantasy is more flexible, individuals are encouraged to observe their hallucinations" and other imagery, and so the threshold for their perception is lower (I. Al-Issa 1977, pp. 576–577; V. R. Adebimpe et al. 1981, p. 519).

It has been noted that hallucinations without other "symptoms," that is, among sane individuals, "seem more common" among Africans than other peoples. And in schizophrenia, in some depressions, and probably in other mental disorders, hallucinations are more frequent among Africans than Westerners (E. Corin & H. B. M. Murphy 1979, p. 155; S. T. C. Ilechukwu 1991, p. 187). A worldwide cross-cultural survey of schizophrenic patients found that visual hallucinations are least frequent in "*urban* Euro-Americans," and most frequent in "peoples of Africa and the Near East" (H. B. M. Murphy et al. 1963, p. 240). A study of a random sample of adults in the United States found a higher rate of hallucinations among blacks than whites (J. J. Schwab, et al., "A study of reported hallucinations in a southeastern county," *Social Order and Mental Health,* New York: Brunner/Mazel, 1979, cited by V. R. Adebimpe et al., op. cit.). As for psychiatric patients in the United States, with a few exceptions studies show the same results. A plausible explanation is that psychological problems express themselves more readily through hallucinations in blacks than whites because blacks are culturally preconditioned for, and whites against, experiences at variance with consensual reality. **Schizophrenia:** M. M. Vitols et al. (1963); A. De Hoyos & G. De Hoyos (1965). **Mixed matched diagnoses:** J. L. Liss et al. (1973); A. Welner et al. (1973); R. M. Costello (1973); B. D. Singer (1977). **Dementias (such as Alzheimer's):** C. I. Cohen & L. Carlin (1993). **Alcoholism:** J. Viamontes & B. J. Powell, "Demographic characteristics of black and white male alcoholics," *International Journal of Addiction* 9:489–494, cited by C. C. Bell et al. (1985), p. 717. **Contrary findings: no racial difference. Schizophrenia:** R. J. Simon et al. (1973). **Affective disorders:** S. B. Guze et al. (1975).

Not all of the visions: The black male prisoners were the only group specifically polled as to whether their visions were seen in physical or mental space. Of the thirteen out of twenty-five (52%) who had had visions, 54% experienced them in mental space only, 8% in physical space only, and 38% in both.

It's important to realize: J. E. Wideman (1992a [1981]), p. 72.

In addition to Wideman: The woman who found her father in the kitchen is interviewee #112. Madame C. J. Walker asserted that her first hair care formula, containing secret ingredients from Africa, was revealed to her by an old man in what we may consider an ancestor vision (K. Russell et al. 1992, p. 44).

106 *Two interviewees:* S. L. Lightfoot (1988), pp. 59–60. S. T. Haizlip (1994), pp. 20, 155, 218, 262.

107 *Three interviewees told stories:* Visions of spirits of the living occur in novels by Ishmael Reed (1978a [1972], p. 150) and Paule Marshall (1991, p. 18).

Visions, like dreams: In his autobiography, Malcolm X recounts the story of his mother's predictive vision hours before Malcolm's father was lynched in Lansing, Michigan. Malcolm's parents had been arguing, and "my father was so angry he slammed on out of the front door and started walking up the road toward town. It was then that my mother had this vision. . . . My father was well up the road when my mother ran screaming out onto the porch. . . . [H]e waved at her, but he kept on going. She told me later, my mother did, that she had a vision of my father's end" (1966 [1965], p. 9 [paragraphing omitted]). Malcolm's brother Philbert X tells the story somewhat differently. Without mentioning the argument, he says their mother warned her husband not to go to town after she fell asleep and then woke up with a premonition, presumably from a dream (O. Bagwell 1994).

The interviews yielded: The woman who saw the shaft of light is interviewee #114.

108 *After asking about visions:* The comparison of blacks (46%) and whites (37%) for hearing voices is in the expected direction but doesn't reach statistical significance: by a 2-tailed t-test, t-value = −1.11, p = .267.

As with visual hallucinations, studies indicate that more black than white psychiatric patients in the United States experience auditory hallucinations. And again, the probable explanation is that cultural preconditioning lowers the boundary against hallucinations for blacks, while raising it for whites. **Schizophrenia:** M. M. Vitols et al. (1963); V. R. Adebimpe et al. (1982). **Mixed matched diagnoses:** I. Sletten et al. (1972); J. L. Liss et al. (1973); A. Welner et al. (1973); R. M. Costello (1973); H. Fabrega Jr. et al. (1988). **Bipolar affective disorder:** J. E. Helzer (1975); S. Mukherjee et al. (1983).

Like visions, voices: Again, the prisoners were the only group specifically polled on this question. Of the eleven out of twenty-five (44%) who reported voices, 45% experienced them in mental space only, 18% in physical space only, and 27% in both. One gave an unclear answer and was excluded.

109 *For Joe Cheeks:* "A voice spoke to me as plain as day," said an ex-slave of his conversion experience, "but it was inward." And another: "A voice that seemed loud enough for everyone to hear would cry on the inside . . . " (C. H. Johnson 1969, pp. 59, 101).

Ann Eskridge: When I later interviewed Carole Morisseau herself, she volunteered the same story, with minor discrepancies, plus one major discrepancy: she said she was asleep throughout. Her explanation when I told her Ann Eskridge's version was instructive: "Over the years I guess I've begun to believe that I really wasn't awake during that. But when I told Ann, I was probably very certain that 'I was awake! I was awake!' I think at one point earlier, I was much, much more a spiritual person than I am now. I think living has made me less spiritual and more pragmatic."

111 Hearing one's name called: For the folk belief mentioned here, see J. M. Brewer (1968), p. 294.

113 *It's curious:* I found the same absence of predictive voices but examples of guiding voices in literature: J. Lester (1976), pp. 81, 269; N. Shange (1982), p. 29; L. Teish (1988 [1985]), p. 43; W. Mosley (1991 [1990]), pp. 96–97.

Creative guidance: J. E. Wideman (1995 [1994]), p. 71. I. Reed (1978b), p. 132.

In fact, all of the voice phenomena: **Ancestor visitations:** H. Van Dyke (1965), p. 214; T. Morrison (1988 [1987]), p. 244; L. Forrest (1992), pp. 122–123, 126; D. Pinckney (1993 [1992]), p. 302; B. Wade (1992), pp. 146, 217. **Spirits:** B. Jones (1989 [1983]), pp. 74–75; H. Dumas (1988), pp. 7, 19–20; C. E. Lincoln (1989 [1988]), p. 186; J. E. Noll (1991), pp. 30–31. **Spirits of the living:** C. Burnett (1990). **Hearing one's name called:** E. J. Gaines (1983), pp. 192–193; W. Mosley (1997), p. 10. **Name called by someone about to die:** R. M. Dorson (1956), p. 121. **Divine and demonic voices:** T. R. Gray (1966), p. 232; Z. N. Hurston (1981), p. 29; R. Wright (1966 [1945]), p. 82; L. Bennett Jr. (1963), pp. 283–284; J. M. Brewer (1968), pp. 554–557; S. Terkel (1993 [1992]), p. 26.

In spite of such overlaps: By a 2-tailed t-test, t-value = −2.52, p = .013. Whites are more likely than blacks to connect the word "presence" with something global, such as "Holy Spirit" or "nature," rather than with a certain spirit in a certain location. Such globals were not counted as presences in these calculations.

114 *How are unseen, unheard:* Literature containing mentions of felt presences includes the following works: L. Jeffers (1983), pp. 75, 78; D. Pinckney (1993 [1992]), p. 238; A. D. Pate (1994), p. 133; D. West (1995), p. 153; S. Jackson-Opoku (1997), pp. 311, 317.

115 *Several people had stories:* The prisoner touched on the shoulder is No. 5.

A few people said: A Nigerian author (A. Omoyajowo 1965, p. 9) states that the average African is aware of ancestral presences in the house by "the petty stealing, especially food and money, which they indulge in."

Stewart said also: Interviewee #110 smells her father's cigars.

In a classic: As to whether these experiences occur during sleep or waking, the following percentages include only those individuals who said they had experienced at least one out-of-body experience *and* specified what state they were in at the time. **Awake (or some other nonsleep state) only:** interviewees: 32%; prisoners: 25%; whites: 38%. **Asleep only:** interviewees: 55%; prisoners: 33%; whites: 52%. **Both awake and asleep, on different occasions:** interviewees: 13%; prisoners: 42%; whites: 10%.

116 *The percentage of interviewees:* The comparison between interviewees and whites leans in the expected direction, but doesn't reach statistical significance: by a 2-tailed t-test, t-value = −1.36, p = .173.

Not all out-of-body experiences: In African American literature, I encountered several other precipitating factors. These include: **sex:** R. Kenan (1990 [1989]), p. 172; T. McMillan (1993b [1992]), p. 57; **drugs:** R. D. Pharr (1997 [1978]), p. 74; R. McKnight (1992), p. 78; **rage:** A. Young (1980), p. 226; **life crisis:** L. Teish (1988 [1985]), p. 38; **grief:** E. Southerland (1979), p. 37; and **witchcraft:** K. Corthron (1994), pp. 64, 67.

Following are some other published mentions of out-of-body experience not cited elsewhere in this chapter: H. Dumas (1976), p. 125; A. Walker (1977 [1976]), p. 58; V. Arvey (1984), p. 72; D. T. Clardy (1987 [1985]), p. 226; J. E. Noll (1991), p. 159 passim.

One precipitating factor: S. T. Haizlip (1994), p. 228. In Brent Wade's novel *Company Man* (1992, p. 178), the self-alienation of a black executive is symbolized by an out-of-body experience that overtakes him in the midst of betraying his fellow black employees to the head of the firm.

117 *A number of interviewees:* The additional interviewees to associate out-of-body experiences with death are Yusuf Abdullah, Kimberly Camp, Adrienne Edmond, Kai EL Zabar, Frances Freeman-Williams, and Alice Stephens.

Few interviewees were familiar: The same conclusion can be drawn from the scarcity of descriptions of lucid dreaming in African American literature. I encountered only six sure depictions of lucid dreaming: D. Goines (1975), p. 30; J. E. Wideman (1990), p. 94; L. Raymond (1994), p. 209; T. Due (1995), p. 197; W. Mosley (1995), pp. 156–157; idem (1998), p. 133. I also came across three debatable instances of lucid dreaming: M. Taylor (1990), p. 281; A. French (1993), p. 145; T. McMillan (1993b [1992]), p. 364.

I found that only 70 percent: By a 2-tailed t-test, t-value = 2.56, p = .011. According to one questionnaire survey (R. Gruber 1995), lucidity rates are virtually identical in black and white college students, with blacks just slightly higher. The other survey (J. Palmer 1974), also conducted by questionnaire, reported that 76% of blacks said they had dreamed lucidly, but only 53% of whites.

Recently, lucid dreaming: For a full discussion of lucid dreaming, see A. Shafton (1995), ch. 14.

118 *I found a similar division:* Rates of dream control turned out to be a major difference between the interviewees and the prisoners. Whereas only just over a third of the interviewees had ever controlled dreams, 71%, or over two-thirds, of the prisoners had. Perhaps control over dreams compensates the prisoners for the loss of control over their lives by incarceration.

But other interviewees: Other interviewees to say that control interferes with the dream's message are Oscar Edmond, Beatriz Penso-Buford, Ethel Smith, Angie Williams, and interviewee #114.

Dreams in which two: J. Dollard (1988 [1937]), pp. 456–457. In the terminology of one specialist (L. L. Magallón 1997), the father and older daughter dreamed *meshing* dreams, that is, mutual dreams which merely have scenes, symbols, or actions in common. A rarer and more extraordinary type of mutual dream is the *meeting* dream, in which the dreamers appear to encounter one another in the very same dreamscape.

119 *Experiences of this type:* **Folklore: mutual dreams:** *South Carolina Folk Tales* (1941), pp. 58–60; H. M. Hyatt (1970–1978), pp. 27, 4585; **mutual visions:** N. N. Puckett (1926), p. 115; R. M. Dorson (1956), p. 130; H. M. Hyatt (1970–1978), p. 4509; M. H. B. Roberson (1983), p. 164; K. W. Heyer (1981), pp. 185–186; H. L. Gates Jr. (1994), p. 120; **mutual voices or sounds:** N. N. Puckett (1926), p. 115. **Literature: mutual dreams:** J. A. Williams (1968 [1967]), p. 88; T. Morrison (1981 [1973]), pp. 43–44; E. Southerland (1979), p. 5; M. Dixon (1989), pp. 50, 58–59; A. Kennedy (1990), p. 8; E. Danticat (1995), p. 169 passim; S. Jackson-Opoku (1997), pp. 38, 365; S. Youngblood (1997), p. 87; **mutual visions:** C. Cullen (1991 [1932]), p. 529; T. Morrison (1978 [1977]), p. 110; idem (1997), pp. 97–98; C. McElroy (1990), p. 167 ff; **mutual voices or sounds:** M. Dixon (1989), pp. 241–242 passim.

Judy Still: This was not a meeting dream. Judy Still said that there were others present in the dream when Lane arrived, but she couldn't identify them. And the other two women didn't say that she was present in their dreams. Still also told about a friend and her father who "both dreamed that they were both crying on Christmas." Their mother/wife subsequently "died just before Christmas." Still's own father also recorded a mutual dream (W. G. Still, "Praise, Prayer, Truth, Testimony," manuscript in the Still archives at the University of Arkansas, p. 25, read to me over the telephone from a copy by Judy Still).

120 *In addition to these examples:* The five additional stories about mutual dreams were told by Kimberly Camp, Eileen Cherry, Illana Jordan, Nicole Smith, and interviewee #112.

Half a dozen interviewees: In addition to interviewee #113, who with her mother saw a tall man, shared visions were experienced by Joe Cheeks, Oscar Edmond, Katie Jones (see the next paragraph), Angela Powell, and Regina Reed.

Mutual voices: The museum in Detroit has since moved. Horse's hooves were heard by interviewee #113.

10. Take Me Through: Dreams and Dreamlike States in Religion

122 *The Christianized slaves:* C. Joyner (1984), p. 160. E. D. Genovese (1974), p. 233.

123 *What matters for our purposes:* Z. N. Hurston (1981), p. 91. J. R. Washington (1972), p. 205. M. J. Herskovits (1990 [1958/1941]), pp. 125, 220–221. E. E. H. Griffith et al. (1980), p. 122.

124 *Nevertheless, almost a third:* C. C. Bell et al. (1985), pp. 720–721. Psychiatrist Carl Bell also finds (p. 726) that only half as many black psychiatric patients as healthy individuals have experienced this altered state, which is therefore associated with normalcy, not with pathology.

It's no surprise that shouting is another staple motif of African American literature: E. S. Griggs (1969 [1899]), p. 19; C. Cullen (1991 [1932]), p. 361; A. Young (1981 [1970]), p. 11; idem (1980), p. 80; A. Murray (1989 [1974]), p. 92; N. Shange (1982), p. 17; L. Jeffers (1983), p. 17; M. Golden (1989), p. 57; Cecil Brown (1993), pp. 74–75; E. Danticat (1995), p. 117; A. J. Verdelle (1995), p. 137; D. West (1995), p. 123; E. Hill (1996), p. 76; S. Youngblood (1997), p. 28; C. Johnson (1998), p. 78; R. Ellison (1999), p. 99.

The mysticism of the early Baptist: M. Sobel (1988 [1979]), pp. xx, 82, 98–101.

125 *In his novel:* J. Baldwin (1954 [1952]), pp. 167–180. M. Sobel (1988 [1979]), pp. 107–108. Other versions of the traditional travel, with an agonizing descent followed by ascent and coming through, may be found in Z. N. Hurston (1981), pp. 87–89; H. Powdermaker (1939), p. 263; J. M. Brewer (1968), p. 257; R. M. Dorson (1956), p. 132; M. Sobel, op. cit., passim.

The treatment of conversion experiences in African American literature is a mixed bag. Nella Larsen (1928, pp. 141–142), Sterling A. Brown (1932, p. 2), and Richard Wright (1966 [1945], p. 129) all treated the subject with ironical skepticism. Like James Baldwin (1954 [1952], pp. 167–180), Julius Lester (1984, pp. 42–44) draws on childhood family experience to give a naturalistic description. Lester also ties his conversion to Judaism to a vision (1988, p. 160). Lance Jeffers (1983, p. 48) uses "coming through" as a metaphor for profound sexual experience. Randall Kenan (1990 [1989], p. 234) describes a conversion experience in reverse: carried to heights, only to end in self-destructive despair. Kenan seems to be allegorizing the deficiency of today's rational Euro-American culture for a young black man's growth. And Ralph Thurmon (1991, pp. 29–32) shows a character stimulated by jazz in a semiliturgical setting undergoing a sort of conversion which concludes with him screaming, "Mamaaaaa, Mamaaaaa Afrikaaaaa." He then peremptorily abandons his white wife on account of her color.

An element of certain versions: M. Sobel (1988 [1979]), pp. 112–113. Out-of-body experience is also an element in two fictional accounts of conversion-like experiences: A. Walker (1977 [1976]), p. 58; D. T. Clardy (1987 [1985]), p. 226.

126 *One type of conversion vision:* M. Eliade (1966), p. 332. Z. N. Hurston (1981), p. 89 (see also N. N. Puckett 1926, p. 540).

In addition to these traditional scenarios: Z. N. Hurston (1981), p. 85. H. Powdermaker (1939), pp. 263, 265. E. J. Gaines (1981 [1971]), pp. 134–135.

Hurston's account: Z. N. Hurston (1981), p. 85; idem (1991 [1942]), pp. 198–199.

127 *To undertake a retreat:* C. Joyner (1984), p. 161. M. Sobel (1988 [1979]), p. 147. Z. N. Hurston (1981), p. 85. H. Powdermaker (1939), p. 260. N. N. Puckett (1926), p. 536. A "mourner" was a sinner actively seeking Christ.

What do we hear: H. Powdermaker (1939), p. 269.

130 *Here is another description:* H. M. Hyatt (1970–1978), pp. 4703–4705. Literary works by August Wilson (1990, pp. 24–25) and C. Eric Lincoln (1989 [1988], pp. 3–4) mention calls to preach coming in dreams. In Wilson's play, as in the novels by James Baldwin (1954 [1952], p. 84) and Julius Lester (1984, pp. 42–44) already mentioned, conversion experiences are also calls to preach.

It's tempting to see: E. Corin & G. Bibeau (1980), p. 223. S. G. Lee (1958), pp. 265–266.

The so-called Independent: S. Charsley (1992), pp. 160, 164. M. Chinkwita (1993), pp. 72–73. A. Omoyajowo (1965), p. 15.

131 *One woman, though no cynic:* The woman who doubts the claims of ministers is interviewee #114.

132 *A singer:* The singer is interviewee #112. There is a book about a healer who was called in a dream (B. J. Robinson 1990, quoting her own *Aunt [Ant] Phyllis*, 2nd ed. [Oakland: Regent Press, 1988], pp. 18–19). H. M. Hyatt interviewed a healer and two root doctors who were inspired by dreams (1970–1978, pp. 273–274, 1094–1095, 4684). Outsider artist Joseph Yoakum "was in his mid-seventies when he was inspired by a dream to begin drawing" (L. Warren 1982, p. 47). Novelist Wallace Thurman (1992 [1932], p. 82) depicted a character called in a dream to be a racewoman.

In The Autobiography of Miss Jane Pittman: E. J. Gaines (1981 [1971]), p. 135. Z. N. Hurston (1991 [1942]), p. 198.

While conversion is still a topic: E. E. H. Griffith et al. (1980), p. 122. E. E. H. Griffith & M. A. Mathewson (1981), p. 1024. By a 2-tailed t-test, t-value = −3.21, p = .002. The percentage of black male prisoners who had heard dreams talked about in church during their childhoods was even higher, 77 percent, significantly higher than the interviewees' 42 percent: t-value = −3.21, p = .003.

134 *Among African American Christians:* Religious dreams and visions of one sort or another abound in African American literature, from Jean Toomer's (1969 [1923], p. 31) reference to a Georgia woman who "saw the mother of Christ and drew her in charcoal on the courthouse wall," to Ishmael Reed's (1982, p. 108 passim) satirical concoction of President Clift's (read Reagan's) visions of hell, to Eleanor Taylor Bland's (1995, pp. 3–4) recent dig at traditional beliefs—drug dealers in her crime novel throw an undercover cop off the top of a parking garage: "Across the street, from a third-floor room, a woman watched from her hospital bed as an angel flew past her window. 'Thank you, Jesus,' she murmured, smiling."

135 *Momentous dreams and visions:* For the motif of being welcomed to death by a loved person, see Walter Mosley (1995), p. 266. Folklorist H. M. Hyatt (1970–1978, p. 2212) heard often about angels appearing before death. Sometimes, however, the figures encountered before death are not welcoming or angelic, but menacing in the extreme. James Baldwin (1954 [1952], p. 59), August Wilson (1986, pp. 11–12), and Walter Mosley (1991 [1990], p. 34) have all written on this theme. Wilson and Mosley both borrowed a folkloric element in their stories: successful defiance of the figure of death.

136 *The founder was Elijah Muhammad:* Malcolm X (1966 [1965]), pp. 205, 250.

   Malcolm X's own "pre-vision": Malcolm X (1966 [1965]), pp. 186–187, 189.

137 *In 1989, Minister Louis Farrakhan:* L. Farrakhan (1989).

138 *An internal publication:* J. Muhammad (1986).

11. All Life Passes Through Water: Dreams in Hoodoo

139 *The hoodoo path:* A. R. Flowers (1985), p. 82.

   Voodoo came from Haiti: M. Sobel (1988 [1979]), p. 48. L. Barrett (1974). E. D. Genovese (1974), p. 220. R. Bastide (1971), p. 147. J. G. Mulira (1990), p. 64. For sources of the word "Voodoo," see: M. Wade-Lewis (1988), p. 187; L. Teish (1988 [1985]), p. x; R. F. Thompson (1984 [1983]), p. 273 n. 29; I. Reed (1978b), p. 9.

   As voodoo spread: M. Wade-Lewis (1988), p. 187.

140 *The slaves regarded hoodoo:* A. J. Robateau (1978), p. 284. N. N. Puckett (1926), pp. 220, 233, 241. W. K. Vass (1979), pp. 110–114. R. F. Thompson (1984 [1983]), p. 131. M. Wade-Lewis (1988), p. 186.

   Hand is the most general term for "a magic helper." A *mojo* or a *toby* usually has drawing power. A *bodyguard* is a protective hand. A *jack* assists divination. A *trick* causes a harmful spell. These are H. M. Hyatt's (1970–1978) definitions, as analyzed by M. E. Bell (1980, p. 350). Other terms include *root, guide, jomo, hoodoo bag, gri-gri (gris-gris, gre-gre), juju, wanga,* and *wuwu.*

   But some elements of hoodoo: K. M. Golden (1977), p. 1425. N. E. Whitten Jr. (1962), p. 406. M. E. Bell (1980), pp. 343, 415. R. Bastide (1971), p. 161.

   By 1926 (p. 579), folklorist Newbell Niles Puckett could point to the "enormous" sales of *Albertus Magnus Egyptian Secrets* and *The Sixth and Seventh Books of Moses* to Negroes in New Orleans. These titles were the sourcebooks most frequently referred to by the practitioners interviewed by Harry Middleton Hyatt (1970–1978) in the 1930s and 1970s. *Albertus Magnus* contains a peculiar collection of European remedies, recipes, and incantations, for everything from removing freckles, to curing sweeny ("Sloth and Slough") in man and beast, to detecting and fending off witches. Melville J. Herskovits (1990 [1958/1941], p. 235) mentioned that *Albertus Magnus* was popular in West Africa as well. The supposedly found lost *Books of Moses*—"the so-called Black Bible" (R. M. Dorson 1956, p. 155)—is an arcane collection of cabalistic, Talmudic, Egyptian, and European mystical philosophy and lore. Other books with an impact on hoodoo are *Pow-Wows, or, Long Lost Friend: A Collection of Mysterious and Invaluable Arts and Remedies* and *The Great Book of Magical Art, Hindu Magic, and Indian Occultism.* The former, written by John George Hohman, a Pennsylvania Dutchman, around 1820, "includes spells and charms familiar in Europe during the Middle Ages" (H. Powdermaker 1939, p. 396). The latter, by L. W. deLaurence and published by the deLaurence Company, a small Chicago firm still in business, was written in 1915. This book "served as a handbook to the old-time root-doctors of the South" (C. M. Long 2001).

Notwithstanding European contributions: M. Sobel (1988 [1979]), p. 46. E. D. Genovese (1974), pp. 212, 217. J. Haskins (1974), pp. 20–21, 46, 50. C. Cullen (1991 [1932]), pp. 448–449. Harry Menton, the ambiguous down-home character in Charles Burnett's film *To Sleep with Anger* (1990), says, "I don't believe in sin, though there is good and evil."

141 *Harry Middleton Hyatt's:* H. M. Hyatt (1970–1978), pp. 1163, 1323, 1672, 1870 (hereafter in this chapter's notes simply Hyatt).

Ishmael Reed: I. Reed (1978b), p. 127. Hyatt, pp. 2341, 2472.

142 *Unfortunately, Hyatt:* Hyatt, pp. 4500, 4742.

In the world of hoodoo: A. Omoyajowo (1965), p. 17. R. M. Wintrob (1973), p. 320. Hyatt, p. 179.

The night before another: Hyatt, p. 368 (see also p. 180).

Another woman: Hyatt, p. 451. For other fixes and remedies divined in dreams, see Hyatt, pp. 179, 179–180, 180, 182–185, 502, 762, 1953–1954, 3202.

143 *In a case from the 1980s:* L. A. Camino (1986), p. 231 and personal communication, 1994. Dream incubation by all sorts of means is a common practice around the world (A. Shafton 1995, pp. 393–430), including Africa (H. W. Turner 1967, vol. 2, p. 103; V. Crapanzano 1975, p. 149; H. J. Fisher 1979, p. 230; R. F. Thompson 1984 [1983], p. 134; L. Mullings 1984, pp. 98, 138–139; E. De Rosny 1985, pp. 266–267; M. Chinkwita 1993, p. 66; B. C. Ray 1993, p. 276).

For hoodoo dream incubations not mentioned elsewhere in the text, see: **for gambling luck:** Hyatt, pp. 245, 695, 1318, 1488, 4014; **for discovering a future mate:** Hyatt, pp. 1901, 4105–4106; N. N. Puckett (1926), pp. 329, 496–497; **for "clear dreams":** J. M. Brewer (1968), p. 289.

Doctors sometimes dream: Hyatt, p. 4171 (see also Hyatt, pp. 1210–1211; *Drums and Shadows* 1973 [1940], pp. 57–58).

Dreams can play: Hyatt, pp. 1188–1189 (see also C. W. Chesnutt 1969a [1899], pp. 77, 155; A. Shafton 1995, pp. 281–282, quoting L. F. Snow, unpublished manuscript).

A boy called Stableboy: N. E. Whitten Jr. (1962), p. 404 (see also Hyatt, pp. 3219–3220).

A hoodoo doctor claimed: Hyatt, pp. 4618–4619.

144 *Suppose a dream visitation:* Hyatt, p. 27.

You can get "some of your peoples": Hyatt, 545–546.

Another way to get luck: Hyatt, p. 2183.

As part of obtaining power: Hyatt, pp. 2300–2301 (see also pp. 1183, 1318, 1349, 3268, 3367, 3587).

Hoodoo can draw the spirits: Hyatt, pp. 1403, 1888.

To catch a thief: Hyatt, p. 1245 (see also pp. 1109–1110, 2173).

145 *Some hoodoo practices:* Hyatt, p. 2287.

Some variants of the grisly ritual: Hyatt, p. 74 (for other versions, see passim; for versions with the Lord and angels, see pp. 1716–1717, 2031, 3920, 3936).

If you want to see evil spirits: Hyatt, pp. 1067, 3922, 4006 passim, 4237.

There are a multitude: Hyatt, pp. 2728–2729, 3367, 3884, 3986.

The following is a list of pages in Hyatt on which one or more examples of in-sleep rituals appear. **To cure a fix:** 426. **To protect against a fix:** 4054. **To cure double pneumonia:** 3127–3128. **To cure impotence:** 3986, 3989–3990. **To stop a man from drinking whiskey:** 3164. **To quiet an angry person:** 4101, 4353. **To lay the ghost of a person you have killed:** 2153. **To get a spirit to act for you:** 3367, 3419–3420, 3442. **To protect against spirits and bring luck:** 4288. **To bring luck:** 4352, 4407. **To get your man to give you money:** 3751, 4443. **To kill someone:** 2870–2871, 2975–2976, 3083–3084, 3339, 3341, 3349, 3381, 3867, 4110, 4456, 4495. **To drive someone crazy and kill them:** 3884. **To cause "falling-out fits":** 2943. **To cause swollen veins:** 3204. **To get someone cut:** 4395. **To cause bad luck:** 4073. **To overcome a love rival:** 3594, 4019, 4337, 4420. **To give someone (lover, rival, etc.) a "hot foot" (make them restless, have to leave, want to travel):** 2981, 3041, 3743, 3745, 3793, 3958, 4064, 4140–4141, 4229, 4466–4467. **To "draw" (attract) someone:** *using underwear, shirt:* 2602–2603, 2603– 2604, 2694, 4061, 4124; *socks, shoes, foot track, foot:* 2713, 2720, 2728–2729, 2739, 2749, 2753, 2815, 2832, 2855, 2861, 2876, 2927, 3073, 4417–4418, 4421; *hair, hat:* 2894, 2983, 3002, 4124; *photo:* 2133, 3419, 3441–3442, 3445, 3453, 3484–3488, 3494–3495; *name:* 3498, 3502, 3572–3573, 3576–3579, 3607, 3866–3867, 4072, 4358; *miscellaneous:* 3231, 3770, 4034, 4089, 4281, 4384, 4470. **To "bind" someone (strengthen an attachment):** *using body fluids (including "dishrag" and other wipes of sexual fluids):* 2405, 2525, 2994, 3975–3978, 3981–3983, 3991–3992, 4309, 4377, 4411, 4412, 4473; *underwear, body clothing, hat:* 2664, 2669, 2670, 2690, 4120, 4124, 4140, 4471, 4472, 4661; *hair:* 2974, 2979, 2987, 3008, 4260, 4272; *socks, shoes, foot track:* 2749, 2753, 2773, 2884, 3858, 3860, 3983, 4443–4444; *string that measures the target person:* 3209–3210, 3993, 4449; *combinations and miscellaneous:* 2532, 2581, 3742, 3814, 3889, 3902, 4147, 4284, 4306, 4454, 4471. **To "tie" someone (make them stay asleep so they can't, or you can, go out and cheat):** *using shoes, socks:* 1538, 2007–2008, 2072, 2105, 3174–3181, 4421; *underwear, etc.:* 1898, 1953, 2024, 2032, 2083, 2097, 2207, 3167–3174, 3176–3177, 3180–3185, 4421; *pants, etc.:* 3173–3174, 3178–3180; *broom:* 3166–3167, 3182; *graveyard items:* 1920–1921, 3181– 3182, 3298–3299, 3349; *crosses:* 3167, 3178, 3182; *names:* 3183; *water:* 2072, 3184–3185; *miscellaneous:* 3183–3184. **To make someone sleep-talk:** 1135–1136, 1619, 2055, 2087, 2176, 3149, 3151, 3794, 4487–4488. **All-purpose graveyard dirt:** 3348–3349, 3366, 3373.

146 *We've already seen that some rituals:* M. E. Bell (1980), p. 193. L. Herron & A. M. Bacon (1895), pp. 363–364. R. Bass (1930), p. 383. M. E. Bell, personal communication, 1995.

One group of in-sleep fixes: For references, see the long note just above. Interviewee Douglas Howard mentioned an "old saying" that seems to have some reference to hoodoo beliefs about induced sleep-talk: "People that talk in their sleep, moaning and groaning, it's something they did to somebody. And they having dreams about it. And, you know, it can be kind of dangerous."

Sleep rituals involving water: Hyatt, pp. 32, 2072, 2087, 2176, 3260, 3485, 3671, 4284, 4407. Z. N. Hurston (1981), p. 20. Here is a summary of rituals involving water in combination with photos, from Hyatt (pp. 3484–3488, 3494–3495). A glass or cup of water is used (rarely, boiling water; rarely, alcohol). Something may be added to the water: nine drops of Hearts Cologne or Blue Moon Perfume; spice and cloves; sugar; a fingernail paring. The glass usually goes under the bed (the head; the edge; the north side); or in a dark corner; or on the dresser. The whole or a corner of the photo may be submerged, or just the image of the head. But usually, the photo goes face down over the glass. The photo may also be tied to the head of the bed; have four threads sewn into it; be weighted down; be covered with a mirror face down. His photo can be placed over hers, face-to-face. Often the ritual is conducted for nine days, and one talks to or prays over the photo, at night or at sunrise. The picture may change—the face or the whole image may fade. The latter eventuality is associated with running someone crazy-restless.

But one water ritual: Hyatt, pp. 545–546. D. J. Hufford (1982), p. 226. L. Teish (1988 [1985]), pp. 19–20 (see also pp. 98–99). *Drums and Shadows* (1973 [1940]), p. 59. Hyatt, pp. 157, 2240.

Another practice involving water: N. N. Puckett (1926), p. 110. M. Sobel (1988 [1979]), p. 47.

147 *The European contribution:* Hyatt, p. 4288.

Hyatt was told: Hyatt, pp. 4525, 4576. K. M. Golden (1977), p. 1425. V. J. Stitt Jr. (1983), p. 721. Gerald G. Jackson, personal communication, 1991. C. M. Long (2001).

Obviously, hoodoo is: The following works containing references to hoodoo (Voodoo, etc.) were published in the decades indicated. **1850s–1860s:** M. R. Delany (1970 [1859–1862]), p. 9 passim. **1890s:** C. W. Chesnutt (1899), passim; idem (1969a [1899]), pp. 77, 155, 173. **1900s:** C. W. Chesnutt (1901), p. 394. **1910s:** W. E. B. Du Bois (1989 [1911]), p. 19 passim. **1920s:** C. McKay (1928), p. 186. **1930s:** A. Bontemps (1933), p. 52; idem (1959 [1931]), pp. 3, 10, 175; idem (1968 [1936]), passim; C. Cullen (1991 [1932]), pp. 383–384, 448–449, 515–516; R. Fisher (1992 [1932]), p. 81; L. Hughes (1935), pp. 72, 86; Z. N. Hurston (1978 [1937]), pp. 126–129, 188; idem (1990 [1935]), passim. **1940s:** Z. N. Hurston (1991 [1942]), pp. 23, 59, 139–140; A. Petry (1985 [1946]), pp. 120, 122–123; D. West (1982 [1948]), p. 230. **1950s:** J. Baldwin (1954 [1952]), p. 59; R. Ellison (1972 [1952]), pp. 56, 172–173, 256, 265; C. Himes (1989b [1954]), p. 282; L. Hughes (1958), p. 18; P. Marshall (1981 [1959]), pp. 71–75, 78, 81, 259; J. S. Redding (1989 [1950]), p. 95. **1960s:** M. Angelou (1971 [1969]), p. 133; Claude Brown (1965), pp. 27, 40, 286; L. Elder III (1965), p. 130; C. Gordon (1969), pp. 409, 411–412; K. Hunter (1964), pp. 84–85; W. M. Kelley (1967), p. 190; J. A. McPherson (1970 [1969]), pp. 13–15; R. Ottley (1965), p. 12; J. J. Phillips (1985 [1966]), pp. 61, 88–89, 117–118, 128–130, 175; I. Reed (1990 [1967]), passim; M. Walker (1967 [1966]), p. 56; C. Wright (1966), p. 42. **1970s:** R. L. Fair (1970), pp. 3–4; E. J. Gaines (1981 [1971]), pp. 96, 121; G. Davis (1984 [1971]), p. 79; K. Hunter (1975), pp. 122, 255, 258, 260; G. Jones (1991 [1977]), p. 150; J. A. McPherson (1977), p. 33; T. Morrison (1981 [1973]), pp. 98, 108–109; idem (1978 [1977]), pp. 125, 132; A. Murray (1989 [1974]), pp. 64, 81, 106; R. D. Pharr (1997 [1978]), p. 78; I. Reed (1978a [1972]), passim; J. E. Wideman (1986 [1973]), p. 252. **1980s:** T. M. Ansa (1989), p. 17; T. C. Bambara (1980), pp. 50, 51, 60, 156; idem (1981), p. 164; Cecil Brown (1983), pp. 17–18, 62, 73; M. Dixon (1989), pp. 1, 28–29, 46, 52–53, 60–65, 146; H. Dumas (1988), pp. 3 passim, 106; A. R. Flowers (1985), passim; M. Golden (1989), p. 4; B. Jones (1989 [1983]), p. 72; R. Kenan (1990 [1989]), p. 25; J. Kincaid (1986), pp. 14–15, 69, 109–110, 116–118, 123–125, 134; J. Lester (1984), pp. 82–83; S. L. Lightfoot (1988), p. 59; A. Lorde (1982), pp. 10, 12; C. Major (1987), pp. 13, 145, 183; P. Marshall (1983a), pp. 28–29, 43, 94; C. J. McElroy (1988 [1987]), pp.

30, 55, 80, 84, 128, 142; R. McKnight (1988), p. 501; T. Morrison (1982 [1981]), p. 150; (1988 [1987]), pp. 256–257; G. Naylor (1993 [1988]), passim; N. Shange (1982), passim; idem (1985), pp. 107, 175; J. E. Wideman (1992c [1983]), pp. 374, 452; S. A. Williams (1986), pp. 19, 86, 226; A. Wilson (1988), p. 24 passim; A. Young (1980), pp. 80, 152; S. Youngblood (1989), pp. 57 passim, 95–100. **1990s:** T. M. Ansa (1996), passim; P. Beatty (1996), pp. 5, 139; Cecil Brown (1993), p. 17; X. Cartiér (1992 [1991]), p. 41; M. Clair (1994), p. 31, 84, 144, 162; E. Danticat (1995), pp. 7, 92, 95, 126, 170, 212; T. Due (1995), p. 230 passim; R. Ellison (1996), pp. 68, 77; idem (1999), p. 54; A. E. Eskridge (1994), pp. 22, 38; S. Jackson-Opoku (1997), pp. 80, 181 passim; G. Jones (1998), p. 15; P. Marshall (1991), p. 163; C. McElroy (1990), pp. 25, 116, 167, 179, 229, 262; T. Morrison (1993b [1992]), p. 121; idem (1997), pp. 244, 271; W. Mosley (1992 [1991]), pp. 146–147; idem (1994), p. 107; idem (1995), pp. 109, 141–142, 144, 167; idem (1997), pp. 41, 174; D. Pinckney (1993 [1992]), pp. 45, 301; A. Rahman (1994), p. 308; J. P. Rhodes (1993), passim; C. W. Sherman (1994 [1993]), p. 19 passim; R. "C." Thurmon (1991), pp. 14, 59–65; A. J. Verdelle (1995), pp. 56, 145; D. West (1995), pp. 133–134; J. E. Wideman (1998), p. 44; A. Wilson (1993), pp. 90, 98 passim; J. Woodson (1995), p. 47; S. Youngblood (1997), p. 4.

Some authors dismiss: **Dismissive remarks:** Claude Brown (1965), p. 286 (see also pp. 62–63). For other dismissive treatments of hoodoo, see R. Ottley (1965), p. 12; B. Jones (1989 [1983]), p. 72; C. Major (1987), p. 13; D. West (1995), pp. 133–134. **Metaphorical usages:** L. Hughes (1958), p. 18; C. Himes (1989b [1954]), p. 282 (see also Cecil Brown 1983, pp. 17–18; C. Major 1987, p. 183; X. Cartiér 1992 [1991], p. 41).

148   *Three novels:* I. Reed (1978a [1972]). See especially pp. 9, 12, 25–26, 159, 173, 233.

    In De Mojo Blues: A. R. Flowers (1985), p. 156.

    We've seen that the role: T. Morrison (1981 [1973]), p. 109. C. W. Sherman (1994 [1993]), p. 142. S. Youngblood (1989), p. 73; idem, personal communication, 1995.

    As for visions: W. Mosley (1995), pp. 131, 141–142.

149   *As for rituals during sleep:* A. Wilson (1988), p. 24. D. Pinckney (1993 [1992]), p. 301. R. Ellison (1972 [1952]), p. 56.

151   *For a number of interviewees:* The woman who spoke of hoodoo murder is interviewee #113.

    A few interviewees: Interviewee #111 experimented with menstrual blood.

153   *Katie Jones:* Katie Jones's story makes an exception to the rule noted by folklorist M. E. Bell: "In the often malicious world of hoodoo, children seem to be spared as a matter of course" (1980, p. 124).

    Ntozake Shange: N. Shange (1982), p. 15.

12. Little Stirrups: Witches Riding You and Sleep Paralysis

155   *"Maybe it wuz uh witch":* Z. N. Hurston (1978 [1937]), p. 259 (for other literary mentions of witches riding, see C. W. Chesnutt 1899, p. 13; C. Cullen 1991 [1932]; A. R. Flowers 1985, p. 88; C. Himes 1989a [1959], p. 141; T. M. Ansa 1989, p. 39).

Another woman told this story: The woman was interviewee #113.

156 *These two accounts:* **Alaska:** J. D. Bloom & R. D. Gelardin (1976). **Philippines:** M. D. Ramos, *The Aswang Syncrasy in Philippine Folklore,* Philippine Folklore Society Paper no. 3 (n.p.: Philippine Folklore Society, 1971), p. 2. Cited by D. J. Hufford (1982), p. 236. **Caribbean:** R. C. Ness (1978), p. 140 (see also P. Marshall 1991, p. 126; E. Danticat 1995, pp. 36–38). **Newfoundland:** R. C. Ness, op. cit., pp. 123–124; D. J. Hufford, op. cit.

In African American folk beliefs: **"Witch":** *Drums and Shadows* (1973 [1940]), pp. 19, 80; L. Saxon et al. (1945), p. 545; R. M. Dorson (1958), pp. 239–240; D. J. Hufford (1982), pp. 212–213. **"Hag":** *Southern Workman,* Feb. 1894, pp. 26–27; *Drums and Shadows,* op. cit., p. 34; *South Carolina Folk Tales* (1941), p. 47; K. W. Heyer (1981), p. 201. **Ridden like horses:** H. M. Hyatt (1970–1978), pp. 141 ff (hereafter in this chapter shown simply as Hyatt); N. N. Puckett (1926), pp. 151–152; W. C. Hendricks (1943), p. 87; J. Mellon (1988), p. 90 (see also C. W. Chesnutt 1969a [1899], pp. 177, 179–180).

It's been speculated: M. Sobel (1988 [1979]), pp. 20, 69.

Perhaps the slaves did bring: J. U. Ohaeri (1992), p. 522. In African American folklore also, the witch can appear as an animal, usually a black cat (N. N. Puckett 1926, pp. 151–152) or a rat (R. M. Dorson 1956, p. 139). The animal was sometimes thought of as a conjurer's helper (Hyatt, p. 135).

157 *In the United States:* **Witch:** B. Jones (1989 [1983]), p. 72 passim. **Hired conjure woman:** *Drums and Shadows* (1973 [1940]), p. 19. **Devil:** A. Lorde (1982), p. 38; Hyatt, pp. 135, 157–158. **Haint:** K. Hunter (1975), p. 260.

The folklore literature records: **Prevention by placation: using water:** *Drums and Shadows* (1973 [1940]), p. 59; N. N. Puckett (1926), p. 157. **Prevention by intimidation: using gunpowder:** *South Carolina Folk Tales* (1941), p. 47; **new lumber:** Hyatt, passim; **sharp objects:** Hyatt, passim; **curses:** Hyatt, p. 2156; **purifiers such as salt:** Hyatt, passim; **brooms:** Puckett, op. cit., p. 156; Hyatt, p. 152. **Prevention by delay: using water:** Hyatt, p. 2240; **horseshoes:** Puckett, op. cit., p. 158; **irritants:** Puckett, p. 16; **exploiting witches' compulsions:** K. W. Heyer (1981), p. 69; Hyatt, passim; **to count (a fatal instinct, witches are too stupid):** Puckett, op. cit., p. 162, 164–165; Hyatt, passim; M. E. Bell (1980), p. 90; B. Jones (1989 [1983]), p. 74. **Trapping: before being ridden: using forks:** *Southern Workman,* Mar. 1894, p. 46; Mar. 1895, p. 49; **water:** Hyatt, p. 3997; **sieves:** Puckett, op. cit., p. 163; Hyatt, p. 1687; **bottles:** Hyatt, p. 1715. **Trapping: after being ridden: using force:** *Drums and Shadows* (1973 [1940]), p. 6; **bottles:** *Southern Workman,* Mar. 1894, p. 46. **Trapped witches turn into:** old rags, snake, worm, insect, screech owl, leather strap, lump of jellied blood, jellyfish, little piece of red meat, little doll (Hyatt, passim). **Escape while being ridden:** count silver money and chew tobacco, both kept handy under the pillow; alternatively, urinate in a bottle (Hyatt, passim).

According to one widespread folk belief: *Drums and Shadows* (1973 [1940]), pp. 80–81. Hyatt, pp. 138, 141 passim. *South Carolina Folk Tales* (1941), p. 91. *Southern Workman,* Feb. 1894, p. 26 (see also Mar. 1894, p. 47). N. N. Puckett (1926), pp. 154–155, 158, 474. M. J. Herskovits (1990 [1958/1941]), p. 259. There's a story about "Brer Rabbit disposing of the last witch in the world by putting pepper in her vacated skin" (M. Sobel 1988 [1979], p. 41).

While some of the other countermeasures: M. E. Bell (1980), p. 90. C. Joyner (1984), p. 151. *Drums and Shadows* (1973 [1940]), p. 246.

158 *These characteristics:* M. J. Thorpy (1990), p. 166. M. Aldrich (1993), p. 569. **Pleasant or ecstatic:** H. C. Everett (1963), p. 297. Hortense Powdermaker (1939, pp. 268–269) collected the story of a woman whose coming through occurred with sleep paralysis. **Out-of-body experience:** L. Levitan & S. LaBerge (1991), p. 2. D. J. Hufford (1982), p. 242. Interviewee #112 believes she experiences paralysis when she doesn't get "completely back in the body" following an out-of-body experience. Ayanna Udongo has out-of-body experiences in the midst of waking paralysis following sleep. Kai EL Zabar awakens with paralysis after struggling to reenter her body so that she can wake up. In the Eskimo folk tradition, an alternative explanation to witches is that the sleeper's soul leaves the body, a condition which, if prolonged, terminates in death (J. D. Bloom & R. D. Gelardin 1976, p. 119). Similarly, one of Hyatt's informants (p. 21) explained sleep paralysis by the spirit not returning in a timely way when it travels from the body, just as it does in death. This man believed, in fact, that death sometimes ensues. The belief that death can result from being ridden was mentioned by Douglas Gills. In folklore of former days, the cause of death usually associated with being ridden was exhaustion (Hyatt, p. 136; *Drums and Shadows* 1973 [1940], p. 19; *South Carolina Folk Tales* 1941, p. 93).

The cause of sleep paralysis: J. A. Hobson (1988), p. 207. C. H. Schenck et al. (1989).

Is sleep paralysis at the bottom: C. C. Bell et al. (1986). J. U. Ohaeri (1992). D. J. Hufford (1982), pp. 32 ff, 113, 169, 202.

Just how common is sleep paralysis?: **International: Chinese university students: 58%** (J. McClenon 1990, p. 2); **"hagging" in a Newfoundland fishing village: 62%** (R. C. Ness 1978, p. 128); **Newfoundland college students (ISP): 23%** (D. J. Hufford 1982, p. 19); **Canadian college students: 41.9%** (K. Fukuda et al. 1998, p. 61); **Japanese college students: 38.9%** (K. Fukuda et al., op. cit., p. 61); **Nigerian medical students: 26.2%** (J. U. Ohaeri et al. 1989, p. 806); **Nigerian psychiatric nursing students: 44.2%** (Ohaeri et al. 1992, p. 68). **U.S. white or general population: adolescents: 5%** (M. Aldrich 1993, p. 570); **medical students: 4.7%** (G. B. Goode 1962, cited by H. C. Everett 1963, p. 284); **15.4%** (H. C. Everett 1963, p. 284); **adults: 10–25%** (Hufford, op. cit., p. 50); **college students: 40–50%** (W. Dement, cited by Hufford, op. cit., p. 159 n. 89). **U.S. blacks: 41%** (C. C. Bell et al. 1984, p. 504). **U.S. black and white college students compared: blacks: 50%; whites: 32–37%** (J. McClenon 1994, p. 124). **This study: blacks: 61%; whites: 42%** (by a 2-tailed t-test, t-value $= -2.54$, $p = .012$). The incidence for the prisoners was 67%. Of eight preadolescent and adolescent children questioned at the Cabrini Green housing project in Chicago, 50% had experienced sleep paralysis.

159 *Bell further concludes:* C. C. Bell et al. (1986), p. 650, citing D. J. Hufford (1982).

Bell considers several factors: C. C. Bell et al. (1984), pp. 506–507.

Something like Bell's "survival fatigue": Interviewee #113 wondered about the genetic component.

The high rates of sleep paralysis: C. C. Bell et al. (1986), pp. 651, 658. C. C. Bell et al. (1988). J. U. Ohaeri (1992), p. 70 (see also D. J. Hufford 1982, pp. 38, 48).

Remarkably, neither Barbara Pulliam: J. E. Wideman (1990), p. 171; idem (1989), pp. 209–210.

161 *As for* devils: Interviewee #115 was told by her mother it was the devil holding her down.

Many interviewees saw or sensed: A vague *somebody* was seen or sensed by Zachary Brown, Kimberly Camp, Dorothy Carter, Cecile Jackson, Preston Jackson, Gloria Naylor, Ivan Watkins, and interviewees #113, #115, and #116. Interviewee #114 referred to "the teacher."

It was almost as usual: Sleep paralysis without imagery apart perhaps from the room was experienced by Marva Pitchford Jolly, Sherry McKinney, Frances Callaway Parks, Alice Stephens, and Winford Williams. Paralysis without imagery or even pressure or difficulty breathing was experienced by Douglas Howard, Carole Morisseau, Gwen Robinson, and Norma Adams Wade. Experiencing only a heaviness, weight, or pressure with paralysis were Ronald Childs, Douglas Gills, and Matthew Stephens.

162 *A few interviewees:* The woman seeking reassurance was interviewee #113.

163 *Before closing this chapter:* See A. Moody (1976 [1968]), p. 85. The woman who asked, "Is it your blood not circulating or something?" was interviewee #113. One interviewee, Yusuf Abdullah, said that during sleep the blood stops circulating, but he didn't draw a connection to sleep paralysis.

Two interviewees put forward: The "blood standing still" is also an alternative explanation of the old hag among Newfoundlanders, some of whom think there's an interaction between physical and spiritual causes; "informants may view blood stagnation as the *proximate* cause and a hostile individual as the *ultimate* cause" (R. C. Ness 1978, pp. 125–126; see also D. J. Hufford 1982, p. 10).

164 *If you believe:* Many narcoleptics have sleep paralysis, but that rare disorder accompanies fewer than 1% of all cases of sleep paralysis (D. J. Hufford 1982, p. 150, citing Constantin R. Soldatos et al., "Narcolepsy: evaluation and treatment," *Journal of Psychedelic Drugs* 10:319, 1978). Even for narcoleptics, the sleep paralysis in itself carries no danger. For the remaining 99+%, the technically correct term is *isolated sleep paralysis* (ISP), in token of the fact that no other problems are associated with it. The only suggested complication of ISP is anxiety or depression, which occasionally results from undergoing the experience (M. J. Thorpy 1990, p. 167). Also, ISP may be a warning marker for hypertension, because some people who have ISP also have panic attacks, and these create stress contributing to hypertension (C. C. Bell et al. 1988).

13. The Same Old Nightmare: Race in Dreams

165 *The South has always frightened me:* J. Baldwin (1962 [1954]), pp. 83–84.

166 *To shed light on this question:* By a 2-tailed t-test, t-value = -4.35, $p = .001$.

The next question to blacks: Never was scored as 1, seldom as 2, sometimes as 3, and often as 4. The mean for the interviewees was 3.23; for the whites, 2.10. By a 2-tailed t-test, t-value = -8.37, $p = .001$. For the black male prisoners the mean was 2.57, significantly lower than for the black interviewees (t-value = 2.89, $p = .005$).

It's perfectly possible: This difference doesn't reach statistical significance.

I then asked, "how frequently": Never was again scored as 1, seldom as 2, sometimes as 3, and often as 4. The mean for the interviewees was 1.75; for the whites, 1.50. By a 2-tailed t-test, t-value = -2.05, $p = .042$.

With this information in hand: Correlation coefficient for blacks, $p = .092$; for whites, $p = .001$.

167 *I had frankly expected:* J. E. Wideman (1992g), p. 84.

Even people whose work: S. T. Haizlip (1994).

168 *Osuurete Adesanya:* The opposite point was made by interviewee #115.

Wideman also speculated: T. Morrison (1993a [1992]), p. 57. A. H. Jenkins (1995), p. 41. J. E. Williams & J. K. Morland (1976).

It's possible, of course: The findings and surmises presented here are based on self-reports about dreams, not on dreams gathered in sleep laboratories or even from dream journals. The advantages of self-reports are that dreamers can survey their whole life spans, and they can pull out significant remembered dreams. The disadvantages are that memory is imperfect and that people consciously or unconsciously suppress things.

170 *Ralph Ellison aptly described:* R. Ellison (1966), p. 96 (the first ellipsis is Ellison's); idem (1972 [1952]), pp. 56–59. For another example of the convergence of personal and racial concerns in a dream, see R. Lucas (1949), p. 57.

171 *A word of caution:* A. Thomas & S. Sillen (1991 [1972]), pp. 57–58. R. E. Haskell (1985).

172 *Another woman:* This is interviewee #116.

Angela Jackson had a dream: In my samples, 70% of blacks had flown or levitated in dreams, 75% of whites. Of the black male prisoners, sixteen of twenty-five (64%) had flown in dreams. Of the sixteen fliers, eight (50%) had flown while in prison. When asked directly, 100% of these eight connected the dreams with their wish for freedom. For some the wish was personal only; for some, also political. For example, prisoner No.14 wrote: "A recent strong and lingering dream of flying over mountains, oceans, trees, rustic landscapes, I am high in the clouds, the stratosphere, blossoming into a reality of going to court in New Jersey soon— and if successful—the system will set me free." Prisoner No. 20 wrote: "It was a few days ago when I had a dream of myself flying over the communities really getting a clear view of our repressed conditions, seeing things that thought it was unseen!" Prisoner No.19, at Pelican Bay, regards himself as a political prisoner. He wrote: "This particular dream I feel symbolized my refusal to allow my confinement to undermine my strong commitment to free my people. My flight was a declaration of war on Amerikkkan racism!"

In addition to Toni Morrison's novel (1978 [1977]), the flying Africans are alluded to elsewhere: **in fiction:** J. A. Walker (1968), p. 360; J. Lester (1970 [1969]), pp. 147–152; J. E. Wideman (1992a [1981]), p. 83; I. Reed (1982), p. 46; C. W. Sherman (1994 [1993]), p. 145; **in children's books:** V. Hamilton (1985); F. Ringgold (1991); idem (1992); **in memoirs:** K. Porter (1946); Cecil Brown (1993), p. 35; **in film:** H. Gerima (1993); and, of course, **in folklore collections:** *Drums and Shadows* (1973 [1940]), p. 17 passim; B. A. Botkin (1945), p. 189; J. M. Brewer (1968), p. 309.

Flying itself is a motif in spirituals such as "Free at Last." While flying there signifies ascent to Heaven ("Gwineter meet my Jesus in de middle of the air"), this Christian theme is almost surely imbued with the slave legend about flying Africans, for the whole spiritual tradition has a subtext of liberation in this world ("Some glad morning, some glad day, I'll fly away") (D. Randall 1971, p. 31; C. L. Taulbert 1989, p. 91). And then there's the comic relief to the sober spiritual tradition in the folk story about the first black man to get to Heaven and earn angel's wings. In Langston Hughes's version (1951, pp. 640–641), this original Air Jordan tears around Heaven, disrupting everything and refusing to be suppressed in his aerobatic virtuosity and euphoria, until finally God Himself stops him. "Saint Peter just looked at him and said, 'Just like a Negro!'" In the version told in *Black Rage* by black psychiatrists William Grier and Price Cobbs (1969 [1968], p. 95), the grounded black man says of his lost wings, "But I was a flying son of a bitch while I had 'em, wasn't I?" This reveals the lighthearted flier's kinship to the heroic badmen of black folklore, such as Stagolee, whose excesses seem a courageous and even rational choice in a world totally weighted against blacks. (See also R. Ellison 1944, p. 142; R. M. Dorson 1956, pp. 79–81, 216; R. Wright 1986 [1963], p. 185; L. Forrest 1992, pp. 98 ff.)

173 *There is a grim companion:* J. Baldwin (1993 [1960]), p. 382.

In his memoir: E. Harris (1993), p. 57. The book is appropriately titled *South of Haunted Dreams*.

Sara Lawrence-Lightfoot's mother: S. L. Lightfoot (1988), p. 304.

Author Audre Lorde: A. Lorde (1982), pp. 198–199 (italics omitted).

174 *Today black people are still:* Paul Beatty has satirically portrayed dreams of being caught between the races (1996, pp. 51–52, 103, 173, 188–189, 208–209). James Baldwin (1968, p. 89) and Walter Mosley (1993 [1992], p. 271) have both written characters who dream of being criticized by other blacks for going with white women.

Another set: For dreams expressing race-related money and status conflicts in literature, see J. S. Redding (1989 [1950]), p. 153; B. Wade (1990), pp. 158–161.

177 *This type of dream:* See P. Marshall (1962), pp. 78–79; T. Morrison (1972 [1970]); J. E. Wideman (1992c [1983]), pp. 447–448; M. Golden (1989), p. 317; K. Russell et al. (1992).

But dreams of being white: Illana Jordan herself wasn't sure her dream was about race. "Maybe," she speculated, "I was just hiding from the world that day." She also regarded the dream as predictive.

Jungian analyst Michael Vannoy Adams (1996, pp. 211, 213) discusses alternative interpretations of two apparently wish-fulfilling race-change dreams of black Africans. One dreamer seems to be criticizing himself for going white, while the other seems to be giving himself permission for "a perfectly realistic adaptation" to the "less than ideal situation" of postcolonial Africa.

Regina Reed dreamed: Charles Chesnutt's short story "Mars Jeems's Nightmare" (in 1969a [1899]) concerns a white man's race-change dream. A conjure woman uses "goopher" to give a vicious white master "a monsr'us bad dream" in which he undergoes the experience of being a black slave, and in consequence mends his ways. Eighty-odd years later, when Mars Jeems's modern counterpart Archie Bunker of *All in the Family* finds himself, against every impulse, about to go on stage in black-face at a lodge minstrel show, he exclaims, "This is every nightmare I ever had come true."

178 *In a variant of the race-change dream:* The woman who gloated is interviewee #113. D. Randall (1971), p. 84. L. Hughes (1965), pp. 127–132. To dream of triumphant role reversal may be uncommon, but to characterize life for blacks in this country as a "nightmare" is not. Recall what Leon Forrest said about "the nightmarish quality" for blacks of "getting shortchanged on the American Dream." Forrest was reflecting on Malcolm X's saying, "The American dream was my nightmare." I noted this metaphor for black life in over a score of writings: M. Angelou (1971 [1969]), p. 2; J. Baldwin (1960), p. 149; Cecil Brown (1983), p. 139; idem (1993), pp. 218, 221; C. Chesnutt (1969a [1899]); H. Dumas (1976),

pp. 80, 91, 133; R. Ellison (1972 [1952]), p. 566; R. L. Fair (1966), p. 21; S. Greenlee (1969), p. 82; S. E. Griggs (1971 [1902]), p. 187; E. L. Harris (1993), pp. 14, 42; C. Himes (1989b [1954]), p. 146; L. Hughes, op. cit.; C. Johnson (1998), pp. 38, 123; J. Lester (1984), p. 118; C. Major (1987), p. 75; P. Marshall (1981 [1959]), p. 254; N. McCall (1995 [1994]), p. 160; R. Milner (1971), p. 142; A. Moody (1976 [1968]), p. 136; W. Mosley (1995), p. 266 passim; A. Murray (1991), p. 180; R. D. Pharr (1969), p. 212; W. Thurman (1969 [1929]), p. 236; D. J. Travis (1981), p. 36; M. Walker (1967 [1966]), p. 314 passim; D. West (1982 [1948]), p. 126; idem (1995), p. 172; S. A. Williams (1986), p. 58; Malcolm X (1966 [1965]), ch. 1.

Judy Still's father: J. A. Still (1990), pp. 73–74. The recurring dreams are in W. G. Still's manuscript "Praise, Prayer, Truth, Testimony" in the Still archives at the University of Arkansas, described to me by Judy Still.

181 *In the early 1950s:* J. A. Kennedy (1952), p. 324.

Dreams like this one: The prisoner is No. 7.

182 *The following dream:* H. Powdermaker (1939), pp. 267–268.

183 *A woman in psychotherapy:* J. A. Kennedy (1952), p. 316. The therapist self-servingly read this image of quasi-rape and impregnation as revealing the patient's "unconscious hope that treatment would make her white and thus cure her illness." Cecil Brown (1991 [1969]), p. 124.

184 *Lori Kinnard:* Langston Hughes wrote a poem about an outsider dream which is also a race-change dream. In a "nightmare" poem in *Montage of a Dream Deferred* (1994, p. 418), suddenly the "million" surrounding "faces black as me . . . *Turned dead white!*"

185 *The feeling of humiliation:* J. Dollard (1988 [1937]), pp. 311–312. Claude Brown (1965), p. 296. For examples of this motif in fiction, see R. Ellison (1996), p. 125; C. Himes (1994 [1983]), p. 96; P. Marshall (1991), p. 383.

186 *Humiliation was expressed:* T. J. Cottle (1974), pp. 127–130. Another excellent commentary on a dream is on pp. 98–104.

In the 1930s: J. Dollard (1988 [1937]), pp. 310–311, 312. In fiction, see C. Major (1987), p. 130.

187 *Osuurete Adesanya dreamed:* The interviewees with dream themes from the Civil Rights era are Diane Dujon, Richard Hunt, Preston Jackson, Marva Pitchford Jolly, Sherry McKinney, and Jim Taylor. For dreams about lynchings in literature, see L. Hughes (1931), p. 30; G. S. Schuyler (1989 [1931]), p. 24; R. Wright (1987 [1958]), pp. 82–83; M. D. Taylor (1976), p. 150; J. E. Wideman (1986 [1973]), p. 68; idem (1990), pp. 93–94.

188 *Each of the dreams just related:* For a dream in which "mansions" were "allusions to a historically residual 'plantation mentality'" that affected a woman's frame of mind when confronting white-dominated institutions, see M. V. Adams (1997), pp. 8–9.

190 *Post-traumatic stress:* Post-traumatic stress nightmares typically occur immediately after the traumatizing episode, then dissipate, but may recur, sometimes years later, when something happens to reevoke the original trauma. PTSD nightmares replay the event, usually with small variations, but depart progressively from the event as healing progresses. Trauma dreams are rare in the general population, but not for "those living in inner cities and many parts of the Third World. . . . For them trauma is an almost constant presence and dreams often reflect this" (E. Hartmann 1996).

Nightmares following every sort of trauma: **Violent death: by murder:** A. French (1993), pp. 113–114; E. T. Bland (1995), pp. 23–24; **by accident:** A. Lorde (1982), p. 211; **by suicide:** C. Major (1987), p. 192; R. Kenan (1990 [1989]), p. 36; W. Mosley (1992 [1991]), pp. 151, 168; idem (1998), p. 82. **Witnessing murder:** W. Mosley (1993 [1992]), pp. 33–34, 160; idem (1994), pp. 9–11 passim. **Perpetrating murder:** D. Goines (1973), pp. 88–90, 130–132; W. Mosley (1997), p. 241. **Attack:** Claude Brown (1965), p. 12; J. A. McPherson (1973), p. 364; J. E. Wideman (1992a [1981]), pp. 52 ff.; T. McMillan (1993a [1989]), p. 350. **Rape/sexual abuse:** A. Lorde (1982), p. 49; M. Dixon (1989), p. 185 passim; S. Youngblood (1989), p. 72; idem (1997), p. 114; B. M. Campbell (1992), pp. 231–232; W. Mosley (1995), p. 53 passim. **Separation/abandonment:** A. Walker (1977 [1976]), pp. 90–91; J. Kincaid (1986), pp. 43–45. **Vietnam:** A. R. Flowers (1982), p. 30; J. E. Wideman (1992a [1981]), p. 121; C. McElroy (1990), p. 231. **Accidental injury:** C. Himes (1989b [1954]), p. 242. **Imprisonment:** G. Cain (1972 [1970]), p. 8. **Abortion:** J. Mayfield (1989 [1957]), pp. 37–38.

Lynching: W. Thurman (1992 [1932]), p. 80; R. Milner (1971), p. 142; L. Forrest (1988 [1973]), p. 17; J. Cameron (1994 [1982]), p. 37; N. Shange (1982), pp. 206–208; M. D. Taylor (1990), pp. 188–189; B. M. Campbell (1992), pp. 86, 144, 165; E. Hill (1996), p. 152. **Civil rights:** J. Baldwin (1964), pp. 120–121; P. Marshall (1983a), p. 31; idem (1991), p. 229; M. Golden (1989), p. 185; R. Perry (1989), pp. 554–555. **Miscellaneous racism:** J. Baldwin (1964), pp. 35, 130; idem (1968), pp. 178, 180; A. Moody (1976 [1968]), pp. 11, 147; H. Dumas (1988), p. 161; I. Reed (1986), p. 8; J. E. Wideman (1990), p. 20.

191 *White-on-black violence:* In a Walter Mosley novel (1998, p. 153), violence against whites is one motif in the nightly violent dreams of a man incarcerated for decades. And in *Reuben,* a John Edgar Wideman novel (1987, pp. 24–25, 119, 200), the character dreams he's in a baseball stadium where "an endless row" of bald, fat white heads are stuck on "letter-high posts." He steps up and bats one over the fence to the cheers of the crowd. He wants to hit more and more, "as many as he can bash in a lifetime." Later in the novel, it turns out that the character has already committed the murder of a white man, an act of totally random vengeance. The character remembers how good it felt and he thinks about repeating the act "till the hate was gone"—just as in his dream he wants to hit head after head. Still later, the possibility is raised that the murder itself was only dreamed by the character. Wideman implies that from a certain point of view, to murder and to dream of murder have the same significance—which, of course, reflects at once on the novelist's role as "dreamer" of the story, therefore as spokesperson for all who recognize the impulse of random vengeance.

Dreams aside, random violence against whites is actually a fairly common element in African American literature, where it takes every form from mere verbal exclamations of the wish for vengeance at random to book-length fantasies of genocide. W. E. B. Du Bois (1974 [1928]). L. Hughes (1931), p. 23. W. Thurman (1992 [1932]), p. 218. G. S. Schuyler (1991 [1936–1938]), pp. 14, 98, 125, 127. C. Himes (1973 [1945]), p. 74; idem (1994 [1983]). J. Baldwin (1948), p. 76; idem 1954 [1952]), p. 123; idem (1964), pp. 34–35. R. Ellison (1972 [1952]), p. 11. R. Wright (1987 [1958]), p. 310. P. Marshall (1981 [1959]), p. 216; idem (1983), pp. 129–130. R. Ottley (1965), pp. 78, 81. W. M. Kelley (1969 [1962]), p. 174; idem (1967), p. 165. S. Greenlee (1969), p. 181. J. A. Williams (1968 [1967]), pp. 92, 100; idem (1969), p. 149. A. Moody (1976 [1968]), p. 187. E. Cleaver (1968), p. 14. N. Giovanni (1968), p. 49. Cecil Brown (1991 [1969]), pp. 112, 205; idem (1983), pp. 128–129. G. Cain (1972 [1970]), p. 69. R. Milner (1971), pp. 139, 144–145. E. Bullins (1973), pp. 49, 50. L. Jeffers (1983), pp. 151, 203. S. A. Williams (1986), p. 20. H. Dumas (1988), p. 85. J. E. Wideman (1990), pp. 164–166. W. Mosley (1994), p. 6. J. Lester (1994), pp. 102–103. N. McCall (1995 [1994]), pp. 3–4, 83, 375. E. L. Harris (1996), p. 253.

I can't explain why violence toward whites in dreams almost always has a very specific target, while in literature black-on-white violence is almost always deliberately random. In this regard, at least, the processes of dreaming and of creative imagining tap into different portions of the psyche. One apparent exception to this generalization is the murder in Richard Wright's *Native Son*. Bigger Thomas murders Mary Dalton in front of her blind mother and then disposes of her body in a furnace. Wright once cooperated with psychoanalyst Frederic Wertham (1944) in seeking the "unconscious determinant" of this plot line. According to Wertham, Wright agreed that his choice of plot was unconsciously determined by an event in his adolescence, the memory of which was only recovered during analysis with Wertham. At fifteen, Wright had worked for a white family. His main duty was tending the fireplaces (hence the furnace). One morning, while engaged in his duties, he opened a door without knocking and came across the attractive young woman of the house undressed, and was severely reprimanded. A dream of Wright's quoted by Wertham led to still earlier associations between white female nudity and punishment. Furthermore, when he chose the family name Dalton, Wright was unconsciously aware that "Daltonism" is the name of a form of color blindness. "I am sure that this . . . was the soil out of which *Native Son* came," Wright affirmed.

Another researcher: R. E. Haskell (1985).

192 *And that is the total:* Prisoner No. 20 dreamed about the FBI, No. 21 about the Aryan Brotherhood.

It's quite remarkable: L. Hansberry (1970 [1969]), pp. 52, 249.

193 *Many whites in this society:* R. Ellison (1966), p. 57 (see also Malcolm X 1966 [1965], p. 204; T. Morrison 1993a [1992], passim; J. E. Wideman 1995 [1994], pp. 78–79).

194 *Moreover, I specifically went after:* A still greater percentage of whites, 77%, dream of threats coming from beings who are either not recognizable by race or not human.

Now the question is: A still greater percentage of blacks, 93%, dream of threats coming from beings who are either not recognizable by race or not human.

195 *Another factor:* The black transgressor dream typical for prisoners belongs to No. 17.

A further explanation: See also N. Shange (1994), p. 323. Salim Muwakkil was interviewed by Studs Terkel (1993 [1992], p. 169).

There's one more factor that might also contribute to the occurrence of black transgressors in the dreams of blacks, but all the more in the dreams of whites. The color black carries negative symbolism: black market, blackmail, a black day, and so on. The associations of black with evil, dirt, and ugliness in England and Europe predate contact with Africans in the sixteenth century. So do the opposite associations with the color white. Furthermore, people all over the world seem to prefer white to black. In a study of color words in twenty-three Asian, European, and American languages, white was evaluated as better than black in all twenty-three languages, and black had the most negative rating of all colors in twenty-one of the twenty-three (J. E. Williams & J. K. Morland 1976, pp. 37–38, 54–55; M. V. Adams 1996, p. 20).

In Africa itself, color symbolism is both more diverse and less dualistic than in Europe. Yet it's probably safe to generalize that white is a positive color, even when regarded as a token of death, since death is associated with the ancestors; and that black in Africa has many of the same associations as in Europe—impurity, sorcery, death—but that it also sometimes signifies correlated qualities which are positive: fertility, strength, and power (Victor Turner, *The Forest of Symbols: Aspects of Ndembu Ritual* [Ithaca, N.Y.: Cornell University Press, 1967], cited by L. Mullings 1984, p. 124 and M. V. Adams, op. cit., p. 24; W. MacGaffey 1968, p. 173; J. E. Williams & J. K. Morland, op. cit., pp. 40–41; R. F. Thompson 1984 [1983], passim; J. P. Kiernan 1985, p. 307; R. M. Shain 1988; W. F. S. Miles 1993, p. 113; E. B. Bynum 1995).

However, the picture for Africa is confused by the fact that many traditional African languages possess only three or four color terms, so that "white" and "black" comprehend what we classify as additional colors. Thus in the Tiv language (Nigeria), for example, "black" comprehends what we call black, plus green, plus some blues and grays. Discussions of color symbolism in traditional cultures rarely take this linguistic circumstance into account (B. Berlin & P. Kay 1969; D. G. Hays et al. 1972).

All in all, there does appear to be a near-universal opposition between the colors black and white, with white preferred. Many have speculated that the preference has a biological basis in aversion to nighttime darkness and attraction to daytime light (C. A. Pinderhughes 1973, p. 94; J. E. Williams & J. K. Morland, op. cit., 1976, p. 239; M. V. Adams, op. cit., p. 22 passim). An interesting indication that the preference has more than just a cultural basis is that both Euro-American and African American preschoolers tend to prefer white already by the age of three. What's more, the preference is actually heightened in children of that age if exposed to a black consciousness curriculum taught by black teachers. Evidently the training heightens the children's awareness of color distinctions at an age when they're still governed by the natural preference, and before they're able to absorb the positive cultural valuation placed on blackness by the training (J. E. Williams & J. K. Morland, op. cit., citing Ph.D. dissertations by John L. McAdoo and Patricia Walker).

Racism enters the mix, according to the same thinkers, when the natural color preference becomes conflated with the skin colors of certain humans, or with their relative lightness and darkness, or with the terms "white" and "black" used to designate them, even if the humans aren't, strictly speaking, either white or black. Several African American authors have called attention to this misassociation (D. West 1982 [1948], p. 208; H. Dumas 1976, p. 79; L. Hughes 1961, p. 25; R. Milner 1971 [1968], p. 193; L. Forrest 1988 [1973], p. 51).

But as far as dreams go, my data don't really support this idea. One would expect such an effect to show up, if anywhere, in the dreams of white people. And yet, as we saw, only 21% of whites say they have *ever* dreamed about black transgressors, while 45% have dreamed of white transgressors. Moreover, many times I heard anonymous transgressors described as "dark" without that leading to a racial identification.

195 *The next question is:* In addition to Gloria Naylor, the following interviewees told what could be white "shadow" dreams: Ralph Arnold, Diane Dujon, Betty Holcomb, Illana Jordan, Beatriz Penso-Buford, Ivan Watkins, Winford Williams, and interviewee #115. The phrase "depreciated reciprocal" is from B. Wade (1992), p. 205. The "shadow" is a term from the psychology of C. G. Jung.

14. What My Mother Does: Dream Sharing and the Future

197 *Every mornin when all us chillen got up:* A. J. Verdelle (1995), p. 112 (italics omitted).

198 *Furthermore, talk about dreams:* Here are a few reminders and further suggestions about books that highlight different strands of the fabric of the dream culture. For ancestor dreams, read P. Marshall (1983a) and T. Morrison (1988 [1987]); for predictive dreams, E. J. Gaines (1981 [1971]) and J. E. Wideman (1992a [1981]); for numbers, R. Wright (1986 [1963]) and R. D. Pharr (1969); for waking/dreaming boundaries, W. Demby (1965) and C. Himes (1989b [1954]); for visions, H. Dumas (1976) and L. Jeffers (1983); for religion, J. Baldwin (1954 [1952]) and A. Wilson (1988). I can't single out any literary work for dreams in hoodoo, but two outstanding novels about hoodoo generally are I. Reed (1978a [1972]) and G. Naylor (1993 [1988]).

An impressive number of literary works by African American authors not only depict the strands of the dream fabric in the course of storytelling, but actually use dreams and dreamlike experiences as key structural elements. In addition to most of the works mentioned in the previous paragraph, *Invisible Man,* by Ralph Ellison, comes to mind.

There are also a great many instances of dreams or visions introduced incidentally as storytelling devices, to provide flashbacks, insights into character, and so on. Some of this abundance of dream material springs from traditional beliefs, while some owes nothing to ethnicity except a general affinity for dreams. Examples occur in D. Goines (1973), pp. 88–90, 130–132, 140–145; A. Young (1980), pp. 13–14; and S. A. Williams (1986), pp. 11–14, 75–81, 83–86.

Several fiction authors nowadays write in a dream-rich style that blends traditional beliefs with magical realism and New Age spirituality. Toni Morrison is the best-known (and best) practitioner of this approach. Others are C. W. Sherman (1994 [1993]) and T. Due (1995).

For yet another group of African American writers, virtuosity in storytelling with dreams becomes interwoven with the notion that a story is itself a kind of dream, and so literature in and of itself is a sort of collective dream sharing. Walter Mosley (1994, p. 18 passim) and John Edgar Wideman (1995 [1994], pp. 21, 50–51 passim) share an acute sensitivity to the harmonic between dreamlike variations of reality and the ever-encroaching background of nothingness, the ultimately real unreality. For both authors, fiction is a dreamlike alternate reality which mitigates that nothingness. Love also mitigates the nothingness. But love is no sure thing: it's one motion of the unstable dream of life. For Chester Himes (1973 [1945]; 1989b [1954], pp. 84, 344) the nihilistic background of life is meaninglessness, and literature is the dream in which to escape from life's insupportable pain. (For Himes, love is a constant hunger, seldom satisfied, as much a dismal constant of life as racism.)

Of course there are dream-poor works of African American literature, just as there are individuals with little or no interest in dreams. For example, see C. McKay (1928); G. W. Henderson (1988 [1934]); A. Murray (1989 [1974]); C. Briscoe (1994). Note that some authors choose to ignore dream material in one novel while introducing it in another. For example, in his first novel (*The Blacker the Berry*), Wallace Thurman emphasized the aspects of black life unique to northern urbanity, while later (*Infants of the Spring*) he gave a more rounded image of Harlem culture, including dreams, visions, and voices. And Melvin

Dixon's *Vanishing Rooms* contains next to no dream material, while his *Trouble the Water* is thoroughly impregnated with it. Also, there are authors who take both a traditional and a Euro-American psychological approach to dreams. Thus Shay Youngblood passes from the traditional beliefs and values honored in *The Big Mama Stories* to a psychological approach to dreams in *Soul Kiss* without perceptible conflict. Then there is Alice Walker, whose *Possessing the Secret of Joy* celebrates a commitment to Jungian psychology.

199 *Children's dreams:* J. S. Redding (1934), p. 542.

200 *With adults, what usually happens:* By a 2-tailed t-test, t-value = -2.38, $p = .019$.

202 *In fact, the largest part:* By a 2-tailed t-test, t-value = -2.16, $p = .032$.

203 *Reluctance to speak about dreams:* In whites' homes, open talk about one's dreams may be suppressed for a reason opposite to reverence. The Freudian theory of dreams, a simplified version of which is still alive in Euro-American popular opinion, holds that dreams reveal unseemly innermost desires and neurotic personality disturbances. This approach to dreams prevails in few black homes, but where it does, it has a predictably dampening effect on dream sharing. Nelson Peery grew up in Minnesota. His mother was a schoolteacher whose absorption of Freud's wish-fulfillment theory of dreams colored the family's attitude. "I don't remember anybody ever really telling me this, but thinking back, I got from them the impression that dreams are your wishes. And that's why we were ashamed of them." Peery later became acquainted with "the traditional black dream, here's God talking to you or your ancestors talking to you, or something like that," when he "got around mainly southern-born blacks." Dorothy Carter's mother, also a teacher, read Freud, Bruno Bettelheim, and other psychologists. Carter learned not to tell her mother when she dreamed. "Not as a child, but as a teenager, I wouldn't tell my mother, because she would interpret it. She would think, 'Oh, my daughter's'—you know—'something's wrong with her.' I would feel she would judge me." By the time she got married and encountered "the black tradition of dreams" in the person of her mother-in-law, Carter believed only in "brain chemistry."

Another restraint on open conversation: The African American trait of closeness about private business has been noted by C. McKay (1928), p. 23; N. Larsen (1929), p. 263; H. Preece (1937), p. 37; R. Wright (1966 [1945]), p. 280; idem (1987 [1958]), passim; R. D. Pharr (1969), p. 24; A. Murray (1989 [1974]), pp. 67–68; M. D. Taylor (1976), pp. 98–99 passim; J. P. Comer (1988), p. xxii; J. Mellon (1988), pp. 225, 271, 412; D. Pinckney (1993 [1992]), p. 8; b. hooks (1993), pp. 22, 23, 27; C. L. Taulbert (1992), p. 122; W. Mosley (1994), p. 22.

The first saying is from R. Wright (1986 [1963]), p. 57 (see also M. Walker 1967 [1966], p. 378), the second from J. M. Brewer (1933), p. 249 (see also T. C. Bambara 1980, p. 9). There is, in fact, a whole cluster of African American sayings around this theme. "A still tongue makes a wise head" (F. Douglass 1960 [1845], p. 43). "If you ask a Negro where he's been, he'll tell you where he's going" (M. Angelou 1971 [1969], p. 165). "The tongue is steel, but a closed mouth is a shield" (J. L. Gwaltney 1981 [1980], p. 33). "The less you know, the less trouble you find" (W. Mosley 1991 [1990], p. 13). "Somebody had they mouth talking when they should be walking" (C. McElroy 1990, p. 103). There are also the common idiomatic expressions critical of "running your mouth" and "putting someone's business in the street."

Closeness was obviously ingrained: M. J. Herskovits (1990 [1958/1941]), p. 156. M. Angelou (1971 [1969]), p. 164. Evidently "Talking Bones," a southern folktale in the Old Marster and John cycle which teaches this moral, was originally an African tale. The version in R. M. Dorson (1956, pp. 62–63) goes as follows (paragraphing omitted): "They used to carry the slaves out in the woods and leave them there, if they killed them—just like dead animals. There wasn't any burying then. It used to be a secret, between one plantation and another, when they beat up their hands and carried them off. So John was walking out in the woods and seed a skeleton. He says: 'This looks like a human. I wonder what he's doing out here.' And the skeleton said, 'Tongue is the cause of my being here.' So John ran back to Old Marster and said, 'The skeleton at the edge of the woods is talking.' Old Marster didn't believe him and went down to see. And a great many people came too. They said, 'Make the bones talk.' But the skeleton wouldn't talk. So they beat John to death, and left him there. And then the bones talked. They said, 'Tongue brought us here, and tongue brought you here.'"

204 *Yet many of these same people:* **Blues:** R. D. Abrahams (1970), p. 6. **Rootwork:** C. McElroy (1988 [1987]), p. 30. **Names:** J. E. Wideman (1992f), p. 43. **Conversion:** D. West (1982 [1948]), p. 53. **Watermelon:** L. Hughes (1956), p. 125.

205 *In sketching her own history:* For gifts skipping a generation, see L. Teish (1988 [1985]), p. 167; C. McElroy (1988 [1987]), pp. 56–57; T. M. Ansa (1989), p. 105 passim. A companion adage goes that "the Devil skips a generation" (K. Hunter 1964, p. 6). As for the "old sociological law," I wrote this quote down from a broadcast, but can't identify the source.

Still one more facet of closeness: W. D. Hand (1961), p. 408 (see also S. A. Williams 1986, p. 85). A nineteenth-century rhyme went, "Friday night dream / Sat'day morning told, / Comes to behold / Before nine days old" (*Southern Workman,* Feb. 1894, p. 26). Folklorists have observed this taboo in Europe and among Euro- and Hispanic Americans as well as African Americans. For the variant belief, see N. N. Puckett (1926), p. 496; H. M. Hyatt (1970–1978), p. 1589.

206 *I can't estimate just how widespread:* Daniel Wideman was alone in applying the principle to good dreams: "One of the things why MLK's 'I Have a Dream' speech resonated so powerfully within the culture is that we all knew that by speaking that, he was gonna make it happen, take a step toward bringing it to reality." Wideman added that when it comes to hoped-for outcomes, a conflicting principle also operates, "that if you say something great's gonna happen, then it won't come true"—or as Wideman the elder said, "If you really want something, you probably shouldn't talk a lot about it. Jinxing it." Wideman the younger qualified the jinx principle: it may only operate *if the person who is told is a main actor in the critical situation.* "For instance, MLK's speech. Those were things that were broad enough."

207 *In the course of discussion:* The person who dreamed Mr. C.'s death is interviewee #114.

208 *This brings us to yet another side:* T. Morrison (1972 [1970]), pp. 22, 111. E. M. Smith (1994), p. 13. L. Teish (1988 [1985]), pp. 13–14 (see also A. Young 1981 [1970], p. 14; C. Burnett 1978; N. McCall 1995 [1994], p. 38; S. Jackson-Opoku 1997, p. 142).

How can knowledge be transmitted: L. Teish (1988 [1985]), pp. 13–14. Z. N. Hurston (1991 [1942]), p. 25. B. Jones (1989 [1983]), p. 61 (see also J. Baldwin 1957, p. 98; Cecil Brown 1993, p. 86; R. Ellison 1999, p. 210).

210 *The Widemans' extended family:* The woman from the patriarchal family is interviewee #114.

212 *In fact,* there are no significant differences: By contrast, gender differences do emerge in the white comparison sample on half of the ten features mentioned, all in the direction of higher scores for the women. Correlation coefficients reveal significant gender differences among whites in the following features: ancestor dreams (p = .003), dreams for another person (p = .001), visions (p = .007), voices (p = .001), and knowledge of witch riding you (p = .05).

Interestingly, dream sharing is apparently common among black male prisoners. It goes on "all the time," said twenty-year-old Josh Taifa, a former prisoner. Of the questionnaire sample of twenty-five black male prisoners, nearly half share dreams with fellow prisoners often (16%) or sometimes (32%), while over three-quarters often (20%) or sometimes (60%) hear fellow prisoners talk about their dreams. These figures are especially interesting, both because men are generally less verbal about dreams than women, and because the sample is relatively young.

213 *What are the prospects:* With the interviewees grouped accord to age—twenty-nine and younger versus thirty and older—an analysis of variance (ANOVA) for age in relation to eight variables reveals that knowing an African American person's age does not help to predict the presence or absence of any of these eight variables (ancestor dreams, predictive dreams, déjà vu based on predictive dreams, dreams for another person, experiences at the waking/dreaming boundary, familiarity with dream signs, familiarity with witches riding you, and familiarity with numbers dreams). A relationship with age approached significance for only one variable, familiarity with numbers dreams (p = .077). And a multivariable analysis of variance (MANOVA) reveals no significant relationship between age and the same cluster of variables taken as a whole (p > .05). (For the purposes of these analyses, the boundary experiences of visions, voices, and presences have been pooled as a single variable.)

REFERENCES

Abrahams, Roger D. (1970). *Deep Down in the Jungle* . . . Rev. ed. Chicago: Aldine Publishing.

Adams, Michael Vannoy (1996). *The Multicultural Imagination: "Race", Color, and the Unconscious.* London: Routledge.

Adams, Michael Vannoy (1997). The beast of racism, the cultural unconscious, and the heroic task: a contemporary Jungian perspective. Paper presented to the Conference on Disenfranchisement at Adelphi University, November 15.

Adebimpe, Victor R., Chung-Chou Chu, Helen E. Klein & Marcia H. Lange (1982). Racial and geographic differences in the psychopathology of schizophrenia. *American Journal of Psychiatry* 139:888–891.

Adebimpe, Victor R., Helen E. Klein & Jeffrey Fried (1981). Hallucinations and delusions in black psychiatric patients. *Journal of the National Medical Association* 73:517–520.

Akiga (1965 [1939]). (Rupert East, annot. and trans.) *Akiga's Story.* London: Oxford University Press.

Albertus Magnus Egyptian Secrets, or, White and Black Art for Man and Beast. N.p: n.d.

Aldrich, Michael (1993). Sleep paralysis. In Mary A. Carskadon, ed. *Encyclopedia of Sleep and Dreaming.* New York: Macmillan Publishing.

Al-Issa, Ihsan (1977). Social and cultural aspects of hallucinations. *Psychological Bulletin* 84:570–587.

Angelou, Maya (1971 [1969]). *I Know Why the Caged Bird Sings.* New York: Bantam Books.

Angelou, Maya (1982 [1981]). *The Heart of a Woman.* New York: Bantam Books.

Angelou, Maya (1993 [1974]). *Gather Together in My Name.* New York: Bantam Books.

Ansa, Tina McElroy (1989). *Baby of the Family.* San Diego: Harcourt, Brace.

Ansa, Tina McElroy (1996). *The Hand I Fan With.* New York: Doubleday (Bantam Doubleday Dell).

Arvey, Verna (1984). *In One Lifetime.* Fayetteville: University of Arkansas Press.

Asante, Molefi Kete (1993). Racism, consciousness, and Afrocentricity. In Early (1993).

Asbury, Herbert (1938). *Sucker's Progress: An Informal History of Gambling in America from the Colonies to Canfield.* New York: Dodd, Mead.

Attaway, William (1993 [1941]). *Blood on the Forge.* New York: Anchor Books (Doubleday).

Bagwell, Orlando (1994). *Malcolm X: Make It Plain.* Boston: Blackside and Roja Productions, for *The American Experience* (WGBH).

Baldwin, James (1948). Previous condition. In Baldwin (1988).

Baldwin, James (1954 [1952]). *Go Tell It on the Mountain.* New York: Signet Books (New American Library).

Baldwin, James (1957). Sonny's Blues. In Baldwin (1988).

Baldwin, James (1960). This morning, this evening, so soon. In Baldwin (1988).

Baldwin, James (1962 [1954]). *Nobody Knows My Name: More Notes of a Native Son.* New York: Delta.

Baldwin, James (1964). *Blues for Mister Charlie.* New York: Dell Publishing.

Baldwin, James (1968). *Tell Me How Long the Train's Been Gone.* New York: Laurel (Dell Publishing).

Baldwin, James (1993 [1960]). *Another Country.* New York: Vintage Books (Random House).

Bambara, Toni Cade (1966). The hammer man. In Bambara (1981).

Bambara, Toni Cade (1972). Basement. In Bambara (1981).

Bambara, Toni Cade (1980). *The Salt Eaters.* New York: Random House.

Bambara, Toni Cade (1981). *Gorilla, My Love.* New York: Vintage Books (Random House).

Bambara, Toni Cade (1993). Deep sight and rescue missions. In Early (1993).

Baraka, Imamu Amiri (1971). *Junkies Are Full of (SHHH . . .).* (Drama.) In King & Milner (1971).

Barrett, Leonard (1974). African religions in the Americas. In Lincoln (1974).

Bass, Ruth (1930). Mojo. In Dundes (1981 [1973]).

Bass, Ruth (1935). The little man. In Dundes (1981 [1973]).

Bastide, Roger (1971). *African Civilisations in the New World.* New York: Harper Torchbooks (Harper & Row).

Beatty, Paul (1996). *The White Boy Shuffle.* Boston: Houghton Mifflin.

Bell, Carl C. (1982). Black intrapsychic survival skills: alteration of states of consciousness. *Journal of the National Medical Association* 74:1017–1020.

Bell, Carl C., Dora D. Dixie-Bell & Belinda Thompson (1986). Further studies on the prevalence of isolated sleep paralysis in black subjects. *Journal of the National Medical Association* 78:649–659.

Bell, Carl C., Maurine Fayen & Gail Mattox (1988). Training psychiatric residents to treat blacks. *Journal of the National Medical Association* 80:637–641.

Bell, Carl C., Carolyn J. Hildreth, Esther J. Jenkins & Cynthia Carter (1988). The relationship of isolated sleep paralysis and panic disorder to hypertension. *Journal of the National Medical Association* 80:289–294.

Bell, Carl C., Bambade Shakoor, Belinda Thompson, Donald Dew, Eugene Hughley, Raymond Mays & Kumea Shorter-Gooden (1984). Prevalence of isolated sleep paralysis in black subjects. *Journal of the National Medical Association* 76:501–508.

Bell, Carl C., Belinda Thompson, Kumea Shorter-Gooden, Raymond Mays & Bambade Shakoor (1985). Altered states of consciousness profile: an Afro-centric intrapsychic evaluation tool. *Journal of the National Medical Association* 77:715–728.

Bell, Michael Edward (1980). Pattern, structure, and logic in Afro-American hoodoo performance. Ph.D. diss., Indiana University.

Bennett, Lerone, Jr. (1963). The convert. In Clarke (1966).

Berlin, Brent & Paul Kay (1969). *Basic Color Terms: Their Universality and Evolution.* Berkeley: University of California Press.

Black Herman (1938 [?]). *Secrets of Magic-Mystery and Legerdermain* [sic]. Dallas: Dorene Publishing.

Bland, Eleanor Taylor (1995). *Done Wrong.* New York: St. Martin's Press.

Bloom, Joseph D. & Richard D. Gelardin (1976). *Uqamairineq* and *uqumanigianiq:* Eskimo sleep paralysis. In Simons & Hughes (1985).

Bontemps, Arna (1933). A summer tragedy. In Major (1993).

Bontemps, Arna (1959 [1931]). *God Sends Sunday.* New York: Harcourt, Brace.

Bontemps, Arna (1968 [1936]). *Black Thunder.* Boston: Beacon Press.

Botkin, B. A., ed. (1945). *Lay My Burden Down: A Folk History of Slavery.* Chicago: University of Chicago Press.

Bradley, David (1986). *South Street*. New York: Charles Scribner's Sons.

Brent, Linda (1861). *Incidents in the Life of a Slave Girl*. In Gates (1987).

Brewer, J. Mason (1933). Old-time Negro proverbs. In Dundes (1981 [1973]).

Brewer, J. Mason (1968). *American Negro Folklore*. Chicago: Quadrangle Books.

Briscoe, Connie (1994). *Sisters and Lovers*. New York: Ivy Books (Ballantine Books).

Brown, Cecil (1983). *Days without Weather*. New York: Farrar, Straus & Giroux.

Brown, Cecil (1991 [1969]). *The Life and Loves of Mr. Jiveass Nigger*. New York: Echo Press.

Brown, Cecil (1993). *Coming Up Down Home: A Memoir of a Southern Childhood*. Hopewell, N.J.: Echo Press.

Brown, Claude (1965). *Manchild in the Promised Land*. New York: Signet Books (New American Library).

Brown, Sterling A. (1932). Seeking religion. In *Southern Road*. New York: Harcourt, Brace.

Bullins, Ed (1973). *The Reluctant Rapist*. New York: Harper & Row.

Burnett, Charles (1978). *The Killer of Sheep*. (Film.) Charles Burnett Productions.

Burnett, Charles (1990). *To Sleep with Anger*. (Film.) Samuel Goldwyn.

Bynum, Edward Bruce (1993). *Families and the Interpretation of Dreams*. New York: Harrington Park Press (Haworth Press).

Bynum, Edward Bruce (1995). Dreams, extended family systems, and the African unconscious. Invited address at the Twelfth Conference of the Association for the Study of Dreams in New York City, June 20–24.

Cain, George (1972 [1970]). *Blueschild Baby*. New York: Laurel (Dell Publishing).

Caldwell, Lewis A. H. (1945). *The Policy King*. Chicago: New Vistas Publishing House.

Caldwell, Verne (pseud. for George S. Schuyler) (1933). Lucky number: 742. *Pittsburgh Courier*, Nov. 25.

Cameron, James (1994 [1982]). *A Time of Terror: A Survivor's Story*. Baltimore: Black Classic Press.

Camino, Linda Anne (1986). Ethnomedical illnesses and non-orthodox healing practices in a black neighborhood in the American South: how they work and what they mean. Ph.D. diss., University of Virginia.

Campbell, Bebe Moore (1992). *Your Blues Ain't Like Mine*. New York: G. P. Putnam's Sons.

Carlson, Gustav G. (1941). Number gambling: a study of a culture complex. Ph.D. diss., University of Michigan.

Cartiér, Xam (1992 [1991]). *Muse-Echo Blues*. New York: Ballantine Books.

Chari, C. T. K. (1964). On some types of *déjà vu* experiences. *Journal of the American Society for Psychical Research* 58:186–203.

Charles, Martie (1971). *Black Cycle*. (Drama.) In King & Milner (1971).

Charsley, Simon (1992). Dreams in African churches. In Jędrej & Shaw (1992).

Chesnutt, Charles W. (1901). Superstitions & folklore of the South. In Dundes (1981 [1973]).

Chesnutt, Charles W. (1969a [1899]). *The Conjure Woman*. Ann Arbor: University of Michigan Press.

Chesnutt, Charles W. (1969b [1899]). *The Wife of His Youth: And Other Stories of the Color Line*. Ann Arbor: University of Michigan Press.

Chesnutt, Charles Waddell (1899). The goophered grapevine. In Clarke (1966).

Chinkwita, Mary (1993). *The Usefulness of Dreams: An African Perspective*. London: Janus Publishing.

Clair, Maxine (1994). *Rattlebone*. New York: Farrar, Straus & Giroux.

Clardy, Daniel T. (1987 [1985]). Open grave. In Carole A. Parks, ed. *NOMMO: A Literary Legacy of Black Chicago (1967–1987)*. Chicago: OBAhouse.

Clark, Kenneth B. (1964). *Dark Ghetto*. New York: Harper Torchbooks (Harper & Row).

Clarke, John Henrik, ed. (1966). *American Negro Short Stories.* New York: Hill and Wang.

Clarke, John Henrik, ed. (1971). *Harlem, U.S.A.* Rev. ed. New York: Collier Books.

Cleaver, Eldridge (1968). *Soul on Ice.* New York: Delta Books (Dell Publishing).

Clifton, Lucille (1969). Good times. In Randall (1971).

Cohen, Carl I. & Lorna Carlin (1993). Racial differences in clinical and social variables among patients evaluated in a dementia assessment center. *Journal of the National Medical Association* 85:379–384.

Comer, James P. (1988). *Maggie's American Dream: The Life and Times of a Black Family.* New York: New American Library.

Corin, Ellen & Giles Bibeau (1980). Psychiatric perspectives in Africa. Part II: The traditional viewpoint. *Transcultural Psychiatric Research Review* 17:205–233.

Corin, Ellen & H. B. M. Murphy (1979). Psychiatric perspectives in Africa. Part I: The Western viewpoint. *Transcultural Psychiatric Research Review* 16:147–178.

Corthron, Kia (1994). *Cage Rhythm.* (Drama.) In Mahone (1994a).

Costello, Raymond M. (1973). Item level differences on the MMPI. *Journal of Social Psychology* 91:161–162.

Cottle, Thomas J. (1974). *Black Children, White Dreams.* Boston: Houghton Mifflin.

Crapanzano, Vincent (1975). Saints, Jnun, and dreams: an essay in Moroccan ethnopsychiatry. *Psychiatry* 38:145–159.

Crouch, Stanley (1990). *Notes of a Hanging Judge: Essays and Reviews, 1979–1989.* New York: Oxford University Press.

Cullen, Countee (1991 [1932]). *One Way to Heaven.* In Gerald Early, ed. *My Soul's High Song: The Collected Writings of Countee Cullen.* New York: Anchor Books (Doubleday).

Danticat, Edwidge (1995). *Krik? Krak!* New York: Soho Press.

Davis, George (1984 [1971]). *Coming Home.* Washington, D.C.: Howard University Press.

Davis, James Allan & Tom W. Smith (1990). *General Social Surveys, 1972–1990.* Machine readable data file. Chicago: National Opinion Research Center.

Dean, Philip Hayes (1971). *The Owl Killer.* (Drama.) In King & Milner (1971).

De Hoyos, Arturo & Genevieve De Hoyos (1965). Symptomatology differentials between negro and white schizophrenics. *International Journal of Social Psychiatry* 11: 245–255.

Delany, Martin R. (1970 [1859–1862]). *Blake; or the Huts of America.* Boston: Beacon Press.

deLaurence, L. W. (1915). *The Great Book of Magical Art, Hindu Magic, and Indian Occultism.* Chicago: deLaurence Company.

Demby, William (1965). *The Catacombs.* New York: Pantheon Books (Random House).

Demby, William (1972 [1950]). *Beetlecreek.* Chatham, N.J.: Chatham Bookseller.

De Rosny, Eric (1985). *Healers in the Night.* Maryknoll, N.Y.: Orbis Books.

Dixon, Melvin (1989). *Trouble the Water.* Boulder: Fiction Collective Two (University of Colorado).

Dixon, Melvin (1991). *Vanishing Rooms.* New York: Dutton (Penguin Group).

Dollard, John (1988 [1937]). *Caste and Class in a Southern Town.* Madison: University of Wisconsin Press.

Dorson, Richard M. (1956). *Negro Folktales in Michigan.* Cambridge, Mass.: Harvard University Press.

Dorson, Richard M. (1958). *American Negro Folktales.* New York: Fawcett Publications.

Douglass, Frederick (1960 [1845]). *Narrative of the Life of Frederick Douglass.* Cambridge, Mass.: Belknap Press of Harvard University Press.

Douglass, Frederick (1968 [1855]). *My Bondage and My Freedom.* New York: Arno Press and New York Times.

Drake, St. Clair & Horace R. Cayton (1945). *Black Metropolis: A Study of Negro Life in a Northern City*. New York: Harcourt, Brace.

Drums and Shadows: Survival Studies among the Georgia Coastal Negroes (1973 [1940]). Georgia Writers' Project. Westport, Conn.: Greenwood Press.

Du Bois, W. E. B. (1974 [1928]). *Dark Princess: A Romance*. Millwood, N.Y.: Kraus-Thomson Organization.

Du Bois, W. E. B. (1989 [1911]). *The Quest of the Golden Fleece*. Boston: Northeastern University Press.

Du Bois, W. E. Burghardt (1961 [1903]). *The Souls of Black Folk*. New York: Dodd, Mead.

Due, Tananarive (1995). *The Between*. New York: HarperCollins Publishers.

Dumas, Henry (1976). *Jonoah and the Green Stone*. New York: Random House.

Dumas, Henry (1988). *Goodbye, Sweetwater: New and Selected Stories*. New York: Thunder's Mouth Press.

Dunbar, Paul Laurence (1900). The ingrate. In Major (1993).

Dundes, Alan, ed. (1981 [1973]). *Mother Wit from the Laughing Barrel: Readings in the Interpretation of Afro-American Folklore*. New York: Garland Publishing.

Early, Gerald, ed. (1993). *Lure and Loathing*. New York: Penguin Books.

Ebony (1953). What happened to the Jones Brothers? *Ebony*, July: 63–70.

Edwards, Junius (1963). *If We Must Die*. Garden City, N.Y.: Doubleday.

Egen, Frederick W. (1959). *Plainclothesman: A Handbook of Vice and Gambling Investigation*. New York: Arco Publishing.

Elder, Lonnie, III (1965). *Ceremonies in Dark Old Men*. New York: Farrar, Straus & Giroux.

Eliade, Mircea (1966). Initiation dreams and visions among Siberian shamans. In G. E. Grunebaum & Roger Caillois, eds. *The Dream and Human Societies*. Berkeley: University of California Press.

Ellison, Ralph (1944). Flying home. In Major (1993).

Ellison, Ralph (1966). *Shadow and Act*. New York: Signet Books (New American Library).

Ellison, Ralph (1972 [1952]). *Invisible Man*. New York: Vintage Books (Random House).

Ellison, Ralph (1996). *Flying Home and Other Stories*. New York: Random House.

Ellison, Ralph (1999). *Juneteenth*. New York: Random House.

Eskridge, Ann E. (1994). *The Sanctuary*. New York: Cobblehill Books (Penguin Books U.S.A.).

Everett, Henry C. (1963). Sleep paralysis in medical students. *Journal of Nervous and Mental Disease* 123:283–287.

Fabian, Ann (1990). *Card Sharps, Dream Books, and Bucket Shops: Gambling in 19th-Century America*. Ithaca, N.Y.: Cornell University Press.

Fabrega, Horacio, Jr., Juan Mezzich & Richard F. Ulrich (1988). Black-white differences in psychopathology in an urban psychiatric population. *Comprehensive Psychiatry* 29:285–297.

Fair, Ronald L. (1966). *Hog Butcher*. New York: Harcourt, Brace & World.

Fair, Ronald L. (1970). *World of Nothing: Two Novellas*. New York: Harper & Row.

Farrakhan, Louis (1989). The announcement. Statement of Minister Louis Farrakhan, National Representative of the Honorable Elijah Muhammad and the Nation of Islam, October 24, 1989, J. W. Marriott Hotel, Washington, D.C.

Fauset, Jessie Redmon (1989 [1924]). *There Is Confusion*. Boston: Northeastern University Press.

Fisher, Humphrey J. (1979). Dreams and conversion in black Africa. In Nehemia Levtzion, ed. *Conversion to Islam*. New York: Holmes & Meier.

Fisher, Rudolph (1992 [1932]). *The Conjure-Man Dies: A Mystery Tale of Dark Harlem*. Ann Arbor: University of Michigan Press.

Flowers, A. R. (1985). *De Mojo Blues: De Quest of HighJohn de Conqueror.* New York: E. P. Dutton.

Forrest, Leon (1988 [1973]). *There Is a Tree More Ancient Than Eden.* Chicago: Another Chicago Press.

Forrest, Leon (1992). *Divine Days.* New York: W. W. Norton.

Fox, John W. (1992). The structure, stability, and social antecedents of reported paranormal experiences. *Sociological Analysis* 53:417–431.

Frankel, Barbara (1977). *Childbirth in the Ghetto: Folk Beliefs of Negro Women in a North Philadelphia Hospital Ward.* San Francisco: R & E Research Associates.

French, Albert (1993). *Billy.* New York: Viking Penguin.

Fukuda, Kazuhiko, Robert D. Ogilvie, Lisa Chilcott, Ann-Marie Vendittelli & Tomoka Takeuchi (1998). The prevalence of sleep paralysis among Canadian and Japanese college students. *Dreaming* 8:59–66.

Funkhouser, Art T. (1983a). A historical review of déjà vu. *Parapsychological Journal of South Africa* 4(1):11–24.

Funkhouser, Art T. (1983b). The "dream" theory of déjà vu. *Parapsychological Journal of South Africa* 4(2):107–123.

Funkhouser, Art (1995). Three types of déjà vu. Paper presented at the Twelfth Conference of the Association for the Study of Dreams in New York City, June 20–24.

Gaines, Ernest J. (1981 [1971]). *The Autobiography of Miss Jane Pittman.* New York: Bantam Books.

Gaines, Ernest J. (1983). *A Gathering of Old Men.* New York: Alfred A. Knopf (Random House).

Gallup, George H. & Frank Newport (1991). Belief in paranormal phenomena among adult Americans. *Skeptical Inquirer* 15:137–146.

Gates, Henry Louis, Jr., ed. (1987). *The Classic Slave Narratives.* New York: Mentor (Penguin Books U.S.A.).

Gates, Henry Louis, Jr. (1994). *Colored People: A Memoir.* New York: Alfred A Knopf (Random House).

Geller, Jesse D. (1988). Racial bias in the evaluation of patients for psychotherapy. In Lillian Comas-Díaz & Ezra E. H. Griffith, eds. *Clinical Guidelines in Cross-Cultural Mental Health.* New York: John Wiley & Sons.

Genovese, Eugene D. (1974). *Roll, Jordan, Roll: The World the Slaves Made.* New York: Pantheon Books (Random House).

Gerima, Haile (1993). *Sankofa.* (Film.) Washington, D.C.: Mypheduh Films.

Giovanni, Nikki (1968). A revolutionary tale. In Mayfield (1972).

Giovanni, Nikki (1993). Black is the noun. In Early (1993).

Goines, Donald (1973). *White Man's Justice, Black Man's Grief.* Los Angeles: Holloway House Publishing.

Goines, Donald (1975). *Inner City Hoodlum.* Los Angeles: Holloway House Publishing.

Golden, Kenneth M. (1977). Voodoo in Africa and the United States. *American Journal of Psychiatry* 134:1425–1427.

Golden, Marita (1989). *Long Distance Life.* New York: Doubleday.

Gordon, Charles (Oyamo) (1969). *The Breakout.* (Drama.) In King & Milner (1971).

Gray, Thomas R. (1966). *The Confession, Trial and Execution of Nat Turner.* In F. Roy Johnson (1966). *The Nat Turner Slave Insurrection.* Murfreesboro, N.C.: Johnson Publishing.

Greaves, Donald (1971). *The Marriage.* (Drama.) In King & Milner (1971).

Greeley, Andrew M. (1975). *The Sociology of the Paranormal.* Beverly Hills, Calif.: Sage Publications.

Greenlee, Sam (1969). *The Spook Who Sat by the Door.* New York: Richard W. Baron.

Grier, William H. & Price M. Cobbs (1969 [1968]). *Black Rage.* New York: Bantam Books.

Griffith, Ezra E. H., Thelouizs English & Violet Mayfield (1980). Possession, prayer, and testimony: therapeutic aspects of the Wednesday night meeting in a black church. *Psychiatry* 43:120–128.

Griffith, Ezra E. H. & Marie A. Mathewson (1981). Communitas and charisma in a black church service. *Journal of the National Medical Association* 73:1023–1027.

Griggs, Sutton E. (1969 [1899]). *Imperium in Imperio: A Study of the Negro Race Problem: A Novel.* New York: Arno Press and New York Times.

Griggs, Sutton E. (1971 [1902]). *Unfettered,* and *Dorlan's Plan.* New York: AMS Press.

Gruber, Russell (1995). Lucid dreaming, waking personality, and cognitive development. Paper presented at the Twelfth Conference of the Association for the Study of Dreams in New York City, June 20–24.

Guze, Samuel B., Robert A. Woodruff Jr. & Paula J. Clayton (1975). The significance of psychotic affective disorders. *Archives of General Psychiatry* 32:1147–1150.

Gwaltney, John Langston (1981 [1980]). *Drylongso: A Self-Portrait of Black America.* New York: Vintage Books (Random House).

Haizlip, Shirlee Taylor (1994). *The Sweeter the Juice.* New York: Simon & Schuster.

Hamilton, Virginia (1985). *The People Could Fly: American Black Folktales.* New York: Alfred A. Knopf (Random House).

Hand, Wayland D., ed. (1961). *The Frank C. Brown Collection of North Carolina Folklore,* vols 6 and 7: *Popular Beliefs and Superstitions from North Carolina.* Durham, N.C.: Duke University Press.

Hansberry, Lorraine (1970 [1969]). (Robert Nemiroff, adapt.) *To Be Young, Gifted and Black.* New York: Signet Books (New American Library).

Harding, Vincent (1992 [1981]). *There Is a River: The Black Struggle for Freedom in America.* New York: Harvest/HBJ.

Harrington, Ollie (1971). How Bootsie was born. In Clarke (1971).

Harris, Eddy L. (1993). *South of Haunted Dreams: A Ride Through Slavery's Old Back Yard.* New York: Simon & Schuster.

Harris, Eddy L. (1996). *Still Life in Harlem.* New York: Henry Holt.

Hartmann, Ernest (1996). Dreaming connects: an outline for a theory on the nature and functions of dreaming. Paper presented at the Thirteenth Conference of the Association for the Study of Dreams at Berkeley, California, July 9–13.

Haskell, Robert E. (1985). Racial content and issues in dream research. *Association for the Study of Dreams Newsletter* 2(1):7–9.

Haskins, James (1974). *Witchcraft, Mysticism and Magic in the Black World.* Garden City, N.Y.: Doubleday.

Hay, David & Ann Morisy (1978). Reports of ecstatic, paranormal, or religious experience in Great Britain and the United States—a comparison of trends. *Journal for the Scientific Study of Religion* 17:255–268.

Hayden, Robert (1966). *Selected Poems.* New York: October House.

Hays, David G., Enid Margolis, Raoul Naroll & Dale Revere Perkins (1972). Color term salience. *American Anthropologist* 74:1107–1121.

Heard, Nathan C. (1968). *Howard Street.* New York: Dial Press.

Helzer, John E. (1975). Bipolar affective disorder in black and white men. *Archives of General Psychiatry* 32:1140–1143.

Henderson, George Wylie (1988 [1934]). *Ollie Miss.* Tuscaloosa: University of Alabama Press.

Hendricks, W. C., ed. (1943). *Bundle of Trouble and Other Tarheel Tales.* Durham, N.C.: Duke University Press.

Herron, Leonora & Alice M. Bacon (1895). Conjuring & conjure-doctors. In Dundes (1981 [1973]).

Herskovits, Melville J. (1990 [1958/1941]). *The Myth of the Negro Past.* Boston: Beacon Press.

Heyer, Kathryn W. (1981). Rootwork: psychosocial aspects of malign magical and illness beliefs in a South Carolina Sea Island community. Ph.D. diss., University of Connecticut.

Hill, Ernest (1996). *Satisfied with Nothin'.* New York: Simon & Schuster.

Hill, Michael Ortiz (1995). Racism and the boundaries of our dreams. Paper presented at the Twelfth Conference of the Association for the Study of Dreams in New York City, June 20–24.

Hill, Paul, Jr. (1992). *Coming of Age: African American Male Rites-of-Passage.* Chicago: African American Images.

Himes, Chester (1972). *The Quality of Hurt: The Autobiography of Chester Himes.* Garden City, N.Y.: Doubleday.

Himes, Chester (1973 [1945]). *If He Hollers Let Him Go.* Chatham, N.J.: Chatham Bookseller.

Himes, Chester (1980). *A Case of Rape.* Washington, D.C.: Howard University Press.

Himes, Chester (1988 [1966]). *The Heat's On.* New York: Vintage Books (Random House).

Himes, Chester (1989a [1959]). *The Crazy Kill.* New York: Vintage Books (Random House).

Himes, Chester (1989b [1954]). *The Third Generation.* New York: Thunder's Mouth Press.

Himes, Chester (1990). *The Collected Stories of Chester Himes.* New York: Thunder's Mouth Press.

Himes, Chester (1994 [1983]). *Plan B.* Jackson: University Press of Mississippi.

Hobson, J. Allan (1988). *The Dreaming Brain.* New York: Basic Books.

Hohman, John George (n.d. [1820]). *Pow-Wow's, or, Long Lost Friend: A Collection of Mysterious and Invaluable Arts and Remedies.* Brooklyn: Fulton Religious Supply.

Holloway, Joseph E., ed. (1990). *Africanisms in American Culture.* Bloomington: Indiana University Press.

hooks, bell (1993). *Sisters of the Yam: Black Women and Self-recovery.* Boston: South End Press.

Hufford, David J. (1982). *The Terror That Comes in the Night: An Experience-Centered Study of Supernatural Assault Traditions.* Philadelphia: University of Pennsylvania Press.

Hughes, Langston (1931). *Mulatto.* In Hughes (1968).

Hughes, Langston (1935). *Little Ham.* In Hughes (1968).

Hughes, Langston (1951). Jokes Negroes tell on themselves. In Dundes (1981 [1973]).

Hughes, Langston (1956). *Simply Heaven.* In Hughes (1968).

Hughes, Langston (1958). *Tambourines to Glory.* New York: John Day.

Hughes, Langston (1961). *The Best of Simple.* New York: Noonday Press (Hill & Wang).

Hughes, Langston (1965). *Simple's Uncle Sam.* New York: Hill & Wang.

Hughes, Langston (1968). (Webster Smalley, ed.) *Five Plays by Langston Hughes.* Bloomington: Midland Books (Indiana University Press).

Hughes, Langston (1969 [1930]). *Not without Laughter.* New York: Collier Books (Macmillan Publishing).

Hughes, Langston (1971). My early days in Harlem. In Clarke (1971).

Hughes, Langston (1994). (Arnold Rampersad, ed.) *The Collected Poems of Langston Hughes.* New York: Alfred A. Knopf (Random House).

Hunter, Kristin (1964). *God Bless the Child.* New York: Charles Scribner's Sons.

Hunter, Kristin (1975). *The Survivors.* New York: Charles Scribner's Sons.

Hurston, Zora Neale (1978 [1937]). *Their Eyes Were Watching God.* Urbana: University of Illinois Press.

Hurston, Zora Neale (1981). (Toni Cade Bambara, ed.) *The Sanctified Church.* Berkeley: Turtle Island Foundation.

Hurston, Zora Neale (1990 [1935]). *Mules and Men.* New York: Harper Perennial (Harper & Row).

Hurston, Zora Neale (1991 [1942]). *Dust Tracks on a Road.* New York: Harper Perennial (Harper & Row).

Hyatt, Harry Middleton (1970–1978). *Hoodoo, Conjuration, Witchcraft, Rootwork: Beliefs Accepted by Many Negroes and White Persons These Being Orally Recorded Among Blacks and Whites.* 5 vols. Hannibal, Mo.: Western Publishing.

Ifill, Gwen (1995). This soldier's story. *Emerge* 7(2): 87–88.

Ilechukwu, S. T. C. (1991). Psychiatry in Africa: special problems and unique features. *Transcultural Psychiatric Research Review* 28:169–218.

Jackson, Angela (1993). *Dark Legs and Silk Kisses: The Beatitudes of the Spinners.* Evanston, Ill.: TriQuarterly Books.

Jackson-Opoku, Sandra (1997). *The River Where Blood Is Born.* New York: One World (Ballantine Books).

James, Phyllis (1975). *Black Shrink.* Los Angeles: Holloway House Publishing.

Jędrej, M. C. & Rosalind Shaw, eds. (1992). *Dreaming, Religion, and Society in Africa.* Leiden, Neth.: E. J. Brill.

Jeffers, Lance (1983). *Witherspoon.* Atlanta: George A. Flippin Press.

Jenkins, Adelbert H. (1995). *Psychology and African Americans: A Humanistic Approach.* 2nd ed. Boston: Allyn & Bacon.

Johnson, Charles (1998). *Dreamer.* New York: Scribner.

Johnson, Clifton H., ed. (1969). *God Struck Me Dead: Religious Conversion Experiences and Autobiographies of Ex-slaves.* Philadelphia: Pilgrim Press.

Jones, Bessie (1989 [1983]). (John Stewart, ed.) *For the Ancestors: Autobiographical Memories.* Athens: Brown Thrasher (University of Georgia Press).

Jones, Gayl (1991 (1977]). *White Rat: Short Stories.* Boston: Northeastern University Press.

Joyner, Charles (1984). *Down by the Riverside: A South Carolina Slave Community.* Urbana: University of Illinois Press.

Kalish, Richard A. & David A. Reynolds (1973). Phenomenological reality and post-death contact. *Journal for the Scientific Study of Religion* 12:209–221.

Karenga, Maulana (1988). *The African American Holiday of Kwanzaa.* Los Angeles: University of Sankore Press.

Kelley, William Melvin (1967). *dem.* Garden City, N.Y.: Doubleday.

Kelley, William Melvin (1969 [1962]). *A Different Drummer.* New York: Anchor Books (Doubleday).

Kenan, Randall (1990 [1989]). *A Visitation of Spirits: A Novel.* New York: Anchor Books (Doubleday).

Kennedy, Adrienne (1990). *Deadly Triplets: A Theatre Mystery and Journal.* Minneapolis: University of Minnesota Press.

Kennedy, Janet A. (1952). Problems posed in the analysis of Negro patients. *Psychiatry* 15:313–327.

Kiernan, J. P. (1985). The social stuff of revelation: pattern and purpose in Zionist dreams and visions. *Africa* 55:304–318.

Kincaid, Jamaica (1986). *Annie John.* New York: Plume Books (New American Library).

King, Johanna (1997). Presidential interview of Johanna King, Ph.D. (interview by Alan Siegel). *Association for the Study of Dreams Newsletter* 14(1):4–5,11.

King, Woodie & Ron Milner, eds. (1971). *Black Drama Anthology*. New York: Signet (New American Library).

Krippner, Stanley (1995). Can dreams predict the future? Panel discussion at the Twelfth Conference of the Association for the Study of Dreams in New York City, June 20–24.

Labov, William, Paul Cohen, Clarence Robins & John Lewis (1968). Toasts. In Dundes (1981 [1973]).

Larsen, Nella (1928). *Quicksand*. In Larson (1992).

Larsen, Nella (1929). *Passing*. In Larson (1992).

Larson, Charles R., ed. (1992). *An Intimation of Things Distant: The Collected Fiction of Nella Larsen*. New York: Anchor Books (Doubleday).

Lawrence-Lightfoot, Sara. See Lightfoot, Sara Lawrence.

Lawson, E. Thomas (1984). *Religions of Africa*. San Francisco: Harper & Row.

Lawson, James R. (1979). The origins of the numbers game. *New York Amsterdam News*, Feb. 10: 25.

Lee, S. G. (1958). Social influences in Zulu dreaming. *Journal of Social Psychology* 47:265–283.

Leeds, Morton (1944). One form of paraamnesia: the illusion of déjà vu. *Journal of the American Society for Psychical Research*. 38(1):24–42.

Lester, Julius (1970 [1969]). *Black Folktales*. New York: Evergreen Black Cat (Grove Press).

Lester, Julius (1976). *All Is Well*. New York: William Morrow.

Lester, Julius (1984). *Do Lord Remember Me*. New York: Holt, Rinehart and Winston.

Lester, Julius (1988). *Lovesong: Becoming a Jew*. New York: Henry Holt.

Lester, Julius (1994). *And All Our Wounds Forgiven*. New York: Arcade Publishing.

Levin, Jeffrey S. (1993). Age differences in mystical experiences. *Gerontologist* 33: 507–513.

Levine, Lawrence W. (1977). *Black Culture and Black Consciousness: Afro-American Folk Thought from Slavery to Freedom*. New York: Oxford University Press.

Levitan, Lynne & Stephen LaBerge (1991). In the mind and out-of-body: OBEs and lucid dreams. *NightLight* 3(2):1–3, 9–11.

Lewis, Reginald Sinclair (n.d.). Fare thee well. Unpublished story manuscript.

Light, Ivan (1974). *Numbers and Policy Gambling in New York City, 1872–1973: Guide to New York Times with Annotations*. Chicago: Council of Planning Librarians.

Lightfoot, Sara Lawrence (1988). [Interviewee Sara Lawrence-Lightfoot.] *Balm in Gilead: Journey of a Healer*. Reading, Mass.: A Merloyd Lawrence Book (Addison-Wesley Publishing).

Lincoln, C. Eric, ed. (1974). *The Black Experience in Religion*. Garden City, N.Y.: Anchor Press (Doubleday).

Lincoln, C. Eric (1989 [1988]). *The Avenue, Clayton City*. New York: Ballantine Books.

Liss, Jay L., Amos Welner, Eli Robins & Marsha Richardson (1973). Psychiatric symptoms in white and black inpatients. I: Record study. *Comprehensive Psychiatry* 14:475–481.

Long, Carolyn Morrow (2001). *Spiritual Merchants: Religion, Magic and Commerce*. Knoxville: University of Tennessee Press.

Long, Doughtry (1970). One time Henry dreamed the number. In Randall (1971).

Lorde, Audre (1982). *Zami: A New Spelling of My Name*. Watertown, Mass.: Persephone Press.

Lucas, Robert (1949). Dreams. *Ebony*, May: 53–58.

MacGaffey, Wyatt (1968). Kongo and the king of the Americans. *Journal of Modern African Studies* 6:171–181.

MacGaffey, Wyatt (1983). *Modern Kongo Prophets*. Bloomington: Indiana University Press.

Magallón, Linda Lane (1997). *Mutual Dreaming*. New York: Pocket Books.

Mahone, Sydné, ed. (1994a). *Moon Marked and Touched by Sun: Plays by African-American Women*. New York: Theatre Communications Group.

Mahone, Sydné (1994b). Introduction. In Mahone (1994a).

Maisel, Albert Q. (1949). Return of the numbers racket. *Collier's*, Jan. 15: 21–23, 71–73.

Major, Clarence (1987). *Such Was the Season*. San Francisco: Mercury House.

Major, Clarence, ed. (1993). *Calling the Wind: Twentieth-Century African-American Short Stories*. New York: Harper Perennial (HarperCollins).

Marshall, Paule (1962). *Reena*. In Marshall (1983b).

Marshall, Paule (1981 [1959]). *Brown Girl, Brownstones*. Old Westbury, N.Y.: Feminist Press.

Marshall, Paule (1983a). *Praisesong for the Widow*. New York: Plume/New American Library (Penguin Books U.S.A.).

Marshall, Paule (1983b). *Reena and Other Stories*. Old Westbury, New York: The Feminist Press.

Marshall, Paule (1991). *Daughters*. New York: Atheneum (Macmillan Publishing).

Mayfield, Julian (1989 [1957]). *The Hit*. In *The Hit and The Long Night*. Boston: Northeastern University Press.

Mayfield, Julian (1989 [1958]). *The Long Night*. In *The Hit and The Long Night*. Boston: Northeastern University Press.

Mayfield, Julian (1960). The numbers writer: a portrait. *Nation* 190(20):424–425.

Mayfield, Julian, ed. (1972). *Ten Times Black: Stories from the Black Experience*. New York: Bantam Books.

McCall, George J. (1963). Symbiosis: the case of Hoodoo and the numbers racket. In Dundes (1981 [1973]).

McCall, Nathan (1995 [1994]). *Makes Me Wanna Holler: A Young Black Man in America*. New York: Vintage Books (Random House).

McClenon, James (1990). A preliminary report on African-American anomalous experiences in northeast North Carolina. *Parapsychology Review* 21:1–4.

McClenon, James (1993). The experiential foundations of shamanic healing. *Journal of Medicine and Philosophy* 18:107–127.

McClenon, James (1994). Surveys of anomalous experience: a cross-cultural analysis. *Journal of the American Society for Psychical Research* 88:117–135.

McElroy, Colleen J. (1988 [1987]). *Jesus and Fat Tuesday*. London: Pandora Press.

McElroy, Colleen (1990). *Driving under the Cardboard Pines*. Berkeley: Creative Arts.

McKay, Claude (1928). *Home to Harlem*. New York: Harper & Brothers.

McKenzie, P. R. (1992). Dreams and visions in nineteenth century Yoruba religion. In Jędrej & Shaw (1992).

McKnight, Reginald (1988). Mali is very dangerous. [From *Moustapha's Eclipse*.] In Major (1993).

McKnight, Reginald (1992). *The Kind of Light That Shines on Texas*. Boston: Little, Brown.

McMillan, Terry (1993a [1989]). *Disappearing Acts*. New York: Pocket Star Books (Simon & Schuster).

McMillan, Terry (1993b [1992]). *Waiting to Exhale*. New York: Pocket Star Books (Simon & Schuster).

McMillan, Terry (1994 [1987]). *Mama*. New York: Pocket Star Books (Simon & Schuster).

McPherson, James Alan (1970 [1969]). *Hue and Cry*. Greenwich, Conn.: Fawcett Publications.

McPherson, James Alan (1973). The story of a scar. In Major (1993).

McPherson, James Alan (1977). *Elbow Room*. Boston: Little, Brown.

McPherson, James Alan (1993). Junior and John Doe. In Early (1993).

Mellon, James, ed. (1988). *Bullwhip Days: The Slaves Remember*. New York: Weidenfeld & Nicolson.

Miles, William F. S. (1993). Hausa dreams. *Anthropologica* 35:105–116.

Milner, Ron (1971). *Who's Got His Own*. In King & Milner (1971).

Mitchell, Francis H. (1957). Numbers boss defies death to go straight. *Jet*, June 13: 48–52.

Moody, Anne (1976 [1968]). *Coming of Age in Mississippi*. New York: Laurel (Dell Publishing).

Morgan, William (1932). Navaho dreams. *American Anthropologist* 34:391–405.

Morrison, Toni (1972 [1970]). *The Bluest Eye*. New York: Washington Square Press (Simon & Schuster).

Morrison, Toni (1978 [1977]). *Song of Solomon*. New York: Signet (Penguin Books U.S.A.).

Morrison, Toni (1981 [1973]). *Sula*. New York: Bantam Books.

Morrison, Toni (1982 [1981]). *Tar Baby*. New York: Plume/New American Library (Penguin Books U.S.A.).

Morrison, Toni (1988 [1987]). *Beloved*. Plume/New American Library (Penguin Books U.S.A.).

Morrison, Toni (1993a [1992]). *Playing in the Dark: Whiteness and the Literary Imagination*. New York: Vintage Books (Random House).

Morrison, Toni (1993b [1992]). *Jazz*. New York: Plume/New American Library (Penguin Books U.S.A.).

Morrison, Toni (1997). *Paradise*. New York: Alfred A. Knopf (Random House).

Mosley, Walter (1991 [1990]). *Devil in a Blue Dress*. New York: Pocket Books (Simon & Schuster).

Mosley, Walter (1992 [1991]). *A Red Death*. New York: Pocket Books (Simon & Schuster).

Mosley, Walter (1993 [1992]). *White Butterfly*. New York: Pocket Books (Simon & Schuster).

Mosley, Walter (1994). *Black Betty*. New York: W. W. Norton.

Mosley, Walter (1995). *RL's Dream*. New York: W. W. Norton.

Mosley, Walter (1997). *Gone Fishin'*. Baltimore: Black Classic Press.

Mosley, Walter (1998). *Always Outnumbered, Always Outgunned*. New York: W. W. Norton.

Muhammad, Jabril (1986). Science and teachings of the Mother Craft. Chicago: Honorable Minister Louis Farrakhan. Internal publication of the Nation of Islam.

Mukherjee, Sukdeb, Sashi Shulka, Joanne Woodle, Arnold M. Rosen & Sylvia Olarte (1983). Misdiagnosis of schizophrenia in bipolar patients: a multiethnic comparison. *American Journal of Psychiatry* 140:1571–1574.

Mulira, Jessie Gaston (1990). The case of Voodoo in New Orleans. In Holloway (1990).

Mullings, Leith (1984). *Therapy, Ideology, and Social Change: Mental Healing in Urban Ghana*. Berkeley: University of California.

Murphy, H. B. M., E. D. Wittkower, J. Fried & H. Ellenberger (1963). A cross-cultural survey of schizophrenic symptomatology. *International Journal of Social Psychiatry*. 9:237–249.

Murray, Albert (1989 [1974]). *Train Whistle Guitar*. Boston: Northeastern University Press.

Murray, Albert (1991). *The Spyglass Tree.* New York: Pantheon Books (Random House).

Naylor, Gloria (1993 [1988]). *Mama Day.* New York: Vintage Books (Random House).

Neal, Larry (1971). Harlem gallery: from the inside. In Randall (1971).

Neppe, Vernon M. (1983). *The Psychology of Déjà Vu: Have I Been Here Before?* Johannesburg: University of Witwatersrand Press.

Ness, Robert C. (1978). The *old hag* phenomenon as sleep paralysis: a biocultural interpretation. In Simons & Hughes (1985).

Noll, Joyce Elaine (1991). *Company of Prophets: African American Psychics, Healers, and Visionaries.* St. Paul, Minn.: Llewellyn Publications.

Ohaeri, Jude Uzoma (1992). Experience of isolated sleep paralysis in clinical practice in Nigeria. *Journal of the National Medical Association* 84:521–523.

Ohaeri, J. U., M. F. Adelekan, A. O. Odejide & B. A. Ikuesan (1992). The pattern of isolated sleep paralysis among Nigerian nursing students. *Journal of the National Medical Association* 84:67–70.

Ohaeri, J. U., A. O. Odejide, B. A. Ikuesan & J. D. Adeyemi (1989). The pattern of isolated sleep paralysis among Nigerian medical students. *Journal of the National Medical Association* 81:805–808.

Oliver, Paul (1990 [1960]). *Blues Fell This Morning.* Cambridge, U.K.: Cambridge University Press.

Omoyajowo, Akinyele (1965). *Your Dreams: An Introductory Study.* Ibadan, Niger.: Daystar Press.

Ottley, Roi (1965). *White Marble Lady.* New York: Farrar, Straus & Giroux.

Our World (1950). Are Negro gamblers dying out? *Our World,* Nov.: 26–28.

Palmer, J. (1974). A community mail survey of psychic experiences. *Research in Parapsychology* 3:130–133.

Pate, Alexs D. (1994). *Losing Absolom.* Minneapolis: Coffee House Press.

Payne-Jackson, Arvilla & John Lee (1993). *Folk Wisdom and Mother Wit: John Lee—An African American Herbal Healer.* Westport, Conn.: Greenwood Press.

Perry, Richard (1989). Going to meet Aaron. In Major (1993).

Petry, Ann (1958). Has anybody seen Miss Dora Dean? In Major (1993).

Petry, Ann (1985 [1946]). *The Street.* Boston: Beacon Press.

Pharr, Robert Deane (1969). *The Book of Numbers.* Garden City, N.Y.: Doubleday.

Pharr, Robert Deane (1997 [1978]). *Giveadamn Brown.* New York: Old School Books (W. W. Norton).

Phillips, J. J. (1985 [1966]). *Mojo Hand: An Orphic Tale.* Berkeley: City Miner Books.

Pinckney, Darryl (1993 [1992]). *High Cotton.* New York: Penguin Books.

Pinderhughes, Charles A. (1973). Racism and psychotherapy. In Charles V. Willie, Bernard M. Kramer & Bertram S. Brown, eds. (1973). *Racism and Mental Health.* Pittsburgh: University of Pittsburgh Press.

Plumpp, Sterling D. (1986). Sanders Bottom. *Open Places* (41):8–17.

Porter, Kenneth (1946). The flying Africans. In Bucklin Moon, ed. *Primer for White Folks.* Garden City, N.Y.: Doubleday.

Powdermaker, Hortense (1939). *After Freedom: A Cultural Study in the Deep South.* New York: Viking Press.

Preece, Harold (1937). The Negro folk cult. In Dundes (1981 [1973]).

Puckett, Newbell Niles (1926). *Folk Beliefs of the Southern Negro.* Chapel Hill: University of North Carolina Press.

Rahman, Aishah (1994). *The Mojo and the Sayso.* In Mahone (1994a).

Randall, Dudley, ed. (1971). *The Black Poets.* New York: Bantam Books.

Ray, Benjamin C. (1993). Aladura Christianity: a Yoruba religion. *Journal of Religion in Africa* 23:266–291.

Raymond, Linda (1994). *Rocking the Babies*. New York: Viking Press.

Redding, J. Saunders (1934). Playing the numbers. *North American Review* 238(6): 533–542.

Redding, J. Saunders (1989 [1950]). *Stranger and Alone*. Boston: Northeastern University Press.

Reed, Ishmael (1978a [1972]). *Mumbo Jumbo*. New York: Bard Books (Avon Books).

Reed, Ishmael (1978b). *Shrovetide in Old New Orleans*. Garden City, N.Y.: Doubleday.

Reed, Ishmael (1982). *The Terrible Twos*. London: Allison & Busby.

Reed, Ishmael (1986). *Reckless Eyeballing*. New York: St. Martin's Press.

Reed, Ishmael (1990 [1967]). *The Free-lance Pallbearers*. London: Allison & Busby.

Reed, Ishmael (1990 [1988]). *Writin' Is Fightin'*. New York: Atheneum (Macmillan Publishing).

Rhodes, Jewell Parker (1993). *Voodoo Dreams: A Novel of Marie Laveau*. New York: St. Martin's Press.

Richardson, T. F. & G. Winokur (1968). Déjà vu—as related to diagnostic categories in psychiatric and neurological patients. *Journal of Nervous and Mental Disease* 146: 161–164.

Ringgold, Faith (1991). *Tar Beach*. New York: Crown Publishers.

Ringgold, Faith (1992). *Aunt Harriet's Underground Railroad in the Sky*. New York: Crown Publishers.

Robateau, Albert J. (1978). *Slave Religion: The "Invisible Institution" in the Antebellum South*. New York: Oxford University Press.

Roberson, Mildred Hopkins Baker (1983). Folk health beliefs and practices of rural black Virginians. Ph.D. diss., University of Utah.

Robinson, Beverly J. (1990). Africanisms and the study of folklore. In Holloway (1990).

Robinson, Major (1975). How the Mafia took the numbers over. *New York Amsterdam News*, Aug. 13: A-2.

Russell, Kathy, Midge Wilson & Ronald Hall (1992). *The Color Complex: The Politics of Skin Color among African Americans*. New York: Harcourt Brace Jovanovich.

Sabshin, Melvin, Herman Diesenhaus & Raymond Wilkerson (1970). Dimensions of institutional racism in psychiatry. *American Journal of Psychiatry* 127:787–793.

Saxon, Lyle, Edward Dreyer & Robert Tallant (1945). *Gumbo Ya-Ya: A Collection of Louisiana Folk Tales*. Boston: Houghton Mifflin.

Schenck, Carlos H., Donna M. Milner, Thomas D. Hurwitz, Scott R. Bundlie & Mark W. Mahowald (1989). A polysomnographic and clinical report on sleep-related injury in 100 adult patients. *American Journal of Psychiatry* 146:1166–1173.

Schuyler, George S. (1989 [1931]). *Black No More: Being an Account of the Strange and Wonderful Workings of Science in the Land of the Free, A.D. 1933–1940*. Boston: Northeastern University Press.

Schuyler, George S. (writing as Samuel I. Brooks) (1991 [1936–1938]). *Black Empire*. Boston: Northeastern University Press.

Seaton, Louis (1954). Racial bias and numbers racket. *New York Amsterdam News*, Aug. 28: 1–2.

Shafton, Anthony (1995). *Dream Reader: Contemporary Approaches to the Understanding of Dreams*. Albany: State University of New York Press.

Shafton, Anthony (1996). Black dreamers in the United States. In Kelly Bulkeley, ed. *Among All These Dreamers*. Albany: State University of New York Press.

Shain, Richard M. (1988). The black and the white: the use of dualities in Etulo historical thought. *Journal of Religion in Africa* 18:237–254.

Shange, Ntozake (1982). *Sassafrass, Cypress and Indigo*. New York: St. Martin's Press.

Shange, Ntozake (1985). *Betsey Brown*. New York: St. Martin's Press.

Shange, Ntozake (1994). *The Resurrection of the Daughter: Liliane*. In Mahone (1994a).

Shaw, Rosalind (1992). Dreaming and accomplishment: power, the individual and Temne divination. In Jędrej & Shaw (1992).

Shepp, Archie (1971). *Junebug Graduates Tonight*. In King & Milner (1971).

Sherman, Charlotte Watson (1994 [1993]). *One Dark Body*. New York: HarperCollins Publishers.

Simon, Robert J., Joseph L. Fleiss, Barry J. Gurland & Pamela R. Stiller (1973). Depression and schizophrenia in hospitalized black and white mental patients. *Archives of General Psychiatry* 28:509–512.

Simons, Ronard C. & Charles C. Hughes, eds. (1985). *The Culture-Bound Syndromes: Folk Illnesses of Psychiatric and Anthropological Interest*. Dordrecht, Neth.: D. Reidel Publishing.

Singer, Benjamin D. (1977). *Racial Factors in Psychiatric Intervention*. San Francisco: R & E Research Associates.

Sithole, Ndabaningi (1977 [1970]). *Obed Mutezo of Zimbabwe*. Nairobi: Oxford University Press.

Sixth and Seventh Books of Moses (?). Brooklyn: Fulton Religious Supply.

Sletten, Ivan, Steven Schuff, Harold Altman & George Ulett (1972). A statewide computerized psychiatric system: demographic, diagnostic and mental health data. *International Journal of Social Psychiatry* 18:30–40.

Smith, Ethel Morgan (1994). A conspiracy of grace. In Nikki Giovanni, ed. *Grand Mothers*. New York: Henry Holt.

Sno, Herman N. & Don H. Linszen (1990).The déjà vu experience: remembrance of things past? *American Journal of Psychiatry* 147:1587–1595.

Snow, Loudell F. (1977). Popular medicine in a black neighborhood. In Edward H. Spicer, ed. *Ethnic Medicine in the Southwest*. Tucson: University of Arizona Press.

Snow, Loudell F. (1993). *Walkin' over Medicine*. Boulder, Colo.: Westview Press.

Sobel, Mechal (1988 [1979]). *Trabelin' On: The Slave Journey to an Afro-Baptist Faith*. Princeton, N.J.: Princeton University Press.

South Carolina Folk Tales (1941). Writers' Program of the Works Projects Administration. Columbia: University of South Carolina Press.

Southerland, Ellease (1979). *Let the Lion Eat Straw*. New York: Charles Scribner's Sons.

Southern Workman (1893–1900). Journal published by the Hampton Institute, Hampton, Virginia.

Sow, I. (1980 [1978]). *Anthropological Structures of Madness in Black Africa*. New York: International Universities Press.

Still, Judith Anne (1990). *William Grant Still: A Voice High-Sounding*. Flagstaff, Ariz.: Master-Player Library.

Stitt, Van J., Jr. (1983). Root doctors as providers of primary care. *Journal of the National Medical Association* 75:719–721.

Taulbert, Clifton L. (1989). *Once Upon a Time When We Were Colored*. Tulsa, Okla.: Council Oak Books.

Taulbert, Clifton L. (1992). *The Last Train North*. Tulsa, Okla.: Council Oak Books.

Taylor, Mildred D. (1976). *Roll of Thunder, Hear My Cry*. New York: Dial Press.

Taylor, Mildred D. (1990). *The Road to Memphis*. New York: Dial Books (Penguin Books U.S.A.).

Teish, Luisah (1988 [1985]). *Jambalaya: The Natural Woman's Book of Personal Charms and Practical Rituals*. San Francisco: Harper & Row.

Terkel, Studs (1993 [1992]). *Race: How Blacks and Whites Think and Feel About the American Obsession*. New York: Anchor Books (Doubleday).

Thomas, Alexander & Samuel Sillen (1991 [1972]). *Racism and Psychiatry.* New York: Citadel Press.

Thompson, Robert Farris (1984 [1983]). *Flash of the Spirit.* New York: Vintage Books (Random House).

Thornton, John (1992). *Africa and Africans in the Making of the Atlantic World, 1400–1680.* Cambridge, U.K.: Cambridge University Press.

Thorpy, Michael J., ed. (1990). *The International Classification of Sleep Disorders.* Rochester, Minn.: American Sleep Disorders Association.

Thurman, Wallace (1969 [1929]). *The Blacker the Berry.* New York: Arno Press and New York Times.

Thurman, Wallace (1992 [1932]). *Infants of the Spring.* Boston: Northeastern University Press.

Thurmon, Ralph "Cheo" (1991). *The Future and Other Stories.* Chicago: Third World Press.

Time (1935). Triple zero. *Time* 26(19):16–17.

Toomer, Jean (1969 [1923]). *Cane.* New York: Perennial Classic (Harper & Row).

Travis, Dempsey J. (1981). *An Autobiography of Black Chicago.* Chicago: Urban Research Institute.

Travis, Dempsey J. (1987). *An Autobiography of Black Politics.* Chicago: Urban Research Institute.

Turner, H. W. (1967). *History of an African Independent Church.* 2 vols. London: Oxford University Press.

Van Dyke, Henry (1965). *Ladies of the Rachmaninoff Eyes.* New York: Farrar, Straus & Giroux.

Van Dyke, Henry (1971). *Dead Piano.* New York: Farrar, Straus & Giroux.

Van Dyke, Henry (1985). Chitterling. In Major (1993).

Vass, Winifred Kellersberger (1979). *The Bantu Speaking Heritage of the United States.* Los Angeles: Center for Afro-American Studies, University of California.

Verdelle, A. J. (1995). *The Good Negress.* Chapel Hill, North Carolina: Algonquin Books.

Vitols, M. M., H. G. Waters & M. H. Keeler (1963). Hallucinations and delusions in white and negro schizophrenics. *American Journal of Psychiatry* 120:472–476.

Wade, Brent (1992). *Company Man.* Chapel Hill, N.C.: Algonquin Books.

Wade-Lewis, Margaret (1988). The African substratum in American English. Ph.D. diss., New York University.

Wakefield, Dan (1960). Harlem's magic numbers. *Reporter* 22(3):25–26.

Walker, Alice (1977 [1976]). *Meridian.* New York: Washington Square Press (Simon & Schuster).

Walker, Alice (1989). *The Temple of My Familiar.* New York: Harcourt Brace Jovanovich.

Walker, Alice (1992). *Possessing the Secret of Joy.* New York: Harcourt Brace Jovanovich.

Walker, Evan K. (1970). Harlem transfer. In Mayfield (1972).

Walker, Joseph A. (1968). *Ododo.* In King & Milner (1971).

Walker, Margaret (1967 [1966]). *Jubilee.* New York: Bantam Books.

Warren, Lynne (1982). Joseph Yoakum. In *Selections from the Dennis Adrian Collection.* Chicago: Museum of Contemporary Art.

Washington, Joseph R. (1972). The Black Holiness and Pentecostal sects. In Lincoln (1974).

Webb, Wilse B. (1994). Retrospective review: Sigmund Freud's *The Interpretation of Dreams. Dreaming* 4:54–58.

Weiss, Harry B. (1944a). Oneirocritica Americana. *Bulletin of the New York Library* 48(6):519–541.

Weiss, Harry B. (1944b). Oneirocritica Americana. Part II—Conclusion: preliminary check list of dream books published in America. *Bulletin of the New York Library* 48(7):642–653.

Welner, Amos, Jay L. Liss & Eli Robins (1973). Psychiatric symptoms in white and black inpatients. II: Follow-up study. *Comprehensive Psychiatry* 14:483–488.

Wertham, Frederic (1944). An unconscious determinant in *Native Son. Journal of Clinical Psychopathology and Psychotherapy* 6:111–115.

West, Dorothy (1940). Jack in the pot. In Major (1993).

West, Dorothy (1982 [1948]). *The Living Is Easy.* Old Westbury, N.Y.: Feminist Press.

West, Dorothy (1995). *The Wedding.* New York: Doubleday.

White, Rhea A. (n.d.). Déjà vu bibliography. Unpublished manuscript.

Whitten, Norman E., Jr. (1962). Contemporary patterns of malign occultism among Negroes in North Carolina. In Dundes (1981 [1973]).

Wideman, Daniel (n.d.). *Going to Meet the Light.* Unpublished production script, draft 6. Produced by Rites & Reason, the theatre of the Afro-American Studies Program at Brown University, May 6–June 5, 1994.

Wideman, John Edgar (1986 [1973]). *The Lynchers.* New York: Owl Book (Henry Holt).

Wideman, John Edgar (1987). *Reuben.* New York: Henry Holt.

Wideman, John Edgar (1989). Fever. In Wideman (1992d).

Wideman, John Edgar (1990). *Philadelphia Fire.* New York: Henry Holt.

Wideman, John Edgar (1992a [1981]). *Damballah.* Collected in *The Homewood Books.* Pittsburgh: University of Pittsburgh Press.

Wideman, John Edgar (1992b [1981]). *Hiding Place.* Collected in *The Homewood Books.* Pittsburgh: University of Pittsburgh Press.

Wideman, John Edgar (1992c [1983]). *Sent for You Yesterday.* Collected in *The Homewood Books.* Pittsburgh: University of Pittsburgh Press.

Wideman, John Edgar (1992d). *The Stories of John Edgar Wideman.* New York: Pantheon Books (Random House).

Wideman, John Edgar (1992e). All stories are true. In Wideman (1992d).

Wideman, John Edgar (1992f). Backseat. In Wideman (1992d).

Wideman, John Edgar (1992g). Signs. In Wideman (1992d).

Wideman, John Edgar (1992h). Welcome. In Wideman (1992d).

Wideman, John Edgar (1995 [1994]). *Fatheralong: A Meditation on Fathers and Sons, Race and Society.* New York: Vintage Books (Random House).

Wideman, John Edgar (1998). *Two Cities.* Boston: Houghton Mifflin Company.

Williams, John A. (1968 [1967]). *The Man Who Cried I Am.* New York: Signet Books (New American Library).

Williams, John A. (1969). *Sons of Darkness, Sons of Light.* Boston: Little, Brown.

Williams, John E. & J. Kenneth Morland (1976). *Race, Color, and the Young Child.* Chapel Hill: University of North Carolina.

Williams, Sherley Anne (1986). *Dessa Rose.* New York: William Morrow.

Wilson, August (1986). *Fences.* New York: Plume (New American Library).

Wilson, August (1988). *Joe Turner's Come and Gone.* New York: Plume (New American Library).

Wilson, August (1990). *The Piano Lesson.* New York: Plume (New American Library).

Wilson, August (1993). *Two Trains Running.* New York: Plume (New American Library).

Wintrob, Ronald M. (1973). The influence of others: witchcraft and rootwork as explanations of behavior disturbances. *Journal of Nervous and Mental Disease* 156: 318–326.

Woodson, Jacqueline (1990). *Last Summer with Maizon*. New York: Delacorte Press (Bantam Doubleday Dell).

Woodson, Jacqueline (1992). *Maizon at Blue Hill*. New York: Yearling Books (Bantam Doubleday Dell).

Woodson, Jacqueline (1993). *Between Madison and Palmetto*. New York: Yearling Books (Bantam Doubleday Dell).

Woodson, Jacqueline (1995). *Autobiography of a Family Photo*. New York: E. P. Dutton.

Wright, Charles (1966). *The Wig*. New York: Farrar, Straus & Giroux.

Wright, Richard (1966 [1945]). *Black Boy*. New York: Perennial Library (Harper & Row).

Wright, Richard (1986 [1963]). *Lawd Today*. Boston: Northeastern University Press.

Wright, Richard (1987 [1958]). *The Long Dream*. New York: Perennial Library (Harper & Row).

X, Malcolm (with Alex Haley) (1966 [1965]). *The Autobiography of Malcolm X*. New York: Grove Press.

Young, Al (1980). *Ask Me Now*. New York: McGraw-Hill.

Young, Al (1981 [1970]). *Snakes*. Berkeley: Creative Arts.

Youngblood, Shay (1989). *The Big Mama Stories*. Ithaca, N.Y.: Firebrand Books.

Youngblood, Shay (1997). *Soul Kiss*. New York: Riverhead Books (G. P. Putnam's Sons).

INDEX

Names preceded by an asterisk (*) also appear in the Index of Interviewees
(Appendix A)

9 781630 260484